WHAT CAN THIS BOOK DO FOR YOU?

Within a few years, your high school experience will lead you into the work world of adults. This book is designed to give you guidance, ideas, and answers about the many options life offers and the steps you will need to take for each.

WHAT FIRST?

Take a few minutes to claim ownership of this book. Write your name in it. In pencil, lay out your career and life goals as you see them today. Consider the obstacles you may have to overcome in order to achieve your goals. If you don't have a formal plan, that's OK. Answering these questions will spark your imagination and help you make one. The first steps might not be easy, but there are no right or wrong answers. As you continue working through this book, refer to these goals and feel free to fill in any blanks you left or to change your ideas.

WHAT NEXT?

Your needs, goals, ideas, and talents are unique to you. What is right for you may not be right for others. But the steps in the process of choosing a career direction (and understanding what education you might need to get there) are the same whether you aspire to repair car engines or design the next generation of space shuttles.

THINK OF THIS BOOK AS A ROAD MAP

Knowing where you want to go and what roads will lead you there is the first step in the process. You can always change your destination and chart a new course. We're providing the map. The rest is up to you.

GETTING A JUMP ON THE ROAD TO SUCCESS

Name _Ashley_

Age _16_

Grade _11th_

Date Started _3/21/07_

My current goal after I graduate from high school is to:

go to college

At school, to reach my goal I'll need:

Curriculum planning:

Clubs, teams, associations:

Career research:

Outside of school, to reach my goal I'll need:

Volunteer work:

Shadowing/mentor program:

Job experience:

Extracurricular activities:

Challenges my goal presents:

Ideas to overcome these challenges:

THOMSON

PETERSON'S

About Thomson Peterson's

Thomson Peterson's (www.petersons.com) is a leading provider of education information and advice, with books and online resources focusing on education search, test preparation, and financial aid. Its Web site offers searchable databases and interactive tools for contacting educational institutions, online practice tests and instruction, and planning tools for securing financial aid. Thomson Peterson's serves 110 million education consumers annually.

For more information, contact Thomson Peterson's, 2000 Lenox Drive, Lawrenceville, NJ 08648; 800-338-3282; or find us on the World Wide Web at www.petersons.com/about.

Editor: Linda Seghers; Production Editor: Alysha Bullock; Manufacturing Manager: Ray Golaszewski; Composition Manager: Michele Able; Interior Design: Michele Able.

ISBN-13: 978-0-7689-2267-7 (Middle Atlantic)
ISBN-10: 0-7689-2267-4 (Middle Atlantic)

ISBN-13: 978-0-7689-2268-4 (Midwest)
ISBN-10: 0-7689-2268-2 (Midwest)

ISBN-13: 978-0-7689-2269-1 (New England)
ISBN-10: 0-7689-2269-0 (New England)

ISBN-13: 978-0-7689-2270-7 (South)
ISBN-10: 0-7689-2270-4 (South)

ISBN-13: 978-0-7689-2271-4 (Texas)
ISBN-10: 0-7689-2271-2 (Texas)

ISBN-13: 978-0-7689-2272-1 (West)
ISBN-10: 0-7689-2272-0 (West)

Printed in the United States of America

10 9 8 7 6 5 4 3 2 1   08 07 06

Eighth Edition

Dear Student:

Whether graduation seems light-years away or alarmingly close, it's never too early—or too late—to think about what comes after high school. Do you know what your next step will be?

Peterson's Get a Jump! can help you figure that out. This book is designed to help you launch your career, whether this means going on for more education or directly entering the workforce. You have a multitude of options and some crucial choices to make. In the pages that follow, we have tried to give you a jumpstart on planning the future that's right for you.

The book is arranged in five parts. Part 1 has all the guidance you'll need to make the transition to high school. Part 2 provides general introductory information about your options after high school and how to use your high school education to plan for the next phase of your life. Part 3 offers more detailed information about postsecondary education, whether you choose a two-year, four-year, vocational/career college, or the military. Part 4 provides useful information about the workplace and how to handle stress, peer pressure, conflict, and other obstacles you may encounter. Finally, Part 5 contains appendices for each state in your geographic region of the United States, including valuable information on two- and four-year colleges and universities in your area and your state's high school graduation requirements, scholarship and financial aid programs, summer opportunities, and vocational and career colleges.

We hope you find this publication helpful as you begin thinking about the rest of your life. If you have questions or feedback on *Peterson's Get a Jump!*, please contact us at: Editor—Get a Jump!
Thomson Peterson's
2000 Lenox Drive
Lawrenceville, NJ 08648

Sincerely,
Thomson Peterson's Editorial Staff

Contents

YOU'RE GOING TO BE A FRESHMAN . . .

You KNOW WHAT IT'S SUPPOSED TO BE LIKE—being a freshman in high school should be COOL. But what will it REALLY be like? Will you be able to figure it all out? Of course you will . . . especially since you are reading this! Your high school years will be like nothing else you have experienced and you are going to have questions about everything. Luckily, it's right here that you will be able to get answers. Whether you are wondering about how to keep your "stuff" organized, choosing your classes, or what is a GPA, we are here to help! So, come on, jump in—you're going to be a FRESHMAN!

To Students, Parents, and Counselors:

It was my pleasure to experiment with using **Peterson's Get a Jump!** in selected high schools and elementary schools in Chicago. While the logistics of how high school students are scheduled and how they move from class to class made the job of getting the material to them and guiding them through it very challenging, the material was well received by the high schools, and those students who were exposed to the book were excited by all of the information provided in this publication.

Conversely, the elementary school (which in Chicago means K-8) students, especially the sixth to eighth graders, were a captive audience and, with assistance from a teacher, were much easier to get together in a group for presentation on a grade-by-grade and class-by-class basis. These students were so attentive and curious about high school and what happens there, and I was more than surprised that the students at both the high schools and elementary schools lacked knowledge about such things as: What is a transcript? What is a GPA? What are class ranks? What are honors classes and AP classes?

When I relayed these "discoveries" back to Thomson Peterson's, the idea of adding a special chapter on just these types of questions and issues facing the middle school student getting ready to make the transition to high school was a natural evolution. "The Big Jump to High School" gives parents, guidance counselors, and, most importantly, students the information they need to successfully make that transition—answering not only the questions about transcripts, GPAs, class ranks, and honors and AP classes but also giving advice on participation in extracurricular activities, how to deal with the differences between middle school and high school, setting goals, staying organized, and how to study. And this advice comes not just from Thomson Peterson's, but also from guidance counselors, parents, and students all over the country!

Finally, as a college administrator who has worked with high schools, elementary schools, and junior high schools for more than thirty years, I find **Peterson's Get a Jump!** to be a book that has been long overdue. It is an excellent vehicle for young people who seek guidance in planning their educational futures! Best of luck to all of you!

Nathaniel Thomas, Ph.D.

Chapter 1

THE BIG JUMP TO HIGH SCHOOL

Even if you've never said anything to anyone else, chances are the thought of your first year of high school is totally scary, especially with all these questions whirling around in your head:

Who will I sit with at lunch **What if my best friends don't have lunch when I do WHERE IS THE VENDING MACHINE** How will I find my way around the halls What will I do when I have only four minutes to get to my next class What happens if I get lost *Will I remember my locker combination* WHAT HAPPENS IF I CAN'T OPEN MY LOCKER **What happens if there aren't any lockers** How will I carry all those books around in my backpack *What if my best friend isn't in the same classes as me* What if I don't know anyone in my classes What if I don't know where the bathroom is What happens if I forget where to go for my class What if, what if, what if the seniors are mean to me and treat me like dirt?!?!??!?

IN MIDDLE SCHOOL, you knew where everything was. You knew exactly who would be sitting next to you at lunch. You knew all the teachers. All the teachers knew you. You were at the top of the heap.

Now you're starting all over again

First of all, take a deep breath, sit back, and realize that it's okay to have the ups and downs, the doubts, and the feelings that zip back and forth between "I can't wait to get into high school" to "I'm hiding under my bed and never coming out." The first few weeks of high school, you're surrounded by a lot of kids who are bigger, who seem to know an awful lot more than you do, and who know exactly where to go. You'll wonder what it will be like, trying out for sports teams or shows and activities with the tenth, eleventh, and twelfth graders.

FROM THE GUIDANCE OFFICE

"Freshmen are afraid the upper class students will pick on them, but honestly, that's not true. Upper class students are not the least bit interested in freshmen."

Helen Erbe
Guidance Counselor
Jackson Memorial High School
Jackson, New Jersey

Second, the friend of a friend's brother who told you he hated ninth grade isn't you. Everyone adjusts to high school in different ways and at different speeds. For some kids, the transition from junior high school/middle school to high school takes a short time, like days or weeks. For others, the adjustment takes longer, especially if they're not admitting to themselves and others what their feelings are and letting others help them get over their insecurities.

ADVICE FROM A SENIOR

Sometimes freshmen give older students too much power. My advice is don't be afraid to be yourself.

Kristen Seghers, Senior
West Windsor-Plainsboro High School South
Princeton Junction, New Jersey

Third, you are not alone. All those big kids ahead of you have gone through the same fears and have had the same feelings, too. They made it through, and you will too. It's most likely that the sophomores, juniors, and seniors are too busy dealing with the problems of being sophomores, juniors, and seniors to be concerned if you forgot your locker combination and have to go slinking off to the school office to find out what it is.

PARENT PERSPECTIVE

"Stephen was nervous about starting ninth grade. It took him only about two to three days to catch on."

Sharon Blumenthal
Parent to Stephen, who is going into the tenth grade.

THE DIFFERENCES: MIDDLE SCHOOL VS. HIGH SCHOOL

There's no getting around it. High school is a different ball game. It's like you're used to playing soccer and all of a sudden in order to score, you're expected to throw the ball, not kick it. Some of the major differences between middle school and high school are:

You are more independent. In middle school, you were part of a group. You did the same things together—ate lunch, took the same classes, goofed off. Same teachers, same schedule. It's a big adjustment to realize that you will have your own schedule of classes that could be very different from your best friend's. You will be in classes with people you don't know because there are different levels of classes. You could be in the middle level of a math class and your friend in the upper-level class.

ADVICE FROM A JUNIOR

"When I was a freshman, I got into band camp and got to know kids in the band. Then when I was walking through the halls I knew more people other than just the freshmen. If you know people around you then you'll feel comfortable. If you feel comfortable then you'll be more willing to do new things. My high school is a huge high school. The idea is to make as many friends as you can. So talk to everybody."

Matt Wolf, Junior
Doherty High School
Colorado Springs, Colorado

You have to take more responsibility. In middle school you probably had fewer choices about which classes you could take. In high school, there are many more choices about your education, especially as you go into your sophomore year. You'll get to choose some classes, or electives as they're called. As a freshman, the choices you have of electives are limited. Most freshmen can choose only one elective. Sophomores only two. At the junior and senior levels, you'll have more and more choices to make, depending on your goals and interests.

The way you are graded is different in high school. Your teachers in junior high school were probably a lot more lenient when it came to late homework. They were more likely to look at your past record and give you a little leeway. Teachers in high school aren't as likely to accept excuses. "I forgot" won't work. In high school your grades are based on numbers. Two points off if you didn't get your homework done and turned in on time.

You have to speak up for yourself. In middle school, your parents probably helped you if you got into a tough situation, say with a teacher. They were the ones making the phone call or visiting the teacher. In high school, there will be times when you will have to deal with situations on your own, such as speaking with a teacher about homework, or getting your voice heard in clubs and activities even though you're the youngest one there. In high school, you have to develop the ability to get advice from your parents and counselors, figure out how to solve the problem, and then take action.

ADVICE FROM A SENIOR

"Speak up if you have a good idea. In sports or clubs, sometimes younger people have good ideas or strategies and ways to help out, but they don't want to say anything."

Kristen Seghers, Senior
West Windsor-Plainsboro High School South
Princeton Junction, New Jersey

THERE'S SO MUCH TO DO!

Your freshman year is a time for you to explore your interests—what's it like being a crime scene investigator, a computer graphics designer, a veterinarian, etc.

Explore your interests via elective classes. One of the main purposes of high school electives is to allow you to investigate career interests. Though you will be required to take a variety of basic classes like math, English, history, and science, your choice of electives can point you in the direction of a future college major. It could very well be that something you enjoy doing as a freshman could end up being the start of your career.

You can take electives in areas like computers, art, accounting, or music. Say you think you'd like to be in business some day, sitting in an office overlooking the city. You can begin to realize that dream by taking accounting as an elective. You may find out you really like working with numbers. Or, you may find out you'd rather be building high-rises instead of sitting in them.

Explore your interests via clubs and activities. In addition to sports, high school offers many clubs and activities outside of what you'll learn in the classroom. You may think these activities are there just so you can have some fun. While that's true, they also give you the opportunity to find out what your interests are. Extracurricular activities can help you find what goals you want to set and then how to reach them.

ADVICE FROM A JUNIOR

I would have definitely joined more clubs and done more activities in my freshman year. Say if you join a drama club as a freshman, you can be at the top when you get to be a junior or senior. If you wait to join when you're a junior, you'll be at the bottom end. Colleges want you to be a leader so you have to start going for the top of activities when you're a freshman.

Matt Wolf, Junior
Doherty High School
Colorado Springs, Colorado

Here's a sample list of clubs and activities in which you can participate. Every school is different, so you'll have to find out what your high school offers, but this list will give you an idea of what you can expect.

- Auto club
- Band
- Bowling club
- Cheerleading
- Choir
- Forensic club
- Math club
- Mock Trial
- Newspaper
- Science club

Explore your interests via volunteer work. High schools often offer opportunities for you to do volunteer work. Are you interested in working with younger kids? In being a lawyer? In helping those who are sick? You can volunteer to help out in a hospital or law office, for instance. By volunteering and working alongside people who are doing the things you may like to do, you can quickly judge if you really do like hospitals or law offices.

TO HONOR OR NOT TO HONOR: CHOOSING CLASSES

One of the most critical decisions you're going to have to make in your first year of high school is whether to take classes on a regular level or on an honors level. You may have heard about AP classes, or Advanced Placement classes. You can't take those until your junior or senior year, but the time to start planning for this high academic level is actually in your freshman year. If your goal is to take college-level courses in high school (that's what AP classes are), you should start in the ninth grade by taking honors classes. AP classes are very competitive with little wiggle room for poor grades or performance as you move from freshman, to sophomore, to junior.

But first you need to know the difference between "regular," honors, and AP classes.

Classes at the "regular" level

Different high schools may have different labels for this level, but basically, if you're in a "regular" level class, you're getting what you need in that subject area to meet the requirements to graduate from high school in four years and go on to college. Do the work expected of you, turn in all your homework, do well on the tests, and you'll get that piece of paper in four years that says you've completed the necessary subjects to become a high school graduate.

Classes at the honors level

Honors level classes require more from you. You'll do more reading and writing that demands more in-depth understanding of the subject matter. Classes at this level develop critical thinking skills by asking you to interpret situations and events. Honors classes are designed to provide you with an in-depth investigation into a subject.

Teachers will expect you to participate in class discussions. You will learn to feel comfortable with a subject so you'll be able to talk about it. For instance, when studying the civil war in an honors class, you'll delve deeper into the conditions that brought the war about, in addition to dates, geographic locations, and famous names. Then you'll look at how the war affected history and learn something about the social and political issues that followed.

Classes at the AP (Advanced Placement) level

In AP classes, you're actually learning at the college level. You are expected to do the assignments and perform on the tests as you would if you were in college. No wonder you can't take AP classes until your junior and senior year. In order to even get into an AP class, you must be a high achiever.

While the hurdles to getting into an AP class are high, the advantages for those who do well in AP classes are huge. The AP exams are given to students across the whole U.S.A. in May and are scored on a level from 1–5, with 5 being tops. If you get a 3, 4, or 5 in the exam of a particular class, you may be able to waive the introductory level of that class in college. Some colleges may even award you college credit! Not only will this save you time and money, but you'll also impress college admissions offices with the fact that you're taking AP classes. Colleges look favorably on students who worked hard in high school and did well in difficult subjects.

During the college admission process, some colleges "weight" the different levels of classes you take. For instance, they'll give you more points for an A in an honors class than they would for an A in a "regular class." An A in a class at a regular level may count as a 4, while an A in an honors level class would count as a 5 and a B in an honors level would count as a 4.

Some things to consider before taking the honors plunge

Many students do well in honors classes. Others struggle, whereas they may have done very well starting off in a "regular" level class. Then, once they've become familiar with the different way classes are taught and what's expected academically of high school students, they may be able to handle an honors class with ease.

You must be honest with yourself and with your parents. Sometimes parents see their kids through rosy glasses and think their sons and daughters are geniuses. Meanwhile, the son or daughter is struggling to cope with the whole change from junior high school to high school, and falls behind. Your mindset has a lot to do with how well you'll do in high school, so it's much better to begin high school at a level that fits you.

If you are terrible at writing, but love science, that's your clue about which honors classes to take and in which sequence. You may take a science honors class your first semester. See how you do. Then you can add an English honors course the second semester.

If you're not confident about your study habits or organizational skills, the first semester of high school is a time to slowly dip your tootsies in the honors pool. Feel the temperature of the water by doing well in a "regular "class, flex your mind muscles, and then dive into honors. The goal is to excel in what you do well and then take the classes that challenge you.

The WORST mistake you can make is to select an honors class because your best friend decided to take it. How well you do in high school determines if many of the doors to your future plans will be open. If you do poorly, you begin to close doors even in your freshman year.

What if you want to be a chef and your parents are determined for you to go to Harvard?

That's a tough situation and the above example is a little on the exaggerated side, but as a freshman, now is the time to address a difference of opinion about your future plans with your parents. So, say you do want to be a chef. You know that honors classes demand a lot more studying and time and that to get into culinary schools or other vocational tracks, you don't need to get As in honors classes. However, your parents know you could get As without too much effort. High school counselors will probably encourage you to take the honors classes. Why not leave your options open? As a freshman, your plans can change a lot before you graduate. If you start out with the plan to be a chef set in concrete and leave no room for change, you could get to your junior year and decide that you hate the smell of burning food. You would rather get a degree in business from a top college. If you'd taken honors classes, you'd be in a good position to go to the university of your choice.

ADVICE FROM A SENIOR

"When you're a freshman, it's hard to see the big picture of your future. I couldn't see it and probably could have done better than I did if I'd talked to some older people or taken a peek at college stuff and seen how important things are."

Kristen Seghers, Senior
West Windsor-Plainsboro High School South
Princeton Junction, New Jersey

Advice for parents

Make sure your child can do well in the honors or AP classes before you start pushing for all As at that level. Each child has different skills. Let's imagine your child takes honors classes in everything that's offered that first year. The child works extremely hard and comes home with a C in science. You're devastated. Your child is devastated. You've never seen a C on a report card. To help your child make the right decisions about honors and AP classes, talk with your child and your child's guidance counselor.

WHAT IN THE WORLD IS A GPA AND WHAT THE HECK IS A TRANSCRIPT?

Your GPA (Grade Point Average). If you haven't already heard about the GPA, those three letters—G, P, and A—are going to mean a lot as you move from freshman to senior. There's no getting around the fact that the GPA is important to your future: what college you can attend, what kind of upper-level high school classes you can take (such as those AP classes), what academic and athletic scholarships you may get, or for what special programs you may qualify.

In short, the GPA is the average of all your grades starting from your freshman year. A little planning in your freshman year can go a long way toward a better GPA when you graduate. If you know the impact a GPA can have, you may do things a little differently in your freshman year.

It's good to know how your GPA is computed. Different schools have their own ways to total up a GPA, but this will give you the basic idea.

In general, schools score letter grades as follows:

A = 4 points

B = 3 points

C = 2 points

D = 1 point

F = 0 points

Some schools give higher points for grades earned in honors courses. That's something you would need to check out in the school office. So, let's take a hypothetical student's grades for one semester:

English	A	4 points
History	B	3 points
Music	A	4 points
Math	C	2 points
Spanish	B	3 points
Physical Education	A	4 points

The points total 20 points. Divide that by the number of classes, which is 6, and you get a GPA of 3.33 for one semester.

Let's take the next semester and see how our student did.

English	A	4 points
History	A	4 points
Music	A	4 points
Math	B	3 points
Spanish	C	2 points
Physical Education	A	4 points

That totals 21 points divided by 6, which equals a 3.5 GPA. Now, add the total number of points over these last two semesters, which is 41 and divide by the number of classes (12) and you get a 3.42 GPA.

This is a simplified version of how schools score GPAs because some high schools give different points to each class level. For instance, an A in English may be worth more points than an A in physical education.

Your transcript. A transcript goes with you through high school and shows the final grade you received in each of your courses. Your transcript is a history of the classes you took and what grade you achieved in that class. It's what colleges ask for to assess what kind of a student you are.

As a freshman, you need to lay a good foundation academically. Competitive colleges that attract thousands of applications look carefully at your transcript. They're not only looking at your final GPA. They're also looking at how you challenged yourself during your high school years. Did you take courses that stretched you academically, like honors and AP classes, or did you take only those classes you were required to take?

Some important things to know about transcripts

Transcripts differ from school to school. You need to find out what your school records on your transcript. For example, say you got good grades but missed a lot of classes because you just didn't feel like showing up. If your transcript shows the number of times you were not in class, and you're going for a top college or university, your good grades (and high GPA) won't look so good.

- Some schools show how many absences you had for each class.

- Some schools are on the trimester system, which means you'll have three sets of grades for each year.

- Some schools show plus and minus grades, such as a B+ or an A−, and some don't.

- Some schools don't count the freshman year when adding up your GPA.

- Some schools don't show your rank in your class, such as 168 out of 388, but instead use a quartile system, such as ranking you in the top 25% of your class.

- Some schools show your GPA as "weighted," which means that you get an extra credit point for an honors or AP class.

- Some schools show your "citizenship" record in classes. Did you contribute to the class or were you disruptive?

- Some schools will send a profile of your school with your transcript to colleges showing the community in which the school is located, the student population, how many honors and AP classes are offered, the number of periods in a day that classes are offered, etc.

WHAT'S WHAT ON YOUR TRANSCRIPT

A. Your personal information:

Name

Address

Social Security Number or Student ID number (if you don't have a social security number)

Date of Birth

Ethnic Code

NOTE: Parents can request that your social security number, date of birth, and ethnic code be deleted from the transcript when it is sent to various colleges.

B. Abbreviations of the classes you've taken.

C. **Term GPA** is the number of grade points you earn each semester. In the transcript example on the following page, each letter grade is given a number of points, with honors classes getting an extra point:

English 1 Honors (with an extra point for honors)	B	= 4 points
Freehand Drawing 1	A	= 4 points
Spanish 1	B	= 3 points
Algebra 1	B	= 3 points
PE 9	B	= 3 points
Intro to Science 1	C	= 2 points
Government/Law 1	B	= 3 points

Add the points up and you get 22 points. Then divide that total (22) by the number of classes this student took, which is 7. Carry that out to 4 decimal points and you get 3.1429 grade points.

Cumulative GPA is found by taking the number of grade points from all your previous semesters and adding them up and then dividing them by the number of semesters. Let's look again at this student's transcript for the second semester:

Computer Apps	B	= 3 points
English 2 Honors (with an extra point for honors)	C	= 3 points
Freehand Drawing 2	A	= 4 points
Spanish 2	B	= 3 points
Algebra 2	B	= 3 points
Intro to Science 2	A	= 4 points
Government/Law 2	B	= 3 points

Add the points up and you get 23 points. Then divide that total (23) by 7 (the number of classes) and carry that figure out 4 decimals to get 3.2857 points. Add the two semesters' points (3.1429 and 3.2857) together and divide by the number of semesters, which is 2, and you get the cumulative GPA of 3.2143.

D. Letter grade you earned in each class.

E. Number of absences in each class.

F. Number of credits you earned in each class—you get one credit per class and you need 44 to graduate at this high school. Every school district has a different number of classes you need to graduate or, in some states, every district might be the same.

G. In this transcript, the letter G instead of an A, B, C, D, or F indicates that this course is not taken into account when figuring out your GPA. An "H" would indicate that you dropped the class without a penalty, like an "F". This student didn't drop any classes.

H. **Unofficial Transcript** means that it hasn't been signed or stamped with an official stamp. Transcripts are mailed directly to the school or colleges of your choice. Sometimes they can be transported by the student in a sealed envelope.

I. The date you entered the high school.

J. The date you left the high school.

K. Overall weighted—if your school gives extra points for honors or AP classes when figuring out your GPA, it will be noted here.

L. Your final cumulative GPA.

M. The total amount of credits you attempted.

N. Your class standing and the number of students who were in your senior class when you graduated. This student was 168 out of 388 students in the senior class.

O. Total Credits Earned in High School.

P. Notes about the clubs, sports, and committees in which you participated can be added here with verification from the person responsible for that extracurricular activity.

Q. Signature—the transcript must be signed and have an official seal in order to be accepted as an official transcript.

Colorado Springs Dist 11 (H)

Unofficial Transcript

Doherty High School   719-328-6400
4515 Barnes Rd
Colorado Springs, CO 80917

Entry Date	Counselor	Graduation Date
09/01/2002 (I)		05/20/2006
Exit Date	Exit Reason	Diploma Type
06/06/2006 (J)	W19-Graduated	High School Diploma
GPA Type	GPA	Crdt Attmpt	Class Rank
Overall Weighted	3.0476	42.0000	168 of 388
(K)	(L)	(M)	(N)

Issued To	Print Date
(A)	09/08/2005
	1 of 1

Total Credits Earned   44.0000 (O)

Subject Cd Course	Mrk1	Abs	Credits
Doherty High School Grd 09 Semester 1			
EN English 1, Honors	B	3	1.0000
HU Frhand Drwng1	A	5	1.0000
HU Spanish 1	B	4	1.0000
MA Algebra 1	B	5	1.0000
PE PE 9	B	7	1.0000
SC Intro to Science 1	C	6	1.0000
SS Gov/Law 1	B	5	1.0000
TERM: GPA 3.1429 CREDITS 7.0000			
CUMULATIVE: GPA 3.1429 CREDITS 7.0000			
Doherty High School Grd 09 Semester 2			
CM Computer Apps	B	1	1.0000
EN English 2, Honors	C	1	1.0000
HU Frhand Drwng2	A	2	1.0000
HU Spanish 2	B	4	1.0000
MA Algebra 2	B	1	1.0000
SC Intro to Science 2	A	1	1.0000
SS Gov/Law 2	B	3	1.0000
TERM: GPA 3.2857 CREDITS 7.0000			
CUMULATIVE: GPA 3.2143 CREDITS 14.0000			
Doherty High School Grd 10 Semester 1			
E3 English 3	B	3	1.0000
HL Health	C	1	1.0000
HU Spanish 3	B	1	1.0000
MA Geometry 1	B	2	1.0000
PA Todays Foods	B	1	1.0000
SC Biology 1	B	3	1.0000
SS World & US History 3	C	2	1.0000
TERM: GPA 2.7143 CREDITS 7.0000			
CUMULATIVE: GPA 3.0476 CREDITS 21.0000			
Doherty High School Grd 10 Semester 2			
E4 English 4	B	11	1.0000
HU Frhand Drwng3	A	6	1.0000
HU Spanish 4	B	6	1.0000
MA Geometry 2	C	3	1.0000
PE PE 10	B	7	1.0000
SC Biology 2	B	7	1.0000
SS World & US History 4	C	6	1.0000
TERM: GPA 2.8571 CREDITS 7.0000			
CUMULATIVE: GPA 3.0000 CREDITS 28.0000			

Subject Cd Course	Mrk1	Abs	Credits
Doherty High School Grd 11 Semester 1			
A1 Hist: US & World 5	C	9	1.0000
E5 English 5	B	9	1.0000
HU Psychology	B	13	1.0000
MA Algebra 3	B	10	1.0000
PA Automotive Tech 1	A	5	1.0000
TERM: GPA 3.0000 CREDITS 5.0000			
CUMULATIVE: GPA 3.0000 CREDITS 33.0000			
Doherty High School Grd 11 Semester 2			
A2 Hist: US & World 6	B	17	1.0000
E6 English 6	B	21	1.0000
EL Student Tutor	G	14	1.0000
HU Psychology, Advanced	A	19	1.0000
MA Algebra 4	B	14	1.0000
TERM: GPA 3.2500 CREDITS 5.0000			
CUMULATIVE: GPA 3.0270 CREDITS 38.0000			
Doherty High School Grd 12 Semester 1			
CE Cons Econ	B	13	1.0000
EN Creative Writing	A	15	1.0000
EN Senior Speed Reading 1	B	17	1.0000
PE PE	A	9	1.0000
PE Physical Ed	G		1.0000
SC College Prep Chem 1	C	19	1.0000
TERM: GPA 3.2000 CREDITS 6.0000			
CUMULATIVE: GPA 3.0476 CREDITS 44.0000			

Mrk 1: Course Grade

Student Notes
(P)

_____
School Official's Signature (Q)

TIPS FOR A SMOOTH START

Write down a list of things you want to accomplish. If you have a rough idea of where you're headed, you'll have an easier time getting there. You've already set goals for yourself. Maybe it was to score more points on a video game than the kid down the street. Maybe it was to ride a bike faster or do more maneuvers on a skateboard. When you get into high school, it's important to set goals for yourself from the start. Obviously, the goals will change over time, but having a list of goals—like I want to make the football team; I want to take some honors classes; I want to run for class president; I want to be the editor of the school yearbook—will help you stay motivated and give you something to work toward.

Make your goals specific. For example:

A vague goal is:

I want to be a better student than I was in middle school.

A specific goal is:

The reason I wasn't a good student in middle school is because I didn't turn in my homework. Starting off in high school, I'm going to turn in all my homework on time.

ADVICE FROM A SENIOR

"When I was a freshman, I was intimidated by the older kids' appearance of greatness and their accomplishments. I thought, 'Wow, I can't get to their level.' But don't give up because you think there's too much competition, especially if it's something you really want to do."

Kristen Seghers, Senior
West Windsor-Plainsboro High School South
Princeton Junction, New Jersey

Get involved in clubs and activities immediately. We've already talked about how clubs and activities help narrow your interests and focus you on what you want to do in the future. But extracurricular activities serve another very important purpose for high school freshmen. You'll find friends who like the same things you do. You'll be with older kids so you'll get to know some juniors and seniors. You'll gain confidence in yourself as you work together with other kids. You'll become comfortable with being in high school a lot quicker than if you hang around on the fringes looking in instead of being in the middle of the action, whether it's on a soccer team, chess club, or—whatever!

Get organized. In high school, being organized does not mean showing up in class on time with your teeth brushed. Being organized is brought to a whole different level in high school. Some kids are naturally this way. In junior high school, they knew what homework had to be done, when it was due, and what was required. In high school, the list of things to organize gets longer. You still have to show up on time and whether your teeth are brushed is up to you, but you do have to have all the supplies you need with you.

PARENT PERSPECTIVE

"Every Friday afternoon before leaving school, Jessica gets her locker organized. It's easy for it to get out of control because kids are stuffing things in there all week. Then they can't find something when they need it and the time between classes is so short."

Jodi Domsky
Parent of Jessica, who just started ninth grade and was very organized in middle school.

That sparkly pink pen in your hand won't do to take the test the teacher just handed you. Your teacher specifically told you to bring a blue or black ballpoint. Now where is it? I thought I put it in my backpack. Oh no, here's the sandwich I forgot to eat yesterday on top of my history homework. Your room may be a disaster, but your notebooks, binders, and calendar need to be in tip-top shape.

You're organizing for more classes and carrying around a lot more books and papers than you ever did in middle school. You're going to be involved in sports and clubs. Unless you're organized, you're going to spend more time dealing with chaos and confusion and moldy sandwiches than getting your homework

"Typically, middle school students get one big binder with four to five dividers. All their classes' materials are in one binder. It doesn't work that way for high school. They have too much. They can't put homework, notes, handouts and other pieces of paper in one section of the binder. When the binder system fails by mid-October, then they take everything that was in the binder and stuff it in a backpack. Now it's a 15-minute ordeal to find something in the backpack."

Heidi Pimentel
Spanish teacher
Pioneer High School
San Jose, California

done and having all the fun there is to have in high school. Each week in high school goes by at blazing speed and things can get out of control very quickly.

This is what organized students know:

- What was assigned in each class
- When the homework is due
- When the next test is scheduled
- What I need to bring to each class
- Where the supplies I need are located

Organization skills will stay with you the rest of your life. Now's a great time to learn how easy your life will be when you're organized.

ADVICE FROM A JUNIOR

I wasn't very organized and should have been. In middle school, you don't have as many classes as in high school. It's harder to plan for seven classes instead of three or four a day.

Matt Wolf, Junior
Doherty High School
Colorado Springs, Colorado

The way to get organized is to set up a system. It can be someone else's system or your own. The important thing is to have some way to keep track of when assignments are due, when tests are coming, and what nights are taken up with practices or meetings. Each week, go through and set up a new schedule for the coming week. It sounds like a lot of work, but when Thursday hits and your head is spinning, you'll be glad you have a schedule to hang on to. You could have three tests on the same day. Wouldn't it be helpful to know that way ahead of time instead of remembering the day of the tests?

Manage your time. Time management is a term that you've probably heard and put into the "I'll deal with that when I get older" category. Guess what, you're older! You have to take your time and manage it, which means figuring out what you have to do and how much time you have to do it.

It's going to be easy to say, "I'll do my homework after dinner," but you have to take into account that basketball practice doesn't end until 8 p.m., and when you get home you'll want something to eat. So, in reality, you're doing homework until 10 or 11 o'clock, and you have to get up at 6 o'clock.

In high school, your workload increases as you move into the upper classes. If you don't learn how to manage your time, you will only have to struggle that much harder. Plus you have all those other activities eating away at the 24 hours in each day.

Ask questions. You've heard the saying, "No question is a stupid question." Well, kids going into ninth grade seem to forget the "NO" part of that sentence and instead rephrase it as "All my questions are stupid." No matter if you went down the wrong hall and can't find your classroom. No matter if you need help in signing up for a club you really want to join. No matter if you didn't understand what the teacher was saying. The guidance counselors and teachers are there to help you get adjusted and pointed in the right direction.

Take advantage of the help the guidance counselors can give you. You'd be amazed at the number of things you can find in the guidance office—advice on good study habits, advice on planning for college, advice about what to do with that class in which you're having a problem. Use it, because it's there for you.

FROM THE GUIDANCE OFFICE

"As students transition to high school, it is important to develop self-advocacy skills. If you need or want something, you will have to seek out the resources to get the help or support that you desire. If you are struggling academically in a particular subject, you need to seek out your teacher for extra help. Your school counselor is an excellent resource to help you develop your self-advocacy skills and to help problem-solve other situations. Once you are in college, your parents will not be there, so start early so you will feel comfortable approaching the resources available."

Leslie Fisher
Lead Counselor
West Windsor-Plainsboro High School South
Princeton Junction, New Jersey

BEWARE OF THE BLACK HOLE OF THE BACKPACK

It looks like an ordinary backpack (or whatever it is you use to carry your books and school papers), but don't be fooled by its innocent appearance. Somewhere between the time you get out of middle school and into high school, it turns into a black hole—casually destroying finished homework, cheerfully ripping through notes you saved for a test, cunningly hiding the special pen you like.

You may have been organized in junior high school, but once you get into high school, the backpack can turn into an endless pit into which you stuff everything; however, whatever it is you need to find in its endless depths cannot be found without a major search and rescue.

The reason for this dilemma that will suddenly appear in your life is that in high school, you've got a lot more papers to organize. Homework is given in most classes. You're getting handouts that have to be saved for a test that will come up in three weeks, along with that list of notes of supplies you're supposed to bring to science class and the day planner you bought.

You must ramp up the way you keep things organized to keep up with high school. One suggestion is to get a three-subject spiral notebook for each class. Section one is for taking notes in class. Section two is for homework. Section three is for tearing out sheets of paper. You now have everything you need for one subject in one notebook. The pages can't come out unless you tear them out and it's chronological, so you can look back at past notes and tell what was discussed when.

With this system, or any other that suits you best, your backpack will turn into an ordinary useful bag, and when your history teacher asks you to pull out the notes from last week's class, you will know exactly where to find them.

TOP 10 MISTAKES

Everyone makes mistakes, but if you can avoid these TOP 10 as you begin your freshman year, you'll be in much better shape. Drum roll, please. We'll start with the worst.

1. **My freshman year doesn't count. My senior year is far away. If I mess up, I can always get back on track in the tenth grade.** While it's true you can make up for bad choices and slip-ups, your freshman year is the foundation upon which the rest of your high school years, and then college, are built. Freshman year isn't practice or a trial period—it's the real thing!

2. **I'm picking this class because my friend is taking it.** Your friend picked the class in beginning biology because she's always liked squiggly green bugs. You don't like looking in microscopes. You won't find out what a mistake you've made until you're way behind on homework and have failed several tests, when you could have been getting As in that writing class you wanted to take but didn't.

3. **I'll just skip this class. One day won't make a difference.** Not so. In high school, attendance counts. Many schools have policies that cause you to lose credits if you miss class a certain number of times. Even the best of students will miss classes because of illness or other unforeseen events. But remember, much of the teaching in high school is cumulative, meaning that each day is built on what happened in the class the day before. If you get out of the loop, it's really hard to get back in.

4. **I don't need to write down that assignment. I'll remember it.** Most likely, you'll only remember the assignment until you leave the classroom, then it's history. By the time you get home, you have a vague recollection of what the teacher said you had to do. Then you have to call someone in the class to ask about the assignment and that person isn't home, so you miss doing the homework.

5. **I spilled soda on my homework and now I'll be late turning it in if I do it over, so I'll just forget about it.** You should talk to your teacher about making up lost or forgotten homework. Even though the teacher will probably take off some points, you guarantee getting no points if you don't turn it in at all! So, while the assignment may be late, at least it will be counted. Don't be afraid to ask your teacher about turning in late assignments—better late than never!

6. **Sorry, I can't join that club, I have to study all the time.** In your freshman year, it's especially important to become part of the school community. Not only will you get to know other kids who like the same things you do, but you'll also explore what you like to do.

7. **Everyone else in this class understood what the teacher just said except me, so I won't ask him to explain it.** You will be surprised to know that if you didn't understand or need more explanation, probably everyone else feels the same way too. Be brave. Ask the question and have everyone else in your class silently thanking you. Plus, more importantly, you'll understand what the teacher was saying.

8. **I don't want to talk to the teacher about the problems I'm having with her class.** Teachers aren't mind readers. They have no clue that you're struggling until they see your work. If you're having problems, it's okay to say, "I just don't get fractions." Teachers love to teach and part of teaching is helping their students understand things.

9. **There's a situation at school that's making me uncomfortable. I'll just tell my friend about it and not go to the counselor's office.** Big or small, serious or not, whatever problems you're having or whatever situations are bothering you, your high school counselors are there to help you, protect you, guide you, comfort you. Your best friend may be able to sympathize with your problem, but chances are your friend can't solve the issue as effectively as a counselor or teacher can.

10. **I really don't need all that much sleep.** That may have been true during the summer when you could sleep late. Now you're up and out with the sunrise. Trouble is, when you go to bed late, you find yourself nodding off in first period. All that brain power you are using to adjust to high school takes energy. Energy comes from a good night's sleep.

MAKE SURE YOUR PARENTS READ THIS!

Some of you have been through the process of transitioning your son or daughter from middle school to high school. For some of you, it's your first time. Helen Erbe, a guidance counselor at Jackson Memorial High School in Jackson, New Jersey, has been a guidance counselor in middle school, elementary school, and now in high school. She says that having been at all levels, the transitions from elementary to middle and middle to high school are the most traumatic for your kids. The range of emotions swings from fearful to happy and back again. The transition brings out all your child's insecurities. But the cumulative wisdom of other parents and guidance counselors can help you help your children. Here are some tried and tested tips.

- Find out what tryouts for high school clubs, activities, and sports take place in the summer and see if your child may be interested in joining.

- While your child is still in middle school, take her to the high school on casual trips, such as to the library, to the swimming pool, to a play, so she will already be familiar with the building and things to do before ninth grade starts.

- Before high school starts, take your child on a test run to walk the halls and meet teachers who are there early to set up their classrooms. Then let him come back by himself for another test run.

- Encourage involvement in school activities other than just sports. In general, the students who are involved in extracurriculars enjoy school and have greater academic success. Advise your child to start gradually in the freshman year with a few activities and then add more as she moves toward her senior year.

- Help your child set up a system to organize homework assignments, test dates, and other activities.

- Give your child space to try things on her own. Get her to advocate for her interests and needs on her own. School administrators and teachers love parent involvement but it's important to let kids deal with some of the issues alone.

- Set realistic goals for your child. It's good for children to be challenged but if the goals are too ambitious, children give up reaching for any goals.

Part 2

JUMP-START YOUR FUTURE

COME ON, ADMIT IT. You know that big question—what will I do when I graduate from high school?—is right around the corner. Some of your classmates know what they want to do, but you're freaking out about all of the decisions you still have to make.

You've got a lot of possibilities from which to choose. Maybe you'll attend a two-year or four-year college or a vocational college or a career college. Or you'll join the armed services. Or perhaps you'll go right into the workplace with a full-time job. But before you march across that stage to get your diploma, *Peterson's Get a Jump!* will help you to begin thinking about your options and to open up doors you never knew existed.

Chapter 2

A LOOK AT YOURSELF

Deciding what to do with your life is a lot like flying. Just look at the many ways you can fly and the many directions your life can take.

A TEACHER ONCE asked her students to bring something to class that flies. Students brought kites, balloons, and models of airplanes, blimps, hot-air balloons, helicopters, spaceships, gliders, and seaplanes. But when class began, the teacher explained that the lesson was about career planning, not flying.

She was making the point that your plans for life after high school can take many forms. How you will make the journey is an individual matter. That's why it's important to know who you are and what you want before taking off.

You may not choose your life's career by reading *Peterson's Get a Jump!* (GAJ), but you'll learn how to become part of the decision-making process and find resources that can help you plan your future.

Ready to Fly?

Just having a high school diploma is not enough for many occupations. But, surprise, surprise, neither is a college degree. Different kinds of work require different kinds of trainings. Knowing how to operate a particular type of equipment, for instance, takes special skills and work experience that you might not learn in college. Employers always want to hire the best-qualified people available, but this does not mean that they always choose those applicants who have the most education. The *type* of education and training you have is just as important as *how much*. Right now, you're at the point in your life where you can choose how much and what kind of education and training you want to get.

If you have a definite career goal in mind, like being a doctor, you probably already know what it will take in terms of education. You're looking at about four years of college, then four years of medical school, and, in most states, one year of residency. Cosmetologists, on the other hand, complete a state-approved training program that ranges from eight to eighteen months.

But for most of you, deciding what to do after high school is not so easy. Perhaps you haven't chosen a field of work yet. You might just know for certain that you want a job that will give you status and a big paycheck. Or maybe you know what you want to do, but you're not sure what kind of education you'll need. For instance, you may love fixing cars, and the idea of being an auto mechanic sounds great. But you need to decide whether to learn on the job, attend a vocational school, seek an apprenticeship, or pursue a combination of these options.

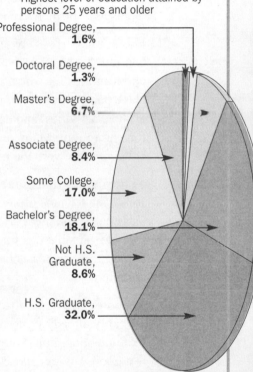

EDUCATIONAL ATTAINMENT
Highest level of education attained by persons 25 years and older

Professional Degree, **1.6%**
Doctoral Degree, **1.3%**
Master's Degree, **6.7%**
Associate Degree, **8.4%**
Some College, **17.0%**
Bachelor's Degree, **18.1%**
Not H.S. Graduate, **8.6%**
H.S. Graduate, **32.0%**

Source: U.S. Census Bureau, Current Population Survey, March 2005

21

THE TOP 10 REASONS TO CONTINUE YOUR EDUCATION

Continuing your education after high school is one choice that can give you a good start no matter what your final career decision is. There are many good reasons to do so. If you think college is not for you at all, take a look at this list. It just might change your mind.

10. **Fulfill a dream—or begin one.** Some people hope to become teachers or scientists. For many, continuing their education provides the opportunity to make that wish a reality for themselves or their family.

9. **Have fun.** Classes are an important part of continued education, but there are plenty of opportunities for some great times outside the classroom. There are hundreds of sports, clubs, groups, activities, and associations just waiting for you to join. Many people say that their college years were the best years of their lives.

8. **Make connections that can link you to future jobs.** The friends, professors, supervisors, and classmates you meet after high school will provide valuable ties for future jobs, committees, and associations within the community.

7. **Become part of a cultural stew.** As you have probably already figured out, not everyone is like you. Nor should they be. Being in college is a good way to expose yourself to many types of people from various backgrounds and geographic locations, with different viewpoints and opinions. You may discover that you like people and things you never knew existed.

6. **Meet new people.** By furthering your education, you will widen your circle of friends and, chances are, form meaningful lifelong relationships.

5. **Do what you love doing and get paid for it.** Have you ever taken a test during which everything clicked or played a video game and caught on immediately? This is what happens when you combine education and training with the right job. Work becomes more like play, which is far more satisfying and rewarding than just going through the motions.

4. **Exercise your mind.** Just as physical exercise keeps your body in shape, mental exercise keeps your mind free of cobwebs. No matter what your area of interest, education holds the key to the most interesting and challenging information you can imagine. Explore your outer limits and become a lifelong learner.

3. **Earn a higher income.** Although money isn't everything, it is necessary for survival. A good education prepares you to become a solid member of society. (See the chart below, "Increase Your Earning Power.")

2. **Learn critical-thinking and analytical skills.** More than any other skill, education teaches you to think. Furthering your learning will help you to think critically, organize and analyze information, and write clearly.

1. **You won't get left behind.** In the twenty-first century, you will need to be prepared to change jobs and continually learn new skills in order to keep up with changes in industry, communications, and technology. Education and training will give you that preparation.

Breaking Down the Barriers to

INCREASE YOUR EARNING POWER

People with more education tend to earn more money. Look at the average yearly earnings of workers over the age of 25 by education level.

Professional Degree	$95,700
Doctoral Degree	$79,400
Master's Degree	$59,500
Bachelor's Degree	$49,900
Associate Degree	$37,600
Some College	$35,700
High School Diploma	$30,800
Less Than High School Diploma	$21,600

Source: U.S. Census Bureau, 2004

Continuing Your Education

Some of you may say, "Forget the reasons why I *should* continue my education. I *can't* because (fill in the blank)." Let's see if your objections stand up.

I can't.

Nobody in my family has ever gone to college.

You can!

You can be the first! It's a little scary and not always easy, but just think how great you'll feel being the first person in your family to receive a degree, diploma, or certificate.

I can't.

My grades are not good enough.

You can!

Don't let less-than-perfect grades stand in your way. Different institutions have different requirements, including what grades they accept. Schools also evaluate you for admission as a whole person, including your participation in extracurricular activities; your talents, such as academics and athletics; and your employment and volunteer history. There are also classes that you can take to improve your skills in various subject areas. Get a tutor now or form a study group to improve your grades as much as possible. Talk to your guidance counselor about what the appropriate curriculum for you is so you'll have more options when making decisions about continuing your education.

I can't.

I can't afford it.

You can!

Many families cannot afford to pay education costs completely out of pocket. That's why there are so many opportunities for financial aid, scholarships, grants, and work-study programs. Federal, state, school-sponsored, private, and career-specific financial aid resources are available to students who take the time to look. Talk to a guidance counselor, go to the library, and look on the Internet. Read the "Financial Aid Dollars and Sense" chapter of this guide for more information about how to finance your continued education. Be creative and persistent. It can happen for you.

I can't.

I don't know how to apply or where I want to go.

You can!

Fortunately, there are resources to help you decide which institution to select. Talk to friends, family members, neighbors, your guidance counselor, pastor, coach, or librarian. Take a look at the Appendix at the back of this guide for listings of two-year and four-year colleges, as well as vocational and career colleges in your state.

I can't.

I think it may be too difficult for me.

You can!

Think back to something you have done in your life that seemed too difficult in the beginning. Didn't you find that once you began, put your mind to it, and stuck with it that you succeeded? You can do almost anything if you set your mind to it and are willing to work for it.

I can't.

I'm not sure I'll fit in.

You can!

One of the best things about furthering your education is the chance to meet new people and be part of new experiences in new surroundings. Colleges and other continuing education options attract a wide variety of students from many different backgrounds. Chances are you won't have any problem finding someone else with interests that are similar to yours. Because schools differ in size, location, student body, and lifestyle, you'll surely find one that meets your needs. Advance visits and interviews can help you determine which school is right for you.

FASTEST-GROWING OCCUPATIONS

Want to have a career that's going places? Check out this chart to see which occupations are expected to grow the fastest by the year 2010 and what type of training you'll need to get the job.

Occupation	Expected Openings	Required Education
Computer Software Engineers, applications	760,000	Bachelor's degree
Computer Support Specialists	996,000	Associate degree
Computer Software Engineers, systems software	601,000	Bachelor's degree
Network and Computer Systems Administrators	416,000	Bachelor's degree
Network Systems and Data Communications Analysts	211,000	Bachelor's degree
Desktop Publishers	63,000	Postsecondary vocational training
Database Administrators	176,000	Bachelor's degree
Personal and Home Care Aides	672,000	On-the-job training
Computer Systems Analysts	689,000	Bachelor's degree
Medical Assistants	516,000	On-the-job-training
Social and Human Service Assistants	418,000	On-the-job training
Physician Assistants	89,000	Bachelor's degree
Medical Records and Health Information Technicians	202,000	Associate degree
Computer and Information Systems Managers	463,000	Master's degree
Home Health Aides	907,000	On-the-job training
Physical Therapist Aides	53,000	On-the-job training
Occupational Therapist Aides	12,000	On-the-job training
Physical Therapist Assistants	64,000	Associate degree
Audiologists	19,000	Master's degree
Fitness Trainers and Aerobics Instructors	222,000	Postsecondary vocational training
Computer and Information Scientists	39,000	Doctoral degree
Veterinary Assistants and Lab Animal Caretakers	77,000	On-the-job training
Occupational Therapist Assistants	23,000	Associate degree
Veterinary Technologists and Technicians	69,000	Associate degree
Speech-language Pathologists	122,000	Master's degree
Mental Health and Substance Abuse Social Workers	116,000	Master's degree
Dental Assistants	339,000	On-the-job training
Dental Hygienists	201,000	Associate degree
Special Education Teachers, grades Pre-K to 6	320,000	Bachelor's degree
Pharmacy Technicians	259,000	On-the-job training

Source: Bureau of Labor Statistics, Occupational Outlook Handbook

I can't.

I don't even know what I want to do with my life.

You can!

Many students don't know this about themselves until they get to experience some of the possibilities. Take the "Self-Assessment Inventory" on page 26 to help you determine what your interests and talents are. Read "Choosing Your Major" on page 97 for a listing of the most popular college majors and their related careers.

I can't.

There is no way I can pursue my education full-time.

You can!

Part-time students are becoming the norm. In fact, a recent study determined that 43 percent of undergraduate students attend school part-time. Most schools offer evening and weekend classes, and many offer work-study opportunities to help students pay for their education. Also, some employers will pay or reimburse you if you are working and want to further your education. If you are enrolled part-time, it does take longer to graduate. But if full-time enrollment is not an option for you, don't give up the opportunity to continue your education. There are many nontraditional ways to achieve your goals.

CHOOSING A CAREER YOU'LL BE HAPPY WITH

Did you know that of the estimated 15 million people searching for employment in the American job market, approximately 12 million are looking for a new occupation or a different employer? That's an awful lot of people who aren't happy with their jobs. Avoid being one of them by taking some time to consider what it is you really want to do now, while you're still in school. Is there a particular type of job you've always dreamed of doing? Or perhaps you're one of the many high school students who say:

"I Kind of Know What I Want, But I'm Not Really Sure."

A good way to gather information about potential occupations is by talking with people who have achieved goals that are similar to yours. Talk to teachers, neighbors, and adult friends about their work experiences. The formal name for that activity is an "informational interview." You're interviewing them about the work they do—not to get a job from them but to gather information about their jobs.

If you don't have any contacts in a field that sparks your interest, do some poking around in the workplace. For instance, if you're interested in a career in nursing, you could visit a hospital, doctor's office, or nursing home. Most people love to talk about themselves, so don't be afraid to ask if they'll chat with you about their profession. Offering to volunteer your services can be the best way to know whether you'll be happy doing that type of work.

"I Don't Have a Clue About What I Want to Do."

If you're completely unsure about what kind of work you'd like to do, contact a career counselor who can help you explore your options and possibly administer some interest and aptitude tests. You also might think about contacting a college career planning and placement office, a vocational school placement office, the counseling services of community agencies, or a private counseling service, which may charge you a fee. Many high schools offer job-shadowing programs, where students actually shadow someone in a particular occupation for an entire day or more. Don't forget that as a high school student, your best resource is your high school guidance counselor. Take a look at the list of the "Fastest-Growing Occupations" on page 24 to get a sampling of the careers with the largest projected job growth in the coming years.

ON THE HUNT FOR INFORMATION

Regardless of how unsure you may be about what you want to do after high school, here's a list of things you can do to get the information you need to head in the right direction. Many people start off thinking they want one career and end up doing something completely different. But this is a good place to begin:

- Investigate careers both in and out of school. Participate in mentoring, job shadowing, and career day opportunities whenever possible.

- Get some on-the-job experience in a field that interests you.

- Research two-year and four-year colleges, vocational/career colleges, and apprenticeship programs.

- Participate in school and state career development activities.

- Prepare for and take aptitude and college entrance tests.

Here are a few Web sites where you can receive valuable direction by completing a career interest questionnaire or by reading about various occupations:

Peterson's

www.petersons.com

On Peterson's Web site, you can read helpful articles about the workplace and search for undergraduate academic and career-oriented degree and certificate programs.

Occupational Outlook Handbook

www.bls.gov/oco

The Bureau of Labor Statistics, an agency within the U.S. Department of Labor, produces this Web site, which offers more information than you'll ever need about specific careers.

SELF-ASSESSMENT INVENTORY

In addition to looking to outside sources for information, there's another rich source of data: yourself. Knowing what you want to do begins with knowing yourself—the real you. The better you understand your own wants and needs, the better you will be able to make decisions about your career goals and dreams. This self-assessment inventory can help.

Who do you admire most, and why?

What is your greatest strength?

What is your greatest talent?

What skills do you already have?

DESCRIBE HOW YOU CURRENTLY USE THESE SKILLS IN YOUR LIFE:

Athletic ability

Mechanical ability

Ability to work with numbers

Leadership skills

Teaching skills

Artistic skills

Analytical skills

CHECK THE AREAS THAT MOST INTEREST YOU:

- ❑ Providing a practical service for people
- ❑ Self-expression in music, art, literature, or nature
- ❑ Organizing and record keeping
- ❑ Meeting people and supervising others
- ❑ Helping others in need, either mentally, spiritually, or physically
- ❑ Solving practical problems
- ❑ Working in forestry, farming, or fishing
- ❑ Working with machines and tools
- ❑ Taking care of animals
- ❑ Physical work outdoors
- ❑ Protecting the public via law enforcement or fire fighting
- ❑ Medical, scientific, or mathematical work
- ❑ Selling, advertising, or promoting

WHAT GIVES YOU SATISFACTION?

Answer the following questions True (T) or False (F).

T F I get satisfaction not from personal accomplishment, but from helping others.

T F I'd like to have a job in which I can use my imagination and be inventive.

T F In my life, money will be placed ahead of job security and personal interests.

T F It is my ambition to have a direct impact on other people's lives.

T F I am not a risk-taker and would prefer a career that offers little risk.

T F I enjoy working with people rather than by myself.

T F I would not be happy doing the same thing all the time.

WHAT MATTERS THE MOST TO YOU?

Rate the items on the list below from 1 to 10, with 10 being extremely important and 1 being not at all important.

___ Good health	___ Seeing the world
___ Justice	___ Love
___ Marriage/family	___ Fun
___ Faith	___ Power
___ Fame	___ Individualism
___ Beauty	___ Charity
___ Safety	___ Honor
___ Friendship	___ Intelligence
___ Respect	___ Wealth
___ Accomplishment	

Mapping Your Future

www.mapping-your-future.org

On this site, you can find out how to choose a career and how to reach your career goals. You can also pick up useful tips on job hunting, resume writing, and job interviewing techniques. This site also provides a ten-step plan for determining and achieving your career goals.

University of Waterloo Career Development Manual

www.cdm.uwaterloo.ca/

This site provides a thorough online career interest survey, and strategies you can use to get the job that's right for you.

LiveCareer

www.livecareer.com

LiveCareer is a San Francisco based company founded by Sigma Assessment Systems, Inc. and a group of leading career professionals and investors. Since 1967, they have developed innovative practical assessment solutions that have helped more than 300,000 people make important career decisions.

HotJobs.com

www.hotjobs.com

Includes information about thousands of job and career fairs, advice on resumes, and much more.

WHAT WOULD YOU DO IF YOU WERE IN A BLIZZARD SURVIVAL SITUATION?

Check the one that would be your most likely role.

- ☐ The leader
- ☐ The one who explains the situation to the others
- ☐ The one who keeps morale up
- ☐ The one who invents a way to keep warm and melt snow for water
- ☒ The one who listens to instructions and keeps the supplies organized
- ☐ The one who positions sticks and rocks to signal SOS

LOOKING AHEAD AND LOOKING BACK

What are your goals for the next five years?
To go to college and get a good Job.

Where would you like to be in ten years?
be interior designer have a family.

What was your favorite course, and why?
Stage Craft b/c I like theatre.

What was your least favorite course, and why?
History I'm not very good at it.

Who was your favorite teacher, and why?
Mrs. kowitz she teaches you step by step.

What are your hobbies?
roller blading. theatre.

What are your extracurricular activities?
theatre.

What jobs have you held?
none yet.

What volunteer work, if any, have you performed?
Cleaned a park.

Have you ever shadowed a professional for a day? If so, what did you learn?
no

Do you have a mentor? If so, who? What have you learned from this person?
no

Do you want to stay close to home, or would you prefer to travel to another city after high school?
close to home

WHAT ARE YOUR CAREER GOALS?

The interests, skills, and knowledge supporting my career goals are: College and design people spaces.

To fulfill my career goals, I will need additional skills and knowledge in: math, biology. Photo.

I will obtain the additional skills and knowledge by taking part in the following educational activities:

I will need a degree, certification, and/or specialized training in: bachlors degree.

When I look in the classified ads of the newspaper, the following job descriptions sound attractive to me: interior designer, zoo keeper

WHAT ARE YOUR IMMEDIATE PLANS AFTER HIGH SCHOOL?

After high school, I plan to:

- ☒ Work full-time
- ☐ Work part-time and attend school
- ☒ Attend college full-time
- ☐ Attend technical college
- ☐ Enter the military

WHAT WILL YOU NEED TO GET WHERE YOU'RE GOING?

The information I have given indicates that I will be selecting courses that are primarily:

- ☐ College path (Four-year or two-year education that offers liberal arts courses combined with courses in your area of interest.)
- ☐ Vocational path (One or more years of education that include hands-on training for a specific job.)
- ☐ Combination of the two

MY PERFECT JOB WOULD BE ...

Let your imagination run wild You can have any job you want. What's it like? Start by describing to yourself the following job conditions:

Work conditions What hours are you willing to work? Do you feel most satisfied in an environment that is indoors/outdoors, varied/regular, noisy/quiet, or casual/traditional?

Duties What duties do you feel comfortable carrying out? Do you want to be a leader, or do you perform best as a team player?

People Do you want to work with other people or more independently? How much people contact do you want/need?

Education How much special training or education is required? How much education are you willing to seek? Can you build upon the education or experience you have to date? Will you need to gain new education or experience?

Benefits What salary and benefits do you expect? Are you willing to travel?

Disadvantages There are disadvantages with almost any job. Can you imagine what the disadvantages may be? Can you confirm or disprove these beliefs by talking to someone or researching the industry or job further? If these disadvantages really exist, can you live with them?

Personal qualities What qualities do you want in the employer you ultimately choose? What are the most important qualities that you want in a supervisor? In your coworkers?

Look over your responses to this assessment. Do you see recurring themes in your answers that start to show you what kind of career you might like? If not, there are many more places to get information to decide where your interests lie. You can go to your guidance counselor for advice. You can take the Campbell ™ Interest and Skills Inventory, the Strong Interest Inventory, the Self-Directed Search, or other assessment tests that your guidance counselor recommends.

3 chapter

THE FIRST STEPS TO A CAREER

Don't be too surprised when your summer job turns into your career.

THE WORD "CAREER" has a scary sound to it when you're still in high school. Careers are for college graduates or those who have been in the workplace for years. But unless you grew up knowing for sure that you wanted to fly airplanes or be a botanist, what will you do? You'll be happy to know that interests you have now can very possibly lead to a college major or into a career. A job at a clothing store, for instance, could lead to a career designing clothes. Perhaps those hours you spend stealing cars in Grand Theft Auto will lead to a career creating video games! Maybe you baby-sit and love being around kids, so teaching becomes an obvious choice. Perhaps cars fascinate you, and you find out you want to fix them for a living.

This chapter will show you how you can begin exploring your interests—sort of like getting into a swimming pool starting with your big toe, rather than plunging in. Vocational/career and tech-prep programs, summer jobs, and volunteering are all ways you can test various career paths to decide if you like them.

THE VOCATIONAL/CAREER EDUCATION PATH

If you're looking for a more real-world education, add yourself to the nearly 11 million youths and adults who are getting a taste of the workplace through vocational and career education programs offered in high schools across the nation. These programs are designed to help you develop competency in the skills you'll need in the workplace as well as in school.

What makes this kind of program different is that you learn in the classroom and in the "real world" of the workplace. Not only do you learn the academics in school, but you also get hands-on training by job shadowing, working under a mentor, and actually performing a job outside of school. Your interests and talents are usually taken into consideration, and you can choose from a variety of traditional, high-tech, and service industry training programs. Take a look at the following categories and see what piques your interest.

STUDENT COUNSEL

Q: What do you like about vocational training?

A: I jumped into the tech center my first year when I was a junior because I thought it was a good way to get out of school. But as the year went on, I said, "Hey, this is a good place to be because it's giving me job experience, and I'm learning how to dress and present myself like I was at a real job." I go during the first 3 or last 3 hours out of the school day. When we're in class, we get to do real jobs for people who ask our instructor for help. Then our teacher lets our creative minds go. We just designed a CD cover. One guy here designed a motorcycle and built it, and now he has three people asking him to come and work for them.

Trisha Younk
Tuscola County Tech Center
Reese High School
Reese, Michigan

Agricultural education. These programs prepare students for careers in agricultural production, animal production and care, agribusiness, agricultural and industrial mechanics, environmental management, farming, horticulture and landscaping, food processing, and natural resource management.

Business education. Students prepare for careers in accounting and finance and computer and data processing as well as administrative/secretarial and management/supervisory positions in professional environments (banking, insurance, law, public service).

Family and consumer sciences. These programs prepare students for careers in child care, food management and production, clothing and interiors, and hospitality and facility care. Core elements include personal development, family life and planning, resource management, and nutrition and wellness.

Trade and industrial and health occupations. Students prepare for careers in auto mechanics, the construction trades, cosmetology, electronics, graphics, public safety, and welding. Health occupation programs offer vocational training for careers in dental and medical assisting, practical nursing, home health care, and medical office assisting.

Marketing education. These programs prepare students for careers in sales, retail, advertising, food and restaurant marketing, and hotel management.

There are many vocational/career education programs available; the kinds listed above represent only a few of the possibilities. To find a program that suits your interests and that is located near you, refer to the college and university listings in the Appendix of this book. Or, you can get more information about vocational education programs by calling 202-245-7700 or e-mailing the U.S. Department of Education, Office of Vocational and Adult Education via its Web site, www.ed.gov/about/offices/list/ovae/index.html.

FROM THE GUIDANCE OFFICE

Q: What if going to college is not for me?

A: When adults ask kids what they want to do as a career, kids feel pressured. They think adults want them to identify with one single career. But there are more than 40,000 job titles a person can hold. We tell kids to pick a path first. When you exit high school, there are three paths you can take. One is to the workplace. One leads to the military as a career or as a stepping stone. The third leads to more education—a professional degree, a four-year degree, or a two-year degree. They have to determine which path they'll take.

One of the main selling points about getting career education in high school is that nearly every employer wants you to have some experience before you are hired. In career tech, students are in a workplace environment and can list their time as work experience, and they'll have previous employers who can vouch for them.

Lenore Lemanski
Counselor, Technology Center
Tuscola ISD
Caro, Michigan

THE TECH-PREP PATH

An even more advanced preparation for the workplace and/or an associate degree from a college is called tech-prep. It's an educational path that combines college-prep and vocational/technical courses of study.

During the sequence of courses, the focus is on blending academic and vocational/technical competencies. When you graduate from high school, you'll be able to jump right into the workforce or get an associate degree. But if you want to follow this path, you've got to plan for it starting in the ninth grade. Ask your guidance counselor for more information.

USING THE SUMMER TO YOUR ADVANTAGE

When you're sitting in class, a summer with nothing to do might seem appealing. But after you've listened to all of your CDs, aced all of your video games, hung out at the same old mall, and talked to your friends on the phone about being bored, what's left? How about windsurfing on a cool, clear New England lake? Horseback riding along breathtaking mountain trails? Parlez français in Paris? Trekking through spectacular canyon lands or living with a family in Costa Rica, Spain, Switzerland, or Japan? Exploring college majors or possible careers? Helping out on an archeological dig or community-service project? Along the way, you'll meet some wonderful people and maybe even make a couple of lifelong friends.

Interested? Get ready to pack your bags and join the 1 million kids and teens who will be having the summer of a lifetime at thousands of terrific camps, academic programs, sports clinics, arts workshops, internships, volunteer opportunities, and travel adventures throughout North America and abroad.

Oh, you don't have the money, you say? Not to worry. There are programs to meet every budget, from $50 workshops to $4,500 world treks and sessions that vary in length from just a couple of hours to a couple of months.

For a list of summer opportunities, take a look at the Appendix in this book. You can also find out about summer opportunities by visiting www.petersons. com.

FROM THE GUIDANCE OFFICE

Q: What options are open to students who take high school career/technology classes and who feel they can't go to college?

A: Students have the opportunity to develop many skills through classes, student organizations, and career/technology classes during high school. These skills form an essential core that they can use to continue on to college, enter the job market, or participate in additional training after graduation. When students can identify those skills and make the connection by applying and expanding their skills as lifelong learners, then the possibilities are endless.

Linda S. Sanchez
Career and Technology Counselor
South San Antonio I.S.D.
Career Education Center
San Antonio, Texas

FLIP BURGERS AND LEARN ABOUT LIFE

A lot of teenagers who are anxious to earn extra cash spend their summers in retail or food service since those jobs are plentiful. If you're flipping burgers or helping customers find a special outfit, you might think the only thing you're getting out of the job is a paycheck. Think again. You will be amazed to discover that you have gained far more.

Being employed in these fields will teach you how to get along with demanding (and sometimes downright unpleasant) customers, how to work on a team, and how to handle money and order supplies. Not only do summer jobs teach you life skills, but they also offer ways to explore potential careers. What's more, when you apply to college or for a full-time job after high school graduation, the experience will look good on your application.

Sometimes, summer jobs become the very thing you want to do later in life. Before committing to a college major, summer jobs give you the opportunity to try out many directions. Students who think they want to be engineers, lawyers, or doctors might spend the summer shadowing an engineer, being a gofer in a legal firm, or volunteering in a hospital.

However, rather than grab the first job that comes along, find out where your interests are and build on what is natural for you. Activities you take for granted provide clues to what you are good at. What about that bookcase you built? Or those kids you love to baby-sit? Same thing with that big party you arranged. The environments you prefer provide other hints, too. Perhaps you feel best in the middle of a cluttered garage instead of surrounded by people. That suggests certain types of jobs.

Getting a summer job while in high school is the first step in a long line of work experiences to come. And the more experience you have, the better you'll be at getting jobs all your life.

TRY YOUR HAND AT AN INTERNSHIP

Each year, thousands of interns work in a wide variety of places, including corporations, law firms, government agencies, media organizations, interest groups, clinics, labs, museums, and historical sites. How popular are internships? Consider the recent trends. In the early 1980s, only 1 in 36 students completed an internship or other experiential learning program. Compare this to 2000, where one study found that 86 percent of college students had completed internships, with 69 percent reporting having had two or more. And an increasing number of high school students are signing up for internships now, too.

The Employer's Perspective

Employers consider internships a good option in both healthy and ailing economies. In healthy economies, managers often struggle to fill their positions with eager workers who can adapt to changing technologies. Internships offer a low-cost way to get good workers into "the pipeline" without offering them a full-time position up front. In struggling economies, on the other hand, downsizing often requires employers to lay off workers without thinking about who will cover their responsibilities. Internships offer an inexpensive way to offset position losses resulting from these disruptive layoffs.

The Intern's Perspective

If you are looking to begin a career or supplement your education with practical training, internships are a good bet for several reasons.

1. **Internships offer a relatively quick way to gain work experience and develop job skills.** Try this exercise. Scan the Sunday want ads of your newspaper. Choose a range of interesting advertisements for professional positions that you would consider taking. List the desired or required job skills and work experiences specified in the ads. How many of these skills

and experiences do you have? Chances are, if you are still in school, you don't have most of the skills and experience that employers require of their new hires. What do you do?

The growing reality is that many entry-level positions require skills and experiences that schools and part-time jobs don't provide. Sure, you know your way around a computer. You have some customer service experience. You may even have edited your school's newspaper or organized your junior prom. But you still lack the relevant skills and on-the-job experiences that many hiring managers require. A well-chosen internship can offer a way out of this common dilemma by providing you job training in an actual career field. Internships help you take your existing knowledge and skills and apply them in ways that will help you compete for good jobs.

2. **Internships offer a relatively risk-free way to explore a possible career path.** Believe it or not, the best internship may tell you what you *don't* want to do for the next ten or twenty years. Think about it. If you put all your eggs in one basket, what happens if your dream job turns out to be the exact opposite of what you want or who you are? Internships offer a relatively low-cost opportunity to "try out" a career field to see if it's right for *you*.

3. **Internships offer real opportunities to do career networking and can significantly increase your chances of landing a good full-time position.** Have you heard the saying: "It's not what you know, but who you know"? The reality is that who you know (or who knows you) can make a big difference in your job search. Studies show that fewer than 20 percent of job placements occur through traditional application methods, including newspaper and trade journal advertisements, employment agencies, and career fairs. Instead, 60 to 90 percent of jobs are found through personal contacts and direct application.

Career networking is the exchange of information with others for mutual benefit. Your career network can tell you where the jobs are and help you compete for them. Isn't it better to develop your networking skills now, when the stakes aren't as high, than later when you are competing with everyone else for full-time jobs? The internship hiring process and the weeks you actually spend on the job provide excellent opportunities to talk with various people about careers, your skills, and ways to succeed.

VOLUNTEERING IN YOUR COMMUNITY

You've probably heard the saying that money isn't everything. Well, it's true, especially when it comes to volunteering and community service. There are a number of benefits you'll get that don't add up in dollars and cents but do add up to open doors in your future.

Community service looks good on a college application. Admissions staff members look for applicants who have volunteered and done community service in addition to earning good grades. You could have gotten top grades, but if that's all that's on your application, you won't come across as a well-rounded person.

Community service lets you try out careers. How will you know you'll like a certain type of work if you haven't experienced it? For instance, you might think you want to work in the health-care field. Volunteering in a hospital will let you know if this is really what you want to do.

Community service is an American tradition. You'll be able to meet some of your own community's needs and join with all of the people who have contributed their talents to our country. No matter what your talents, there are unlimited ways for you to serve your community. Take a look at your interests, and then see how they can be applied to help others.

Here are some ideas to get you started:

- ❑ **Do you like kids?** Volunteer at your local parks and recreation department, for a Little League team, or as a big brother or sister.

- ❑ **Planning a career in health care?** Volunteer at a blood bank, clinic, hospital, retirement home, or hospice. There are also several organizations that raise money for disease research.

- ❑ **Interested in the environment?** Volunteer to assist in a recycling program. Create a beautification program for your school or community. Plant trees and flowers or design a community garden.

- ❑ **Just say no.** Help others stay off drugs and alcohol by volunteering at a crisis center, hotline, or prevention program. Help educate younger kids about the dangers of drug abuse.

- ❑ **Lend a hand.** Collect money, food, or clothing for the homeless. Food banks, homeless shelters, and charitable organizations need your help.

- ❑ **Is art your talent?** Share your knowledge and skills with youngsters, the elderly, or local arts organizations that depend on volunteers to help present their plays, recitals, and exhibitions.

- ❑ **Help fight crime.** Form a neighborhood watch or organize a group to clean up graffiti.

- ❑ **Your church or synagogue may have projects that need youth volunteers.** The United Way, your local politician's office, civic groups, and special interest organizations also provide exceptional opportunities to serve your community. Ask your principal, teachers, or counselors for additional ideas.

For more information on joining in the spirit of youth volunteerism, write to the Federal Citizen Information Center, Pueblo, Colorado 81009, and request the *Catch the Spirit* booklet. Also check out the FCIC's Web site at www.pueblo.gsa.gov.

Part 3

THE ROAD TO MORE EDUCATION

SOME PEOPLE WAKE up at age 3 and announce that they want to be doctors, teachers, or marine biologists—and they do it.

They're the exceptions. Many high school students don't have a clue about what they want to be. They dread the question, "So, what are you going to do after graduation?" Unfortunately, some of those same people are also the ones who end up in careers that don't satisfy them.

You don't have to plan the rest of your life down to the last detail, but you can start to take some general steps toward your future and lay the groundwork. Then, when you do decide what you want to do, you'll be able to seize hold of your dream and go with it.

Chapter 4

PLANNING YOUR EDUCATION WHILE IN HIGH SCHOOL

Some people are planners. Then there are the non-planners. Either way, we've got a plan for you!

NON-PLANNERS see the words "plan" and "future" and say, "Yeah, yeah, I know." Meanwhile, they're running out the door for an appointment they were supposed to be at 5 minutes ago.

Unfortunately, when it comes time to really do something about those goals and future hopes, the non-planners often discover that much of what should have been done wasn't done—which is not good when they're planning their future after high school. What about those classes they should have taken? What about those jobs they should have volunteered for? What about that scholarship they could have had if only they'd found out about it sooner?

But there is hope for poor planners. Now that you've thought about yourself and the direction you might want to go after graduating, you can use this chapter to help you plan what you should be doing and when you should be doing it, while still in high school.

Regardless of what type of education you're pursuing after high school, here's a plan to help you get there.

YOUR EDUCATION TIMELINE

Use this timeline to help you make sure you're accomplishing everything you need to accomplish on time.

Ninth Grade

- As soon as you can, meet with your guidance counselor to begin talking about colleges and careers.

- Make sure you are enrolled in the appropriate college-preparatory or tech-prep courses.

- Get off to a good start with your grades. The grades you earn in ninth grade will be included in your final high school GPA and class rank.

- College might seem a long way off now, but grades really do count toward college admission and scholarships.

- Explore your interests and possible careers. Take advantage of Career Day opportunities.

- Get involved in extracurricular activities (both school and non-school-sponsored).

- Talk to your parents about planning for college expenses. Continue or begin a savings plan for college.

- Look at the college information available in your counselor's office and school and public libraries. Use the Internet to check out college Web sites. Visit Peterson's at www.petersons.com to start a list of colleges that might interest you.

- Tour a nearby college, if possible. Visit relatives or friends who live on or near a college campus. Check out the dorms, go to the library or student center, and get a feel for college life.

Investigate summer enrichment programs. Visit www.petersons.com for some neat ideas about summer opportunities.

Tenth Grade

Fall

In October, take the Preliminary SAT/National Merit Scholarship Qualifying Test (PSAT/NMSQT) for practice. When you fill out your test sheet, check the box that releases your name to colleges so you can start receiving brochures from them.

Ask your guidance counselor about the American College Testing program's PLAN (Pre-ACT) assessment program, which helps determine your study habits and academic progress and interests. This test will prepare you for the ACT Assessment next year.

Take geometry if you have not already done so. Take biology and a second year of a foreign language.

Become familiar with general college entrance requirements.

Participate in your school's or state's career development activities.

PARENT PERSPECTIVE

Q: **When should parents and their children start thinking about preparing for college?**

A: **The discussion needs to start in middle school. If parents don't expose their children to these concepts at that time, then it can be too late in the game. Children need to take the right courses in high school. Many kids here end up going to junior colleges because they don't meet the minimum requirements when they graduate. Many universities and private colleges don't count some of the classes kids take in high school. You can't wait until the child is 18 and then say, "Maybe we should do something about getting into college."**

Kevin Carr
Parent
Oak Park, California

Visit Petersons.com for advice on test taking and general college entrance requirements.

Winter

Discuss your PSAT score with your counselor.

The people who read college applications aren't looking just for grades. Get involved in activities outside the classroom. Work toward leadership positions in the activities that you like best. Become involved in community service and other volunteer activities.

Read, read, read. Read as many books as possible from a comprehensive reading list, like the one on pages 42 and 43.

Read the newspaper every day to learn about current affairs.

Work on your writing skills—you'll need them no matter what you do.

Find a teacher or another adult who will advise and encourage you to write well.

Spring

Keep your grades up so you can have the highest GPA and class rank possible.

Ask your counselor about postsecondary enrollment options and Advanced Placement (AP) courses.

Continue to explore your interests and careers that you think you might like.

Begin zeroing in on the type of college you would prefer (two-year or four-year, small or large, rural or urban). To get an idea of what's available, take a look at college profiles on Petersons.com.

If you are interested in attending a military academy such as West Point or Annapolis, now is the time to start planning and getting information.

Write to colleges and ask for their academic requirements for admission.

- Visit a few more college campuses. Read all of the mail you receive from colleges. You may see something you like.

- Attend college fairs.

- Keep putting money away for college. Get a summer job.

- Consider taking SAT Subject Tests in the courses you took this year while the material is still fresh in your mind. These tests are offered in May and June.

Eleventh Grade

Fall

- Meet with your counselor to review the courses you've taken, and see what you still need to take.

- Check your class rank. Even if your grades haven't been that good so far, it's never too late to improve. Colleges like to see an upward trend.

- If you didn't do so in tenth grade, sign up for and take the PSAT/NMSQT. In addition to National Merit Scholarships, this is the qualifying test for the National Scholarship Service and Fund for Negro Students and the National Hispanic Recognition Program.

- Make sure that you have a social security number.

- Take a long, hard look at why you want to continue your education after high school so you will be able to choose the best college or university for your needs.

- Make a list of colleges that meet your most important criteria (size, location, distance from home, majors, academic rigor, housing, and cost). Weigh each of the factors according to their importance to you.

- Continue visiting college fairs. You may be able to narrow your choices or add a college to your list.

PARENT PERSPECTIVE

Q: How involved should parents get in the selection of a college for their children?

A: Parents are getting more involved than ever before in supporting their children in the college process. This phenomenon is due to two factors:

(1) This generation of parents has been much more involved with their children in dealing with the outside world than were their parents.

(2) The investment made by today's parents is much more than that made by parents 20 or 30 years ago. As parents focus on the cost of this big-ticket item, there's interest to be more involved, to get the proper return.

Parents certainly should be involved in the college selection and application process. Studies clearly indicate that parental support in this process and throughout the college years can make a big difference in the success of a student. But this process also should be a learning opportunity in decision making for students. In that regard, parents shouldn't direct the student but provide input and the framework to assist their students.

Parents should not feel uncomfortable making suggestions to help their children through the thought and selection process—especially when it comes to identifying schools that their pocketbooks can accommodate. However, the child must be comfortable with the final decision and must have ultimate responsibility for the selection of the school. When students have made the final decision, it can help in their level of commitment because they've invested in it. They have a responsibility to do well and complete their academics at that location.

Richard Flaherty
President, College Parents of America

- Speak to college representatives who visit your high school.

- If you want to participate in Division I or Division II sports in college, start the certification process. Check with your counselor to make sure you are taking a core curriculum that meets NCAA requirements.

- If you are interested in one of the military academies, talk to your guidance counselor about starting the application process now.

6 STUDY SKILLS THAT LEAD TO SUCCESS

1. **SET A REGULAR STUDY SCHEDULE. No one at college is going to hound you to do your homework. Develop the study patterns in high school that will lead to success in college. Anyone who has ever pulled an all-nighter knows how much you remember when you are on the downside of your fifth cup of coffee and no sleep—not much! Nothing beats steady and consistent study habits.**

2. **SAVE EVERYTHING. To make sure your history notes don't end up in your math notebook and your English papers don't get thrown at the bottom of your friend's locker, develop an organized system for storing your papers. Stay on top of your materials, and be sure to save quizzes and tests. It is amazing how questions from a test you took in March can miraculously reappear on your final exam.**

3. **LISTEN. Teachers give away what will be on the test by repeating themselves. If you pay attention to what the teacher is saying, you will probably notice what is being emphasized. If what the teacher says in class repeats itself in your notes and in review sessions, chances are that material will be on the test. So really listen.**

4. **TAKE NOTES. If the teacher has taken the time to prepare a lecture, then what he or she says is important enough for you to write down. Develop a system for reviewing your notes. After each class, rewrite them, review them, or reread them. Try highlighting the important points or making notes in the margins to jar your memory.**

5. **USE TEXTBOOKS WISELY. What can you do with a textbook besides lose it? Use it to back up or clarify information that you don't understand from your class notes. Reading every word may be more effort than it is worth, so look at the book intelligently. What is in boxes or highlighted areas? What content is emphasized? What do the questions ask about in the review sections?**

6. **FORM A STUDY GROUP. Establish a group that will stay on task and ask one another the questions you think the teacher will ask. Compare notes to see if you have all the important facts. And discuss your thoughts. Talking ideas out can help when you have to respond to an essay question.**

Winter

- Collect information about college application procedures, entrance requirements, tuition and fees, room and board costs, student activities, course offerings, faculty composition, accreditation, and financial aid. The Internet is a good way to visit colleges and obtain this information. Begin comparing the schools by

the factors that you consider to be most important.

- Discuss your PSAT score with your counselor.

- Begin narrowing down your college choices. Find out if the colleges you are interested in require the SAT, ACT Assessment, or SAT Subject Tests for admission.

- Register for the SAT and additional SAT Subject Tests, which are offered several times during the winter and spring of your junior year (see the "Tackling the Tests" chapter for a schedule). You can take them again in the fall of your senior year if you are unhappy with your scores.

- Register for the ACT Assessment, which is usually taken in April or June. You can take it again late in your junior year or in the fall of your senior year, if necessary.

- Begin preparing for the tests you've decided to take.

- Have a discussion with your parents about the colleges in which you are interested. Examine financial resources, and gather information about financial aid. Check out the "Financial Aid Dollars and Sense" chapter for a step-by-step explanation of the financial aid process.

- Set up a filing system with individual folders for each college's correspondence and printed materials.

Spring

- Meet with your counselor to review senior-year course selection and graduation requirements.

- Discuss ACT Assessment/SAT scores with your counselor. Register to take the ACT Assessment and/or SAT again if you'd like to try to improve your score.

- Discuss the college essay with your guidance counselor or English teacher.

- Stay involved with your extracurricular activities. Colleges look for consistency and depth in activities.

Consider whom you will ask to write your recommendations. Think about asking teachers who know you well and who will write positive letters about you. Letters from a coach, activity leader, or an adult who knows you well outside of school (e.g., volunteer work contact) are also valuable.

Inquire about personal interviews at your favorite colleges. Call or write for early summer appointments. Make necessary travel arrangements.

See your counselor to apply for on-campus summer programs for high school students. Apply for a summer job or internship. Be prepared to pay for college applications and testing fees in the fall.

Request applications from schools you're interested in by mail or via the Internet.

Summer

Visit the campuses of your top-five college choices.

After each college interview, send a thank-you letter to the interviewer.

Talk to people you know who have attended the colleges in which you are interested.

Continue to read books, magazines, and newspapers.

Practice filling out college applications, and then complete the final application forms or apply on line through the Web sites of the colleges in which you're interested.

Volunteer in your community.

Compose rough drafts of your college essays. Have a teacher read and discuss them with you. Polish them, and prepare final drafts. Proofread your final essays at least three times.

Develop a financial aid application plan, including a list of the aid sources, requirements for each application, and a timetable for meeting the filing deadlines.

ADMISSIONS ADVICE

Q: Other than grades and test scores, what are the most important qualities that you look for in students?

A: We consider the types of classes students have taken. A grade of a B in an honors class is competitive to an A in a regular course. We seek not only academically talented students but those who are well rounded. They need to submit their interests and activities, letters of recommendation, and writing samples in addition to their test scores. We look for someone that's involved in his or her community and high school, someone that holds leadership positions and has a balance of activities outside of academics. This gives us a look at that person as a whole.

Cheyenna Smith
Admission Counselor
University of Houston
Houston, Texas

Twelfth Grade

Fall

Continue to take a full course load of college-prep courses.

Keep working on your grades. Make sure you have taken the courses necessary to graduate in the spring.

Continue to participate in extracurricular and volunteer activities. Demonstrate initiative, creativity, commitment, and leadership in each.

To male students: you must register for selective service on your eighteenth birthday to be eligible for federal and state financial aid.

Talk to counselors, teachers, and parents about your final college choices.

Make a calendar showing application deadlines for admission, financial aid, and scholarships.

Check resource books, Web sites, and your guidance office for information on scholarships and grants. Ask colleges about scholarships for which you may qualify. Check out Petersons.com for information on scholarships.

College APP deadline Dec. 3rd 2007

- Give recommendation forms to the teachers you have chosen, along with stamped, self-addressed envelopes so your teachers can send them directly to the colleges. Be sure to fill out your name, address, and school name on the top of the form. Talk to your recommendation writers about your goals and ambitions.

- Give School Report forms to your high school's guidance office. Fill in your name, address, and any other required information. Verify with your guidance counselor the schools to which transcripts, test scores, and letters are to be sent. Give your counselor any necessary forms at least two weeks before they are due or whenever your counselor's deadline is, whichever is earlier.

- Register for and take the ACT Assessment, SAT, or SAT Subject Tests, as necessary.

- Be sure you have requested (either by mail or on line) that your test scores be sent to the colleges of your choice.

- Mail or send electronically any college applications for early decision admission by November 1.

- If possible, visit colleges while classes are in session.

- If you plan to apply for an ROTC scholarship, remember that your application is due by December 1.

- Print extra copies or make photocopies of every application you send.

Winter

- Attend whatever college-preparatory nights are held at your school or by local organizations.

- Send midyear grade reports to colleges. Continue to focus on your schoolwork!

- Fill out the Free Application for Federal Student Aid (FAFSA) and, if necessary, the PROFILE®. These forms can be obtained from your guidance counselor or at

www.fafsa.ed.gov/ to download the forms or to file electronically. These forms may not be processed before January 1, so don't send them before then.

- Mail or send electronically any remaining applications and financial aid forms before winter break. Make sure you apply to at least one college that you know you can afford and where you know you will be accepted.

- Follow up to make sure that the colleges have received all application information, including recommendations and test scores.

- Meet with your counselor to verify that all forms are in order and have been sent out to colleges.

Spring

- Watch your mail between March 1 and April 1 for acceptance notifications from colleges.

- Watch your mail for notification of financial aid awards between April 1 and May 1.

- Compare the financial aid packages from the colleges and universities that have accepted you.

- Make your final choice, and notify all schools of your intent by May 1. If possible, do not decide without making at least one campus visit. Send your nonrefundable deposit to your chosen school by May 1 as well. Request that your guidance counselor send a final transcript to the college in June.

- Be sure that you have received a FAFSA acknowledgment.

- If you applied for a Pell Grant (on the FAFSA), you will receive a Student Aid Report (SAR) statement. Review this notice, and forward it to the college you plan to attend. Make a copy for your records.

- Complete follow-up paperwork for the college of your choice (scheduling, orientation session, housing arrangements, and other necessary forms).

Summer

⏰ If applicable, apply for a Stafford Loan through a lender. Allow eight weeks for processing.

⏰ Receive the orientation schedule from your college.

⏰ Get residence hall assignment from your college.

⏰ Obtain course scheduling and cost information from your college.

⏰ Congratulations! You are about to begin the greatest adventure of your life. Good luck.

CLASSES TO TAKE IF YOU'RE GOING TO COLLEGE

Did you know that classes you take as early as the ninth grade will help you get into college? Make sure you take at least the minimum high school curriculum requirements necessary for college admission. Even if you don't plan to enter college immediately, take the most demanding courses you can handle.

Review the list of Suggested Courses on this page. Some courses, categories, and names vary from state to state, but this list may be used as a guideline. Talk with your guidance counselor to select the curriculum that best meets your needs and skills.

Of course, learning also occurs outside of school. While outside activities will not make up for poor academic performance, skills learned from jobs, extracurricular activities, and volunteer opportunities will help you become a well-rounded student and will strengthen your college or job application.

Getting a Head Start on College Courses

You can take college courses while still in high school so that when you're in college, you'll be ahead of everyone else. The formal name is postsecondary enrollment. (In Texas, the formal names are "dual credit"—academic credit and "articulated credit"—career and technology credit.) What it means is that

SUGGESTED COURSES

College-Preparatory Curriculum

ENGLISH. Four units, with emphasis on composition (English 9, 10, 11, 12)

MATHEMATICS. Three units (algebra I, algebra II, geometry) are essential; trigonometry, precalculus, calculus, and computer science are recommended for some fields of study

SOCIAL SCIENCE. Three units (American history, world history, government/economics)

SCIENCE. Four units (earth science, biology, chemistry, physics)

FOREIGN LANGUAGE. Three units (at least 2 years in the same language)

FINE ARTS. One to 2 units

OTHER. Keyboarding, computer applications, computer science I, computer science II, physical education, health

College-Preparatory Curriculum Combined with a Career Education or Vocational Program

ENGLISH. Four units

MATHEMATICS. Three units (algebra I, algebra II, geometry)

SOCIAL SCIENCE. Three units (American history, world history, government/economics)

SCIENCE. Two units (earth science, biology)

FOREIGN LANGUAGE. Three units (at least 2 years in the same language)

FINE ARTS. One to 2 units

OTHER. Keyboarding, computer applications, physical education, and health and half-days at the Career Center during junior and senior years

some students can take college courses and receive both high school and college credit for the courses taken. It's like a two-for-one deal!

Postsecondary enrollment is designed to provide an opportunity for qualified high school students to experience more advanced academic work. Participation in a postsecondary enrollment program is not intended to replace courses available in high school but rather to enhance the educational opportunities available to students while in high school. There are two options for postsecondary enrollment:

Option A: Qualified high school juniors and seniors take courses for college credit. Students enrolled under Option A must pay for all books, supplies, tuition, and associated fees.

Option B: Qualified high school juniors and seniors take courses for high school and college credit. For students enrolled under this option, the local school district covers the related costs, provided that the student completes the selected courses. Otherwise, the student and parent will be assessed the costs.

Certain preestablished conditions must be met for enrollment, so check with your high school counselor for more information.

SUGGESTED READING LIST FOR GRADES 9 THROUGH 12

Instead of flipping on the TV or putting on those headphones, how about picking up a book instead? Reading not only will take you to wonderful, unexplored worlds through your imagination, but there are practical gains as well. Reading gives you a more well-rounded background. College admissions and future employers pick up on that. And you'll be able to answer the questions, "Did you read that book? What did you think of it?" How many of the books on this list have you read?

Adams, Richard
  Watership Down
Aesop
  Fables
Agee, James
  A Death in the Family
Anderson, Sherwood
  Winesburg, Ohio
Anonymous
  Go Ask Alice
Asimov, Isaac
  Short Stories
Austen, Jane
  Emma
  Northanger Abbey
  Pride and Prejudice
  Sense and Sensibility
Baldwin, James
  Go Tell It on the Mountain
Balzac, Honore de
  Pere Goriot
Beckett, Samuel
  Waiting for Godot
Bolt, Robert
  A Man for All Seasons
Brontë, Charlotte
  Jane Eyre
Brontë, Emily
  Wuthering Heights
Brooks, Gwendolyn
  In the Mecca
  Riot

Browning, Robert
  Poems
Buck, Pearl
  The Good Earth
Butler, Samuel
  The Way of All Flesh
Camus, Albert
  The Plague
  The Stranger
Cather, Willa
  Death Comes for the Archbishop
  My Antonia
Cervantes, Miguel
  Don Quixote
Chaucer, Geoffrey
  The Canterbury Tales
Chekhov, Anton
  The Cherry Orchard
Chopin, Kate
  The Awakening
Collins, Wilkie
  The Moonstone
Conrad, Joseph
  Heart of Darkness
  Lord Jim
  The Secret Sharer
  Victory
Crane, Stephen
  The Red Badge of Courage
Dante
  The Divine Comedy

Defoe, Daniel
  Moll Flanders
Dickens, Charles
  Bleak House
  David Copperfield
  Great Expectations
  Hard Times
  Oliver Twist
  A Tale of Two Cities
Dickinson, Emily
  Poems
Dinesen, Isak
  Out of Africa
Dostoevski, Fyodor
  The Brothers Karamazov
  Crime and Punishment
Douglass, Frederick
  Narrative of the Life of Frederick Douglass
Dreiser, Theodore
  An American Tragedy
  Sister Carrie
Early, Gerald
  Tuxedo Junction
Eliot, George
  Adam Bede
  Middlemarch
  The Mill on the Floss
  Silas Marner

Eliot, T. S.
  Murder in the Cathedral
Ellison, Ralph
  Invisible Man
Emerson, Ralph Waldo
  Essays
Faulkner, William
  Absalom, Absalom!
  As I Lay Dying
  Intruder in the Dust
  Light in August
  The Sound and the Fury
Fielding, Henry
  Joseph Andrews
  Tom Jones
Fitzgerald, F. Scott
  The Great Gatsby
  Tender Is the Night
Flaubert, Gustave
  Madame Bovary
Forster, E. M.
  A Passage to India
  A Room with a View
Franklin, Benjamin
  The Autobiography of Benjamin Franklin
Galsworthy, John
  The Forsyte Saga

Golding, William
  Lord of the Flies
Goldsmith, Oliver
  She Stoops to Conquer
Graves, Robert
  I, Claudius
Greene, Graham
  The Heart of the Matter
  The Power and the Glory
Hamilton, Edith
  Mythology
Hardy, Thomas
  Far from the Madding Crowd
  Jude the Obscure
  The Mayor of Casterbridge
  The Return of the Native
  Tess of the D'Urbervilles
Hawthorne, Nathaniel
  The House of the Seven Gables
  The Scarlet Letter
Hemingway, Ernest
  A Farewell to Arms
  For Whom the Bell Tolls
  The Sun Also Rises
Henry, O.
  Stories

Hersey, John
  A Single Pebble
Hesse, Hermann
  Demian
  Siddhartha
  Steppenwolf
Homer
  The Iliad
  The Odyssey
Hughes, Langston
  Poems
  The Big Sea
Hugo, Victor
  Les Misérables
Huxley, Aldous
  Brave New World
Ibsen, Henrik
  A Doll's House
  An Enemy of the People
  Ghosts
  Hedda Gabler
  The Master Builder
  The Wild Duck
James, Henry
  The American
  Daisy Miller
  Portrait of a Lady
  The Turn of the Screw
Joyce, James
  Dubliners
  A Portrait of the Artist as a Young Man

Kafka, Franz
  The Castle
  The Metamorphosis
  The Trial
Keats, John
  Poems
Kerouac, Jack
  On the Road
Koestler, Arthur
  Darkness at Noon
Lawrence, Jerome, and Robert E. Lee
  Inherit the Wind
Lewis, Sinclair
  Arrowsmith
  Babbitt
  Main Street
Llewellyn, Richard
  How Green Was My Valley
Machiavelli
  The Prince
MacLeish, Archibald
  J.B.
Mann, Thomas
  Buddenbrooks
  The Magic Mountain

Marlowe, Christopher
  Dr. Faustus
Maugham, Somerset
  Of Human Bondage
McCullers, Carson
  The Heart Is a Lonely Hunter
Melville, Herman
  Billy Budd
  Moby-Dick
  Typee
Miller, Arthur
  The Crucible
  Death of a Salesman
Monsarrat, Nicholas
  The Cruel Sea
Naylor, Gloria
  Bailey's Cafe
  The Women of Brewster Place
O'Neill, Eugene
  The Emperor Jones
  Long Day's Journey Into Night
  Mourning Becomes Electra

Orwell, George
  Animal Farm
  1984
Pasternak, Boris
  Doctor Zhivago
Poe, Edgar Allan
  Short Stories
Remarque, Erich Marie
  All Quiet on the Western Front
Rolvaag, O. E.
  Giants in the Earth
Rostand, Edmond
  Cyrano de Bergerac
Salinger, J. D.
  The Catcher in the Rye
Sandburg, Carl
  Abraham Lincoln: The Prairie Years
  Abraham Lincoln: The War Years
Saroyan, William
  The Human Comedy
Sayers, Dorothy
  The Nine Tailors
Shakespeare, William
  Plays and Sonnets

Shaw, George Bernard
  Arms and the Man
  Major Barbara
  Pygmalion
  Saint Joan
Sheridan, Richard B.
  The School for Scandal
Shute, Nevil
  On the Beach
Sinclair, Upton
  The Jungle
Sophocles
  Antigone
  Oedipus Rex
Steinbeck, John
  East of Eden
  The Grapes of Wrath
  Of Mice and Men
Stowe, Harriet Beecher
  Uncle Tom's Cabin
Swift, Jonathan
  Gulliver's Travels
Thackeray, William M.
  Vanity Fair

Thoreau, Henry David
  Walden
Tolstoy, Leo
  Anna Karenina
  War and Peace
Trollope, Anthony
  Barchester Towers
Turgenev, Ivan
  Fathers and Sons
Twain, Mark
  Pudd'nhead Wilson
Updike, John
  Rabbit, Run
Vergil
  The Aeneid
Voltaire
  Candide
Walker, Alice
  The Color Purple
  Meridian
Warren, Robert Penn
  All the King's Men
Waugh, Evelyn
  Brideshead Revisited
  A Handful of Dust
Wharton, Edith
  The Age of Innocence

White, T. H.
  The Once and Future King
  The Sword in the Stone
Wilde, Oscar
  The Importance of Being Earnest
  The Picture of Dorian Gray
Wilder, Thornton
  Our Town
Williams, Tennessee
  The Glass Menagerie
  A Streetcar Named Desire
Wolfe, Thomas
  Look Homeward, Angel
Woolf, Virginia
  Mrs. Dalloway
  To the Lighthouse
Wouk, Herman
  The Caine Mutiny
Wright, Richard
  Black Boy
  Native Sun

Source: The National Endowment for the Humanities.

For more book recommendations, see what college professors suggest in **ARCO Reading Lists for College-Bound Students**, *available at your local bookstore.*

5 Chapter

TACKLING THE TESTS

Unless you've been on another planet for the last two or three years, you've probably heard older high school students buzzing about the alphabet soup list of college entrance exams—SAT, ACT Assessment, and PSAT.

SOME OF THE STUDENTS who are getting ready to take one of these tests look like they're in various states of hysteria. Others have been studying for months on end, so when they open their mouths, out pops the definition for "meretricious" or the answer to "What is the ratio of 3 pounds to 6 ounces?" Well, the talk that you've heard about the tests is partly true. They are a big deal and can be crucial to your academic plans. On the other hand, you don't have to walk in cold. Remember that word "planning"? It's a whole lot nicer than the word "panic." Preparing for the tests takes a lot of planning and time, but if you're reading this chapter, you're already ahead of the game.

A FEW FACTS ABOUT THE MAJOR TESTS

The major standardized tests students take in high school are the PSAT, SAT, and ACT Assessment. Colleges across the country use them to get a sense of a student's readiness to enter their ivy-covered halls. These tests, or "boards" as they are sometimes called, have become notorious because of how important they can be. There is a mystique that surrounds them. People talk about the "magic number" that will get you into the school of your dreams.

Beware! There is a lot of misinformation out there. First and foremost, these are not intelligence tests; they are reasoning tests designed to evaluate the way you think. These tests assess the basic knowledge and skills you have gained through your classes in school, and they also gauge the knowledge you have gained through outside experience. The material on these tests is not curriculum-based, but the tests do emphasize those academic experiences that educational institutions feel are good indicators of your probable success in college.

THE ACT ASSESSMENT

The ACT Assessment is a standardized college entrance examination that measures knowledge and skills in English, mathematics, reading, and science reasoning and the application of these skills to future academic tasks. The ACT Assessment consists of four multiple-choice tests.

Test 1: English

- 75 questions, 45 minutes
- Usage and mechanics
- Rhetorical skills

Test 2: Mathematics

- 60 questions, 60 minutes
- Pre-algebra
- Elementary algebra
- Intermediate algebra
- Coordinate geometry
- Plane geometry
- Trigonometry

Test 3: Reading

- 40 questions, 35 minutes
- Prose fiction
- Humanities
- Social studies
- Natural sciences

Test 4: Science Reasoning

- 40 questions, 35 minutes
- Data representation
- Research summary
- Conflicting viewpoints

Each section is scored from 1 to 36 and is scaled for slight variations in difficulty. Students are not penalized for incorrect responses. The composite score is the average of the four scaled scores. In the 2004–05 school year, an optional writing component was added to the ACT Assessment.

To prepare for the ACT Assessment, ask your guidance counselor for a free guidebook called *Preparing for the ACT Assessment*. Besides providing general test-preparation information and additional test-taking strategies, this guidebook describes the content and format of the four ACT Assessment subject area tests, summarizes test administration procedures followed at ACT Assessment test centers, and includes a practice test. Thomson Peterson's publishes *The Real ACT Prep Guide* that includes three official ACT Assessment tests.

THE SAT

The SAT measures developed verbal and mathematical reasoning abilities as they relate to successful performance in college. It is intended to supplement the secondary school record and other information about the student in assessing readiness for college. There is one unscored, experimental section on the exam, which is used for equating and/or pretesting purposes and can cover either the mathematics or verbal subject area.

STUDENT COUNSEL

Q: What kept you from stressing out about the tests?

A: The best way I found to prepare was to take practice tests to get to know the questions. At first, I'd set the kitchen timer and practice while ignoring the time, just to see what I could do. Practice is the best because they don't really change the type of questions. You read that in every review book, and it's true.

My advice for dealing with the stress on test day? The night before, I watched movies and had popcorn. When you take the test, definitely bring candy. A candy bar in between each section helps.

Theresa-Marie Russo
Edgemont High School
Scarsdale, New York

Critical Reading

- 67 questions, 70 minutes
- Sentence completion
- Passage-based reading

Math

- 54 questions, 70 minutes
- Multiple-choice
- Student-produced response (grid-ins)

Writing

- 49 questions plus essay, 75 minutes
- Identifying sentence errors
- Improving paragraphs
- Improving sentences
- Essay

Students receive one point for each correct response and lose a fraction of a point for each incorrect response (except for student-produced responses). These points are totaled to produce the raw scores, which are then scaled to equalize the scores for slight

WHICH SHOULD I TAKE? THE ACT ASSESSMENT VS. THE SAT

It's not a bad idea to take both. This assures that you will have the test scores required for admission to all schools, because some colleges accept the results of one test and not the other. Some institutions use test results for proper placement of students in English and math courses.

You should take the ACT Assessment and SAT during the spring of your junior year, if not earlier. This enables you to retake the test in the fall of your senior year if you're not satisfied with your scores. Also, this makes it possible for institutions to receive all test scores before the end of January. Institutions generally consider the better score when determining admission and placement. Because most scholarship applications are processed between December and April of the senior year, your best score results can then be included in the application.

variations in difficulty for various editions of the test. The critical reading, writing, and math scaled scores range from 200–800 per section. The total scaled score range is from 600–2400.

To prepare for the SAT, you should carefully review the pamphlet, *Taking the SAT*, which you should be able to get from your guidance counselor. Also, most libraries and bookstores stock a large selection of material about the SAT and other standardized tests.

RECOMMENDED TEST-TAKING DATES

Sophomore Year

October	PSAT/NMSQT and PLAN (for practice, planning, and preparation)
May–June	SAT Subject Tests (if necessary)

Junior Year

October	PSAT/NMSQT (for the National Merit Scholarship Program and practice)
January–June	ACT Assessment and/or SAT, SAT Subject Tests (if necessary—for college admission)

Senior Year

October–December	ACT Assessment and/or SAT, SAT Subject Tests (if necessary—for college admission)

THE PSAT/NMSQT

The Preliminary SAT/National Merit Scholarship Qualifying Test, better known as the PSAT/NMSQT, is a practice test for the SAT. Many students take the PSAT more than once because scores tend to increase with repetition and because it allows students to become more comfortable with taking standardized tests. During the junior year, the PSAT is also used as a qualifying test for the National Merit Scholarship Program and the National Scholarship Service and Fund for Negro Students. It is also used in designating students for the National Hispanic Scholar Recognition Program. The PSAT includes a writing skills section, which consists entirely of multiple-choice questions. There is, however, no essay section on the PSAT.

Critical Reading

- 48 questions, two 25-minute sections
- Sentence completion
- Passage-based reading

Math

- 38 questions, one 30-minute section
- Multiple-choice
- Student-produced response (grid-ins)

Writing

- 39 questions, one 30-minute section
- Identifying sentence errors
- Improving sentences
- Improving paragraphs

Students receive a score in each content area (verbal, math, and writing). Each score ranges from 20 to 80 and is totaled with the others for the combined score. The total score ranges from 60 to 240.

Selection Index (used for National Merit Scholarship purposes)

- Verbal + Math + Writing

- Score Range: 60 to 240
- Mean Junior Score: 147

National Merit Scholarship Program

- Semifinalist Status: Selection Index of 201 to 222
- Commended Student: Selection Index of 199

SAT SUBJECT TESTS

Subject Tests are required by some institutions for admission and/or placement in freshman-level courses. Each Subject Test measures one's knowledge of a specific subject and the ability to apply that knowledge. Students should check with each institution for its specific requirements. In general,

ADMISSIONS ADVICE

Q: What can students who don't have the best grades do to improve their chances of getting into the college of their choice?

A: We encourage students to take the SAT or ACT Assessment more than once and see how they do. There are options for students who may not meet the academic requirements because they've had to work or are gifted in other areas, such as art or athletics, or who perhaps have been through something tragic. We ask them to submit letters of recommendations, a personal statement, and any other documentation that might help support their cases. What were the factors that affected their grades? What else can they offer the university?

We often encourage students who still may not meet the requirements to start at a community college and then transfer. We'll look at their college credit vs. their high school credit. They can prove to us that they can handle a college curriculum.

Cheyenna Smith
Admission Counselor
University of Houston

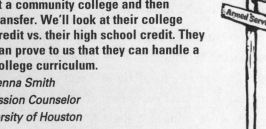

students are required to take three Subject Tests (one English, one mathematics, and one of their choice).

Subject Tests are given in the following areas: biology, chemistry, Chinese, English language proficiency, French, German, Italian, Japanese, Korean, Latin, literature, mathematics, modern Hebrew, physics, Spanish, U.S. history, and world history. These tests are 1 hour long and are primarily multiple-choice tests. Three Subject Tests may be taken on one test date.

Scored like the SAT, students gain a point for each correct answer and lose a fraction of a point for each incorrect answer. The raw scores are then converted to scaled scores that range from 200 to 800.

THE TOEFL INTERNET-BASED TEST (iBT)

The Test of English as a Foreign Language Internet-Based Test (TOEFL iBT) is designed to help assess a student's grasp of English if it is not the student's first language. Performance on the TOEFL test may help interpret scores on the verbal section of the SAT. The test consists of four integrated sections: speaking, listening, reading, and writing. The TOEFL iBT emphasizes integrated skills. The computer- and paper-based versions of the TOEFL will continue to be administered in certain countries until the internet-based version is administered by Educational Testing Service (ETS). For further information, visit www.toefl.org.

WHAT OTHER TESTS SHOULD I KNOW ABOUT?

The AP Program

This program allows high school students to try college-level work and build valuable skills and study habits in the process. Subject matter is explored in more depth in AP courses than in other high school classes. A qualifying score on an AP test—which varies from school to school—can earn you college credit or advanced placement. Getting qualifying grades on enough exams can even earn you a full year's credit and sophomore standing at more than 1,500 higher-education institutions. There are currently thirty-four AP courses in nineteen different subject areas, including art, biology, and computer science. Speak to your guidance counselor for information about your school's offerings.

College-Level Examination Program (CLEP)

The CLEP enables students to earn college credit for what they already know, whether it was learned in school, through independent study, or through other experiences outside of the classroom. Approximately 2,900 colleges and universities now award credit for qualifying scores on one or more of the 34 CLEP exams. The exams, which are 90 minutes in length and are primarily multiple choice, are administered at participating colleges and universities. For more information, check out the Web site at www.collegeboard.com/clep.

Armed Services Vocational Aptitude Battery (ASVAB)

ASVAB is a career exploration program consisting of a multi-aptitude test battery that helps students explore their interests, abilities, and personal preferences. A career exploration workbook gives students information about the workplace, and a career information resource book helps students match their personal characteristics to the working world. Finally, an occupational outlook handbook describes in detail approximately 250 civilian and military occupations. Students can use ASVAB scores for military enlistment up to two years after they take the test. A student can take the ASVAB as a sophomore, junior, or senior, but students cannot use their sophomore scores to enter the armed forces. Ask your guidance counselor or your local recruiting office for more information. Also, see Chapter 11, "The Military Option."

General Educational Development (GED) Test

If you have not completed your high school education, you may earn an equivalence by taking the GED test, sponsored by your state Department of Education. However, taking the GED test is not a legitimate reason for dropping out of school. In fact, it is more

difficult to get into the armed services with only a GED, and some employees have difficulty getting promoted without a high school diploma.

You're eligible to take the GED if you are not enrolled in high school, have not yet graduated from high school, are at least 16 years old, and meet your local requirements regarding age, residency, and length of time since leaving school.

There are five sections to the GED test, covering writing skills, social studies, science, interpreting literature and the arts, and mathematics. Part II of the Writing Skills Test requires writing an essay. The GED costs an average of $35 but can vary from state to state, and the application fee may be waived under certain circumstances. You should contact your local GED office to arrange to take the exam. Call 800-62-MYGED to find your local GED office and for more information.

WHAT CAN I DO TO PREPARE FOR THESE TESTS?

Know what to expect. Get familiar with how the tests are structured, how much time is allowed, and the directions for each type of question. Get plenty of rest the night before the test and eat breakfast that morning.

There are a variety of products, from books to software to videos, available to help you prepare for most standardized tests. Find the learning style that suits you best. As for which products to buy, there are two major categories—those created by the test makers and those created by private companies. The best approach is to talk to someone who has been through the process and find out which product or products he or she recommends.

Some students report significant increases in scores after participating in coaching programs. Longer-term programs (40 hours) seem to raise scores more than short-term programs (20 hours), but beyond 40 hours, score gains are minor. Math scores appear to benefit more from coaching than verbal scores.

Preparation Resources

There are a variety of ways to prepare for standardized tests—find a method that fits your schedule and your budget. But you should definitely prepare. Far too many students walk into these tests cold, either because they find standardized tests frightening or annoying or they just haven't found the time to study. The key is that these exams are standardized. That means these tests are largely the same from administration to administration; they always test the same concepts. They have to, or else you couldn't compare the scores of people who took the tests on different dates. The numbers or words may change, but the underlying content doesn't.

So how do you prepare? At the very least, you should review relevant material, such as math formulas and commonly tested vocabulary words, and know the directions for each question type or test section. You should take at least one practice test and review your mistakes so you don't make them again on test day. Beyond that, you know best how much preparation you need. You'll also find lots of material in libraries or bookstores to help you: books and software from the test makers and from other publishers (including Peterson's) or live courses that range from national test-preparation companies to teachers at your high school who offer classes. Peterson's interactive and personalized SAT Online Course at www.petersonstestprep.com is another resource you'll want to check out.

THE TOP 10 WAYS *NOT* TO TAKE THE TEST

10. Cramming the night before the test.

9. Not becoming familiar with the directions before you take the test.

8. Not becoming familiar with the format of the test before you take it.

7. Not knowing how the test is graded.

6. Spending too much time on any one question.

5. Not checking spelling, grammar, and sentence structure in essays.

4. Second-guessing yourself.

3. Forgetting to take a deep breath to keep from—

2. Losing It!

1. Writing a one-paragraph essay.

THE COLLEGE SEARCH

Now that you have examined your interests, talents, wants, and needs in great detail, it's time to start investigating colleges.

THE BEST RESOURCES

There are thousands of colleges and universities in the United States, so before you start filling out applications, you need to narrow down your search. There are a number of sources that will help you do this.

WELCOME TO *CollegesWantYou*^{SM}!

Is the traditional process of searching for colleges getting old—fast? Well stop looking for colleges and let them find you with *CollegesWantYou*, the new approach to the search and selection process.

Unlike other college search and selection tools, *CollegesWantYou* doesn't expect you to sort through page after page of generic college listings. Instead, enter information on your preferences, test scores, and extracurricular activites into the online form, and before you know it, colleges that meet your specifications will be in touch with you. And the best part is, you only need to enter your personal information once to connect with hundreds of colleges.

Save time. Keep your sanity. Get the information you need directly from colleges and universities across the country and take the next step in college search and selection. You can get to *CollegesWantYou* by going to www.collegeswantyou.com.

Your Guidance Counselor

Your guidance counselor is your greatest asset in the college search process. He or she has access to a vast repository of information, from college bulletins and catalogs to financial aid applications. He or she knows how well graduates from your high school have performed at colleges across the country, and has probably even visited many of the colleges to get some firsthand knowledge about the places she has sent her students to. The more your guidance counselor sees you and learns about you, the easier it is for her to help you. So make sure you stop by her office often, whether it's to talk about your progress or just to say "hi."

Your Teachers

Use your teachers as resources, too. Many of them have had twenty to thirty years of experience in their field. They have taught thousands of students and watched them go off to college and careers. Teachers often stay in contact with graduates and know about their experiences in college and may be familiar with the schools you are interested in attending. Ask your teachers how they feel about the match between you and your choice of schools and if they think you will be able to succeed in that environment.

Your Family

Your family needs to be an integral part of the college selection process, whether they are financing your education or not. They have opinions and valuable advice. Listen to them carefully. Try to absorb all their information and see if it applies to you. Does it fit with who you are and what you want? What works and what doesn't work for you? Is some of what they say dated? How long ago were their experiences, and how relevant are they today? Take in the information, thank them for their concern, compare what they have said with the information you are gathering, and discard what doesn't fit.

Colleges and Universities

Don't forget to go to college fairs. Usually held in large cities in the evening, they are free and sponsored by your local guidance counselors' association and the National Association of College Admissions Counselors (NACAC). The admissions counselors of hundreds of colleges, vocational/career colleges, and universities attend college fairs each year. Whether your questions are as general as what the overall cost of education is at a particular institution or as specific as how many biology majors had works published last year, the admissions office works to assist you in locating the people who can answer your questions. Bring a shopping bag for all the information you will get.

Admissions officers also visit high schools. Don't forget to attend these meetings during your junior and senior years. In general, college admissions counselors come to a school to get a general sense of the high school and the caliber and personality of the student body. Although it is difficult to make an individual impression at these group sessions, the college counselors do take names on cards for later contact, and you will occasionally see them making notes on the cards when they are struck by an astute questioner. It is helpful to attend these sessions because consistent contact between a student and a college is tracked by colleges and universities. An admissions decision may come down to examining the size of your admissions folder and the number of interactions you have had with the school over time.

College and university brochures and catalogs are a good place to look, too. After reading a few, you will discover that some offer more objective information than others. You will also start to learn what information colleges think is essential to present. That's important. If one college's brochure does not present the same information as most of the other college brochures, you have to ask yourself why. What might this say about the college's academic offerings, athletic or extracurricular programs, or campus life? What does the campus look like? How is the campus environment presented in the brochure? The brochures should present clues to what schools feel are their important majors, what their mission is, and on which departments they are spending their budgets. Take the time to do these informational resources

PARENT PERSPECTIVE

Q: Now that you've been through the process of getting three of your children into college, what's your best advice for parents and teens?

A: Apply early and meet deadlines. Both of our older sons were sitting there after high school graduation wondering why they were on college waiting lists: "I have good grades. I can't figure it out." At eighteen, they don't see tomorrow, much less way down the line, but do you want to deal with their heartbreak at not getting into the college where they want to be? It's their future. It's hard because they're in their senior year and you want it to be fun for them. However, you see the reality out there that they will be facing for the rest of their lives. They don't want to look at it, but you have to keep bringing them back to it—not in a preachy way. If they start earlier than their senior year, it won't be as much of a shock when they become seniors.

Jeanette and Amedee Richard
San Antonio, Texas

justice. They have a great deal to say to the careful reader.

A college's Web site can give you a glimpse of campus life that does not appear in the college's brochure and catalog. It is true that the virtual tour will show you the shots that the college marketing department wants you to see, highlighting the campus in the best light, but you can use the home page to see other things, too. Read the student newspaper. Visit college-sponsored chat rooms. Go to the department in the major you are investigating. Look at the Course Bulletin to see what courses are required.

ONLINE HELP

To help you find two-year and four-year colleges or universities in your specific region, take a look at the Appendix in the back of this book for a listing of schools in each state. Then check out the following online resources for additional information on college selection, scholarships, student information, and much more.

Peterson's College Search. Petersons.com provides information and tools that will help you prepare, search, and pay for college. You can search for a

CRITERIA TO CONSIDER

Depending on your personal interests, the following characteristics should play a role in helping you narrow down the field of colleges you are considering.

AFFILIATION
- Public
- Private, independent
- Private, church affiliated
- Proprietary

SIZE
- Very small (fewer than 1,000 students)
- Small (1,000–3,999 students)
- Medium (4,000–8,999 students)
- Large (9,000–19,999 students)
- Very large (more than 20,000 students)

COMMUNITY
- Rural
- Small town
- Suburban
- Urban

LOCATION
- In your hometown
- Less than 3 hours from home
- More than 3 hours from home

HOUSING
- Dorm
- Off-campus apartment
- Home
- Facilities and services for students with disabilities

STUDENT BODY
- All male
- All female
- Coed
- Minority representation
- Primarily one religious denomination
- Primarily full-time students
- Primarily part-time students
- Primarily commuter students
- Primarily residential students

ACADEMIC ENVIRONMENT
- Majors offered
- Student-faculty ratio
- Faculty teaching reputation
- Instruction by professors versus teaching assistants
- Facilities (such as classrooms and labs)
- Libraries
- Independent study available
- International study available
- Internships available

FINANCIAL AID
- Scholarships
- Grants
- Loans
- Work-study program
- Part-time or full-time jobs

SUPPORT SERVICES
- Academic counseling
- Career/placement counseling
- Personal counseling
- Student health facilities

ACTIVITIES/SOCIAL CLUBS
- Clubs, organizations
- Greek life
- Athletics, intramurals

ATHLETICS
- Division I, II, or III
- Sports offered
- Scholarships available

SPECIALIZED PROGRAMS
- Honors programs
- Services for students with disabilities or special needs

school by name or location. In addition to college search and selection tools, Petersons.com also offers tips on financial aid, test preparation, and online applications.

The National Association for College Admission Counseling. This home page offers information for professionals, students, and parents. The Internet address is www.nacac.com.

U.S. Department of Education. This federal agency's National Center for Education Statistics produces reports on every level of education, from elementary to postgraduate. Dozens are available for downloading. You can hook up with these and other links at www.ed.gov/index.jsp.

CAMPUS VISITS

You've heard the old saying, "A picture is worth a thousand words." Well, a campus visit is worth a thousand brochures. Nothing beats walking around a campus to get a feel for it. Some students report that all they needed to know that they loved or hated a campus was to drive through it. Then there is the true story of the guy who applied to a school because it had a prestigious name. Got accepted. Didn't visit, and when he arrived to move into the dorms, discovered to his horror it was an all-male school. A visit would have taken care of that problem.

The best time to experience the college environment is during the spring of your junior year or the fall of your senior year. Although you may have more time to visit colleges during your summer off, your observations will be more accurate when you can see the campus in full swing. Open houses are a good idea and provide you with opportunities to talk to students, faculty members, and administrators. Write or call in advance to take student-conducted campus tours. If possible, stay overnight in a dorm to see what living at the college is really like.

Bring your transcript so that you are prepared to interview with admission officers. Take this opportunity to ask questions about financial aid and other services that are available to students. You can get a good snapshot of campus life by reading a copy of the student newspaper. The final goal of the campus visit is to study the school's personality and decide if it matches yours. Your parents should be involved with the campus visits so that you can share your impressions. Here are some additional campus visit tips:

- ☑ Read campus literature prior to the visit.
- ☑ Ask for directions, and allow ample travel time.
- ☑ Make a list of questions before the visit.
- ☑ Dress in neat, clean, and casual clothes and shoes.
- ☑ Ask to meet one-on-one with a current student.

- Ask to meet personally with a professor in your area of interest.
- Ask to meet a coach or athlete in your area of interest.
- Offer a firm handshake.
- Use good posture.
- Listen, and take notes.
- Speak clearly, and maintain eye contact with people you meet.
- Don't interrupt.
- Be honest, direct, and polite.
- Be aware of factual information so that you can ask questions of comparison and evaluation.
- Be prepared to answer questions about yourself. Practice a mock interview with someone.
- Don't be shy about explaining your background and why you are interested in the school.
- Ask questions about the background and experiences of the people you meet.
- Convey your interest in getting involved in campus life.
- Be positive and energetic.
- Don't feel as though you have to talk the whole time or carry the conversation yourself.
- Relax, and enjoy yourself.
- Thank those you meet, and send thank-you notes when appropriate.

After you have made your college visits, use the "College Comparison Worksheet" on page 56 to rank the schools in which you're interested. This will help you decide not only which ones to apply to, but also which one to attend once you receive your acceptance letters.

THE COLLEGE INTERVIEW

Not all schools require or offer an interview. However, if you are offered an interview, use this one-on-one time to evaluate the college in detail and to sell yourself to the admission officer. The following list of questions can help you collect the information you may need to know.

WRITING TO A COLLEGE FOR INFORMATION

If neither you nor your guidance counselor has an application for a college that you are interested in, write a brief letter to the college admissions office to request an application.

Date

Your Name
Street Address
City, State, Zip

Office of Admission
Name of College
Street Address
City, State, Zip

To Whom It May Concern:

I am a (freshman, sophomore, junior, senior) at (name of your school) and will graduate in (month) (year).

Please send me the following information about your college: a general information brochure, program descriptions, an admission application, financial aid information, and any other information that might be helpful. I am considering _____ as my major field of study (optional, if you know your preferred field of study).

I am interested in visiting your campus, taking a campus tour, and meeting with an admission counselor and a financial aid officer. I would also like to meet with an adviser or professor in the (your preferred field of study) department, if possible. I will contact you in a week to set up a time that is convenient.

If you would like to contact me directly, I can be reached at (your phone number with area code and e-mail address). Thank you.

Sincerely,

(Signature)
Your Name

- How many students apply each year? How many are accepted?
- What are the average GPA and average ACT Assessment or SAT score(s) for those accepted?
- How many students in last year's freshman class returned for their sophomore year?
- What is the school's procedure for credit for Advanced Placement high school courses?

(Continued on page 56)

THE MATCHING GAME Read each question and respond by circling Y (Yes), N (No), or C (Combination). Complete all the questions and return to the top. Highlight each action that coordinates with your answer, and then read it. Where you chose C, highlight both actions. Is there a pattern? Do the questions seem to lead to a certain type of college or university? Certain size? Certain location? Read the suggestions at the end of "The Matching Game" for more ideas.

Question	Yes/No/ Combination	Action
1. Do I have a goal in life?	Y N C	**Y:** State it._____. **N:** Don't worry, many students start college without knowing what they want to do. Look into colleges that specialize in the arts and sciences.
2. Do I know what I want to achieve with a college diploma?	Y N C	**Y:** List specifically what your goals are. _____ **N:** Think about what college can offer you.
3. Do I want to broaden my knowledge?	Y N C	**Y:** Consider a liberal arts college. **N:** You might need to consider other options or educational opportunities.
4. Do I want specific training?	Y N C	**Y:** Investigate technical colleges or professional training programs in universities. **N:** You don't know what you want to study? Don't worry, only 20 pecent of seniors who apply to college are sure.
5. Am I looking for a balanced workload?	Y N C	**Y:** When you are visiting colleges, ask students about how they handle the workload. **N:** Check the workload carefully. If no one is on campus on a sunny day, it may not be the school for you
6. Am I self-directed enough to finish a four-year college program?	Y N C	**Y:** Consider only four-year colleges and universities. **N:** Maybe a two-year junior or community college is a better way to begin your college experience. Also consider a vocational/career college.
7. Do I know what I do well?	Y N C	**Y:** Identify majors related to your abilities. _____ **N:** Spend a little more time asking yourself questions about your interests. Speak to your counselor and do an interest inventory.
8. Do I like to spend time learning any one subject more than others?	Y N C	**Y:** List majors related to that area. _____ _____ **N:** Look at your high school courses. Which ones do you like better than others? _____
9. Do I know what matters to me and what my values are?	Y N C	**Y:** Look for the schools that talk about the values on their campus. Do the values confirm or conflict with your values? **N:** Values are less important to you, so places that really expound their values may seem confining to you.
10. Do I need to be in affluent surroundings?	Y N C	**Y:** Look at the schools that deliver that package. Check the small, private liberal arts colleges. **N:** How strong is your reaction against this setting? If it is strong, check larger, more diverse settings, like an urban school.
11. Am I going to college for the financial gains?	Y N C	**Y:** What majors are going to give you the payback you want? Look at business colleges and professional programs, like premed. **N:** If a big financial payback does not interest you, look at social service majors, like counseling, teaching, and social work.
12. Am I focused?	Y N C	**Y:** Search out the programs that will offer you the best options. **N:** Avoid those schools whose programs are not strong in your focused area.
13. Am I conservative in my views and behavior?	Y N C	**Y:** The political policies of schools are important. Look into them carefully. You might look at the schools in the Midwest or the South. **N:** If you're a liberal, look closely at the political climate. Check the schools in the Northeast and on the West Coast.

14.	Do I need to be around people who are similar to me?	Y N C	**Y:** If you are African American, check the historically black colleges. If socioeconomic level or a certain look is important to you, study the student populations carefully during campus visits. If it is religious orientation you are interested in, look into religiously sponsored colleges and universities. **N:** Look at large, midsize, and small universities in urban settings.
15.	Are the name and prestige of the school important to me?	Y N C	**Y:** Look into the Ivies and the competitive schools to see if you are eligible and what they offer you. Broaden your search to include other colleges and compare their offerings to your specific needs and interests. **N:** Don't exclude the well-known institutions if they fit in every other way.
16.	Do I like sports?	Y N C	**Y:** Large universities with Division I teams will give you all the sports you need—as a competitor or a fan. If you do not want to compete at that level, check schools in other divisions. Look at the liberal arts colleges for athletes. **N:** Look into smaller universities and liberal arts colleges with good teams.
17.	Am I a techie?	Y N C	**Y:** Check for computer engineering courses at technical universities and large universities near research centers and major computer business areas. Ask about hardwiring, e-mail, and computer packages before you enroll. **N:** It still helps to know what computer services are available where you enroll.
18.	Do I need to live in or be near a city?	Y N C	**Y:** How close to a city do you need to be? In the city or an hour away? Do you still want a campus feel? Consider these questions as you visit campuses. **N:** Do you need space, natural beauty, and peaceful surroundings to think? Look into small liberal arts schools in rural and suburban settings. Explore universities in the Midwest and South.
19.	Will I need counseling for support?	Y N C	**Y:** Investigate the quality of student services and the mechanism for accessing them. Smaller schools often pride themselves on their services. Look at liberal arts colleges. Universities connected to medical centers often provide extensive services. **N:** It is still good to know what is offered.
20.	Do I need an environment in which questioning is important?	Y N C	**Y:** Liberal arts colleges, honors colleges, and smaller universities place an emphasis on academic inquiry. **N:** You like to hear others discuss issues, gather as much information and opinions as you can, and think it over by yourself. Try the university setting.

Suggestions

Here are some ideas for you to consider based on the way you answered the questions.

1. If you answered *no* to numbers 2 and 3, why not investigate apprenticeships, vocational/career colleges, armed services options, and certification or two-year college programs?

2. If you answered *yes* to numbers 4, 11, and 17, technical or professional colleges and universities with hands-on training may give you the education you want.

3. If you answered *yes* to numbers 9, 10, and 20, you are leaning toward a liberal arts setting.

4. If you answered *yes* to numbers 5 and 6, examine the competitive and Ivy League colleges.

5. If you answered *no* to numbers 9, 10, 14, and 20 and yes to 16, 17, and 18, larger universities may offer you the best options.

Once you have completed your self-evaluation, made a decision whether college is for you, have some ideas about your personality and likes and dislikes, and can relate them to the different personalities of colleges, it is time to gather information. It needs to be quality information from the right sources. The quality of information you put into your search now will determine whether your list of colleges will represent a good or a bad match.

☑ As a freshman, will I be taught by professors or teaching assistants?

☑ How many students are there per teacher?

☑ When is it necessary to declare a major?

☑ Is it possible to have a double major or to declare a major and a minor?

☑ What are the requirements for the major in which I am interested?

☑ How does the advising system work?

☑ Does this college offer study abroad, cooperative programs, or academic honors programs?

☑ What is the likelihood, due to overcrowding, of getting closed out of the courses I need?

☑ What technology is available, and what are any associated fees?

☑ How well equipped are the libraries and laboratories?

☑ Are internships available?

☑ How effective is the job placement service of the school?

☑ What is the average class size in my area of interest?

☑ Have any professors in my area of interest recently won any honors or awards?

☑ What teaching methods are used in my area of interest (lecture, group discussion, fieldwork)?

☑ How many students graduate in four years in my area of interest?

☑ What are the special requirements for graduation in my area of interest?

☑ What is the student body like? Age? Sex? Race? Geographic origin?

☑ What percentage of students live in dormitories? In off-campus housing?

☑ What percentage of students go home for the weekend?

COLLEGE COMPARISON WORKSHEET

Fill in your top five selection criteria and any others that may be of importance to you. Once you narrow your search of colleges to five, fill in the colleges across the top row. Using a scale of 1 to 5, where 1 is poor and 5 is excellent, rate each college by your criteria. Total each column to see which college rates the highest based upon your criteria.

SELECTION CRITERIA	COLLEGE 1	COLLEGE 2	COLLEGE 3	COLLEGE 4	COLLEGE 5
1.					
2.					
3.					
4.					
5.					
OTHER CRITERIA					
6.					
7.					
8.					
9.					
10.					
TOTAL					

Sample criteria (Use this list as a starting point—there may be other criteria important to you not listed here.): Arts facilities, athletic facilities, audiovisual center, campus setting, class size, classrooms/lecture halls, computer labs, dining hall, dorms, financial aid, fraternity/sorority houses, majors offered, religious facilities, professor profiles, student-faculty ratio, student profile, student union, surrounding community.

- What are some of the regulations that apply to living in a dormitory?
- What are the security precautions taken on campus and in the dorms?
- Is the surrounding community safe?
- Are there problems with drug and alcohol abuse on campus?
- Do faculty members and students mix on an informal basis?
- How important are the arts to student life?
- What facilities are available for cultural events?
- How important are sports to student life?
- What facilities are available for sporting events?
- What percentage of the student body belongs to a sorority/fraternity?
- What is the relationship between those who belong to the Greek system and those who don't?
- Are students involved in the decision-making process at the college? Do they sit on major committees?
- In what other activities can students get involved?
- What percentage of students receive financial aid based on need?
- What percentage of students receive scholarships based on academic ability?

- What percentage of a typical financial aid offer is in the form of a loan?
- If my family demonstrates financial need on the FAFSA (and PROFILE®, if applicable), what percentage of the established need is generally awarded?
- How much did the college increase the cost of room, board, tuition, and fees from last year?
- Do opportunities for financial aid, scholarships, or work-study increase each year?
- When is the admission application deadline?
- When is the financial aid application deadline?
- When will I be notified of the admission decision?
- If there is a deposit required, is it refundable?

Keep in mind that you don't need to ask all these questions—in fact, some of them may have already been answered for you in the catalog, on the Web site, or in the interview. Ask only the questions for which you still need answers.

SHOULD YOU HEAD FOR THE IVY LEAGUE?

Determining whether to apply to one of the eight Ivy League schools is something about which you should think long and hard. Sure, it can't hurt to toss your application into the ring if you can afford the application fee and the time you'll spend writing the essays. But if you want to figure out if you'd be a legitimate candidate for acceptance at one of these top-tier schools, you should understand the type of student that they look for and how you compare, says John Machulsky, a guidance counselor at Lawrence High School in New Jersey. Take a look at these statistics:

- Only 30 percent or fewer applicants are accepted at highly competitive colleges each year.

- Most Ivy League students have placed in the top 10 percent of their class.

- Because Ivy League schools are so selective, they want a diverse student population. That means they want students that represent not only the fifty states but also a wide selection of other countries.

Lirio Jimenez, a guidance counselor at New Brunswick High School in New Jersey, says that being accepted by an Ivy League school is a process that starts in the ninth grade. You should select demanding courses and maintain good grades in those courses throughout all four years of high school. Get involved in extracurricular activities as well, and, of course, do well on your standardized tests. When it comes time to apply for college, select at least three schools: one ideal, one possible, and one shoe-in. Your ideal can be an Ivy League if you wish.

Peterson's Get a Jump! certainly doesn't want to discourage you from applying to one of these prestigious schools. We're in your corner and want to see you get the best education possible. However, students are sometimes more concerned about getting accepted than with taking a hard look at what a school has to offer them. Often, a university or college that is less competitive than an Ivy may have exactly what you need to succeed in the future. Keep that in mind as you select the colleges that will offer you what you need.

STUDENT COUNSEL

Q: What made you choose to apply to an Ivy League school?

A: My mother recommended that I apply to Princeton. She said, "Why not just try? What do you have to lose? All they can tell you is no." I was afraid of being rejected. I wasn't a straight-A student, and I thought they weren't going to want me—they get thousands of applications. Through the whole college process I had a whole lot of self-doubt. Looking back, I realize that you won't know if you don't try. Take the chance and fill out the application. If you don't get in, it doesn't mean you're less intelligent. It just wasn't the correct fit.

Zoelene Hill
Princeton University

MINORITY STUDENTS GO TO COLLEGE

African-American, Hispanic, Asian-American, and Native-American high school students have a lot of doors into higher education opening for them. In fact, most colleges want to respond to the social and economic disadvantages of certain groups of Americans. They want to reflect the globalization of our economy. They want their student populations to look like the rest of America, which means people from many different backgrounds and ethnic groups. This isn't just talk either. You'll find that most colleges have at least one member of the admissions staff who specializes in recruiting minorities.

One of the reasons college admissions staff are recruiting minorities and want to accommodate their needs is because there are more minorities thinking of attending college—and graduating. Let's put some numbers to these statements. According to the Department of Education, in 1976, 16 percent of college students were minorities, compared to 30 percent in 2001. Much of the change can be attributed to rising numbers of Hispanic and Asian students. The proportion of Asian and Pacific Islander students rose from 2 percent to 6 percent, and the Hispanic proportion rose from 4 percent to 9 percent during that same time period. The proportion of African-American students fluctuated during most of the early part of the period before rising slightly to 11 percent in 1997, the last year for which data was collected on this subject.

Peterson's Get a Jump! has a lot of information in this section to help you make decisions about college and paying for college. Perhaps the most important information we can give you is that if you want to go to college, you can. There are a lot of organizations ready to assist you. So go for it. See the list of organizations in this section and check with the colleges in which you're interested to connect with the minority affairs office.

Academic Resources for Minority Students

In addition to churches, sororities and fraternities, and college minority affairs offices, minority students can

SHOULD YOU ATTEND A HISTORICALLY BLACK COLLEGE OR UNIVERSITY?

Choosing which college to attend is usually a difficult decision for anyone to make, but when an African-American student is considering attending a historically black college or university (HBCU), a whole other set of family and cultural issues are raised.

There are many valid reasons that favor one or the other. Some are obvious differences. Parents and their children have to be honest with themselves and take a long, hard look at the needs of the student and how the campus environment can fulfill them. To help you decide, here are some questions to ask:

DO I KNOW WHAT'S REALLY IMPORTANT TO ME?

Look at the reasons why you want a degree and what you want to achieve with it. Is the choice to attend an HBCU yours or your family's? Do you have a particular field of study you want to pursue? Sometimes students can get so caught up in applying to a particular institution, they don't realize it doesn't even offer their major.

HOW WILL THIS CAMPUS FIT MY PLANS FOR THE FUTURE?

There's no substitute for doing your homework about the campuses you're seriously considering. Know the reputation of those campuses in the community and among employers and the general population. Find out about student retention, graduation, and placement rates.

DOES THIS CAMPUS HAVE THE FACILITIES AND LIVING CONDITIONS THAT SUIT MY COMFORT LEVEL?

Finding a campus where you're comfortable is a big factor in choosing a college. What do you want in campus facilities and living conditions? For instance, if you currently attend a small private high school in a suburban setting, perhaps you wouldn't like living on a large urban campus with peers who don't mirror your kind of background.

WHAT LEVEL OF SUPPORT WILL I GET ON CAMPUS?

Students considering institutions where few people are like them should look at the available support systems and organizations that will be available to them. Parents need to feel comfortable with the contact person on campus.

When all the factors that determine the choice of a college are laid out, the bottom line is which institution best meets your needs. For some African-American students, an HBCU is the best choice. For others, it's not. African-American students reflect many backgrounds, and there is no single decision that will be right for everyone.

receive information and assistance from the following organizations:

ASPIRA

ASPIRA's mission is to empower the Puerto Rican and Latino community through advocacy and the education and leadership development of its youth.

1444 Eye Street, NW, Suite 800
Washington, D.C. 20005
202-835-3600
www.aspira.org

INROADS

A national career-development organization that places and develops talented minority youth (African-American, Hispanic-American, and Native-American) in business and industry.

10 South Broadway, Suite 700
St. Louis, Missouri 63102
314-241-7488
www.inroads.org

National Action Council for Minorities in Engineering (NACME)

An organization that aims to provide leadership and support for the national effort to increase the representation of successful African-American, American Indian, and Latino women and men in engineering and technology and math- and science-based careers.

440 Hamilton Avenue, Suite 302
White Plains, New York 10601-1813
914-539-4010
www.nacme.org

National Association for the Advancement of Colored People (NAACP)

The purpose of the NAACP is to improve the political, educational, social, and economic status of minority groups; to eliminate racial prejudice; to keep the public aware of the adverse effects of racial discrimination; and to take lawful action to secure its elimination, consistent with the efforts of the national organization.

4805 Mt. Hope Drive
Baltimore, Maryland 21215
877-NAACP-98 (toll-free)
www.naacp.org

Q: How did you make the decision to attend a historically black college or university?

A: Selecting a college was one of the hardest decisions I've ever had to make. As a recipient of the National Achievement Scholarship and a National History Day winner, I was offered scholarships to a number of colleges across the country, including many HCBUs. I tried to figure out which institution would be able to give me the most help in achieving my goals. I finally decided on Florida A&M University (FAMU) in my hometown of Tallahassee.

There are many pluses to attending college in my hometown. By living on campus, I have the freedom to make my own decisions and live as a young adult while being close to the loving support of my parents. Also, FAMU will help me succeed in my objective of obtaining a bachelor's degree in broadcast journalism. As I look back, I am glad that I, unlike some of my high school peers, did not rush to judgment during the process of choosing a college. I am very happy with my decision.

Larry Rivers
Florida A&M University

The National Urban League

The Campaign for African-American Achievement of the National Urban League provides services for African-Americans and economically disadvantaged people. These services include basic academic development, GED test preparation for youths and adults, after-school tutoring for children, parent training classes, scholarships, an annual tour of historically black colleges and universities, and summer employment for youths.

> 120 Wall Street
> New York, New York 10005
> 212-558-5300
> www.nul.org

United Negro College Fund (UNCF)

The UNCF serves to enhance the quality of education by raising operating funds for its 39 member colleges and universities, providing financial assistance to deserving students, and increasing access to technology for students and faculty at historically black colleges and universities.

> 8260 Willow Oaks Corporate Drive
> P.O. Box 10444
> Fairfax, Virginia 22031-8044
> 800-331-2244 (toll-free)
> www.uncf.org

The American Indian Higher Education Consortium (AIHEC)

AIHEC's mission is to support the work of tribal colleges and the national movement for tribal self-determination through four objectives: maintain commonly held standards of quality in American Indian education; support the development of new tribally controlled colleges; promote and assist in the development of legislation to support American Indian higher education; and encourage greater participation by American Indians in the development of higher education policy.

> 121 Oronoco Street
> Alexandria, Virginia 22314
> 703-838-0400
> www.aihec.org

The Gates Millennium Scholars (GMS)

The Gates Millennium Scholars, funded by a grant from the Bill & Melinda Gates Foundation, was established in 1999 to provide outstanding African-American, American-Indian/Alaska Natives, Asian-Pacific Islander Americans, and Hispanic-American students with an opportunity to complete an undergraduate college education in all discipline areas and a graduate education for those students pursuing studies in mathematics, science, engineering, education, or library science. The goal of GMS is to promote academic excellence and to provide an opportunity for thousands of outstanding students with significant financial need to reach their fullest potential.

> P.O. Box 10500
> Fairfax, Virginia 22031-8044
> 877-690-4677 (toll-free)
> www.gmsp.org

Hispanic Association of Colleges and Universities (HACU)

The Hispanic Association of Colleges and Universities is a national association representing the accredited colleges and universities in the United

States where Hispanic students constitute at least 25 percent of the total student enrollment. HACU's goal is to bring together colleges and universities, corporations, government agencies, and individuals to establish partnerships for promoting the developing Hispanic-serving colleges and universities; improving access to and the quality of postsecondary education for Hispanic students; and meeting the needs of business, industry, and government through the development and sharing of resources, information, and expertise.

8415 Datapoint Drive, Suite 400
San Antonio, Texas 78229
210-692-3805
www.hacu.net

Hispanic Scholarship Fund (HSF)

The Hispanic Scholarship Fund is the nation's leading organization supporting Hispanic higher education. HSF was founded in 1975 with a vision to strengthen the country by advancing college education among Hispanic Americans. In support of its mission, HSF provides the Latino community with college scholarships and educational outreach support.

55 Second Street, Suite 1500
San Francisco, California 94105
877-473-4636 (toll-free)
www.hsf.net

STUDENTS WITH DISABILITIES GO TO COLLEGE

The Americans with Disabilities Act (ADA) requires educational institutions at all levels, public and private, to provide equal access to programs, services, and facilities. Schools must be accessible to students, as well as to employees and the public, regardless of any disability. To ensure such accessibility, they must follow specific requirements for new construction, alterations or renovations, academic programs, and institutional policies, practices, and procedures. Students with specific disabilities have the right to request and expect accommodations, including auxiliary aids and services that enable them to participate in and benefit from all programs and activities offered by or related to a school.

TIPS FOR STUDENTS WITH DISABILITIES

- Document your disability with letters from your physician(s), therapist, case manager, school psychologist, and other service providers.
- Get letters of support from teachers, family, friends, and service providers that detail how you have succeeded despite your disability.
- Learn the federal laws that apply to students with disabilities.
- Research support groups for peer information and advocacy.
- Visit several campuses.
- Look into the services available, the pace of campus life, and the college's programs for students with disabilities.
- Ask about orientation programs, including specialized introductions for, or about, students with disabilities.
- Ask about flexible, individualized study plans.
- Ask if the school offers technology such as voice synthesizers, voice recognition, and/or visual learning equipment to its students.
- Ask about adapted intramural/social activities.
- Ask to talk with students who have similar disabilities to hear about their experiences on campus.
- Once you select a college, get a map of the campus and learn the entire layout.
- If you have a physical disability, make sure the buildings you need to be in are accessible to you. Some, even though they comply with the ADA, aren't as accessible as others.
- Be realistic. If you use a wheelchair, for example, a school with an exceptionally hilly campus may not be your best choice, no matter what other accommodations it has.

To comply with ADA requirements, many high schools and universities offer programs and information to answer questions for students with disabilities and to assist them both in selecting appropriate colleges and in attaining full inclusion once they enter college. And most colleges and universities have disabilities services offices to help students negotiate the system. When it comes time to apply to colleges, write to the ones that you're interested in to find out what kinds of programs they have in place. When it comes time to narrow down your choices, make a request for a visit.

What Is Considered a Disability?

A person is considered to have a disability if he or she meets at least one of three conditions. The individual must:

1. have a documented physical or mental impairment that substantially limits one or more major life activities, such as personal self-care, walking, seeing, hearing, speaking, breathing, learning, working, or performing manual tasks;

2. have a record of such an impairment; or

3. be perceived as having such an impairment.

Physical disabilities include impairments of speech, vision, hearing, and mobility. Other disabilities, while less obvious, are similarly limiting; they include diabetes, asthma, multiple sclerosis, heart disease, cancer, mental illness, mental retardation, cerebral palsy, and learning disabilities.

Learning disabilities refer to an array of biological conditions that impede a person's ability to process and disseminate information. A learning disability is commonly recognized as a significant deficiency in one or more of the following areas: oral expression, listening comprehension, written expression, basic reading skills, reading comprehension, mathematical calculation, or problem solving. Individuals with learning disabilities also may have difficulty with sustained attention, time management, or social skills.

If you have a disability, you will take the same steps to choose and apply to a college as other students, but you should also evaluate each college based on your special need(s). Get organized, and meet with campus specialists to discuss your specific requirements. Then, explore whether the programs, policies, procedures, and facilities meet your specific situation.

It is usually best to describe your disability in a letter attached to the application so the proper fit can be made between you and the school. You will probably need to have your psychoeducational evaluation and testing record sent to the school. Some colleges help with schedules and offer transition courses, reduced course loads, extra access to professors, and special study areas to help address your needs.

Remember, admission to college is a realistic goal for any motivated student. If you invest the time and effort, you can make it happen.

STUDENT COUNSEL

The following quotes are from students who attend a college that offers services for learning disabled students.

"I have delayed development. I need help getting things done, and I need extra time for tests. As long as I'm able to go up to teachers and ask questions, I do well on tests."

—Anita

"I have dyslexia. I thought the term 'disabilities services' was for people with visual and hearing impairments. But when I got here, I found it covered a variety of disabilities. It was like Christmas. You got everything you wanted and more."

—Debra

"I am hard of hearing. I was always afraid I wouldn't be able to hear what [teachers] said. It's hard to read lips and listen at the same time. With note takers, I still get what I need even if the teacher moves around. They want you to make it through."

—Jeannette

DIRECTORY FOR STUDENTS WITH DISABILITIES

The following resources can help students, families, and schools with the legal requirements for accommodating disabilities. They can also link you with other groups and individuals that are knowledgeable in students' rights and the process of transition into postsecondary education.

Also, there are special interest, education, support, and advocacy organizations for persons with particular disabilities. Check with your counselor or contact one of the following organizations for information:

ACT Assessment Administration

Standard-Time National Testing with Accommodations

ACT Test Administration
P.O. Box 168
Iowa City, Iowa 52243-0168
319-337-1510

Extended-Time National Testing (up to 5 hours testing time or 5 hours, 45 minutes if taking the Writing Test)

ACT Registration
P.O. Box 414
Iowa City, Iowa 52243-0414
319-337-1270

Association on Higher Education and Disability (AHEAD)

P.O. Box 540666
Waltham, Massachusetts 02454
781-788-0003
www.ahead.org

Attention Deficit Disorder Association (ADDA)

P.O. Box 543
Pottstown, Pennsylvania 19464
484-945-2101
www.add.org

Children and Adults with Attention-Deficit/ Hyperactivity Disorders (CHADD)

8181 Professional Place, Suite 150
Landover, Maryland 20785
800-233-4050 (toll-free)
www.chadd.org

Council for Learning Disabilities

P.O. Box 4014
Leesburg, Virginia 20177
www.cldinternational.org

HEATH Resource Center National Clearinghouse on Postsecondary Education for Individuals with Disabilities

The George Washington University
HEATH Resource Center
2121 K Street, NW, Suite 220
Washington, D.C. 20037
800-544-3284 (toll-free)
www.heath.gwu.edu

International Dyslexia Association

The Chester Building, Suite 382
8600 LaSalle Road
Baltimore, Maryland 21286-2044
410-296-0232
www.interdys.org

Learning Disabilities Association of America (LDA)

4156 Library Road
Pittsburgh, Pennsylvania 15234
412-341-1515
www.ldanatl.org

National Center for Learning Disabilities (NCLD)

381 Park Avenue South, Suite 1401
New York, New York 10016
888-575-7373 (toll-free)
www.ncld.org

National Dissemination Center for Children with Disabilities

P.O. Box 1492
Washington, D.C. 20013
800-695-0285 (toll-free)
www.nichcy.org

Recording for the Blind & Dyslexic

20 Roszel Road
Princeton, New Jersey 08540
866-RFBD-585
www.rfbd.org

SAT Services for Students with Disabilities

The College Board Services for Students with Disabilities
P.O. Box 6226
Princeton, New Jersey 08541-6226
609-771-7137
www.collegeboard.com

7 Chapter

APPLYING TO COLLEGE

The big moment has arrived. It's time to make some decisions about where you want to apply.

Once your list is finalized, the worst part is filling out all the forms accurately and getting them in by the deadlines. Because requirements differ, you should check with all the colleges that you are interested in attending to find out what documentation is needed and when it is due.

WHAT SCHOOLS LOOK FOR IN PROSPECTIVE STUDENTS

As if you were sizing up the other team to plan your game strategy, you'll need to understand what

admissions committees want from you as you assemble all the pieces of your application.

Academic record: Admission representatives look at the breadth (how many), diversity (which ones), and difficulty (how challenging) of the courses on your transcript.

Grades: You should show consistency in your ability to work to your potential. If your grades are not initially good, colleges look to see that significant improvement has been made. Some colleges have minimum grade point averages that they are willing to accept.

Class rank: Colleges may consider the academic standing of a student in relation to the other members of his or her class. Are you in the top 25 percent of your class? Top half? Ask your counselor for your class rank.

Standardized test scores: Colleges look at test scores in terms of ranges. If your scores aren't high but you did well academically in high school, you shouldn't be discouraged. There is no set formula for admission. Even at the most competitive schools, some students' test scores are lower than you would think.

Extracurricular activities: Colleges look for depth of involvement (variety and how long you participated), initiative (leadership), and creativity demonstrated in activities, service, or work.

Recommendations: Most colleges require a recommendation from your high school guidance counselor. Some ask for references from teachers or other adults. If your counselor or teachers don't know you well, you should put together a student resume, or brag sheet, that outlines what you have done during

---

PARENT PERSPECTIVE

Q: How did you help your daughter get into college?

A: The key is to start early, like in the junior year. We didn't do that. At this point in the fall of our daughter's senior year, deadlines are coming up, and we haven't really looked at any colleges yet or gone on visits. It's kind of like choosing a house to buy without going to the house. The parent's role is to ask a lot of questions to get your child to figure out exactly what it is he or she wants to do. It's a big decision.

We hired a financial aid consultant who is helping us look at different colleges. The biggest worry is the FAFSA form. If you get it wrong, and they send it back to you—you have to start all over again. In the meantime, you're behind and others are getting grants. The whole process is very confusing, and there's no one to walk you through it. We've looked at different colleges on the Internet, and college fairs are a good resource. Plus, our daughter has done a lot on her own.

Doug and Judy Ames
Colorado Springs, Colorado

your four years of high school. In this chapter, you'll find a worksheet that will help you put together your resume.

College interview: An interview is required by most colleges with highly selective procedures. For further information, see "The College Interview" in the previous chapter.

ADMISSION PROCEDURES

Your first task in applying is to get application forms. That's easy. You can get them from your high school's guidance department, at college fairs, or by calling or writing to colleges and requesting applications. (See "Writing to a College for Information" in the previous chapter.) The trend, however, is leaning toward online applications, which are completed at the school's Web site. Admission information can be gathered from college representatives, catalogs, Web sites, and directories; alumni or students attending the college; and campus visits. Take a look at "Dos and Don'ts for Filling out Your Applications" on page 70 for some guidelines.

Which Admissions Option Is Best for You?

One of the first questions you will be asked on applications for four-year colleges and universities is which admission option you want. What they're talking about is whether you want to apply early action, early decision, deferred admission, etc.

Four-year institutions generally offer the following admissions options:

Early admission: A student of superior ability is admitted into college courses and programs before completing high school.

Early decision: A student declares a first-choice college, requests that the college decide on acceptance early (between November and January), and agrees to enroll if accepted. Students with a strong high school record who are sure they want to attend a certain school should consider early decision admission. (See "More on Early Decision," on the next page.)

PARENT PERSPECTIVE

Q: What can parents do to help their children make decisions about colleges?

A: Parents and teens should visit college campuses early and trust their gut feelings about whether the campus feels right. Above all, don't be blinded by name-brand colleges and the strong peer pressure that seems to steer your teen in the direction of prestigious colleges. Just as in shopping for clothing: Would you rather have a name brand or something that fits you well and makes you feel comfortable?

Ask your teen some questions. Do you really want to live in a pressure-cooker for the next four years? Some students thrive in a highly competitive environment, but many do not—even if they are excellent students. Before making a final decision, a teen should spend three or four days at the two colleges that interest him or her the most.

Senior year in high school is a time when teens go through many changes and experiment with many different roles. This can be bewildering to parents. Be patient. Realize that the time is equally bewildering to your son or daughter. Parents can be supportive and understanding, even though their teen may seem to be pushing them away. Offer guidance about choosing the right college, even though your teen might seem to be rejecting it. Teens hear everything, though they might not show it.

Marilyn Wedge, Ph.D.
Parent, family therapist, and educational consultant
Agoura Hills, California

Early action: This is similar to early decision, but if a student is accepted, he or she has until the regular admission deadline to decide whether or not to attend.

Early evaluation: A student can apply under early evaluation to find out if the chance of acceptance is good, fair, or poor. Applications are due before the regular admission deadline, and the student is given an opinion between January and March.

Regular admission: This is the most common option offered to students. A deadline is set for when all applications must be received, and all notifications are sent out at the same time.

Rolling admission: The college accepts students who meet the academic requirements on a first-come, first-served basis until it fills its freshman class. No strict application deadline is specified. Applications are reviewed and decisions are made immediately (usually within two to three weeks). This method is commonly used at large state universities, so students should apply early for the best chance of acceptance.

Open admission: Virtually all high school graduates are admitted, regardless of academic qualifications.

Deferred admission: An accepted student is allowed to postpone enrollment for a year.

If you're going to a two-year college, these options also apply to you. Two-year colleges usually have an "open-door" admission policy, which means that high school graduates may enroll as long as space is available. Sometimes vocational/career colleges are somewhat selective, and competition for admission may be fairly intense for programs that are highly specialized.

More on Early Decision

Early decision is a legally binding agreement between you and the college. If the college accepts you, you pay a deposit within a short period of time and sign an agreement stating that you will not apply to other colleges. To keep students from backing out, some colleges mandate that applicants' high school counselors cannot send transcripts to other institutions.

STUDENT COUNSEL

Q: **What made you want to apply to college early decision?**

A: **I visited lots of schools in Pennsylvania, but the minute I walked on the campus at Gettysburg, I knew I wanted to come here. I liked the way the campus was set up. It was small, and everything was together. The student-teacher ratio was low, and it had a good political science program. It had everything that I wanted.**

But if you want to go early decision, you have to visit the schools to be able to compare and contrast the different campuses. Many of the schools will have the same things, like small class size, but the way you feel about the campus is the largest factor because that's where you will be living. I visited Gettysburg four times, so when I went early decision, I was confident about it. I realized it was a huge step and knew I had to be sure. But after visiting here so many times, I knew I'd be unhappy anywhere else.

Kelly Keegan
Gettysburg College

In many ways, early decision is a win-win for both students and colleges. Students can relax and enjoy their senior year of high school without waiting to see if other colleges have accepted them. And colleges know early in the year who is enrolled and can start planning the coming year.

When Is Early Decision the Right Decision?

For good and bad reasons, early decision is a growing trend, so why not just do it? Early decision is an excellent idea that comes with a warning. It's not a good idea unless you have done a thorough college search and know without a shred of doubt that this is the college for you. Don't go for early decision unless you've spent time on the campus, in classes and dorms, and you have a true sense of the academic and social climate of that college.

Early decision can get sticky if you change your mind. Parents of students who have signed agreements and then want to apply elsewhere get angry at high school counselors, saying they've taken away their rights to choose among colleges. They try to force them to send out transcripts even though their children have committed to one college. To guard against this scenario, some colleges ask parents and students to sign a statement signifying their understanding that early decision is a binding plan. Some high schools now have their own form for students and parents to sign acknowledging that they completely realize the nature of an early decision agreement.

The Financial Reason Against Early Decision

Another common argument against early decision is that if an institution has you locked in, there's no incentive to offer applicants the best financial packages. The consensus seems to be that if you're looking to play the financial game, don't apply for early decision.

However, some folks argue that the best financial aid offers are usually made to attractive applicants. In general, if a student receives an early decision offer, they fall into that category and so would get "the sweetest" financial aid anyway. That doesn't mean that there aren't colleges out there using financial incentives to get students to enroll. A strong candidate who applies to six or eight schools and gets admitted to them all will look at how much money the colleges throw his or her way before making a decision.

Before You Decide...

If you're thinking about applying for early decision at a college, ask yourself these questions first. You'll be glad you did.

- ☑ Why am I applying early decision?

- ☑ Have I thoroughly researched several colleges and do I know what my options are?

- ☑ Do I know why I'm going to college and what I want to accomplish there?

- ☑ Have I visited several schools, spent time in classes, stayed overnight, and talked to professors?

- ☑ Do the courses that the college offers match my goals?

- ☑ Am I absolutely convinced that one college clearly stands out above all others?

MORE MUMBO JUMBO

Besides confusing terms like deferred admission, early decision, and early evaluation, just discussed, you'll most likely stumble upon some additional terms that might bamboozle you. Here, we explain a few more:

Academic Calendar

Traditional semesters: Two equal periods of time during a school year.

Early semester: Two equal periods of time during a school year. The first semester is completed before Christmas.

Trimester: Calendar year divided into three equal periods of time. The third trimester replaces summer school.

Quarter: Four equal periods of time during a school year.

4-1-4: Two equal terms of about four months separated by a one-month term.

Accreditation

Accreditation is recognition of a college or university by a regional or national organization, which indicates that the institution has met its objectives and is maintaining prescribed educational standards. Colleges may be accredited by one of six regional associations of schools and colleges and by any one of many national specialized accrediting bodies.

Specialized accreditation of individual programs is granted by national professional organizations. This is intended to ensure that specific programs meet or exceed minimum requirements established by the professional organization. States may require that students in some professions that grant licenses graduate from an accredited program as one qualification for licensure.

Accreditation is somewhat like receiving a pass/fail grade. It doesn't differentiate colleges and universities that excel from those that meet minimum requirements. Accreditation applies to all programs within an institution, but it does not mean that all programs are of equal quality within an institution. Accreditation does not guarantee transfer recognition by other colleges. Transfer decisions are made by individual institutions.

Affiliation

Not-for-profit colleges are classified into one of the following categories: state-assisted, private/independent, or private/church-supported. The institution's affiliation does not guarantee the quality or nature of the institution, and it may or may not have an effect on the religious life of students.

State-assisted colleges and universities and private/independent colleges do not have requirements related to the religious activity of their students. The influence of religion varies among private/church-supported colleges. At some, religious services or study are encouraged or required; at others, religious affiliation is less apparent.

Articulation Agreement

Articulation agreements facilitate the transfer of students and credits among state-assisted institutions of higher education by establishing transfer procedures and equitable treatment of all students in the system.

One type of articulation agreement links two or more colleges so that students can continue to make progress toward their degree, even if they must attend different schools at different times. For example, some states' community colleges have agreements with their state universities that permit graduates of college parallel programs to transfer with junior standing.

A second type of articulation agreement links secondary (high school) and postsecondary institutions to allow students to gain college credit for relevant vocational courses. This type of agreement saves students time and tuition in the pursuit of higher learning.

Because articulation agreements vary from school to school and from program to program, it is recommended that students check with their home institution and the institution they are interested in attending in order to fully understand the options available to them and each institution's specific requirements.

Cross-Registration

Cross-registration is a cooperative arrangement offered by many colleges and universities for the purpose of increasing the number and types of courses offered at any one institution. This arrangement allows students to cross-register for one or more courses at any participating host institution. While specific cross-registration program requirements may vary, typically a student can cross-register without having to pay the host institution additional tuition.

If your college participates in cross-registration, check with your home institution concerning any additional tuition costs and request a cross-registration form. Check with your adviser and registrar at your home institution to make sure that the course you plan to take is approved, and then contact the host institution for cross-registration instructions. Make sure that there is space available in the course you want to take at the host institution, as some host institutions give their own students registration priority.

To participate in cross-registration, you may need to be a full-time student (some programs allow part-time student participation) in good academic and financial standing at your home institution. Check with both colleges well in advance for all of the specific requirements.

THE COMPLETE APPLICATION PACKAGE

Freshman applications can be filed any time after you have completed your junior year of high school. Colleges strongly recommend that students apply by April (at the latest) of their senior year in order to be considered for acceptance, scholarships, financial aid, and housing. College requirements may vary, so always read and comply with specific requirements. In general, admission officers are interested in the following basic materials:

- A completed and signed application and any required application fee.

- An official copy of your high school transcript, including your class ranking and grade point average. The transcript must include all work completed as of the date the application is submitted. Check with your guidance counselor for questions about these items. If you apply on line, you must inform your guidance counselor and request that he or she send your transcript to the schools to which you are applying. Your application will not be processed without a transcript.

- An official record of your ACT Assessment or SAT scores.

- Other items that may be required include letters of recommendation, an essay,

(Continued on page 70)

COLLEGE APPLICATION CHECKLIST Keep track of your applications by inserting a check mark or the completion date in the appropriate column and row.

	College 1	College 2	College 3	College 4
Campus visit				
Campus interview				
Letters of recommendation				
NAME:				
Date requested				
Date followed-up				
NAME:				
Date requested				
Date followed-up				
NAME:				
Date requested				
Date followed-up				
Counselor recommendation form to counselor				
Secondary school report form to counselor				
Test scores requested				
Transcripts sent				
Application completed				
Essay completed				
All signatures collected				
Financial aid forms enclosed				
Application fee enclosed				
Copies made of all forms and documentation enclosed in application packet				
Postage affixed/return address on envelope				
Letters of acceptance/denial/wait list received				
Colleges notified of intent				
Tuition deposit sent				
Housing and other forms submitted to chosen college				
Orientation scheduled				

the secondary school report form and midyear school report (sent in by your guidance counselor after you fill out a portion of the form), and any financial aid forms required by the college.

Use the "College Application Checklist" on the previous page to make sure you have what you need before you send everything off.

Filling out the Forms

Filling out college applications can seem like a daunting task, but there are six easy steps to follow for the successful completion of this part of the process.

Step 1: Practice Copies

Make a photocopy of each application of each college to which you plan to apply. Since the presentation of your application may be considered an important aspect in the weighting for admission, you don't want to erase, cross out, or use white-out on your final application. Make all your mistakes on your copies. When you think you have it right, then transfer the information to your final original copy or go on line to enter it on the college's electronic application. Remember, at the larger universities, the application packet may be the only part of you they see.

Step 2: Decide on Your Approach

What is it about your application that will grab the admission counselor's attention so that it will be pulled out of the sea of applications on his or her desk for consideration? Be animated and interesting in what you say. Be memorable in your approach to your application, but don't overdo it. You want the admissions counselor to remember you, not your Spanish castle made of popsicle sticks. Most importantly, be honest and don't exaggerate your academics and extracurricular activities. Approach this process with integrity every step of the way. First of all, it is the best way to end up in a college that is the right match for you. Second, if you are less than truthful, the college will eventually learn about it.

DOS AND DON'TS FOR FILLING OUT YOUR APPLICATIONS

One of the most intimidating steps of applying for admission to college is filling out all the forms. This list of dos and don'ts will help you put your best foot forward on your college applications.

DO

- Read applications and directions carefully.
- Make sure that everything that is supposed to be included is enclosed.
- Make copies of applications, and practice filling one out before you complete the original.
- Fill out your own applications. Type the information yourself to avoid crucial mistakes.
- Start with the simple applications and then progress to the more complex ones.
- Type or neatly print your answers, and then proofread the applications and essays several times for accuracy. Also ask someone else to proofread them for you.
- If asked, describe how you can make a contribution to the schools to which you apply.
- Be truthful, and do not exaggerate your accomplishments.
- Keep a copy of all materials you submit to colleges.
- Be thorough and on time.

DON'T

- Use correction fluid. If you type your application, use a correctable typewriter or the liftoff strips to correct mistakes. Better yet, fill out your application on line.
- Write in script. If you don't have access to a computer or typewriter, print neatly.
- Leave blank spaces. Missing information may cause your application to be sent back or delayed while admission officers wait for complete information.
- Be unclear. If the question calls for a specific answer, don't try to dodge it by being vague.
- Put it off!

How will they know? You have to supply support materials to accompany your application, things like transcripts and recommendations. If you tell one story and they tell another, the admissions office will notice the disparity—another red flag!

Step 3: Check the Deadlines

In September of your senior year, organize your applications in chronological order. Place the due dates for your final list of schools next to their names on your stretch, target, and safety list and on your "College Application Checklist." Work on the earliest due date first.

Step 4: Check the Data on You

You need to make sure that the information you will be sending to support your applications is correct. The first thing to double-check is your transcript. This is an important piece because you must send a transcript with each application you send to colleges. Take a trip to the guidance office and ask for a "Transcript Request Form." Fill out the request for a formal transcript, indicating that you are requesting a copy for yourself and that you will pick it up. Pay the fee if there is one.

When you get your transcript, look it over carefully. It will be several pages long and will include everything from the titles of all the courses that you have taken since the ninth grade along with the final grade for each course and community service hours you have logged each year. Check the information carefully. It is understandable that with this much data, it is easy to make an input error. Because this information is vital to you and you are the best judge of accuracy, it is up to you to check it. Take any corrections or questions you have back to your guidance counselor to make the corrections. If it is a questionable grade, your counselor will help you find out what grade should have been posted on your transcript. Do whatever needs to be done to make sure your transcript has been corrected no later than October 1 of your senior year.

Step 5: List Your Activities

When you flip through your applications, you will find a section on extracurricular activities. It is time to hit your computer again to prioritize your list of extracurricular activities and determine the best approach for presenting them to your colleges. Some students will prepare a resume and include this in every application they send. Other students will choose to develop an "Extracurricular, Academic, and Work Experience Addendum" and mark those specific sections of their application as "See attached Addendum."

If you are a powerhouse student with a great deal to say in this area, it will take time to prioritize your involvement in activities and word it succinctly yet interestingly. Your "Brag Sheet" will help (see "The Brag Sheet" on page 72). Put those activities that will have the strongest impact, show the most consistent involvement, and demonstrate your leadership abilities at the top of the list. This will take time, so plan accordingly. If you feel you have left out important information because the form limits you, include either an addendum or your resume as a back-up.

Step 6: Organize Your Other Data

What other information can you organize in advance of sitting down to fill out your applications?

The Personal Data Section

Most of this section is standard personal information that you will not have any difficulty responding to, but some items you will need to think about. For example, you may find a question that asks, "What special college or division are you applying to?" Do you have a specific school in mind, like the College of Engineering? If you are not sure about your major, ask yourself what interests you the most and then enter that college. Once you are in college and have a better sense of what you want to do, you can always change your major later.

The application will provide an optional space to declare ethnicity. If you feel you would like to declare an area and that it would work to your advantage for

(Continued on page 73)

THE BRAG SHEET

At the beginning of this chapter, we described how a student resume can help your guidance counselors and teachers write their letters of recommendation for you. Putting together a list of your accomplishments will also help you organize all of the information you will need to include when you fill out your college applications.

ACADEMICS

GPA (Grade Point Average) _____

THE HONORS COURSES I HAVE TAKEN ARE:

English _____

History _____

Math _____

Science _____

Language _____

Electives _____

THE AP COURSES I HAVE TAKEN ARE:

English _____

History _____

Math _____

Science _____

Language _____

Electives _____

STANDARDIZED TEST SCORES

PSAT _____

1st SAT _____

2nd SAT _____

ACT Assessment _____

SAT SUBJECT TESTS

Test 1 _____ Score _____

Test 2 _____ Score _____

Test 3 _____ Score _____

SPECIAL TALENTS

I have received the following academic awards:

_____

_____

_____

I have performed in these theatrical productions: _____

_____

I lettered in the following sports: _____

I have played on the following traveling teams: _____

_____

_____

I am a member of the following musical groups: _____

_____

EXTRACURRICULAR ACTIVITIES

I participate on a regular basis in the following extracurricular activities: _____

_____

I have held the following offices: _____

_____

_____

I have established the following extracurricular organizations: _____

_____

I have held the following after-school and summer jobs: _____

_____

GOALS

I plan to major in the following area in college: _____

_____

admission, consider completing this section of the application.

You are also going to need your high school's College Entrance Examination Board (CEEB) number. That is the number you needed when you filled out your test packets. It is stamped on the front of your SAT and ACT Assessment packets, or, if you go to the guidance department, they'll tell you what it is.

The Standardized Testing Section

Applications ask you for your test dates and scores. Get them together accurately. All your College Board scores should be recorded with the latest test results you have received. Your latest ACT Assessment record will only have the current scores unless you asked for all your past test results. If you have lost this information, call these organizations or go to your guidance department. Your counselor should have copies. Be sure the testing organizations are sending your official score reports to the schools to which you're applying. If you are planning to take one of these tests in the future, the colleges will want those dates, too; they will wait for those scores before making a decision. If you change your plans, write the admissions office a note with the new dates or the reason for canceling.

The Senior Course Load Section

Colleges will request that you list your present senior schedule by semester. Set this information up in this order: List any AP or honors-level full-year courses first, as these will have the most impact. Then list other required full-year courses and then required semester courses, followed by electives. Make sure you list first-semester and second-semester courses appropriately. Do not forget to include physical education if you are taking it this year.

Your Recommendation Writers

Most schools will require you to submit two or three letters of recommendation from adults who know you well.

Guidance Counselor Recommendations

Nearly all colleges require a letter of recommendation from the applicant's high school guidance counselor. Some counselors will give students an essay question that they feel will give them the background they need in order to structure a recommendation. Other counselors will canvass a wide array of individuals who know a student in order to gather a broader picture of the student in various settings. No one approach is better than the other. Find out which approach is used at your school. You will probably get this information as a handout at one of those evening guidance programs or in a classroom presentation by your school's guidance department. If you are still not sure you know what is expected of you or if the dog has eaten those papers, ask your guidance counselor what is due and by what date. Make sure that you complete the materials on time and that you set aside enough of your time to do them justice.

Teacher Recommendations

In addition to the recommendation from your counselor, colleges may request additional recommendations from your teachers. Known as formal recommendations, these are sent directly to the colleges by your subject teachers. Most colleges require at least one formal recommendation in addition to the counselor's recommendation. However, many competitive institutions require two, if not three, academic recommendations. Follow a school's directions regarding the exact number. A good rule-of-thumb is to have recommendations from teachers in two subject areas (e.g., English and math).

Approach your recommendation writers personally to request that they write for you. If they agree, provide them with a copy of your Brag Sheet. On the other hand, you may be met with a polite refusal on the order of "I'm sorry, but I'm unable to write for you. I've been approached by so many seniors already that it would be difficult for me to accomplish your recommendation by your due dates." This teacher may really be overburdened with requests for recommendations, especially if this is a senior English teacher, or the teacher may be giving you a signal that someone else may be able to write a stronger piece for you. Either way, accept the refusal politely, and seek another recommendation writer.

How do you decide whom to ask? Here are some questions to help you select your writers:

- ☑ How well does the teacher know you?

- ☑ Has the teacher taught you for more than one course? (A teacher who taught you over a two- to three-year period has seen your talents and skills develop.)

- ☑ Has the teacher sponsored an extracurricular activity in which you made a contribution?

- ☑ Do you get along with the teacher?

- ☑ Does the college/university indicate that a recommendation is required or recommended from a particular subject-area instructor?

- ☑ If you declare an intended major, can you obtain a recommendation from a teacher in that subject area?

Other Recommendation Writers

Consider getting recommendations from your employer, your rabbi or pastor, the director of the summer camp where you worked for the last two summers, and so on—but only if these additional letters are going to reveal information about you that will have a profound impact on the way a college will view your candidacy. Otherwise, you run the risk of overloading your application with too much paper.

Writing the Application Essay

Application essays show how you think and how you write. They also reveal additional information about you that is not in your other application material. Not all colleges require essays, and those that do often have a preferred topic. Make sure you write about the topic that is specified and keep to the length of pages or words. If the essay asks for 300 words, don't submit 50 or 500. Some examples of essay topics include:

Tell us about yourself. Describe your personality and a special accomplishment. Illustrate the unique aspects of who you are, what you do, and what you want out of life. Share an experience that made an impact on you, or write about something you have learned from your parents.

Tell us about an academic or extracurricular interest or idea. Show how a book, experience, quotation, or idea reflects or shapes your outlook and aspirations.

Tell us why you want to come to our college. Explain why your goals and interests match the programs and offerings of that particular school. This question requires some research about the school. Be specific.

Show us an imaginative side of your personality. This question demands originality but is a great opportunity to show off your skills as a writer. Start writing down your thoughts and impressions well before the essay is due. Think about how you have changed over the years so that if and when it comes time to write about yourself, you will have plenty of information. Write about something that means a lot to you, and support your thoughts with reasons and examples. Then explain why you care about your topic.

The essay should not be a summary of your high school career. Describe yourself as others see you, and

---

FROM THE GUIDANCE OFFICE

Q: Why are essays so important to the college application?

A: Students focus more on grades than anything else. They think grades are the be-all and end-all and that an SAT score will get them in. For most selective schools, that's just one piece of the pie. Many of the schools in the upper 20 percent of competitive schools consider the essay more heavily. Essays show whether the student is a thinker, creative, and analytical. They're looking for the type of personality that can shine rather than one that simply can spit out names and dates. When everyone has high SATs in a pool of applicants, the essay is what makes one student stand out over another.

Patsy Lovelady
Counselor
MacArthur High School
San Antonio, Texas

---

use a natural, conversational style. Use an experience to set the scene in which you will illustrate something about yourself. For example, you might discuss how having a disabled relative helped you to appreciate life's simple pleasures. Or you may use your athletic experiences to tell how you learned the value of teamwork. The essay is your chance to tell something positive or enriching about yourself, so highlight an experience that will make the reader interested in you.

Outline in the essay what you have to offer the college. Explain why you want to attend the institution and how your abilities and goals match the strengths and offerings at the university. Write, rewrite, and edit. Do not try to dash off an essay in one sitting. The essay will improve with time and thought. Proofread and concentrate on spelling, punctuation, and content. Have someone else take a look at your essay. Make copies and save them after mailing the original.

Admission officers look for the person inside the essay. They seek students with a breadth of knowledge and experiences, someone with depth and perspective. Inner strength and commitment are admired, too. Not everyone is a winner all the time. The essay is a tool you can use to develop your competitive edge. Your essay should explain why you should be admitted over other applicants.

As a final word, write the essay from the heart. It should have life and not be contrived or one-dimensional. Avoid telling them what they want to hear; instead, be yourself.

SPECIAL INFORMATION FOR ATHLETES

If you weren't a planner before, but you want to play sports while in college or go to college on an athletic scholarship, you'd better become a planner now. There are many regulations and conditions you need to know ahead of time so that you don't miss out on possible opportunities.

First, think about whether or not you have what it takes to play college sports. It's a tough question to ask, but it's a necessary one. In general, playing college sports requires both basic skills and natural

SAMPLE APPLICATION ESSAY

Here is one student's college application essay. She answered the question, "Indicate a person who has had a significant influence on you, and describe that influence."

Mrs. Morrone did not become my guidance counselor until my sophomore year of high school. During my first meeting with her, I sat across from her in an uncomfortable vinyl chair and refused to meet her eyes as I told her about my long and painful shyness, how I detested oral reports, and how I feared raising my hand in class or being called on to answer a question—all because I didn't want to be the center of attention.

She did not offer me advice right away. Instead, she asked me more about myself—my family, my friends, what kinds of music, books, and movies I liked. We talked easily, like old friends, and it was not long before I began to look forward to our weekly meetings. Her office was one of the few places where I felt like I could be myself and let my personality shine through, where I knew that I was accepted and liked unconditionally.

In November of that year, the drama club announced auditions for the spring play, The Glass Menagerie. I had studied it in English class and it was one of my favorites; not surprisingly, I identified strongly with the timid Laura. I talked with Mrs. Morrone about the play and how much I liked theater. At one point I sighed, "I'd love to play Laura."

"Why don't you try out for the show?" Mrs. Morrone suggested.

The very idea of performing, onstage, in a spotlight, in front of dozens of people frightened me. She did not press the matter, but at the end of the session she encouraged me to bring a copy of the play to our next few meetings and read some of the character's lines, "just for fun." I did, and found myself gradually transforming into Laura as I recited her lines with increasing intensity.

After a couple of these amateur performances, she told me that I was genuinely good as Laura, and she would love to see me at least audition for the part. "I would never force you to do it," she said, "but I would hate to see you waste your potential." I insisted that I was too frightened, but she promised that she would come and watch my audition. She told me to pretend she was the only person in the audience.

A week later, I did read for the part of Laura. Mrs. Morrone beamed with pride in the back of the auditorium. I discovered that I truly enjoyed acting; slipping into another character cracked the shell that I had built around myself. I did not get the part, but I had found a passion that enriched my life in immeasurable ways. I owe Mrs. Morrone so much for putting me on the path to becoming a professional actress and for helping me to finally conquer my shyness. Without her quiet support and strength, none of this would have come to pass.

FROM THE GUIDANCE OFFICE

Q: What's a big mistake high school athletes make when thinking about college?

A: Some athletes think that their athletic ability alone will get them a scholarship and do not believe that their academics must be acceptable. The Division I or II schools cannot offer scholarships if the student has not met the academic standards required by the school for admission. Our counselors start reminding students in the freshman year and every year after that the courses they take do make a difference in how colleges view their transcripts. Students can't start preparing in their senior year of high school.

Sue Bradshaw
Guidance Counselor
Sterling High School
Baytown, Texas

ability, a solid knowledge of the sport, overall body strength, speed, and sound academics. Today's athletes are stronger and faster because of improved methods of training and conditioning. They are coached in skills and techniques, and they begin training in their sport at an early age. Remember, your talents will be compared with those from across the U.S. and around the world.

Second, know the background. Most college athletic programs are regulated by the National Collegiate Athletic Association (NCAA), an organization that has established rules on eligibility, recruiting, and financial aid. The NCAA has three membership divisions: Division I, Division II, and Division III. Institutions are members of one or another division according to the size and scope of their athletic programs and whether they provide athletic scholarships.

If you are planning to enroll in college as a freshman and you wish to participate in Division I or Division II athletics, you must be certified by the NCAA Initial-Eligibility Clearinghouse (www.ncaaclearinghouse.net). The Clearinghouse was established as a separate organization by the NCAA member institutions to ensure consistent interpretation of NCAA initial-eligibility requirements for all prospective student athletes at all member institutions.

You should start the certification process when you are a junior in high school. Check with your counselor to make sure you are taking a core curriculum that meets NCAA requirements. Also, register to take the ACT Assessment or SAT as a junior. Submit your Student Release Form (available in your guidance counseling office) to the Clearinghouse by the beginning of your senior year.

Initial Eligibility of Freshman Athletes for Division I and II

Students who plan to participate in NCAA Division I or II college sports must obtain the Student Release Form from their high school, complete it, and send it to the NCAA Clearinghouse. This form authorizes high schools to release student transcripts, including test scores, proof of grades, and other academic information, to the Clearinghouse. It also authorizes the Clearinghouse to release this information to the colleges that request it. The form and corresponding fee must be received before any documents will be processed. (Fee waivers are available for economically disadvantaged students. Check with your counselor for fee waiver information.)

Students must also make sure that the Clearinghouse receives ACT Assessment and/or SAT score reports. Students can have score reports sent directly to the Clearinghouse by entering a specific code (9999) printed in the ACT Assessment and SAT registration packets.

Once a year, high schools will send an updated list of approved core courses, which lists each course offering that meets NCAA core course requirements. The Clearinghouse personnel will validate the form. Thereafter, the Clearinghouse will determine each student's initial eligibility. Collegiate institutions will request information from the Clearinghouse on the initial eligibility of prospective student-athletes. The Clearinghouse will make a certification decision and report it directly to the institution.

Three types of eligibility are possible:

1. Certification of eligibility for expense-paid campus visits.

2. Preliminary certification of eligibility to participate in college sports (appears likely to meet all NCAA requirements but not yet graduated).

ATHLETIC RESUME

Name _____

Address _____

_____

High school address and phone number

_____

_____

_____

Coach's name _____

Height/weight _____

Foot speed (by specific event) _____

Position played _____

Weight classification _____

GPA _____

Class rank _____

ACT Assessment or SAT scores (or when you plan to take them) _____

_____

Athletic records held _____

_____

All-state teams _____

Special awards _____

Off-season accomplishments _____

Weightlifting exercises _____

Vertical jumps _____

Push-ups _____

Bench jumps _____

Shuttle run _____

Leadership characteristics _____

Former successful athletes from your high school

_____

Outstanding capabilities _____

Citizenship _____

Alumni parents/relatives _____

Include the following with your resume:

- Team schedule with dates and times
- Videotape with jersey number identified
- Newspaper clippings about you and/or your team

3. Final certification granted when proof of graduation is received.

Additional information about the Clearinghouse can be found in the *Guide for the College-Bound Student-Athlete*, published by the NCAA. To get a copy of this guide, call 800-638-3731 (toll-free). You can also visit the NCAA Web site at www2.ncaa.org.

National Association of Intercollegiate Athletics (NAIA) Regulations

The National Association of Intercollegiate Athletics (NAIA) has different eligibility requirements for student-athletes. To be eligible to participate in intercollegiate athletics as an incoming freshman, two of the following three requirements must be met:

1. Have a 2.0 (C) or higher cumulative final grade point average in high school.

2. Have a composite score of 18 or higher on the ACT Assessment or an 860 total score or higher on the SAT Critical Reading and Math sections.

3. Have a top-half final class rank in his or her high school graduating class.

Student-athletes must also have on file at the college an official ACT Assessment or SAT score report from the appropriate national testing center. Results reported on the student's high school transcript are not acceptable. Students must request that their test scores be forwarded to the college's admission office.

If you have additional questions about NAIA eligibility, contact them at:

NAIA
23500 W. 105th Street
Olathe, Kansas 66051
913-791-0044
www.naia.org

AUDITIONS AND PORTFOLIOS

If you decide to study the arts, such as theater, music, or fine arts, you may be required to audition or show your portfolio to admissions personnel. The following tips will help you showcase your talents and skills when preparing for an audition or portfolio review.

Music Auditions

High school students who wish to pursue a degree in music, whether it is vocal or instrumental, typically must audition. If you're a singer, prepare at least two pieces in contrasting styles. One should be in a foreign language, if possible. Choose from operatic, show music, or art song repertories, and make sure you memorize each piece. If you're an instrumentalist or pianist, be prepared to play scales and arpeggios, at least one etude or technical study, and a solo work. Instrumental audition pieces need not be memorized. In either field, you may be required to do sight-reading.

When performing music that is sight-read, you should take time to look over the piece and make certain of the key and time signatures before proceeding with the audition. If you're a singer, you should bring a familiar accompanist to the audition.

"My advice is to ask for help from teachers, try to acquire audition information up front, and know more than is required for the audition," says one student. "It is also a good idea to select your audition time and date early."

"Try to perform your solo in front of as many people as you can as many times as possible," says another student. "You may also want to try to get involved in a high school performance."

Programs differ, so students are encouraged to call the college and ask for audition information. In general, music departments seek students who demonstrate technical competence and performance achievement.

Admission to music programs varies in degree of competitiveness, so you should audition at a minimum of three colleges and a maximum of five to amplify your opportunity. The degree of competitiveness varies also by instrument, especially if a renowned musician teaches a certain instrument. Some colleges offer a second audition if you feel you did not audition to your potential. Ideally, you will be accepted into the music program of your choice, but keep in mind that it's possible to not be accepted. You must then make the decision to either pursue a music program at another college or consider another major at that college.

Dance Auditions

At many four-year colleges, an open class is held the day before auditions. A performance piece that combines improvisation, ballet, modern, and rhythm is taught and then students are expected to perform the piece at auditions. Professors look for coordination, technique, rhythm, degree of movement, and body structure. The dance faculty members also assess your ability to learn and your potential to complete the curriculum. Dance programs vary, so check with the college of your choice for specific information.

Art Portfolios

A portfolio is simply a collection of your best pieces of artwork. The pieces you select to put in your portfolio should demonstrate your interest and aptitude for a serious education in the arts. A well-developed portfolio can help you gain acceptance into a prestigious art college and increase your chances of being awarded a scholarship in national portfolio competitions. The pieces you select should show diversity in technique and variety in subject matter. You may show work in any medium (oils, photography, watercolors, pastels, etc.) and in either black-and-white or color. Your portfolio can include classroom assignments as well as independent projects. You can also include your sketchbook.

Specialized art colleges request that you submit an average of ten pieces of art, but remember that quality is more important than quantity. The admission office staff will review your artwork and transcripts to assess your skill and potential for success. Usually, you will present your portfolio in person; however, some schools allow students to mail slides if distance is an issue. There is no simple formula for success other than hard work. In addition, there is no such thing as a "perfect portfolio," nor any specific style or direction to achieve one.

Tips for Pulling Your Portfolio Together:

- ☑ Try to make your portfolio as clean and organized as possible.

- ☑ It is important to protect your work, but make sure the package you select is easy to handle and does not interfere with the viewing of the artwork.

- ☑ Drawings that have been rolled up are difficult for the jurors to handle and view. You may shrink-wrap the pieces, but it is not required.

- ☑ Avoid loose sheets of paper between pieces. Always spray fixative on any pieces that could smudge.

- ☑ If you choose to mount or mat your work (not required), use only neutral gray tones, black, or white.

- ☑ Never include framed pieces or three-dimensional work.

- ☑ A slide portfolio should be presented in a standard 8 × 11 plastic slide sleeve.

- ☑ Be sure paintings are completely dry before you place them in your portfolio.

- ☑ Label each piece with your name, address, and high school.

Theater Auditions

Most liberal arts colleges do not require that students who audition be accepted into the theater department unless the college offers a Bachelor of Fine Arts (B.F.A.) degree in theater. You should apply to the college of your choice prior to scheduling an audition. You should also consider spending a full day on campus so that you may talk with theater faculty members and students, attend classes, meet with your admission counselor, and tour the facilities.

Although each college and university has different requirements, you should prepare two contrasting monologues taken from plays of your choice if you're auditioning for a B.F.A. acting program. Musical theater requirements generally consist of one up-tempo musical selection and one ballad, as well as one monologue from a play or musical of your choice. The total of all your pieces should not exceed 5 minutes. Music for the accompanist, a resume of your theater experience, and a photo are also required.

Tips to Get You Successfully through an Audition:

- ☑ Choose material suitable for your age.

- ☑ If you choose your monologue from a book of monologues, you should read the entire play and be familiar with the context of your selection.

- ☑ Select a monologue that allows you to speak directly to another person; you should play only one character.

- ☑ Memorize your selection.

- ☑ Avoid using characterization or style, as they tend to trap you rather than tapping deeper into inner resources.

FINANCIAL AID DOLLARS AND SENSE

Getting financial aid can be intimidating—but don't let that stop you.

FINDING THE MONEY you need to attend a two- or four-year institution or vocational/career college is a challenge, but you can do it if you devise a strategy well before you actually start applying to college. Financial aid comes from a lot of different sources. But this is where GAJ comes in. You'll find lots of help in this guide in locating those sources and where to get advice. Financial aid is available to help meet both direct educational costs (tuition, fees, books) and personal living expenses (food, housing, transportation).

Times have changed to favor the student in the financial aid process. Because the pool of potential traditional college students is somewhat limited, colleges and universities are competing to attract the top students to their school. In fact, some colleges and universities not only use financial aid as a method to help students fund their college education but often as a marketing and recruitment tool. This puts students and families at an advantage, one that should be recognized and used for bargaining power.

It used to be that colleges and universities offered need-based and merit-based financial aid to only needy and/or academically exceptional students. Now some schools offer what might be called incentive or tuition discount aid to encourage students to choose them over another college. This aid, which is not necessarily based on need or merit, is aimed at students who meet the standards of the college but who wouldn't necessarily qualify for traditional kinds of aid.

A BIRD'S-EYE VIEW OF FINANCIAL AID

You and your family should be assertive in negotiating financial aid packages. It used to be that there was no room for such negotiation, but in today's environment, it is wise to be a comparison shopper. Families should wait until they've received all of their financial offers and then talk to their first-choice college to see if the college can match the better offers from other colleges.

To be eligible to receive federal/state financial aid, you must maintain satisfactory academic progress toward a degree or certificate. This criterion is established by each college or university. You'll also need a valid social security number, and all male students must register for selective service on their eighteenth birthday.

You apply for financial aid during your senior year. Every school requires the Free Application for

PROJECTED COLLEGE EXPENSES

The following chart estimates the cost of one year of college education, including tuition, room, and board. Estimates are based on a 6 percent annual increase.

School Year	Public 4-Year	Private 4-Year
2006–2007	$12,127	$29,026
2007–2008	13,580	32,500
2010–2011	16,000	38,350
2014–2015	19,800	47,500

Source: The College Entrance Examination Board, "Trends in College Pricing, 2004"

FINANCIAL AID GLOSSARY

ASSETS. The amount a family has in savings and investments. This includes savings and checking accounts, a business, a farm or other real estate, and stocks, bonds, and trust funds. Cars are not considered assets, nor are such possessions as stamp collections or jewelry. The net value of the principal home is counted as an asset by some colleges in determining their own awards but is not included in the calculation for eligibility for federal funds.

CITIZENSHIP/ELIGIBILITY FOR AID. To be eligible to receive federally funded college aid, a student must be one of the following:

1. A United States citizen;

2. A non-citizen national;

3. A permanent resident with an I-151 or I-551 without conditions;

4. A participant in a suspension of deportation case pending before Congress; or

5. A holder of an I-94 showing one of the following designations: "Refugee," "Asylum Granted," "Indefinite Parole" and/or "Humanitarian Parole," "Cuban/Haitian Entrant, Status Pending," or "Conditional Entrant" (valid if issued before April 1, 1980).

Individuals in the U.S. on an F1 or F2 visa or on a J1 or J2 exchange visa cannot get federal aid.

COOPERATIVE EDUCATION. A program offered by many colleges in which students alternate periods of enrollment with periods of employment, usually paid, and that can lengthen the usual baccalaureate program to five years.

EXPECTED FAMILY CONTRIBUTION (EFC). A figure determined by a congressionally mandated formula that indicates how much of a family's resources should be considered "available" for college expenses. Factors such as taxable and nontaxable income and the value of family assets are taken into account to determine a family's financial strength. Allowances for maintaining a family and future financial needs are then taken into consideration before determining how much a family should be able to put toward the cost of college.

INDEPENDENT STUDENT. A student who reports only his or her own income and assets (and that of a spouse, if relevant) when applying for federal financial aid. Students are automatically considered independent at 24 years of age. Students who are under 24 will be considered independent if they are:

- married as of the date of filing the FAFSA.
- provide more than half the support of a legal dependent other than a spouse.
- a veteran of the U.S. Armed Forces.
- an orphan or ward of the court.
- classified as independent by a college's financial aid administrator because of other unusual circumstances.
- a graduate or professional student.

MERIT-BASED AID. Any form of financial aid awarded on the basis of personal achievement or individual characteristics without reference to financial need.

SUBSIDIZED LOAN. While enrolled at least half-time, this loan does not accure interest. For Subsidized Federal Stafford and/or Direct Loans, the government pays the interest to the lender on behalf of the borrower while the student is in college and during approved grace periods.

Federal Student Aid (FAFSA), which cannot be filed until after January 1 of your senior year. Your application will be processed in about 4 weeks if you use the paper application or about one week if you apply on line at www.fafsa.ed.gov. You'll then receive a Student Aid Report (SAR), which will report the information from the FAFSA and show your calculated Expected Family Contribution (EFC—the number used in determining your eligibility for federal student aid). Each school you listed on the application, as well as your state of legal residence, will also receive your FAFSA information. If you are applying to higher-cost colleges or some scholarship programs, you also may have to file the PROFILE® application. This should be completed in September or October of your senior year. More information on the PROFILE is available from your high school guidance office or on the Web at www.collegeboard.org. There is a fee charged with the PROFILE.

COLLEGE FUNDS AVAILABLE

Use this chart to estimate resources that will be available for college expenses. Check your progress at the end of your sophomore and junior years to see if your plans for seeking financial aid need to be revised.

YOUR RESOURCES	Estimated amount available	Actual amount: 11th grade	Actual amount: 12th grade
Savings and other assets			
Summer earnings			
Part-time work during school year			
Miscellaneous			
PARENTS' RESOURCES			
From their current income			
From college savings			
Miscellaneous (insurance, annuities, stocks, trusts, home equity, property assets)			
TOTAL			

Source: American College Testing Program

You must reapply for federal aid every year. Also, if you decide to transfer to another school, your aid doesn't necessarily go with you. Check with your new school to find out what steps you must take to continue receiving aid. You should plan any transfer at least three months in advance.

Once you've decided to which schools you want to apply, talk to the financial aid officers of those schools. There is no substitute for getting information from the source when it comes to understanding your financial aid options. That personal contact can lead you to substantial amounts of financial aid.

If you qualify for admission, don't let the sticker price of the college or program scare you away, because you may get enough financial assistance to pay for the education you want. Don't rule out a private institution until you have received the financial aid package from the school. Private colleges, in order to attract students from all income levels, offer significant amounts of financial aid. Public-supported institutions tend to offer less financial aid because the lower tuition acts as a form of assistance (see "Projected College Expenses"). In addition, students attending school in their home state often have more aid possibilities than if they attend an out-of-state college. Use the "College Funds Available" chart to determine how much you and your family can contribute to your education and the "College Cost Comparison Worksheet" to figure out which schools best suit you financially.

TYPES OF FINANCIAL AID

Be sure that you understand the differences between the types of financial aid so you are fully prepared to apply for each. One or more of these financial resources may make it possible to pursue the education you want.

Grants: Grants are usually given to students with financial need. But the term is also used for athletics (Division I only), academics, demographics, and special talents. Grants do not have to be repaid.

Scholarships: Scholarships, also called "merit aid," are awarded for academic excellence or other special talents or abilities. Repayment is not required.

Loans: Student loans, which have very favorable terms and conditions, are sponsored by the federal government, state governments, and through commercial lending institutions. The Financial Aid Office is the best source of information on student loans. These must be repaid, generally after you graduate or leave school.

College Work-Study: College Work-Study is a federally sponsored program that enables colleges to hire students for employment. If eligible, students work a limited number of hours throughout the school year. Many colleges use their own funds to hire students to work in the many departments and offices on campus. If you do not receive a federal work-study grant, you should contact the Student Employment Office or the Financial Aid Office to help locate nonfederal work-study positions that may be available.

Financial Aid Programs: The federal government is the single largest source of financial aid for students, making more than an estimated $90 billion available in loans, grants, and other aid to millions of students. In addition, a number of sources of financial aid are available to students from state governments, private lenders, foundations, and private sources, and the colleges and universities themselves.

FEDERAL GRANTS

The federal government offers a number of educational grants, which are outlined below:

Federal Pell Grant

The Federal Pell Grant is the largest grant program in the nation; about 5.3 million students receive awards annually. This grant is intended to be the base or starting point of assistance for lower-income families. Eligibility for a Federal Pell Grant depends on the EFC, or Expected Family Contribution. (See the "Financial Aid Glossary" for a description of commonly used terms.) The actual Pell Grant award amounts depend on how much funds are appropriated by Congress each year. The maximum for the 2005–06 school year was $4,050. How much you will receive depends not only on your EFC, but also on your cost of attendance and whether you're a full-time or part-time student.

Federal Supplemental Educational Opportunity Grant (FSEOG)

As its name implies, the Federal Supplemental Educational Opportunity Grant (FSEOG) provides additional need-based federal grant money to supplement the Federal Pell Grant. Each participating college is given funds to award to especially needy students. The maximum award is $4,000 per year, but the amount a student receives depends on the college's policy, the availability of FSEOG funds, the total cost of education, and the amount of other aid awarded.

COLLEGE COST COMPARISON WORKSHEET

Chart your course to see which college or university best fits your financial resources. Your totals in expenses and funds available should be the same amount. If not, you have a funding gap, meaning that you have more expenses than funds available.

	College 1	College 2	College 3	College 4
EXPENSES				
Tuition and fees	$	$	$	$
Books and supplies	$	$	$	$
Room and board	$	$	$	$
Transportation	$	$	$	$
Miscellaneous	$	$	$	$
TOTAL	$	$	$	$
FUNDS AVAILABLE				
Student and parent contributions	$	$	$	$
Grants	$	$	$	$
Scholarships	$	$	$	$
Work-study	$	$	$	$
TOTAL	$	$	$	$
Funding gap	$	$	$	$

FEDERAL SCHOLARSHIPS

The following comprise the scholarships available through the federal government:

ROTC Scholarships

The Armed Forces (Army, Air Force, Navy, Marines) may offer up to a four-year scholarship that pays full college tuition plus a monthly allowance; however, these scholarships are very competitive and based upon GPA, class rank, ACT Assessment or SAT scores, and physical qualifications. Apply as soon as possible before December 1 of your senior year. Contact the headquarters of each of the armed forces for more information: Army, 800-USA-ROTC; Air Force, 800-423-USAF; Navy, 800-USA-NAVY; Marines, 800-MARINES (all numbers are toll-free).

Scholarships from Federal Agencies

Federal agencies, such as the CIA, NASA, Department of Agriculture, and Office of Naval Research, offer an annual stipend as well as a scholarship. In return, the student must work for the agency for a certain number of years or else repay all the financial support. See your counselor for more information.

Robert C. Byrd Honors Scholarship

To qualify for this state-administered scholarship, you must demonstrate outstanding academic achievement and excellence in high school as indicated by class rank, high school grades, test scores, and leadership activities. Award amounts of $1,500 are renewable for four years. Contact your high school counselor for application information. Deadlines may vary per state, so also contact your state's Department of Education.

FINANCIAL AID ADVICE

Q: What do you wish students and their parents knew about financial aid?

A: They don't know they should get their financial application filed early enough, so if we run into snags, it can be corrected. They make mistakes, such as not answering the question about the amount of taxes paid the previous year. A lot of parents think that if they didn't send in a check to the IRS, they didn't pay taxes. Something as simple as that causes a lot of problems. If their financial information is recorded incorrectly, it can really mess them up. They should read all the information on the financial aid form, and if they have questions, they should ask someone. Speaking from my experience, if you can't get in touch with the college you're child is thinking of attending, then call a local college. Any time an application doesn't go through the system smoothly, it can cause major problems.

Now that you can apply over the Internet, the applications are much simpler and worded in layman's terms. If applicants miss filling in some information, that will trigger a warning that they omitted something. I realize that not all students have access to the Internet, but they can go to the public library and look into getting onto the Internet there.

Trudy Masters, Financial Aid Officer

Lee College

Baytown, Texas

FEDERAL LOANS

Following are methods through which you may borrow money from the federal government:

Federal Perkins Loan

This loan provides low-interest (5 percent) aid for students with exceptional financial need. The Federal Perkins Loans are made through the college's Financial Aid Office—that is, the college is the lender. For undergraduate study, you may borrow a maximum of $4,000 per year for up to five years of undergraduate study and may take up to ten years to repay the loan, beginning nine months after you graduate, leave school, or drop below half-time status. No interest accrues while you are in school and, under certain conditions (e.g., if you teach in a low-income area, work in law enforcement, are a full-time nurse or medical technician, or serve as a Peace Corps or VISTA volunteer), some or all of your loans may be either partially paid or cancelled in full. Payments also can be deferred under certain conditions, such as unemployment.

FFEL Stafford Loan

A Federal Family Education (FFEL) Stafford Loan may be borrowed from a participating commercial lender, such as a bank, credit union, or savings and loan association. This is a variable rate loan, capped at a maximum of 8.25 percent. If you qualify for a need-based subsidized FFEL Stafford Loan, the interest is paid by the federal government while you are enrolled in school. There is also an unsubsidized FFEL Stafford Student Loan that is not based on need and for which you are eligible, regardless of your family income.

The maximum amount you may borrow as a dependent student is $2,625 for freshman, $3,500 for sophomores, and $5,500 for juniors and seniors, with a maximum of $23,000 for your undergraduate program. The maximum amount for independent students is $6,625 for freshman, $7,500 for sophomores, and $10,500 for juniors and seniors, with a maximum of $46,000 for your undergraduate program. (The subsidized amount for independent students is the same as for dependent students, based on financial need.) There may be up-front origination fees charged for these loans that are deducted from the loan proceeds.

To apply for an FFEL Stafford Student Loan, you must first complete a FAFSA to determine eligibility for the subsidized amount of your loan. You should contact your school's Financial Aid Office to determine the most efficient method of selecting a lender, since many schools have established a preferred lender list. If your school does not have a preferred lender list, contact any local financial institution in your area or your state's Department of Higher Education for assistance. The lender will help you through the process, including a one-time signing of a promissory note. The proceeds of the loan, less any fees, will be sent to your college to be credited to your account.

If you qualify for a subsidized Stafford Loan, you don't have to pay interest while in school. For an unsubsidized Stafford Loan, you will be responsible for paying the interest from the time the loan is disbursed. However, most FFEL lenders will permit you to delay making payments and will add the interest to your loan. Once the repayment period starts, you should contact the lender and/or your school's Financial Aid Office to discuss repayment options. For many students, it is wise to consider consolidating all of your student loans into one loan program.

William D. Ford Federal Direct Loans

The Federal Direct Loan program is very similar to the FFEL Stafford Loan program except that the school serves as the lender. There is no need to contact a private financial institution for your student loans. About 30 percent of all U.S. colleges participate in the Direct Loan program. The terms and conditions of the two loan programs are essentially the same. There are many repayment plans available to meet your needs, and these will be explained to you during your "exit interview" during your final term of school.

FINANCIAL AID RESOURCES

You can use these numbers for direct access to federal and state agencies and processing services.

FEDERAL STUDENT AID INFORMATION CENTER

Provides duplicate student aid reports and aid applications to students. Also answers questions on student aid, mails Department of Education publications, makes corrections to applications, and verifies college federal aid participation. Call 800-4-Fed-Aid (toll-free) or visit their Web site at www.studentaid.ed.gov.

VETERANS BENEFITS ADMINISTRATION

Provides dependent education assistance for children of disabled veterans. College-bound students should call the VBA to determine whether or not they qualify for assistance, what the benefits are, and if a parent's disability qualifies them for benefits. Call 800-827-1000 (toll-free) or visit their Web site at www.gibill.va.gov.

ACT FINANCIAL AID NEED ESTIMATOR (FANE)

Mails financial tabloids to students, provides information on filling out financial aid forms, and estimates financial aid amounts. Also mails financial need estimator forms. Forms are also accessible on line. Go to www.ACT.org or call 319-337-1000.

COLLEGE SCHOLARSHIP SERVICE (PROFILE)

Provides free applications and registration forms for federal student aid. Helps students fill out applications. Call 305-829-9793 or visit http://profileonline.collegeboard.com/index.jsp.

COLLEGE FOR TEXANS

Here is everything a Texan needs to know about preparing for, applying for and paying for college or technical school. And it's all in one up-to-date, easy-to-navigate site as big as the state itself. And remember $3 billion is available every year to help Texans attend college. Go to www.collegefortexans.com for more information.

Parent Loans for Undergraduate Students (PLUS)

The PLUS loans are for parents of dependent students and are designed to help families with cash-flow problems. There is no needs test to qualify, and the loans are made by FFEL lenders or directly by the Department of Education. The loan has a variable interest rate that cannot exceed 9 percent, and there is no specific yearly limit; parents can borrow up to the cost of your education, less other financial aid received. Repayment begins sixty days after the money is advanced. There may be an origination fee of up to 4 percent charged for these loans. Parent borrowers must generally have a good credit record to qualify for PLUS loans.

The PLUS loan will be processed under either the Direct or the FFEL system, depending on the type of loan program for which the college has contracted.

Nursing Student Loan Program

These loans are awarded to nursing students with demonstrated financial need. This loan has a 5 percent interest rate, repayable after completion of studies. Repayment is to be completed within ten years. Contact your college's Financial Aid Office for deadline and other information, including maximum borrowing amounts.

THINKING AHEAD TO PAYING BACK YOUR STUDENT LOAN

More than ever before, loans have become an important part of financial assistance. The majority of students find that they must borrow money to finance their education. If you accept a loan, you are incurring a financial obligation. You will have to repay the loan in full, along with all of the interest and any additional fees (collection, legal, etc.). Since you will be making loan payments to satisfy the loan obligation, carefully consider the burden your loan amount will impose on you after you leave college. Defaulting on a student loan can jeopardize your financial future. Borrow intelligently.

Some Repayment Options

A number of repayment options are available to borrowers of federally guaranteed student loans.

The Standard Repayment Plan requires fixed monthly payments (at least $50) over a fixed period of time (up to ten years). The length of the repayment period depends on the loan amount. This plan usually results in the lowest total interest paid because the repayment period is shorter than under the other plans.

The Extended Repayment Plan allows loan repayment to be extended over a period from generally twelve to thirty years, depending on the total amount borrowed. Borrowers still pay a fixed amount each month (at least $50), but usually monthly payments will be less than under the Standard Repayment Plan. This plan may make repayment more manageable; however, borrowers usually will pay more interest because the repayment period is longer.

The Graduated Repayment Plan allows payments to start out low and increase every two years. This plan may be helpful to borrowers whose incomes are low initially but will increase steadily. A borrower's monthly payments must be at least half but may not be more than one-and-a-half times what he or she would pay under Standard Repayment. As in the Extended Repayment Plan, the repayment period will usually vary from twelve to thirty years, depending on the total amount borrowed. Again, monthly payments may be more manageable at first because they are lower, but borrowers will pay more interest because the repayment period is longer.

The Income Contingent Repayment Plan bases monthly payments on adjusted gross income (AGI) and the total amount borrowed. This is currently only available to students who participate in Direct Loans; however, some FFEL lenders and guaranty agencies provide income-sensitive repayment plans. As income rises or falls each year, monthly payments will be adjusted accordingly. The required monthly payment will not exceed 20 percent of the borrower's discretionary income as calculated under a published formula. Borrowers have up to twenty-five years to repay; after that time, any unpaid amount will be discharged, and borrowers must pay taxes on the amount discharged. In other words, if the federal government forgives the balance of a loan, the amount is considered to be part of the borrower's income for that year.

OTHER FEDERAL PROGRAMS

The following programs offer alternative ways to earn money for college:

Federal Work-Study (FWS)

The Federal Work-Study program provides both on- and off-campus jobs to students who have financial need. Funding for this program is from federal grants to the institutions, plus a partial match from the employer. Students work on an hourly basis and are paid at least the minimum wage. Students are allowed to work up to the amount of the grant authorized by the college. Contact the Financial Aid Office for more information.

AmeriCorps

AmeriCorps is a national service program for a limited number of students. Participants work in a public or private nonprofit agency that provides service to the community in one of four priority areas: education, human services, the environment, and public safety. In exchange, they earn a stipend for living expenses and up to $4,725 a year to apply toward college expenses. Students can work either before, during, or after they go to college and can use the funds to either pay current educational expenses or repay federal student loans. If you successfully complete one full-time term of service (at least 1,700 hours over one year or less), you will be eligible for an award of $4,725. If you successfully complete one part-time term of service (at least 900 hours over two years or less), you will be eligible for an award of $2,362.50. You should speak to your college's Financial Aid Office for more details about this program and any other initiatives available to students or visit the Web at www.americorps.org.

FAMILIES' GUIDE TO TAX CUTS FOR EDUCATION

Many new tax benefits for adults who want to return to school and for parents who are sending or planning to send their children to college are now available. These tax cuts effectively make the first two years of college universally available, and they give many more working Americans the financial means to go back to school if they want to choose a new career or upgrade their skills. Millions of families are eligible for the HOPE and Lifetime Learning tax credits each year, as well as the taxable income deduction allowed for tuition and fees.

HOPE Scholarship Tax Credit

The HOPE Scholarship tax credit helps make the first two years of college or career school universally available. Students receive a 100 percent tax credit for the first $1,000 of tuition and required fees and a 50 percent credit on the second $1,000. This credit is available for tuition and required fees minus grants, scholarships, and other tax-free educational assistance.

The credit is gradually reduced for families with Adjusted Gross Incomes between $42,000 and $52,000 if single, or between $85,000 and $105,000 if married. These limits are adjusted for inflation every year. The credit can be claimed in two years for students who are in their first two years of college or career school and who are enrolled on at least a half-time basis in a degree or certificate program for any portion of the year. The taxpayer can claim a credit for his own tuition expense or for the expenses of his or her spouse or dependent children.

The Lifetime Learning Tax Credit

This tax credit is targeted at adults who want to go back to school, change careers, or take a course or two to upgrade their skills and to college juniors, seniors, graduate, and professional degree students. A family will receive a 20 percent tax credit for tuition and required fees paid each year and for the first $10,000 with the minimum credit being $2,000. Just like the HOPE Scholarship tax credit, the Lifetime Learning tax credit is available for tuition and required fees minus grants, scholarships, and other tax-free educational assistance. The maximum credit is determined on a per-taxpayer (family) basis, regardless of the number of postsecondary students in the family, and is phased out at the same income levels as the HOPE Scholarship tax credit. Families will be able to claim the Lifetime Learning tax credit for some members of their family and the HOPE Scholarship tax credit for others who qualify in the same year.

Tuition and Fees Tax Deduction

The Tuition and Fees Tax Deduction can reduce the amount of your taxable income by as much as $4,000 per year. This deduction is subtracted from your income, which means you can claim this deduction even if you do not itemize your deductions on Schedule A of Form 1040. This deduction may benefit you if you do not qualify for the HOPE or Lifetime Learning Tax Credits because your income is too high. This program is available for four years, 2002 through 2005. Participating in the HOPE and/or

Lifetime Tax credits does not preclude participation in this program, as long as the same student is not used as the basis for each deduction, credit, or exclusion and the family does not exceed the Lifetime Learning maximum per family. The income cut-off for single tax payers is $65,000 (Modified Adjusted Gross Income) and $130,000 for married filers. Single tax payers under $80,000 and married filers under $160,000 qualify for a reduced amount. Check with the IRS or your accountant for more information.

APPLYING FOR FINANCIAL AID

Applying for financial aid is a process that can be made easier when you take it step by step.

1. **You must complete the Free Application for Federal Student Aid (FAFSA) to be considered for federal financial aid.** Pick up the FAFSA from your high school guidance counselor or college financial aid office or download it from the Department of Education's Web site at www.fafsa.ed.gov. The FAFSA can be filed after January 1 of the year you will be attending school. Submit the form as soon as possible but never before the first of the year. If you need to estimate income tax information, it is easily amended later in the year.

2. **Apply for any state grants. Most states use the FASFA for determining state aid, but be sure to check out the specific requirements with your state Higher Education Assistance agency.** Your high school guidance office can answer most questions about state aid programs.

3. **Some schools (usually higher cost private colleges) require an additional form know as the PROFILE®.** This application is needed for institutional grants and scholarships controlled by the school. Check to see if the schools you are applying to require the PROFILE form. Additional information is available from your high school guidance office or online through the College Board at www.collegeboard.com.

CHECKLIST FOR SENIORS

Applying for financial aid can become confusing if you don't record what you've done and when. Use this chart to keep track of important information. Remember to keep copies of all applications and related information.

COLLEGE APPLICATIONS	COLLEGE 1	COLLEGE 2	COLLEGE 3	COLLEGE 4
Application deadline				
Date sent				
Official transcript sent				
Letters of recommendation sent				
SAT/ACT Assessment scores sent				
Acceptance received				
INDIVIDUAL COLLEGE FINANCIAL AID AND SCHOLARSHIP APPLICATIONS				
Application deadline				
Date sent				
Acceptance received				
FREE APPLICATION FOR FEDERAL STUDENT AID (FAFSA), FINANCIAL AID FORM (FAF), AND/OR PROFILE®				
Form required				
Date sent				
School's priority deadline				
PROFILE® ACKNOWLEDGMENT (if filed)				
Date received				
Correct (Y/N)				
Date changes made, if needed				
Date changes were submitted				
STUDENT AID REPORT				
Date received				
Correct (Y/N)				
Date changes made, if needed				
Date changes were submitted				
Date sent to colleges				
FINANCIAL AWARD LETTERS				
Date received				
Accepted (Y/N)				

Source: The Dayton-Montgomery County Scholarship Program

There is a fee associated with this form. Some schools may require an institutional aid application. This is usually found with the admission application. Contact each college you are considering to be sure you have filed the required forms.

4. **Complete individual colleges' required financial aid application forms on time.** These deadlines are usually before March 15, but check to be sure.

5. **Make sure your family completes the required forms during your senior year of high school.**

6. **Always apply for grants and scholarships before applying for student loans.** Grants and scholarships are essentially free money. Loans must be repaid with interest.

Use the "Checklist for Seniors" above to keep track of the financial aid application process.

NATIONAL, STATEWIDE, AND LOCAL SCHOLARSHIPS

Without a doubt, the best source for up-to-date information on private scholarships is the Internet. There are a variety of excellent Web sites to explore, including www.petersons.com, among others. The most important thing to be careful about is scholarship scams, where you are asked either to pay for a scholarship search by an independent organization or pay a "processing fee" to a particular organization to receive their scholarship.

State and Local Scholarships

It is not possible within the scope of this book to list all of the sources of state and local scholarship dollars. The following are excellent resources for seeking financial assistance:

- Your guidance counselor
- A high school teacher or coach
- Your high school and elementary school PTA (yes, many elementary school PTAs award scholarships to alumni)
- The local librarian
- College admissions office
- Your parents' alma mater
- Your employer
- Your parents' employer
- Professional and social organizations in your community
- The local Financial Aid Office of a college in your area
- Your state Higher Education Assistance Agency

SCHOLARSHIPS FOR MINORITY STUDENTS

The following is just a sample of the many scholarships available to minority students.

Bureau of Indian Affairs Higher ED Grant Programs
1849 C Street, NW/MS 3512-MIB
Washington, D.C. 20240-001
www.oiep.bia.edu

The Gates Millennium Scholars
P.O. Box 10500
Fairfax, Virginia 22031-5044
www.gmsp.org

Hispanic Scholarship Fund College Scholarship Program
55 Second Street, Suite 1500
San Francisco, California 94105
877-473-4636
www.hsf.net

National Achievement® Scholarship Program
1560 Sherman Avenue, Suite 200
Evanston, Illinois 60201-4897
847-866-5100
www.nationalmerit.org

National Association of Minority Engineering Program Administrators National Scholarship Fund
1133 West Morse Boulevard, Suite 201
Winter Park, Florida 32789
407-647-8839
www.namepa.org

Jackie Robinson Foundation Scholarship
3 West 35th Street, 11th Floor
New York, New York 10001
212-290-8600
www.jackierobinson.org

APPLYING FOR SCHOLARSHIPS

Here are some tips to help make a success of your scholarship hunt.

1. Start early. Your freshman year is not too early to plan for scholarships by choosing extracurricular activities that will highlight your strengths, and getting involved in your church and community—all things that are important to those who make scholarship decisions.

2. **Search for scholarships.** The best source of scholarships can be found on the Internet. There are many great Web sites that are free, including www.petersons.com. For more information, you should also check www.finaid.org and www.ed.gov/studentaid. Scholarship information is also available at your local library.

TYPES OF ATHLETIC SCHOLARSHIPS

Colleges and universities offer two basic types of athletic scholarships: the institutional grant, which is an agreement between the athlete and the college, and the conference grant, which also binds the college to the athlete. The difference is that the athlete who signs an institutional grant can change his or her mind and sign with another team. The athlete who signs a conference contract cannot renegotiate another contract with a school that honors conference grants. Here are the various ways that a scholarship may be offered:

Full four-year. Also known as full ride, these scholarships pay for room, board, tuition, and books. Due to the high cost of awarding scholarships, this type of grant is being discouraged by conferences around the country in favor of the one-year renewable contract or the partial scholarship.

Full one-year renewable contract. This type of scholarship, which has basically replaced the four-year grant, is automatically renewed at the end of each school year for four years if the conditions of the contract are met. The recruiter will probably tell you in good faith that the intent is to offer a four-year scholarship, but he is legally only allowed to offer you a one-year grant. You must ask the recruiter as well as other players what the record has been of renewing scholarships for athletes who comply athletically, academically, and socially. Remember—no athlete can receive more than a full scholarship.

One-year trial grant (full or partial). A verbal agreement between you and the institution that at the end of the year, your renewal will be dependent upon your academic and athletic performance.

Partial scholarship. The partial grant is any part of the total cost of college. You may be offered room and board but not tuition and books, or you may be offered just tuition. The possibility exists for you to negotiate to a full scholarship after you complete your freshman year.

Waiver of out-of-state fees. This award is for out-of-state students to attend the college or university at the same fee as an in-state student.

3. **Apply, apply, apply.** One student applied for nearly sixty scholarships and was fortunate enough to win seven. "Imagine if I'd applied for five and only gotten one," she says.

4. **Plan ahead.** It takes time to get transcripts and letters of recommendation. Letters from people who know you well are more effective than letters from prestigious names who you know.

5. **Be organized.** In the homes of scholarship winners, you can often find a file box where all relevant information is stored. This method allows you to review deadlines and requirements every so often. Computerizing the information, if possible, allows you to change and update information quickly.

6. **Follow directions.** Make sure that you don't disqualify yourself by filling the forms out incorrectly, missing the deadline, or failing to supply important information. Type your applications, if possible, and have someone proofread them.

WHAT YOU NEED TO KNOW ABOUT ATHLETIC SCHOLARSHIPS

Whether you're male or female or interested in baseball, basketball, crew, cross-country, fencing, field hockey, football, golf, gymnastics, lacrosse, sailing, skiing, soccer, softball, swimming and diving, tennis, track and field, volleyball, or wrestling, there may be scholarship dollars available for you. But, here's that word again—planning. You must plan ahead if you want to get your tuition paid for in return for your competitive abilities.

At the beginning of your junior year, ask your guidance counselor to help you make sure that you take the required number and mix of academic courses and to inform you of the SAT and ACT Assessment score minimums that must be met to play college sports. Also ask your counselor about academic requirements, because you must be certified by the NCAA Clearinghouse, and this process must be started by the end of your junior year.

But before you do all that, think. Do you want and need an athletic scholarship? Certainly, it is prestigious to receive an athletic scholarship, but some athletes compare having an athletic scholarship to having a job at which you are expected to perform. Meetings, training sessions, practices, games, and (don't forget!) studying take away from social and leisure time. Also, with very few full-ride scholarships available, you will most likely receive a partial scholarship or a one-year renewable contract. If your scholarship is not renewed, you may be left scrambling for financial aid. So ask yourself if you are ready for the demands and roles associated with accepting an athletic scholarship.

If you decide that you want an athletic scholarship, you need to market yourself to beat the stiff competition. Think of yourself as a newly designed sports car, and you're selling your speed, look, and all those other goodies to a waiting public. The point is that you're going to have to sell, or market, your abilities to college recruiters. You're the product, and the college recruiter is the buyer. What makes you stand out from the rest?

College recruiters look for a combination of the following attributes when awarding athletic scholarships: academic excellence, a desire to win, self-motivation, ability to perform as a team player, willingness to help others, cooperation with coaching staff, attitude in practice, attitude in games/matches, toughness, strength, optimal height and weight, and excellence.

In order to successfully sell your skills to a college or university, you'll need to take three main steps: 1) locate the colleges and universities that offer scholarships in your sport, 2) contact the institution in a formal manner, and 3) follow up each lead.

Finding and Getting Athletic Scholarships

Ask your coach or assistant coaches for recommendations; learn about the conference or institution from newspaper or television coverage; ask your guidance counselor; review guidebooks, reference books, and the Internet; ask alumni; or attend a tryout or campus visit. You can also call the NCAA to request a recruiting guide for your sport. The following steps can help you snag that scholarship:

1. **Contact the school formally.** Once you make a list of schools in which you are interested, get the names of the head coaches and write letters to the top twenty schools on your list. Then compile a factual resume of your athletic and academic accomplishments. Put together 10 to 15 minutes of video highlights of your athletic performance (with your jersey number noted), get letters of recommendation from your high school coach and your off-season coach, and include a season schedule.

2. **Ace the interview.** When you meet a recruiter or coach, exhibit self-confidence with a firm handshake, by maintaining eye contact, and by making sure that you are well groomed. According to recruiters, the most effective attitude is quiet confidence, respect, sincerity, and enthusiasm.

3. **Ask good questions.** Don't be afraid to probe the recruiter by getting answers to the following questions: Do I qualify athletically and academically? If I am recruited, what would the parameters of the scholarship be? For what position am I being considered? It's okay to ask the recruiter to declare what level of interest he or she has in you.

4. **Follow up.** Persistence pays off when it comes to seeking an athletic scholarship, and timing can be everything. There are four good times when a follow-up letter from your coach or a personal letter from you is extremely effective: prior to your senior season, during or just after the senior season, just prior to or after announced conference-affiliated signing dates or national association signing dates, and mid-to late summer, in case other scholarship offers have been withdrawn or declined.

To sum up, you know yourself better than anyone, so you must look at your skills—both athletic and academic—objectively. Evaluate the skills you need to improve, and keep the desire to improve alive in your heart. Develop your leadership skills, and keep striving for excellence with your individual achievements. Keep your mind open as to what school you want to attend, and keep plugging away, even when you are tired, sore, and unsure. After all, athletes are trained to be winners!

MYTHS ABOUT SCHOLARSHIPS AND FINANCIAL AID

The scholarship and financial aid game is highly misunderstood by many high school students. And high school guidance counselors often lack the time to fully investigate scholarship opportunities and to inform students about them. The myths and misconceptions persist while the truth about scholarships remains hidden, the glittering prizes and benefits unknown to many teenagers.

Myth 1: Scholarships are rare, elusive awards won only by valedictorians, geniuses, and whiz kids.

The truth is that with proper advice and strategies, private scholarships are very much within the grasp of high school students who possess talent and ability in almost any given field. Thousands of high school students like you compete and win.

Myth 2: My chances of being admitted to a college are reduced if I apply for financial aid.

The truth is that most colleges have a policy of "need-blind" admissions, which means that a student's financial need is not taken into account in the admission decision. However, there are a few colleges that do consider ability to pay before deciding whether or not to admit a student. There are a few more that look at ability to pay of those whom they placed on a waiting list to get in or those students who applied late. Some colleges will mention this in their literature, others may not. In making decisions about the college application and financing process,

however, families should apply for financial aid if the student needs the aid to attend college.

Myth 3: All merit scholarships are based on a student's academic record.

The truth is that many of the best opportunities are in such areas as writing, public speaking, leadership, science, community service, music and the arts, foreign languages, and vocational-technical skills. So that means you don't always have to have a 3.99 GPA to win if you excel in a certain area.

Myth 4: You have to be a member of a minority group to get a scholarship.

The truth is that there are indeed some scholarships that are targeted toward women and minority students. There are also scholarships for which you must be a member of a specific national club or student organization (such as 4-H and the National Honor Society), which makes these scholarships just as exclusive. But most scholarship opportunities are not exclusive to any one segment of the population.

Myth 5: If you have need for and receive financial aid, it's useless to win a scholarship from some outside organization because the college will just take away the aid that the organization offered.

It's true that if you receive need-based aid, you can't receive more than the total cost of attendance (including room and board, books, and other expenses, not just tuition). If the financial aid that you've been awarded meets the total cost and you win an outside scholarship, colleges have to reduce something. But usually, they reduce the loan or work-study portion of your financial aid award before touching the grant portion that they've awarded you. This means that you won't have to borrow or earn as much. Also, most colleges don't meet your full financial need when you qualify for need-based financial aid. So, if you do win an outside scholarship, chances are that your other aid will not be taken away or reduced.

SCHOLARSHIP SCAMS

Although most scholarship sponsors and most scholarship search services are legitimate, schemes that pose as either legitimate scholarship search services or scholarship sponsors have cheated thousands of families.

These fraudulent businesses advertise in campus newspapers, distribute flyers, mail letters and postcards, provide toll-free phone numbers, and even have sites on the Web. The most obvious frauds operate as scholarship search services or scholarship clearinghouses. Another quieter segment sets up as a scholarship sponsor, pockets the money from the fees and charges that are paid by thousands of hopeful scholarship seekers, and returns little, if anything, in proportion to the amount it collects. A few of these frauds inflict great harm by gaining access to individuals' credit or checking accounts with the intent to extort funds.

The Federal Trade Commission (FTC), in Washington, D.C., has a campaign called Project $cholar$cam to confront this type of fraudulent activity. There are legitimate services; however, a scholarship search service cannot truthfully guarantee that a student will receive a scholarship, and students almost always will fare as well or better by doing their own homework using a reliable scholarship information source, such as *Peterson's Scholarships, Grants & Prizes* or www.petersons.com, than by wasting money and time with a search service that promises a scholarship.

The FTC warns you to be alert for these six warning signs of a scam:

1. **"This scholarship is guaranteed or your money back."** No service can guarantee that it will get you a grant or scholarship. Refund guarantees often have impossible conditions attached. Review a service's refund policies in writing before you pay a fee.

2. **"The scholarship service will do all the work."** Unfortunately, nobody else can fill out the personal information forms, write the essays, and supply the references that many scholarships may require.

3. **"The scholarship will cost some money."** Be wary of any charges related to scholarship information services or individual scholarship applications, especially in significant amounts. Before you send money to apply for a scholarship, investigate the sponsor.

4. **"You can't get this information anywhere else."** In addition to Peterson's, scholarship directories from other publishers are available in any large bookstore, public library, or high school guidance office.

5. **"You are a finalist"** or **"You have been selected by a national foundation to receive a scholarship."** Most legitimate scholarship programs almost never seek out particular applicants. Most scholarship sponsors will contact you only in response to an inquiry because they generally lack the budget to do anything more than this. Should you think that there is any real possibility that you may have been selected to receive a scholarship, before you send any money, investigate first to be sure that the sponsor or program is legitimate.

6. **"The scholarship service needs your credit card or checking account number in advance."** Never provide your credit card or bank account number on the telephone to the representative of an organization that you do not know. Get information in writing first. An unscrupulous operation does not need your signature on a check. It will scheme to set up situations that will allow it to drain a victim's account with unauthorized withdrawals.

In addition to the FTC's six signs, here are some other points to keep in mind when considering a scholarship program:

- Fraudulent scholarship operations often use official-sounding names, containing words such as *federal, national, administration, division, federation,* and *foundation.* Their names are often a slight variant of the name of a legitimate government or private organization. Do not be fooled by a name that seems reputable or official, an official-looking seal, or a Washington, D.C., address.

If you win a scholarship, you will receive written official notification by mail, not by telephone. If the sponsor calls to inform you, it will follow up with a letter in the mail. If a request for money is made by phone, the operation is probably fraudulent.

Be wary if an organization's address is a box number or a residential address. If a bona fide scholarship program uses a post office box number, it usually will include a street address and telephone number on its stationery.

Beware of telephone numbers with a 900-area code. These may charge you a fee of several dollars a minute for a call that could be a long recording that provides only a list of addresses or names.

Watch for scholarships that ask you to "act now." A dishonest operation may put pressure on an applicant by saying that awards are on a "first-come, first-serve" basis. Some scholarship programs will give preference to the earlier qualified applications. However, if you are told, especially on the telephone, that you must respond quickly but that you will not hear about the results for several months, there may be a problem.

Be wary of endorsements. Fraudulent operations will claim endorsements by groups with names similar to well-known private or government organizations. The Better Business Bureau (BBB) and government agencies do not endorse businesses.

Don't pay money for a scholarship to an organization that you've never heard of before or whose legitimacy you can't verify. If you have already paid money to such an organization and find reason to doubt its authenticity, call your bank to stop payment on your check, if possible, or call your credit card company and tell it that you think you were the victim of consumer fraud.

To find out how to recognize, report, and stop a scholarship scam, you may write to the Federal Trade Commission's Consumer Response Center at 600 Pennsylvania Avenue NW, Washington, D.C. 20580. On the Web, go to www.ftc.gov, or call 877-FTC-HELP (toll-free). You can also check with the Better Business Bureau (BBB), which is an organization that maintains files of businesses about which it has received complaints. You should call both your local BBB office and the BBB office in the area of the organization in question; each local BBB has different records. Call 703-276-0100 to get the telephone number of your local BBB, or look at www.bbb.org for a directory of local BBBs and downloadable BBB complaint forms.

FINANCIAL AID ON THE WEB

A number of good financial aid resources exist on the Web. It is quick and simple to access general financial aid information, links to relevant Web sites, loan information, employment and career information, advice, scholarship search services, interactive worksheets, forms, and free Expected Family Contribution (EFC) calculators.

Also visit the Web sites of individual colleges to find more school-specific financial aid information.

FAFSA Online

The Free Application for Federal Student Aid (FAFSA) can be filed on the Web at www.fafsa.ed.gov. You can download a worksheet from this Web site, since the questions are formatted differently from the paper application. FAFSA on the Web is a much quicker process and helps eliminate errors. To file electronically, the student and one parent will need an electronic signature Personal Identification Number (PIN). To get a PIN, go to www.pin.ed.gov. The pin number will be sent to you within 24 hours.

FIND MONEY FOR COLLEGE

Don't have enough money to pay for college? Afraid your family makes too much and you can't get financial aid? Regardless of your financial situation, BestCollegeDeals® helps you quickly and easily identify each college's unique financial aid packages—student loans, grants, discounts, scholarships—and little-known financial deals you've probably never even heard of.

How does it work? It's simple!

1. **Provide financial information about your family in a safe, secure environment that ensures your privacy.**

2. **Calculate, with help from BestCollegeDeals®, your Estimated Expected Family Contribution (EFC), the amount of money you may be expected to pay toward your college education.**

3. **Choose location, enrollment size, and whether you're interested in a public, private, all-women's, or all-men's college or university.**

4. **Get a list of colleges, and information about their financial aid offerings, that match your preferences.**

5. **Discover great need- and merit-based (merit awards include scholarships, grants, and prizes that are given for academic achievement) financial deals that you can't find anywhere else!**

No matter what your level of income, BestCollegeDeals® gives your family personalized support. BestCollegeDeals® helps you and your family better understand the financial aid process. Go to www.bestcollegedeals.com to learn more!

The Education Resource Institute (TERI)

TERI is a private, not-for-profit organization that was founded to help middle-income Americans afford a college education. This site contains a database describing programs that aim to increase college attendance from underrepresented groups. (The target population includes students from low-income families and those who are the first in their family to pursue postsecondary education.) Visit TERI's Web site at www.teri.org.

FinAid

This Web site offers numerous links to valuable financial aid information, including scholarship search engines. You can find the site at www.finaid.org.

Mapping Your Future

This site is sponsored by a group of guaranty agencies that participate in the Federal Family Education Loan Program (FFELP). They are committed to providing information about higher education and career opportunities. Information is available to help parents of middle school students plan for college and for adults returning to higher education to learn new skills. You can find this site at www.mapping-your-future.org.

Student Financial Assistance Information, U.S. Department of Education

This page takes you to some of the major publications on student aid, including the latest edition of *The Student Guide*. Visit www.ed.gov/finaid.html.

Petersons.com

Get advice on finding sources to pay for college and search for scholarships at www.petersons.com/finaid.

AES

American Education Services (AES) is a division of PHEAA, which has grown from a small student loan guarantor with a volume of only 4,600 student loans in 1964, to one of the largest, full-service financial aid organizations in the nation. AES helps students succeed by giving them the tools to plan for higher education and find money for school, as well as allowing them to manage student loan accounts online. Visit them at www.aessuccess.org.

Chapter 9

WHAT TO EXPECT IN COLLEGE

If you were going on a long trip, wouldn't you want to know what to expect once you reached your destination? The same should hold true for college.

GET A JUMP! CAN'T FILL IN all the details of what you'll find once you begin college. However, we can give you information about some of the bigger questions you might have, such as how to choose your classes or major and how you can make the most of your life outside the classroom.

CHOOSING YOUR CLASSES

College is designed to give you freedom, but at the same time, it teaches you responsibility. You will probably have more free time than in high school, but you will also have more class material to master. Your parents may entrust you with more money, but it is up to you to make sure there's enough money in your bank account when school fees are due. The same principle applies to your class schedule: You will have more decision-making power than ever, but you also need to know and meet the requirements for graduation.

To guide you through the maze of requirements, all students are given an adviser. This person, typically a faculty member, will help you select classes that meet your interests and graduation requirements. During your first year or two at college, you and your adviser will choose classes that meet general education requirements and select electives, or non-required classes, that pique your interests. Early on, it is a good idea to take a lot of general education classes. They are meant to expose you to new ideas and help you explore possible majors. Once you have selected a major, you will be given an adviser for that particular area of study. This person will help you understand and meet the requirements for that major.

In addition to talking to your adviser, talk to other students who have already taken a class you're interested in and who really enjoyed how a professor taught the class. Then try to get into that professor's class when registering. Remember, a dynamic professor can make a dry subject engaging. A boring professor can make an engaging subject dry.

As you move through college, you will notice that focusing on the professor is more important than focusing on the course title. Class titles can be cleverly crafted. They can sound captivating. However, the advice above still holds true: "Pop Culture and Icons" could turn out to be awful, and "Beowulf and Old English" could be a blast.

When you plan your schedule, watch how many heavy reading classes you take in one semester. You don't want to live in the library or the dorm study lounge. In general, the humanities, such as history, English, philosophy, and theology, involve a lot of reading. Math and science classes involve less reading; they focus more on solving problems.

Finally, don't be afraid to schedule a fun class. Even the most intense program of study will let you take a few electives. So take a deep breath, dig in, and explore!

CHOOSING YOUR MAJOR

You can choose from hundreds of majors—from accounting to zoology—but which is right for you? Should you choose something traditional or select a major from an emerging area? Perhaps you already know what career you want, so you can work backward to decide which major will best help you achieve your goals.

If you know what you want to do early in life, you will have more time to plan your high school curriculum, extracurricular activities, jobs, and community service to coincide with your college major. Your college selection process may also focus upon the schools that provide strong academic programs in a certain major.

Where Do I Begin?

Choosing a major usually starts with an assessment of your career interests. Once you have taken the self-assessment test in Part 1, you should have a clearer understanding of your interests, talents, values, and goals. Then review possible majors, and try several on for size. Picture yourself taking classes, writing papers, making presentations, conducting research, or working in a related field. Talk to people you know who work in your fields of interest and see if you like what you hear. Also, try reading the classified ads in your local newspaper. What jobs sound interesting to you? Which ones pay the salary that you'd like to make? What level of education is required in the ads you find interesting? Select a few jobs that you think you'd like and then consult the following list of majors to see which major(s) coincide. If your area of interest does not appear here, talk to your counselor or teacher about where to find information on that particular subject.

Majors and Related Careers

Agriculture

Many agriculture majors apply their knowledge directly on farms and ranches. Others work in industry (food, farm equipment, and agricultural supply companies), federal agencies (primarily in the Departments of Agriculture and the Interior), and state and local farm and agricultural agencies. Jobs might be in research and lab work, marketing and sales, advertising and public relations, or journalism and radio/TV (for farm communications media). Agriculture majors also pursue further training in biological sciences, animal health, veterinary medicine, agribusiness management, vocational agriculture education, nutrition and dietetics, and rural sociology.

Architecture

Architecture and related design fields focus on the built environment as distinct from the natural environment of the agriculturist or the conservationist. Career possibilities include drafting, design, and project administration in architectural, engineering, landscape design, interior design, industrial design, planning, real estate, and construction firms; government agencies involved in construction, housing, highways, and parks and recreation; and government and nonprofit organizations interested in historic or architectural preservation.

Area/Ethnic Studies

The research, writing, analysis, critical thinking, and cultural awareness skills acquired by area/ethnic studies majors, combined with the expertise gained in a particular area, make this group of majors valuable in a number of professions. Majors find positions in administration, education, public relations, and communications in such organizations as cultural, government, international, and (ethnic) community agencies; international trade (import-export); social service agencies; and the communications industry (journalism, radio, and TV). These studies also provide a good background for further training in law, business management, public administration, education, social work, museum and library work, and international relations.

Arts

Art majors most often use their training to become practicing artists, though the settings in which they work vary. Aside from the most obvious art-related career—that of the self-employed artist or craftsperson—many fields require the skills of a visual artist. These include advertising; public relations; publishing; journalism; museum work; television, movies, and theater; community and social service agencies concerned with education, recreation, and entertainment; and teaching. A background in art is also useful if a student wishes to pursue art therapy, arts or museum administration, or library work.

Biological Sciences

The biological sciences include the study of living organisms from the level of molecules to that of populations. Majors find jobs in industry; government agencies; technical writing, editing, or illustrating; science reporting; secondary school teaching (which usually requires education courses); and research and laboratory analysis and testing. Biological sciences are also a sound foundation for further study in medicine, psychology, health and hospital administration, and biologically oriented engineering.

Business

Business majors comprise all the basic business disciplines. At the undergraduate level, students can major in a general business administration program or specialize in a particular area, such as marketing or accounting. These studies lead not only to positions in business and industry but also to management positions in other sectors. Management-related studies include the general management areas (accounting, finance, marketing, and management) as well as special studies related to a particular type of organization or industry. Management-related majors may be offered in a business school or in a department dealing with the area in which the management skills are to be applied. Careers can be found throughout the business world.

Communication

Jobs in communication range from reporting (news and special features), copywriting, technical writing, copyediting, and programming to advertising, public relations, media sales, and market research. Such positions can be found at newspapers, radio and TV stations, publishing houses (book and magazine), advertising agencies, corporate communications departments, government agencies, universities, and firms that specialize in educational and training materials.

Computer, Information, and Library Sciences

Computer and information science and systems majors stress the theoretical aspects of the computer and emphasize mathematical and scientific disciplines. Data processing, programming, and computer technology programs tend to be more practical; they are more oriented toward business than to scientific applications and to working directly with the computer or with peripheral equipment. Career possibilities for computer and information science majors include data processing, programming, and systems development or maintenance in almost any setting: business and industry, banking and finance, government, colleges and universities, libraries, software firms, service bureaus, computer manufacturers, publishing, and communications.

STUDENT COUNSEL

Q: Why did you choose a seven-year premed program instead of a traditional four-year college program?

A: I'm one of those people who knew what I wanted to do since I was very little, so that made choosing easier. If I was not 100 percent sure that I wanted to go into medicine, I would not be in this seven-year program. For students who are interested but not really sure that they want to go into medicine, they should pick a school they will enjoy, get a good education, and then worry about medical school. That way, if they decide in their junior year that medicine is not for them, they have options.

Elliot Servais
Premed
Boston University

Library science gives preprofessional background in library work and provides valuable knowledge of research sources, indexing, abstracting, computer technology, and media technology, which is useful for further study in any professional field. In most cases, a master's degree in library science is necessary to obtain a job as a librarian. Library science majors find positions in public, school, college, corporate, and government libraries and research centers; book publishing (especially reference books); database and information retrieval services; and communications (especially audiovisual media).

Education

Positions as teachers in public elementary and secondary schools, private day and boarding schools, religious and parochial schools, vocational schools, and proprietary schools are the jobs most often filled by education majors. However, teaching positions also exist in noneducational institutions, such as museums, historical societies, prisons, hospitals, and nursing homes, as well as jobs as educators and trainers in government and industry. Administrative (nonteaching) positions in employee relations and personnel, public relations, marketing and sales, educational publishing, TV and film media, test development firms, and government and community social service agencies also tap the skills and interests of education majors.

Engineering and Science Technology

Engineering and science technology majors prepare students for practical design and production work rather than for jobs that require more theoretical, scientific, and mathematical knowledge. Engineers work in a variety of fields, including aeronautics, bioengineering, geology, nuclear engineering, and quality control and safety. Industry, research labs, and government agencies where technology plays a key role, such as in manufacturing, electronics, construction communications, transportation, and utilities, hire engineering as well as engineering technology and science technology graduates regularly. Work may be in technical activities (research, development, design, production, testing, scientific programming, or systems analysis) or in nontechnical areas where a technical degree is needed, such as marketing, sales, or administration.

Foreign Language and Literature

Knowledge of foreign languages and cultures is increasingly recognized as important in today's international world. Language majors possess a skill that is used in organizations with international dealings as well as in career fields and geographical areas where languages other than English are prominent. Career possibilities include positions with business firms with international subsidiaries; import-export firms; international banking; travel agencies; airlines; tourist services; government and international agencies dealing with international affairs, foreign trade, diplomacy, customs, or immigration; secondary school foreign language teaching and bilingual education (which usually require education courses); freelance translating and interpreting (high level of skill necessary); foreign

(Continued on page 103)

MAKING THAT MAJOR DECISION: REAL-LIFE ADVICE FROM COLLEGE SENIORS

Somewhere between her junior and senior year in high school, Karen Gliebe got the psychology bug. When choosing a major in college, she knew just what she wanted. Justin Bintrim, on the other hand, did a complete 180. He thought he'd study physics, then veered toward philosophy. It wasn't until he took survey courses in literature that he found where his heart really lay, and now he's graduating with a degree in English.

You might find yourself at either end of this spectrum when choosing a major. Either you'll know just what you want or you'll try on a number of different hats before finally settling on one. To give you a taste of what it could be like for you, meet four college seniors who have been through the trials and errors of choosing their majors. Hopefully you'll pick up some pointers from them or at least find out that you don't have to worry so much about what your major will be.

From Grove City College, a liberal arts school in Pennsylvania, meet Karen Gliebe, who will graduate with a degree in psychology, and English major Justin Bintrim. From Michigan State University, meet computer engineering major Seth Mosier and Kim Trouten, who is finishing up a zoology degree. Here's what they had to say:

HOW THEY CHOSE THEIR MAJORS

Karen: During high school, I volunteered at a retirement center, and my supervisor gave me a lot of exposure to applied psychology. After my freshman year in college, I talked to people who were using a psychology degree. You put in a lot of work for a degree and can wonder if it's worth all the work. It helps to talk to someone who has gone through it so you can see if that's what you want to be doing when you graduate.

Justin: I wasn't sure about what my major would be. One professor told me to take survey courses to see if I was interested in the subject. I took English literature, math, psychology, and philosophy. I liked English the best and did well in it. The next semester, I took two English courses and decided to switch my major. My professors told me not to worry about choosing a major. They said to get my feet wet and we'll talk about your major in two years. I decided that if they're not worried about a major, I wouldn't be either, but I still had it on my mind. I was around older students who were thinking about their careers, so I talked to them about the jobs they had lined up.

Seth: I liked computers in high school. In college, I started out in computer science but got sick of coding. My interest in computers made me pick computer science right off the bat. I didn't know about computer engineering until I got to college.

Kim: I wanted to be a veterinarian but after two years decided that I didn't want to go to school for that long. I was still interested in animals and had two options. One was in animal science, which is working more with farm animals, or going into zoology. I decided to concentrate on zoo and aquarium science. Besides being a vet, the closest interaction with animals would be being a zookeeper.

THE ELECTIVES THEY TOOK AND WHY

Karen: My adviser told me to take different classes, so I took philosophy, art, religion, and extra psychology classes that weren't required.

Justin: I was planning to do a double major, but my professors said to take what interested me. English majors have lots of freedom to take different courses, unlike science majors.

Seth: Because I'm in computer engineering, I don't get to take a lot of electives. I am taking a swimming class right now and took a critical incident analysis class where we looked at major accidents. I wanted something that wasn't computer engineering-related but extremely technical.

Kim: I took a kinesiology class, which was pretty much an aerobics class. I needed to work out and figured I could get credit for it. I also took sign language because I'm interested in it.

WHAT THEY'RE GOING TO DO WITH THEIR DEGREES

Karen: I want to go to graduate school and hopefully get some experience working with kids.

Justin: I'm applying to graduate school in English literature and cultural studies. I want to do research and become a college professor.

Seth: I'm going to work for the defense department. It's not the highest offer I've gotten, but it will be the most fun, which is more important to me than the money.

Kim: My goals have changed again. I don't plan on using my degree. I just got married a year ago, and my husband and I want to go into full-time ministry. I'll work for a while, and then we'll go overseas.

THE CHANGES THEY WOULD MAKE IN THE CLASSES THEY TOOK IF THEY COULD

Karen: There are classes I wouldn't necessarily take again. But even though I didn't learn as much as I wanted to, it was worth it. I learned how to work and how to organize my efforts.

Justin: I should have worried less about choosing a major when I first started college. I didn't have the perspective as to how much time I had to choose.

Seth: I have friends who would change the order in which they took their humanities classes. I was lucky enough to think ahead and spread those classes out over the entire time. Most [engineering] students take them their freshman year to get them all out of the way. Later on, they're locked in the engineering building all day. Because I didn't, it was nice for me to get my mind off engineering.

Kim: Something I can't change are the labs. They require a lot of work, and you only get one credit for 3 hours. Some labs take a lot of work outside of class hours. I had a comparative anatomy lab, which kept me busy over entire weekends. I suggest you don't take a lot of classes that require labs all at once.

THEIR ADVICE FOR YOU

Karen: You don't have to know what you want to do with the rest of your life when you get to college. Most people don't even stay with the major they first choose. Colleges recognize that you will see things you may have not considered at first. Some high school students say they won't go to college unless they know what they want to do.

Justin: If it's possible, take a little of this and a little of that. If you're an engineering student, you'll have it all planned out [for you], but if you're a liberal arts major and are not sure, you probably can take something from each department.

Seth: If possible, take AP exams in high school. You'll be able to make a decision about a major. Freshmen who think they want to do engineering suffer through math and physics classes. Then by their sophomore or junior year, they realize they don't want to be engineers. If they'd taken AP classes, they'd know by their freshman year.

Kim: When I changed my major, I was worried that I might have spent a year in classes that wouldn't count toward my new major. But you shouldn't be scared to change majors because if you stick with something you don't like, you'll have to go back and take other classes anyway.

Though these four seniors arrived at a decision about which major they wanted in different ways, they had similar things to say:

- It's okay to change your mind about what you want out of college.

- To find out which major you might want, start with what you like to do.

- Talk to professionals who have jobs in the fields that interest you.

- Ask your professors about what kinds of jobs you could get with the degree you're considering.

- Talk to seniors who will be graduating with a degree in the major you're considering.

- Take electives in areas that interest you, even though they may have nothing to do with your major.

- College is a time to explore many different options, so take advantage of the opportunity.

language publishing; and computer programming (especially for linguistics majors).

Health Sciences

Health professions majors, while having a scientific core, are more focused on applying the results of scientific investigation than on the scientific disciplines themselves. Allied health majors prepare graduates to assist health professionals in providing diagnostics, therapeutics, and rehabilitation. Medical science majors, such as optometry, pharmacy, and the premedical profession sequences, are, for the most part, preprofessional studies that comprise the scientific disciplines necessary for admission to graduate or professional school in the health or medical fields. Health service and technology majors prepare students for positions in the health fields that primarily involve services to patients or working with complex machinery and materials. Medical technologies cover a wide range of fields, such as cytotechnology, biomedical technologies, and operating room technology.

Administrative, professional, or research assistant positions in health agencies, hospitals, occupational health units in industry, community and school health departments, government agencies (public health, environmental protection), and international health organizations are available to majors in health fields, as are jobs in marketing and sales of health-related products and services, health education (with education courses), advertising and public relations, journalism and publishing, and technical writing.

Home Economics and Social Services

Home economics encompasses many different fields—basic studies in foods and textiles as well as consumer economics and leisure studies—that overlap with aspects of agriculture, social science, and education. Jobs can be found in government and community agencies (especially those in education, health, housing, or human services), nursing homes, child-care centers, journalism, radio/TV, educational media, and publishing. Types of work also include marketing, sales, and customer service in consumer-related industries, such as food processing and packaging, appliance manufacturing, utilities, textiles, and secondary school home economics teaching (which usually requires education courses).

Majors in social services find administrative positions in government and community health, welfare, and social service agencies, such as hospitals, clinics, YMCAs and YWCAs, recreation commissions, welfare agencies, and employment services. See the "Law and Legal Studies" section for information on more law-related social services.

Humanities (Miscellaneous)

The majors that constitute the humanities (sometimes called "letters") are the most general and widely applicable and the least vocationally oriented of the liberal arts. They are essentially studies of the ideas and concerns of human kind. These include classics, history of philosophy, history of science, linguistics, and medieval studies. Career possibilities for humanities majors can be found in business firms, government and community agencies, advertising and public relations, marketing and sales, publishing, journalism and radio/TV, secondary school teaching in English and literature (which usually requires education courses), freelance writing and editing, and computer programming (especially for those with a background in logic or linguistics).

Law and Legal Studies

Students of legal studies can use their knowledge of law and government in fields involving the making, breaking, and enforcement of laws; the crimes, trials, and punishment of law breakers; and the running of all branches of government at local, state, and federal levels. Graduates find positions of all types in law firms, legal departments of other organizations, the court or prison system, government agencies (such as law enforcement agencies or offices of state and federal attorneys general), and police departments.

Mathematics and Physical Sciences

Mathematics is the science of numbers and the abstract formulation of their operations. Physical sciences involve the study of the laws and structures of physical matter. The quantitative skills acquired through the study of science and mathematics are especially useful for computer-related careers. Career possibilities include positions in industry (manufacturing and processing companies, electronics firms, defense contractors, consulting firms); government agencies (defense, environmental protection, law enforcement); scientific/technical writing, editing, or illustrating; journalism (science reporting); secondary school teaching (usually requiring education courses); research and laboratory analysis and testing; statistical analysis; computer programming; systems analysis; surveying and mapping; weather forecasting; and technical sales.

Natural Resources

A major in the natural resources field prepares students for work in areas as generalized as environmental conservation and as specialized as groundwater contamination. Jobs are available in industry (food, energy, natural resources, and pulp and paper companies), consulting firms, state and federal government agencies (primarily the Departments of Agriculture and the Interior), and public and private conservation agencies. See the "Agriculture" and "Biological Sciences" sections for more information on natural resources-related fields.

Psychology

Psychology majors involve the study of behavior and can range from the biological to the sociological. Students can study individual behavior, usually that of humans, or the behavior of crowds. Students of psychology do not always go into the obvious clinical fields, the fields in which psychologists work with patients. Certain areas of psychology, such as industrial/organizational, experimental, and social, are not clinically oriented. Psychology and counseling careers can be in government (such as mental health agencies), schools, hospitals, clinics, private practice, industry, test development firms, social work, and personnel. The careers listed in the "Social Sciences" section are also pursued by psychology and counseling majors.

Religion

Religion majors are usually seen as preprofessional studies for those who are interested in entering the ministry. Career possibilities for religion also include casework, youth counseling, administration in community and social service organizations, teaching in religious educational institutions, and writing for religious and lay publications. Religious studies also prepare students for the kinds of jobs other humanities majors often pursue.

Social Sciences

Social sciences majors study people in relation to their society. Thus, social science majors can apply their education to a wide range of occupations that deal with social issues and activities. Career opportunities are varied. People with degrees in the social sciences find careers in government, business, community agencies (serving children, youth, and senior citizens), advertising and public relations, marketing and sales, secondary school social studies teaching (with education courses), casework, law enforcement, parks and recreation, museum work (especially for anthropology, archaeology, geography, and history majors), preservation (especially for anthropology, archaeology, geography, and history majors), banking and finance (especially for economics majors), market and survey research, statistical analysis, publishing, fundraising and development, and political campaigning.

Technologies

Technology majors, along with trade fields, are most often offered as two-year programs. Majors in technology fields prepare students directly for jobs; however, positions are in practical design and production work rather than in areas that require more theoretical, scientific, and mathematical knowledge.

Engineering technologies prepare students with the basic training in specific fields (e.g., electronics, mechanics, or chemistry) that are necessary to become technicians on the support staffs of engineers. Other technology majors center more on maintenance and repair. Work may be in technical activities, such as production or testing, or in nontechnical areas where a technical degree is needed, such as marketing, sales, or administration. Industries, research labs, and government agencies in which technology plays a key role—such as in manufacturing, electronics, construction, communications, transportation, and utilities—hire technology graduates regularly.

Still Unsure?

Relax! You don't have to know your major before you enroll in college. More than half of all freshmen are undecided when they start school and prefer to get a feel for what's available at college before making a decision. Most four-year colleges don't require students to formally declare a major until the end of their sophomore year or beginning of their junior year. Part of the experience of college is being exposed to new subjects and new ideas. Chances are your high school never offered anthropology. Or marine biology. Or applied mathematics. So take these classes and follow your interests. While you're fulfilling your general course requirements, you might stumble upon a major that appeals to you, or maybe you'll discover a new interest while you're volunteering or involved with other extracurricular activities. Talking to other students might lead to new options you'll want to explore.

Can I Change My Major If I Change My Mind?

Choosing a major does not set your future in stone, nor does it necessarily disrupt your life if you need to change your major. However, there are advantages to choosing a major sooner rather than later. If you wait too long to choose, you may have to take additional classes to satisfy the requirements, which may cost you additional time and money.

THE OTHER SIDE OF COLLEGE: HAVING FUN!

There is more to college than writing papers, reading books, and sitting through lectures. Your social life plays an integral part in your college experience.

Meeting New People

The easiest time to meet new people is at the beginning of something new. New situations shake people up and make them feel just uncomfortable enough to take the risk of extending their hand in friendship. Fortunately for you, college is filled with new experiences. There are the first weeks of being the newest students. This can be quickly followed by being a new member of a club or activity. And with each passing semester, you will be in new classes with new teachers and new faces. College should be a time of constantly challenging and expanding yourself, so never feel that it is too late to meet new people.

But just how do you take that first step in forming a relationship? It's surprisingly easy. The first few weeks of school will require you to stand in many lines. Some will be to buy books; others will be to get meals. One will be to get a student I.D. card. Another will be to register for classes. While standing in line, turn around and introduce yourself to the person behind you. Focus on what you have in common and try to downplay the differences. Soon you will find the two of you have plenty to talk about. When it is time to leave the line, arrange to have coffee later or to see a movie. This will help you form relationships with the people you meet.

Be open to the opportunities of meeting new people and having new experiences. Join clubs and activities. Investigate rock-climbing. Try ballet. Write for the school paper. But most of all, get involved.

Campus Activities

College life will place a lot of demands on you. Your classes will be challenging. Your professors will expect more from you. You will have to budget and manage your own money. But there is a plus side you probably haven't thought of yet: college students do have free time.

The average student spends about three hours a day in class. Add to this the time you will need to spend studying, eating, and socializing, and you will still have time to spare. One of the best ways to use this time is to participate in campus activities.

Intramural Sports

Intramurals are sports played for competition between members of the same campus community. They provide competition and a sense of belonging without the same level of intensity in practice schedules. Anyone can join an intramural sport. Often there are teams formed by dormitories, sororities, or fraternities that play team sports such as soccer, volleyball, basketball, flag-football, baseball, and softball. There are also individual intramural sports such as swimming, golf, wrestling, and diving. If you want to get involved, just stop by the intramural office. Usually it is located near the student government office.

Student Government

Student government will be set up in a way that is probably similar to your high school. Students form committees and run for office. However, student government in college has more power than in high school. The officers address all of their class's concerns directly to the President of the college or university and the Board of Trustees. Most student governments have a branch responsible for student activities that brings in big name entertainers and controversial speakers. You may want to get involved to see how such contacts are made and appearances negotiated.

Community Service

Another aspect of student life is volunteering, commonly called community service. Many colleges offer a range of opportunities. Some allow you to simply commit an afternoon to a cause, such as passing out food at a food bank. Others require an ongoing commitment. For example, you might decide to help an adult learn to read every Thursday at 4 p.m. for three months. Some colleges will link a service commitment with class credit. This will enhance your learning, giving you some real-world experience. Be sure to stop by your community service office and see what is available.

Clubs

There are a variety of clubs on most college campuses spanning just about every topic you can imagine. Amnesty International regularly meets on most campuses to write letters to help free prisoners in foreign lands. Most college majors band together in a club to discuss their common interests and career potential. There are also clubs that are based on the use of certain computer software or that engage in outdoor activities like sailing or downhill skiing. The list is endless. If you cannot find a club for your interest, consider starting one of your own. Stop by the student government office to see what rules you will need to follow. You will also need to find a location to hold meetings and post signs to advertise your club. When you hold your first meeting, you will probably be surprised at how many people are willing to take a chance and try a new club.

Greek Life

A major misconception of Greek life is that it revolves around wild parties and alcohol. In fact, the vast majority of fraternities and sororities focus on instilling values of scholarship, friendship, leadership, and service in their members. From this point forward, we will refer to both fraternities and sororities as fraternities.

Scholarship

A fraternity experience helps you make the academic transition from high school to college. Although the classes taken in high school are challenging, they'll be even harder in college. Fraternities almost always require members to meet certain academic standards. Many hold mandatory study times, keep old class notes and exams on file for study purposes, and personal tutors are often available. Members of a fraternity have a natural vested interest in seeing that other members succeed academically, so older members often assist younger members with their studies.

Friendship

Social life is an important component of Greek life. Social functions offer an excellent opportunity for freshmen to become better acquainted with others in the chapter. Whether it is a Halloween party or a formal dance, there are numerous chances for members to develop poise and confidence. By participating in these functions, students enrich friendships and build memories that will last a lifetime. Remember, social functions aren't only parties; they can include such activities as intramural sports and Homecoming.

Leadership

Because fraternities are self-governing organizations, leadership opportunities abound. Students are given hands-on experience in leading committees, managing budgets, and interacting with faculty members and administrators. Most houses have as many as ten officers, along with an array of committee members. By becoming actively involved in leadership roles, students gain valuable experience that is essential for a successful career. Interestingly, although Greeks represent less than 10 percent of the undergraduate student population, they hold the majority of leadership positions on campus.

Service

According to the North-American Interfraternity Council, fraternities are increasingly becoming involved in philanthropies and hands-on service projects. Helping less fortunate people is a major focus of Greek life. This can vary from work with Easter Seals, blood drives, and food pantry collections to community upkeep, such as picking up trash, painting houses, or cleaning up area parks. Greeks also get involved in projects with organizations such as Habitat for Humanity, the American Heart Association, and Children's Miracle Network. By being involved in philanthropic projects, students not only raise money for worthwhile causes, but they also gain a deeper insight into themselves and their responsibility to the community.

ROOMMATES

When you arrive on campus, you will face a daunting task: to live peacefully with a stranger for the rest of the academic year.

To make this task easier, most schools use some type of room assignment survey. This can make roommate matches more successful. For example, two people who prefer to stay up late and play guitar can be matched, while two people who prefer to rise at dawn and hit the track can be a pair. Such differences are easy to ask about on a survey and easy for students to report. However, surveys cannot ask everything, and chances are pretty good that something about your roommate is going to get on your nerves.

HOMESICKNESS

Homesickness in its most basic form is a longing for the stuff of home: your parents, friends, bedroom, school, and all of the other familiar people and objects that make you comfortable. But on another level, homesickness is a longing to go back in time. Moving away to college forces you to take on new responsibilities and begin to act like an adult. This can be scary.

While this condition is often described as a "sickness," no pill will provide a quick fix. Instead, you need to acknowledge that your feelings are a normal reaction to a significant change in your life. Allow yourself to feel the sadness of moving on in life and be open to conversations about it that may crop up in your dorm or among your new friends. After all, everyone is dealing with this issue. Then, make an effort to create a new home and a new life on campus. Create new habits and routines so that this once-strange place becomes familiar. Join activities and engage in campus life. This will help you to create a feeling of belonging that will ultimately be the key to overcoming homesickness.

In order to avoid conflict, plan ahead. When you first meet, work out some ground rules. Most schools have roommates write a contract together and sign it during the first week of school. Ground rules help eliminate conflict from the start by allowing each person to know what is expected. You should consider the following areas: privacy, quiet time, chores, and borrowing.

When considering privacy, think about how much time alone you need each day and how you and your roommate will arrange for private time. Class schedules usually give you some alone time. Be aware of this; if your class is cancelled, consider going for a cup of coffee or a browse in the bookstore instead of immediately rushing back to your room. Privacy also relates to giving your roommate space when he or she has had a bad day or just needs time to think. Set up clear hours for quiet time. Your dorm will already have some quiet hours established. You may choose to simply reiterate those or add additional time. Just be clear.

Two other potentially stormy issues are chores and borrowing. If there are cleaning chores that need to be shared, make a schedule and stick to it. No one appreciates a sink full of dirty dishes or a dingy shower. Remember the golden rule: do your chores as you wish your roommate would. When it comes to borrowing, set up clear rules. The safest bet is to not allow it; but if you do, limit when, for how long, and what will be done in case of damage.

Another issue many students confront is whether or not to live with a best friend from high school who is attending the same college. Generally, this is a bad idea for several reasons. First, you may think you know your best friend inside and out, but you may be surprised by her personal living habits. There is nothing like the closeness of a dorm room to reveal the annoying routines of your friend. Plus, personalities can change rapidly in college. Once you are away from home, you may be surprised at how you or your friend transforms from shy and introverted to late night partygoer. This can cause conflict. A final downfall is that the two of you will stick together like glue in the first few weeks and miss out on opportunities to meet other people.

Armed with this information, you should have a smooth year with your new roommate. But just in case you are the exception, most colleges will allow students who absolutely cannot get along to move. Prior to moving, each student must usually go through a dispute resolution process. This typically involves your Resident Adviser, you, and your roommate trying to work through your problems in a structured way.

Living with a roommate can be challenging at times, but the ultimate rewards—meeting someone new, encountering new ideas, and learning how to compromise—will serve you well later in life. Enjoy your roommate and all the experiences you will have, both good and bad, for they are all part of the college experience.

COMMUTING FROM HOME

For some students, home during the college years is the same house in which they grew up. Whether you are in this situation because you can't afford to live on campus or because you'd just rather live at home with your family, some basic guidelines will keep you connected with campus life.

By all means, do not just go straight home after class. Spend some of your free time at school. Usually there is a student union or a coffee shop where students gather and socialize. Make it a point to go there and talk to people between classes. Also, get involved in extracurricular activities, and visit classmates in the dorms.

If you drive to school, find other students who want to carpool. Most schools have a commuters' office or club that will give you a list of people who live near you. Sharing a car ride will give you time to talk and form a relationship with someone else who knows about the challenges of commuting.

Commuters' clubs also sponsor a variety of activities throughout the year—give them a try! Be sure also to consider the variety of activities open to all members of the student body, ranging from student government to community service to intramural sports. You may find this takes a bit more effort on your part, but the payoff in the close friendships you'll form will more than make up for it.

WHAT IF YOU DON'T LIKE THE COLLEGE YOU PICK

In the best of all worlds, you compile a list of colleges, find the most compatible one, and are accepted. You have a great time, learn a lot, graduate, and head off to a budding career. However, you may find the college you chose isn't the best of all worlds. Imagine these scenarios:

1. Halfway through your first semester of college, you come to the distressing conclusion that you can't stand being there for whatever reason. The courses don't match your interests. The campus is out in the boonies, and you don't ever want to see another cow. The selection of extracurricular activities doesn't cut it.

2. You have methodically planned to go to a community college for two years and move to a four-year college to complete your degree. Transferring takes you nearer to your goal.

3. You thought you wanted to major in art, but by the end of the first semester, you find yourself more interested in English lit. Things get confusing, so you drop out of college to sort out your thoughts and now you want to drop back in, hoping to rescue some of those credits.

4. You didn't do that well in high school— socializing got in the way of studying. But you've wised up, have gotten serious about your future, and two years of community college have brightened your prospects of transferring to a four-year institution.

Circumstances shift, people change, and, realistically speaking, it's not all that uncommon to transfer. Many people do. The reasons why students transfer run the gamut, as do the institutional policies that govern them. The most common transfers are students who move from a two-year to a four-year university or the person who opts for a career change midstream.

Whatever reasons you might have for wanting to transfer, you will be doing more than just switching academic gears. Aside from potentially losing credits, time, and money, transferring means again adjusting to a new situation. This affects just about all transfer students, from those who made a mistake in choosing a college to those who planned to go to a two-year college and then transferred to a four-year campus. People choose colleges for arbitrary reasons. That's why admissions departments try to ensure a good match between the student and campus before classes begin. Unfortunately, sometimes students don't realize they've made a mistake until it's too late.

The best way to avoid transferring is to extensively research a college or university before choosing it. Visit the campus and stay overnight, talk to admissions and faculty members, and try to learn as much as you can.

10 Chapter

OTHER OPTIONS AFTER HIGH SCHOOL

Years ago, most young people went directly to work after high school. Today, most young people first go to school for more training, but the majority don't go to traditional four-year colleges.

ACCORDING TO SHANNON MCBRIDE, Director of the Golden Crescent Tech Prep Partnership in Victoria, Texas, "Only 40 percent of high school graduates attempt to go to a four-year college, and of those, only 25 percent get their degree. And of that 25 percent, only 37 percent use the degree they got in that area."

So why aren't the remaining 60 percent of students choosing a traditional four-year college? The reasons are as varied as the students. Life events can often interfere with plans to attend college. Responsibilities to a family may materialize that make it impossible to delay earning an income for four years. One may have to work and go to school. And traditional colleges demand certain conventions, behaviors, and attitudes that don't fit every kind of person. Some people need a lot of physical activity to feel satisfied, while others just aren't interested in spending day after day sitting, reading, memorizing, and analyzing. Years of strict time management and postponed rewards are more than they can stand.

If any of these reasons ring true with you, there are still postsecondary options for you, all of which will not only allow you to pursue further education but also will train you for a career. Let's take a look at some of these educational directions you can follow.

DISTANCE LEARNING

As a future college student, can you picture yourself in any of these scenarios?

1. You need some information, but the only place to find it is at a big state university. Trouble is, it's hundreds of miles away. No problem. You simply go to your local community college and hook up electronically with the university. Voilà! The resources are brought to you.

2. That ten-page paper is due in a few days, but you still have some last-minute questions to ask the professor before you turn it in. Only one problem: you won't be able to see the professor until after the paper is due. Being a night owl, you also want to work on it when your roommate is asleep. Not to worry. Since you have the professor's e-mail address, just like all the other students in the class, you simply e-mail your question to her. She replies. You get your answer, finish the paper, and even turn it in electronically.

3. After graduating from high school, you can't go to college right away, but your employer has a neat hook up with a college that offers courses via the Internet. During your lunch hours, you and several of your work buddies log in to a class and get college credit.

Not too long ago, if you'd offered these scenarios to high school graduates as real possibilities, they would have thought you were a sci-fi freak. Distance education was not common at all—or if it was, it usually meant getting courses via snail mail or on videotape. Well, today you are in the right place at the right time. Distance education is a reality for countless high school graduates.

What distance education now means is that you can access educational programs and not have to physically be in a classroom on a campus. Through such technologies as cable or satellite television, videotapes and audiotapes, fax, computer modem, computer conferencing and videoconferencing, and other means of electronic delivery, the classroom comes to you—sometimes even if you're sitting in your room in your bunny slippers and it's 2 in the morning.

Distance learning expands the reach of the classroom by using various technologies to deliver university resources to off-campus sites, transmit college courses into the workplace, and enable you to view class lectures in the comfort of your home.

Where and How Can I Take Distance Learning Courses?

The technology for new, cheaper telecommunications technology is getting better all the time, and there is a growing demand for education by people who can't afford either the time or money to be a full-time, on-campus student. To fill that demand, educational networks also are growing and changing how and when you can access college courses.

Most states have established new distance learning systems to advance the delivery of instruction to schools, postsecondary institutions, and state government agencies. Colleges and universities are collaborating with commercial telecommunication entities, including online information services, such as America Online and cable and telephone companies, to provide education to far-flung student constituencies. Professions such as law, medicine, and accounting, as well as knowledge-based industries, are utilizing telecommunications networks for the transmission of customized higher education programs to working professionals, technicians, and managers.

Ways in Which Distance Learning May Be Offered:

- **Credit courses.** In general, if these credit courses are completed successfully, they can be applied toward a degree.

- **Noncredit courses and courses offered for professional certification.** These programs can help you acquire specialized knowledge in a concentrated, time-efficient manner and stay on top of the latest developments in your field. They provide a flexible way for you to prepare for a new career or study for professional licensure and certification. Many of these university programs are created in cooperation with professional and trade associations so that courses are based on real-life workforce needs, and the practical skills learned are immediately applicable in the field.

The Way Distance Learning Works

Enrolling in a distance learning course may simply involve filling out a registration form, making sure that you have access to the equipment needed, and paying the tuition and fees by check, money order, or credit card. In these cases, your applications may be accepted without entrance examinations or proof of prior educational experience.

Other courses may involve educational prerequisites and access to equipment not found in all geographic locations. Some institutions offer detailed information about individual courses, such as a course outline, upon request. If you have access to the Internet and simply wish to review course descriptions, you may be able to peruse an institution's course catalogs electronically by accessing the institution's home page on the Web.

Time Requirements

Some courses allow you to enroll at your convenience and work at your own pace. Others closely adhere to a traditional classroom schedule. Specific policies and time limitations pertaining to withdrawals, refunds, transfers, and renewal periods can be found in the institutional catalog.

Admission to a Degree Program

If you plan to enter a degree program, you should consult the academic advising department of the institution of your choice to learn about entrance requirements and application procedures. You may find it necessary to develop a portfolio of your past experiences and accomplishments that may have resulted in college-level learning.

How Do I Communicate with My Instructor?

Student-faculty exchanges occur using electronic communication (through fax and e-mail). Many institutions offer their distance learning students access to toll-free numbers so students can talk to their professors or teaching assistants without incurring any long-distance charges.

Responses to your instructor's comments on your lessons, requests for clarification of comments, and all other exchanges between you and your instructor will take time. Interaction with your instructor—whether by computer, phone, or letter—is important, and you must be willing to take the initiative.

What Else Does Distance Learning Offer?

Distance learning comes in a variety of colors and flavors. Along with traditional college degrees, you can earn professional certification or continuing education units (CEUs) in a particular field.

College Degrees

There are opportunities for you to earn degrees at a distance at the associate, baccalaureate, and graduate levels. Two-year community college students are now able to earn baccalaureate degrees—without relocating—by transferring to distance learning programs offered by four-year universities. Corporations are forming partnerships with universities to bring college courses to worksites and encourage employees to continue their education. Distance learning is especially popular among people who want to earn their degree part-time while continuing to work full-time. Although on-campus residencies are sometimes required for certain distance learning degree programs, they generally can be completed while employees are on short-term leave or vacation.

Professional Certification

Certificate programs often focus on employment specializations, such as hazardous waste management or electronic publishing, and can be helpful to those seeking to advance or change careers. Also, many states mandate continuing education for professionals such as teachers, nursing home administrators, or accountants. Distance learning offers a convenient way for many individuals to meet professional certification requirements. Health care, engineering, and education are just a few of the many professions that take advantage of distance learning to help their professionals maintain certification.

Many colleges offer a sequence of distance learning courses in a specific field of a profession. For instance, within the engineering profession, certificate programs in computer-integrated manufacturing, systems engineering, test and evaluation, waste management education, and research consortium are offered via distance learning.

Business offerings include distance learning certification in information technology, total quality management, and health services management.

Within the field of education, you'll find distance learning certificate programs in areas such as early reading instruction and special education for the learning handicapped.

Continuing Education Units (CEUs)

If you choose to take a course on a noncredit basis, you may be able to earn continuing education units (CEUs). The CEU system is a nationally recognized system to provide a standardized measure for accumulating, transferring, and recognizing participation in continuing education programs. One CEU is defined as 10 contact hours of participation in an organized continuing education experience under responsible sponsorship, capable direction, and qualified instruction.

COMMUNITY COLLEGES

Two-year colleges or community colleges, are often called "the people's colleges." With their open-door policies (admission is open to individuals with a high school diploma or its equivalent), community colleges provide access to higher education for millions of Americans who might otherwise be excluded from higher education. Community college students are diverse, of all ages, races, and economic backgrounds. While many community college students enroll full-time, an equally large number attend on a part-time basis so they can fulfill employment and family commitments as they advance their education.

Today, there are more than 1,800 community colleges in the United States. They enroll more than 7.4 million students, who represent more than 50 percent of all undergraduates in the United States. As you can see, millions of first-time freshmen begin their higher education in a community college.

Community colleges are also referred to as either technical or junior colleges, and they may either be under public or independent control. What unites all two-year colleges is that they are regionally accredited, postsecondary institutions, whose highest credential awarded is the associate degree. With few exceptions, community colleges offer a comprehensive curriculum, which includes transfer, technical, and continuing education programs.

Important Factors in a Community College Education

The student who attends a community college can count on receiving quality instruction in a supportive learning community. This setting frees the student to pursue his or her own goals, nurture special talents, explore new fields of learning, and develop the capacity for lifelong learning.

From the student's perspective, four characteristics capture the essence of community colleges:

- They are community-based institutions that work in close partnership with high schools, community groups, and employers in extending high-quality programs at convenient times and places.

- Community colleges are cost effective. Annual tuition and fees at public community colleges average approximately half those at public four-year colleges and less than 15 percent of private four-year institutions. In addition, since most community colleges are generally close to their students' homes, these students can also save a significant amount of money on the room, board, and transportation expenses traditionally associated with a college education.

- They provide a caring environment, with faculty members who are expert instructors, known for excellent teaching and for meeting students at the point of their individual needs, regardless of age, sex, race, current job status, or previous academic preparation. Community colleges join a strong curriculum with a broad range of counseling and career services that are intended to assist students in making the most of their educational opportunities.

A SCHOLARSHIP FOR CAREER COLLEGE STUDENTS

The Imagine America Scholarship can help those who dream of a career but might not be able to achieve it through traditional college education.

What is the Imagine America Scholarship?

Introduced in 1998 by the Career College Foundation, the *Imagine America* Scholarship aims to reduce the growing "skills gap" in America. Any graduating high school senior can be considered for selection for one of the three scholarships awarded to his or her high school. The *Imagine America* Scholarship gives thousands of graduating high school seniors scholarships of $1,000 to be used at more than 400 participating career colleges and schools across the country.

You are eligible for the Imagine America Scholarship if:

- You attend any private postsecondary institution that is accredited by an agency recognized by the U.S. Department of Education.

- You are graduating from high school this year.

To find out more about the Imagine America Scholarship Program, talk to your high school counselor or visit www.imagine-america.org for more information.

- Many offer comprehensive programs, including transfer curricula in such liberal arts programs as chemistry, psychology, and business management, that lead directly to a baccalaureate degree and career programs that prepare students for employment or assist those already employed in upgrading their skills. For those students who need to strengthen their academic skills, community colleges also offer a wide range of developmental programs in mathematics, languages, and learning skills, designed to prepare the student for success in college studies.

Getting to Know Your Two-Year College

The best way to learn about your college is to visit in person. During a campus visit, be prepared to ask a lot of questions. Talk to students, faculty members, administrators, and counselors about the college and its programs, particularly those in which you have a special interest. Ask about available certificates and

MOST POPULAR MAJORS FOR COMMUNITY COLLEGE GRADS

The American Association of Community Colleges conducted a survey in the year 2004 to see what the most popular majors for community college students were. The top 15 majors and their average starting salaries follow:

MAJOR	AVERAGE STARTING SALARY
1. Registered Nursing	$38,419
2. Law Enforcement	$31,865
3. Licensed Practical Nursing	$27,507
4. Radiology	$35,612
5. Computer Technologies	$35,469
6. Automotive	$32,498
7. Nursing Assistant	$16,754
8. Dental Hygiene	$35,956
9. Health Information Technology	$26,578
10. Construction	$34,414
11. Education	$30,810
12. Business	$31,366
13. Networking	$35,938
14. Electronics	$32,734
15. Medical Assistant	$22,953

associate degrees. Don't be shy. Do what you can to dig below the surface. Ask college officials about the transfer rate to four-year colleges. If a college emphasizes student services, find out what particular assistance is offered, such as educational or career guidance. Colleges are eager to provide you with the information you need to make informed decisions.

The Money Factor

For many students, the decision to attend a community college is often based on financial factors. If you aren't sure what you want to do or what talents you have, community colleges allow you the freedom to explore different career interests at a low cost. For those students who can't afford the cost of university tuition, community colleges let them take care of their basic classes before transferring to a four-year institution. Many two-year colleges can now offer you instruction in your own home through cable television or public broadcast stations or through home study courses that can save both time and money. Look into all your options, and be sure to add up all the costs of attending various colleges before deciding which is best for you.

Working and Going to School

Many two-year college students maintain full-time or part-time employment while they earn their degrees. Over the past decades, a steadily growing number of students have chosen to attend community colleges while they fulfill family and employment responsibilities. To enable these students to balance the demands of home, work, and school, most community colleges offer classes at night and on weekends.

For the full-time student, the usual length of time it takes to obtain an associate degree is two years. However, your length of study will depend on the course load you take: the fewer credits you earn each term, the longer it will take you to earn a degree. To assist you in moving more quickly toward your degree, many community colleges now award credit through examination or for equivalent knowledge gained through relevant life experiences. Be certain to find out the credit options that are available to you at the college in which you are interested. You may discover that it will take less time to earn a degree than you first thought.

Preparation for Transfer

Studies have repeatedly shown that students who first attend a community college and then transfer to a four-year college or university do at least as well academically as the students who entered the four-year institutions as freshmen. Most community colleges have agreements with nearby four-year institutions to make transfer of credits easier. If you are thinking of transferring, be sure to meet with a counselor or faculty adviser before choosing your courses. You will want to map out a course of study with transfer in mind. Make sure you also find out the credit-transfer requirements of the four-year institution you might want to attend.

New Career Opportunities

Community colleges realize that many entering students are not sure about the field in which they want to focus their studies or the career they would like to pursue. Community colleges have the resources to help students identify areas of career interest and to set challenging occupational goals.

Once a career goal is set, you can be confident that a community college will provide job-relevant, high-quality occupation and technical education. About half of the students who take courses for credit at community colleges do so to prepare for employment or to acquire or upgrade skills for their current job. Especially helpful in charting a career path is the assistance of a counselor or a faculty adviser, who can discuss job opportunities in your chosen field and help you map out your course of study.

In addition, since community colleges have close ties to their communities, they are in constant contact with leaders in business, industry, organized labor, and public life. Community colleges work with these individuals and their organizations to prepare students for direct entry into the world of work. For example, some community colleges have established partnerships with local businesses and industries to provide specialized training programs. Some also provide the academic portion of apprenticeship training, while others offer extensive job-shadowing and cooperative education opportunities. Be sure to examine all of the career-preparation opportunities offered by the community colleges in which you are interested.

VOCATIONAL/CAREER COLLEGES

Career education is important for every employee as technology continues to change. From the largest employers, such as the U.S. military, defense contractors, IBM, aviation, and health care, down to the company with one and two employees, issues of keeping up with technology and producing goods and services cheaper, faster, and at less cost requires—indeed demands—a skilled, world-class workforce. In good or bad economic times, you will always have a distinct advantage if you have a demonstrable skill and can be immediately productive while continuing to learn and improve. If you know how to use technology, work collaboratively, and find creative solutions, you will always be in demand.

Career colleges offer scores of opportunities to learn the technical skills required by many of today's and tomorrow's top jobs. This is especially true in the areas of computer and information technology, health care, and hospitality (culinary arts, travel and tourism, and hotel and motel management). Career colleges range in size from those with a handful of students to universities with thousands enrolled. They are located in every state in the nation and share one common objective—to prepare students for a successful career in the world of work through a focused, intensive curriculum.

America's career colleges are privately owned and operated for-profit companies. Instead of using tax support to operate, career colleges pay taxes. Because career colleges are businesses, they must be responsive to the workforce needs of their communities or they will cease to exist.

SNAPSHOT OF A CAREER COLLEGE STUDENT

Katrina Dew
Network Systems Administration
Silicon Valley College
Fremont, California

ABOUT KATRINA

Right after high school, Katrina headed for junior college, but she felt like she was spinning her wheels. She wanted something that was goal-oriented. Community college offered too many options. She needed to be focused in one direction.

At first, Katrina thought she would become a physical therapist. Then she realized how much schooling she would need to begin working. Turning to the computer field, she saw some definite benefits. For one, she had messed around with them in high school. She could get a degree and get out in two years. She saw that computer careers are big and getting bigger. Plus, there weren't a lot of women in that field, which signaled more potential for her. But before she switched schools, she visited the career college, talked to students, and sat in on lectures. She really liked the way the teachers related to their students. Along with her technical classes, she's taken algebra, psychology, English composition, and management communication.

WHAT I LIKE ABOUT BEING A CAREER STUDENT

"Career colleges are for fast-track-oriented students who want to get out in the work field and still feel that they have an appropriate education."

Nicholas Cecere
Automotive Techniques Management
Education America/Vale Technical Institute
Blairsville, Pennsylvania

ABOUT NICHOLAS

Nicholas has completely repainted his 1988 Mercury Topaz, redone all the brakes, put in a brand-new exhaust system, and lots of smaller stuff here and there. But he says that's nothing compared to the completely totaled cars some of his classmates haul into the school. Talk about hands-on: they're able to completely restore them while going through the program.

Nicholas didn't always have gasoline running through his veins. In fact, he just recently discovered how much he likes automotives. After graduating from high school, he went to a community college, and after one semester, he left to work at a personal care home. Standing over a sink of dirty dishes made him realize he wanted more than just a job. He started thinking about what he wanted to do and visited a few schools and the body shop where his brother worked. Where others saw twisted car frames, Nicholas saw opportunity and enrolled in the program.

WHAT I LIKE ABOUT BEING A CAREER STUDENT

"I compare career college to a magnifying glass that takes the sun and focuses it. You learn just what you need to learn."

Generally, career colleges prepare you for a specific career. Some will require you to take academic courses such as English or history. Others will relate every class you take to a specific job, such as computer-aided drafting or interior design. Some focus specifically on business or technical fields. Bob Sullivan, a career counselor at East Brunswick High School in East Brunswick, New Jersey, points out that the negative side to this kind of education is that if you haven't carefully researched what you want to do, you could waste a lot of time and money. "There's no room for exploration or finding yourself as opposed to a community college where you can go to find yourself and feel your way around," he explains.

So how do you find the right career college for you? A good place to start is knowing generally what you want to do. You don't have to know the fine details of your goals, but you should have a broad idea, such as a career in allied health or business or computing.

After you've crossed that hurdle, the rest is easy. Since professional training is the main purpose of career colleges, its graduates are the best measure of a school's success. Who hires the graduates? How do their jobs relate to the education they received? Career colleges should be able to provide that data to prospective students. "Career colleges have a different customer than other institutions," notes Stephen Friedheim, President of ESS College of Business in Dallas, Texas. In addition to focusing on the needs of their students, career colleges also want to ensure they meet the needs of the employers who are hiring their graduates. "The assumption is that if you can please the employer, you will please the student," Friedheim explains.

Checking the credentials of a career college is one of the most important steps you should take in your career college search. Though not every career college has to be accredited, it is a sign that the college has gone through a process that ensures quality. It also means that students can qualify for federal grant and loan programs. Furthermore, you should see if the college has met the standards from professional training organizations. In fields such as court reporting and health-related professions, those criteria are paramount.

FINANCIAL AID OPTIONS FOR CAREER AND COMMUNITY COLLEGES

The financial aid process is basically the same for students attending a community college, a career college, or a technical institute as it is for students attending a four-year college. However, there are some details that can make the difference between getting the maximum amount of financial aid and only scraping by.

As with four-year students, the federal government is still your best source of financial aid. Most community colleges and career and technical schools participate in federal financial aid programs. To get detailed information about federal financial aid programs and how to apply for them, read through Chapter 8: "Financial Aid Dollars and Sense." In the meantime, here are some quick tips on where to look for education money.

Investigate federal financial aid programs. You should definitely check out a Federal Pell Grant, which is a need-based grant available to those who can't pay the entire tuition themselves. The Federal Supplemental Educational Opportunity Grant (FSEOG) is for those students with exceptional financial need. You also can take advantage of the Federal Work-Study programs that provide jobs for students with financial aid eligibility in return for part of their tuition. Many two-year institutions offer work-study, but the number of jobs tends to be limited. Also, federal loans make up a substantial part of financial aid for two-year students. Student loans, which have lower interest rates, may be sponsored by the institution or federally sponsored, or they may be available through commercial financial institutions. They are basically the same as those for the traditional four-year college student, such as the Federal Perkins Loan and the Direct Stafford Loan and the Federal Family Education Stafford Loan. In fact, some private career colleges and technical institutes only offer federal loans. You also can find more specific information about federal loans in Chapter 8.

Don't overlook scholarships. What many two-year students don't realize is that they could be

WHAT TO LOOK FOR IN A CAREER COLLEGE

A tour of the college is a must! While visiting the campus, do the following:

- **Get a full explanation of the curriculum, including finding out how you will be trained.**

- **Take a physical tour of the classrooms and laboratories and look for cleanliness, modern equipment/computers, and size of classes. Observe the activity in classes: Are students engaged in class, and are lectures dynamic?**

- **Ask about employment opportunities after graduation. What are the placement rates (most current) and list of employers? Inquire about specific placement assistance: resume preparation, job leads, etc. Look for "success stories" on bulletin boards, placement boards, and newsletters.**

- **Find out about tuition and other costs associated with the program. Ask about the financial aid assistance provided to students.**

- **Find out if an externship is part of the training program. How are externships assigned? Does the student have any input as to externship assignment?**

- **Ask if national certification and registration in your chosen field is available upon graduation.**

- **Inquire about the college's accreditation and certification.**

- **Also find out the associations and organizations to which the college belongs. Ask what awards or honors the college has had bestowed.**

- **Ask if the college utilizes an advisory board to develop employer relationships.**

- **Ask about the rules and regulations. What GPA must be maintained? What is the attendance policy? What are grounds for termination? What is the refund policy if the student drops or is terminated? Is there a dress code? What are the holidays of the college?**

Source: Arizona College of Allied Health, Phoenix, Arizona

eligible for scholarships. Regrettably, many make the assumption that scholarships are only for very smart students attending prestigious universities. You'd be surprised to learn how many community and career colleges offer scholarships. It's critical to talk to the financial aid officer of each school you plan to attend to find out what scholarships might be available.

Two-year students should find out how their state of residence can help them pay for tuition. Every state in the union has some level of state financial aid that goes to community college students. The amounts are dependent on which state you live in, and most aid is in the form of grants.

APPRENTICESHIPS

Some students like working with their hands and have the skill, patience, and temperament to become expert mechanics, carpenters, or electronic repair technicians. If you think you'd enjoy a profession like this and feel that college training isn't for you, then you might want to think about a job that requires apprenticeship training.

To stay competitive, America needs highly skilled workers. But if you're looking for a soft job, forget it. An apprenticeship is no snap. It demands hard work and has tough competition, so you've got to have the will to see it through. An apprenticeship is a program formally agreed upon between a worker and an employer where the employee learns a skilled trade through classroom work and on-the-job training. Apprenticeship programs vary in length, pay, and intensity among the various trades. A person completing an apprenticeship program generally becomes a journeyperson (skilled craftsperson) in that trade.

The advantages of apprenticeships are numerous. First and foremost, an apprenticeship leads to a lasting lifetime skill. As a highly trained worker, you can take your skill anywhere you decide to go. The more creative, exciting, and challenging jobs are put in the hands of the fully skilled worker, the all-around person who knows his or her trade inside out.

Skilled workers advance much faster than those who are semiskilled or whose skills are not broad enough to equip them to assume additional responsibilities in a career. Those who complete an apprenticeship have also acquired the skills and judgment that are necessary to go into business for themselves if they choose.

What to Do If You're Interested in an Apprenticeship

If you want to begin an apprenticeship, you have to be at least 16 years old, and you must fill out an application for employment. These applications may be available year-round or only at certain times during the year, depending on the trade in which you're interested.

Federal regulations prohibit anyone under the age of 16 from being considered for an apprenticeship. Some programs require a high school degree or certain course work. Other requirements may include passing certain aptitude tests, proof of physical ability to perform the duties of the trade, and possession of a valid driver's license.

Once you have met the basic program entrance requirements, you'll be interviewed and awarded points on your interest in the trade, your attitude toward work in general, and personal traits, such as appearance, sincerity, character, and habits. Openings are awarded to those who have achieved the most points.

Because an apprentice must be trained in an area where work actually exists and where a certain pay scale is guaranteed upon completion of the program, the wait for application acceptance may be pretty long in areas of low employment. This standard works to your advantage, however. Just think: You wouldn't want to spend one to six years of your life learning a job where no work exists or where the wage is the same as, or just a little above, that of an unskilled or semiskilled laborer.

If you're considering an apprenticeship, the best sources of assistance and information are vocational or career counselors, local state employment security agencies, field offices of state apprenticeship agencies, and regional offices of the Bureau of Apprenticeship and Training (BAT). Apprenticeships are usually registered with the BAT or a state apprenticeship council. Some apprenticeships are not registered at all, although that doesn't necessarily mean that the program isn't valid. To find out if a certain apprenticeship is legitimate, contact your state's apprenticeship agency or a regional office of the BAT. Addresses and phone numbers for these regional offices are listed on the following page. You can also visit the Bureau's Web site at www.doleta.gov/atels_bat/bat.cfm.

BUREAU OF APPRENTICESHIP AND TRAINING OFFICES

NATIONAL OFFICE
Office of Apprenticeship Training
Bureau of of Apprenticeship and Training
Frances Perkins Building
200 Constitution Avenue, NW
Washington, DC 20210
Phone: 877-US-2JOBS (toll-free)

REGION I: BOSTON

Mr. John M. Griffin Jr.	Connecticut
Regional Director	Maine
USDOL/ETA/OATELS	Massachusetts
JFK Federal Building	New Hampshire
Room E-370	New Jersey
Boston, MA 02203	New York
Telephone: 617-788-0177	Puerto Rico
Fax: 617-788-0304	Rhode Island
E-mail: Griffin.John@dol.gov	Vermont
	Virgin Islands

REGION II: PHILADELPHIA

Mr. Joseph T. Hersh	Delaware
Regional Director	District of Columbia
USDOL/ETA/OATELS	Maryland
Suite 820-East	Pennsylvania
170 S. Independence Mall West	Virginia
Philadelphia, PA 19106-3315	West Virginia
Telephone: 215-861-4830	
Fax: 215-861-4833	
E-mail: Hersh.Joseph@dol.gov	

REGION III: ATLANTA

Mr. Garfield G. Garner, Jr.	Alabama
Regional Director	Florida
USDOL/ETA/OATELS	Georgia
61 Forsyth Street SW, Rm. 6T71	Kentucky
Atlanta, GA 30303	Mississippi
Telephone: 404-562-2335	North Carolina
Fax: 404-562-2329	South Carolina
E-mail: Garner.Garfield@dol.gov	Tennessee

REGION IV: DALLAS

Mr. Steve Opitz	Arkansas
Regional Director	Colorado
USDOL/ETA/OATELS	Louisiana
Federal Building	Montana
525 S. Griffin Street. Rm. 317	North Dakota
Dallas, TX 75202	South Dakota
Telephone: 214-767-4993	Texas
Fax: 214-767-4995	Utah
E-mail: Opitz.Steve@dol.gov	Wyoming

REGION V: CHICAGO

Mr. Terrence Benewich	Illinois
Regional Director	Indiana
USDOL/ETA/OATELS	Iowa
230 South Dearborn Street, Rm. 656	Kansas
Chicago, IL 60604	Michigan
Telephone: 312-596-5500	Minnesota
Fax: 312-596-5501	Missouri
E-mail: Benewich.Terrence@dol.gov	Nebraska
	Ohio
	Wisconsin

REGION VI: SAN FRANCISCO

Mr. Michael W. Longeuay	Alaska
Deputy Regional Director	Arizona
USDOL/ETA/OATELS	California
71 Stevenson Street, Suite 815	Hawaii
San Francisco, CA 94105	Idaho
Phone: 415-975-4007	Nevada
Fax: 415-975-4010	Oregon
E-mail: Longeuay.Michael@dol.gov	Washington

THE MILITARY OPTION

Bet you didn't know that the United States military is the largest employer in the country. There's got to be a good reason that so many people get their paychecks from Uncle Sam.

SHOULD I OR SHOULDN'T I WORK FOR THE LARGEST EMPLOYER IN THE U.S.?

Every year, thousands of young people pursue a military career and enjoy the benefits it offers. Yet thousands more consider joining the military and decide against it. Their reasons vary, but many choose not to enlist because they lack knowledge of what a career in the military can offer. Others simply mistrust recruiters based on horror stories they've heard. Sadly, many make the decision against joining the military without ever setting foot in the recruiting office.

But if you are an informed "shopper," you will be able to make an informed choice about whether the military is right for you.

People rarely buy anything based on their needs: Instead, they buy based on their emotions. We see it on a daily basis in advertising, from automobiles to soft drinks. We rarely see an automobile commercial that gives statistics about how the car is engineered, how long it will last, the gas mileage, and other technical specifications. Instead, we see people driving around and having a good time.

The reason for this is that advertising agencies know that you will probably buy something based on how you feel rather than what you think. Because of this tendency to buy with emotion rather than reason, it is important to separate the feelings from the facts. That way, you can base your decision about whether to join the military primarily on the facts.

There are two big questions that you must answer before you can come to any conclusions. First, is the military right for me, and second, if the first answer is yes, which branch is right for me?

Suppose that you have to decide whether to buy a new car or repair your current car. The first choice you make will determine your next course of action. You will have to weigh the facts to determine if you will purchase a new car or not. Once you've decided to buy a car rather than repair your old one, you must then decide exactly what make and model will best suit your needs.

NO HYPE, JUST THE FACTS

So you didn't wake up one morning and know for sure that you're going to join the Navy. One minute you think you'd like the Army, but then you talk to your cousin who convinces you to follow him into the Air Force. But then the neighbor down the street is a Marine, and he's gung ho for you to join up with them. What to do?

Well, a helpful Web site is the answer. Go to www.spear.navy.mil/profile for some really straightforward and non-partisan information about each branch of the military. You'll be able to compare the benefits that each service offers plus pick up other helpful tips and information. The Web site is designed specifically for high school students considering the military.

"Normally the first question we get from people interested in the Air Force is 'What does the Air Force have to offer me?' But I back off and ask them about their qualifications. Sometimes it's easier to go to an Ivy League school than to join the Air Force because of our stringent requirements."

Master Sergeant Timothy Little
United States Air Force

You should make a list of the reasons why you want to join the military before you ever set foot in the recruiter's office. Whether your list is long—containing such items as money for college, job security, opportunity to travel, technical training, and good pay—or contains only one item, such as having full-time employment, the number of items on your list is not what's important. What is important is that you are able to satisfy those reasons, or primary motivators.

Whatever your list contains, the first course of action is to collect your reasons to join the military and put them in order of importance to you. This process, known as rank-ordering, will help you determine if you should proceed with the enlistment process.

"Take two people with the same qualifications who are looking for jobs. The person with the Army background will be that much more competitive. That's due to the fact that he or she is disciplined and knows how to act without being told what to do."
Staff Sergeant Max Burda
United States Army

Rank-ordering your list is a simple process of deciding which motivators are most important to you and then listing them in order of importance. List your most important motivator as number one, your next most important as number two, and so on.

If we apply the car-buying scenario here, your primary motivators may be finding a car that costs under $20,000, gets at least 30 miles to the gallon, has leather interior, is available in blue, and has a sunroof. If you put those motivators in rank order, your list might look something like this:

1. Costs under $20,000

2. Gets at least 30 mpg

3. Has a sunroof

4. Has leather interior

5. Available in blue

You'll notice that the number one, or most important, motivator in this case is cost, while the last, or least important, motivator is color. The more important the motivator, the less likely you'll be willing to settle for something different or to live without it altogether.

After you've rank-ordered your motivators, go down your list and determine whether those motivators can be met by enlisting in the military. If you find that all your motivators can be met by enlisting, that's great; but even if only some of your motivators can be met, you may still want to consider enlisting. Seldom does a product meet all our needs and wants.

CHOOSING WHICH BRANCH TO JOIN

"If you like to travel, we offer more than anyone else. The longest you're underway is generally two to three weeks, with three to four days off in every port and one day on the ship. Prior to pulling in, you can even set up tours."
Chief Petty Officer Keith Horst
United States Navy

If you are seriously considering joining the military, you probably have checked out at least two of the branches. Check them all out, even if it means just requesting literature and reviewing it. A word of caution though: Brochures do not tell the complete story, and it is very difficult to base your decision either for or against a military branch on the contents of a brochure alone. Would you buy a car based solely on the information contained in a brochure? Probably not!

"I tell people that you get paid the same in all the services, and the benefits are the same. What's different about each branch is the environment."
Sergeant Ian Bonnell, Infantry Sergeant
United States Marines

The process of choosing the right branch of the military for you is basically the same process that you used to determine if joining the military was right for you. You should start with your list of primary

I'M JOINING THE AIR FORCE

It didn't take Brian Filipek long to decide he wanted to join the Air Force. But that's if you don't count the times he talked to people who had served in the Air Force or the research he did on the Internet to gather information—and that was before he even set foot inside the recruiter's office. By the time an Air Force recruiter responded to a card Brian had sent in, he was pretty sure he liked what he'd seen so far. "The recruiter didn't have to do any work to convince me," says Brian. After that, it was a matter of going through the pre-qualifying process, like whether he met the height and weight qualifications, and the security forms he had to fill out.

After he enlisted, Brian didn't stop gathering information. Long before he was sent to Basic Training, he found out about Warrior Week, which is held on one of the last weeks in Basic Training. He was already looking forward to it. "I'm an outdoors kind of person," he says. "I want to do the obstacle course and ropes course."

Though the idea of testing his endurance and strength appeals to him, being away from family will be hard. "Granted, your food is cooked for you, but you're still on your own," he says. However, he knows that it's worth it to achieve his goal of education and free job training. Brian acknowledges that the military is not for everyone, but as far as he's concerned, he's sure he's made the right choice.

Brian Filipek, Enlistee
U.S. Air Force

motivators and use the "yes/no" method to determine whether each branch can meet all or some of those motivators. Once you've determined which branch or branches can best meet your motivators, it's time to compare those branches. Remember to look for the negative aspects as well as the motivators of each of the branches as you compare.

After making your comparisons, you may still find yourself with more than one choice. What do you do then? You could flip a coin, but that's not the wisest idea! Instead, look at some of these factors:

Length of enlistment—Some branches may require a longer term for offering the same benefits that you could receive from another branch.

Advanced pay grade—You may be entitled to an advanced rank in some branches based on certain enlistment options.

"In the Army, you can get training in everything from culinary arts to truck driving and all the way to aviation mechanics, military intelligence, and computer networking."
Staff Sergeant Max Burda
United States Army

Length and type of training—How long will your training take? Usually the longer the training, the more in-depth and useful it is. You'll also want to consider how useful the training will be once you've left the military.

Enlistment bonuses—Be careful when using an enlistment bonus as the only factor in deciding which branch to choose. If it comes down to a tie between two branches and only one offers a bonus, it's not a bad reason to choose that branch.

Additional pay and allowances—There may be additional pay you'd be entitled to that can only be offered by a particular branch. For instance, if you join the Navy, you may be entitled to Sea Pay and Submarine Pay, something obviously not available if you join the Air Force.

Ability to pursue higher education—While all the military branches offer educational benefits, you must consider when you will be able to take advantage of these benefits. If your job requires 12-hour shifts and has you out in the field a lot, when will you be able to attend classes?

"Everyone in the Navy learns how to fight a fire. You get qualified in First Aid and CPR. That's mandatory for every sailor. The only jobs we don't have in the Navy are veterinarians, forest rangers, and rodeo stars."
Chief Petty Officer Keith Horst
United States Navy

Once you have considered these factors, and perhaps some of your own, you should be able to decide which branch is right for you. If you still haven't been able to select one branch over another, though, consider the following:

- Ask your recruiter if you can speak to someone who has recently joined.

- If there is a base nearby, you may be able to get a tour to look at its facilities.

- If you are well versed in Internet chat rooms, you may want to look for ones that cater to military members—then ask a lot of questions.

- Talk to friends and family members who are currently serving in the military. Be careful, however, not to talk to people who have been out of the military for a while, as they probably aren't familiar with today's military. Also, avoid people who left the military under less-than-desirable conditions (for example, someone who was discharged from Basic Training for no compatibility).

If you choose to continue with processing for enlistment, your next step will probably be to take the Armed Services Vocational Aptitude Battery (ASVAB).

THE ASVAB

The ASVAB, a multiple-aptitude battery of tests designed for use with students in their junior or senior year in high school or in a postsecondary school, as well as those seeking military enlistment, was developed to yield results useful to both students and the military. The military uses the results to determine the qualifications of candidates for enlistment and to help place them in military occupational programs. Schools use ASVAB test results to assist their students in developing future educational and career plans.

Frequently Asked Questions About the ASVAB

What is the Armed Services Vocational Aptitude Battery (ASVAB)?

The ASVAB, sponsored by the Department of Defense, is a multi-aptitude test battery consisting of nine short individual tests covering Word Knowledge, Paragraph Comprehension, Arithmetic Reasoning, Mathematic Knowledge, General Science, Auto and Shop Information, Mechanical Comprehension, Electronics Information, and Assembling Objects. Your ASVAB results provide scores for each individual test, as well as three academic composite scores—Verbal, Math, and Academic Ability—and two career exploration composite scores.

Why should I take the ASVAB?

As a high school student nearing graduation, you are faced with important career choices. Should you go on to college, technical, or vocational school? Would it be better to enter the job market? Should you consider a military career? Your ASVAB scores are measures of aptitude. Your composite scores measure your aptitude for higher academic learning and give you ideas for career exploration.

When and where is the ASVAB given?

ASVAB is administered annually or semiannually at more than 14,000 high schools and postsecondary schools in the United States.

Is there a charge or fee to take the ASVAB?

ASVAB is administered at no cost to the school or to the student.

How long does it take to complete the ASVAB?

ASVAB testing takes approximately 3 hours. If you miss class, it will be with your school's approval.

If I wish to take the ASVAB but my school doesn't offer it (or I missed it), what should I do?

See your school counselor. In some cases, arrangements may be made for you to take it at another high school. Your counselor should call 800-323-0513 (toll-free) for additional information.

How do I find out what my scores mean and how to use them?

Your scores will be provided to you on a report called the ASVAB Student Results Sheet. Along with your scores, you should receive a copy of *Exploring Careers: The ASVAB Workbook*, which contains information that will help you understand your

ASVAB results and show you how to use them for career exploration. Test results are returned to participating schools within thirty days.

What is a passing score on the ASVAB?

No one "passes" or "fails" the ASVAB. The ASVAB enables you to compare your scores to those of other students at your grade level.

If I take the ASVAB, am I obligated to join the military?

No. Taking the ASVAB does not obligate you to the military in any way. You are free to use your test results in whatever manner you wish. You may use the ASVAB results for up to two years for military enlistment if you are a junior, a senior, or a postsecondary school student. The military services encourage all young people to finish high school before joining the armed forces.

If I am planning to go to college, should I take the ASVAB?

Yes. ASVAB results provide you with information that can help you determine your capacity for advanced academic education. You can also use your ASVAB results, along with other personal information, to identify areas for career exploration.

Should I take the ASVAB if I plan to become a commissioned officer?

Yes. Taking the ASVAB is a valuable experience for any student who aspires to become a military officer. The aptitude information you receive could assist you in career planning.

Should I take the ASVAB if I am considering entering the Reserve or National Guard?

Yes. These military organizations also use the ASVAB for enlistment purposes.

What should I do if a service recruiter contacts me?

You may be contacted by a service recruiter before you graduate. If you want to learn about the many opportunities available through military service, arrange for a follow-up meeting. However, you are under no obligation to the military as a result of taking the ASVAB.

Is the ASVAB administered other than in the school testing program?

Yes. ASVAB is also used in the regular military enlistment program. It is administered at approximately sixty-five Military Entrance Processing Stations located throughout the United States. Each year, hundreds of thousands of young men and women who are interested in enlisting in the uniformed services (Army, Navy, Air Force, Marines, and Coast Guard) but who did not take the ASVAB while in school are examined and processed at these military stations.

Is any special preparation necessary before taking the ASVAB?

Yes. A certain amount of preparation is required for taking any examination. Whether it is an athletic competition or a written test, preparation is a *must* in order to achieve the best results. Your test scores reflect not only your ability but also the time and effort in preparing for the test. The uniformed services use ASVAB to help determine a person's qualification for enlistment and to help indicate the vocational areas for which the person is best suited. Achieving your maximum score will increase your vocational opportunities. So take practice tests to prepare.

BASIC TRAINING: WHAT HAVE I GOTTEN MYSELF INTO?

The main objective of Basic Training is to transform civilians into well-disciplined military personnel in a matter of weeks. Performing such a monumental task takes a lot of hard work, both mentally and physically. For most people, Basic Training ends with a parade on graduation day. For others, though, it ends somewhere short of graduation. It is those "horror stories" that make Basic Training the one biggest fear, or anxiety-inducer, for those considering military enlistment.

Unlike the boot camp you may have heard about from your Uncle Louie or seen on television, today's Basic Training doesn't include the verbal and physical abuse of yesterday. All of the military branches are ensuring that new enlistees are treated fairly and with dignity. Not that enlistees aren't yelled at (because they are); however, the vulgarity and demeaning verbal attacks are a thing of the past. There are, from time to time, incidents involving instructors who contradict the military's policies. These violations, however, receive a lot of attention, are thoroughly investigated, and usually end up with disciplinary action taken against those involved in the abuse.

"A lot of kids are worried about Marine boot camp. They've seen movies or heard stories. Boot camp is not set up to make you fail. It's challenging, but that's the purpose of it. You're learning that no matter what life throws at you, you will be able to improvise, adapt, and overcome."

Sergeant Ian Bonnell, Infantry Sergeant
United States Marines

I SURVIVED BASIC TRAINING

Although Michael Hipszky was eager to join the Navy, it didn't take long for doubts about his decision to hit him. While he was riding the bus to the Navy's Basic Training facility, he asked himself THE QUESTION—"Why am I putting myself through this mess?" Recalls Michael, "It crosses everyone's mind. As far as I know, in my division, everyone had the same thought. 'I want to go home.' Those first few days are intense."

He figures it's because you lose control the minute you walk through the door on the first day of Basic Training. Someone's telling you (in a very loud voice) how to stand at attention, how to stand in line, how to do just about everything. "So many things go through your head," says Michael. He soon found that if he followed three rules, life got a whole lot easier:

1. KEEP YOUR MOUTH SHUT. "Your mouth is your biggest problem," he warns, "talking when you aren't supposed to and saying dumb things."

2. PAY ATTENTION TO DETAIL. "They'll say things like, 'Grab the door knob, turn it half to the right, and go through.' A lot of people will just pull it open and get yelled at. They teach you how to fold your clothes and clean the head (toilet). Everything is paying attention to detail," Michael advises.

3. DON'T THINK FOR YOURSELF. "Wait to be told what to do," Michael says, recalling the time his group was handed a form and told to wait until ordered to fill it out. Many saw that the form was asking for information like name, date, and division and began filling it out, only to get in trouble because they didn't wait.

Having been through Basic Training, Michael now knows that every little thing—from folding T-shirts the exact way he'd been told to do (arms folded in), to sweeping the floor, to marching—is all part of the training process. "You don't realize it until you're done," he says.

Despite all the yelling and push-ups, Michael values the training he got in the classes. He learned how to put out different kinds of fires, how to manage his money, how to identify aircraft—even etiquette. And that's just for starters.

His lowest point was about halfway through Basic, which, he found out, usually happens for everyone at the same time. "The first half of Basic, everything is so surreal. Then you get halfway through, and finishing up Basic seems so far away. You're always busy, whether you're stenciling your clothes or marching. You march a lot," he says. But then he reached his highest point, which was pass-in review at the end of the training and winning awards. He knew he'd done well. Looking into his future with the Navy, Michael says, "I want to see the world and have the experiences that the Navy can give you." Having finished Basic Training, he's well on his way.

Airman Michael Hipszky
United States Navy

If you are still uncertain of which branch you'd like to join, do not allow the type of Basic Training you'll receive to be your only deciding factor. If, for example, the Marine Corps meets all your needs and is clearly your first choice, do not select the Air Force because its Basic Training seems easier. Conversely, if the Air Force is clearly your first choice, do not select the Marine Corps because it has the "toughest" Basic Training, and you want to prove you are up to the challenge. Basic Training is a means of your transformation from civilian life to military life. It happens in a relatively short period of time compared to the entire length of your enlistment.

Some Words on Getting through Basic Training

No matter what you may have heard or read elsewhere, there are no secrets to getting through Basic Training; only common sense and preparation will get you through. Here are some do's and don'ts that should help you survive Basic Training for any of the services. Although following these guidelines will not ensure your success at Basic Training, your chances for success will be greatly improved by following them.

Before Arriving at Basic Training

DO:

- Start an exercise program.
- Maintain a sensible diet.
- Stay out of trouble. (For example, pay any traffic fines promptly before leaving for Basic Training.)
- Ensure that all of your financial obligations are in order.
- Bring the required items that you are told to bring.
- Give up smoking.

DON'T:

- Skip preparing yourself physically because you think that Basic Training will whip you into shape.
- Abuse drugs and/or alcohol.
- Have a big send-off party and get drunk the night before you leave for Basic Training.
- Leave home with open tickets, summonses, or warrants.

- Get yourself into heavy debt (such as buying a new car).
- Bring any prohibited items.
- Have your hair cut in a radical manner. (This includes having your head shaved. Men will receive a "very close" haircut shortly after arriving at Basic Training.)
- Have any part of your body pierced, tattooed, or otherwise altered.

PAYING FOR COLLEGE THROUGH THE ARMED SERVICES

You can take any of the following three paths into the armed services—all of which provide opportunities for financial assistance for college.

Enlisted Personnel

All five branches of the armed services offer college-credit courses on base. Enlisted personnel can also take college courses at civilian colleges while on active duty.

"In the Air Force, you're not only getting an education, but also experience. You could go to school for a degree in avionics technology, but in the Air Force, you get the teaching and the experience— real-world, hands-on experience—that makes your education marketable."
Master Sergeant Timothy Little
United States Air Force

ROTC

More than 40,000 college students participate in Reserve Officers' Training Corps (ROTC). Two-, three-, and four-year ROTC scholarships are available to outstanding students. You can try ROTC at no obligation for two years or, if you have a four-year scholarship, for one year. Normally, all ROTC classes, uniforms, and books are free. ROTC graduates are required to serve in the military for a set period of time, either full-time on active duty or part-time in the Reserve or National Guard. Qualifying graduates can delay their service to go to graduate or professional school first.

U.S. Service Academics

Openings at the U.S. service academies are few, so it pays to get information early. Every student is on a full scholarship, but free does not mean easy—these intense programs train graduates to meet the demands of leadership and success.

West Point. The U.S. Military Academy (Army) offers a broad-based academic program with forty-two majors in various fields of study. Extensive training and leadership experience go hand in hand with academics. *www.usma.edu*

Annapolis. The U.S. Naval Academy is a unique blend of tradition and state-of-the-art technology. Its core curriculum includes nineteen major fields of study, and classroom work is supported by practical experience in leadership and professional operations. *www.usna.edu*

Air Force Academy. The U.S. Air Force Academy prepares and motivates cadets for careers as Air Force officers. The academy offers a B.S. degree in thirty-two majors. Graduates receive a reserve commission as a second lieutenant in the Air Force. *www.usfa.edu*

Coast Guard Academy. This broad-based education, which leads to a B.S. degree in eight technical or professional majors, includes a thorough grounding in the professional skills necessary for the Coast Guard's work. *www.cga.edu*

Financing Higher Education through the U.S. Armed Forces

The U.S. military provides a number of options to help students and their parents get financial aid for postsecondary education.

The Active Duty Montgomery GI Bill

The Active Duty Montgomery GI Bill, called "ADMGIB" for short, provides up to 36 months of education benefits to eligible veterans for college, business, technical or vocational courses,

WHAT'S MY JOB?—OH, I JUST DRIVE AN ARMORED CARRIER AROUND

Justin Platt thought maybe he would join the Army, but first he had a few doubts to overcome. A big one was his reluctance to be away from friends and family. Another one was the overseas duty—something he definitely didn't want. But his desire to get his foot in the door of medical training won out. When he found out that he could get an education in the Army to become a nurse, his fears flew out the window, and Justin joined the Army. He's glad he did.

Stationed at Fort Carson in Colorado, Justin's been through Basic Training and is on his first stint of active duty working in—you guessed it—the medical field. "I work in an aid station, which is like a mini hospital," he says. He's the one who does the screening for anyone in his battalion who comes into sick call. Okay, it's from 5 a.m. to 7 p.m., but Justin doesn't mind.

Justin's job on active duty doesn't just consist of handing out Band-Aids and cough drops. He's also learning how to drive an armored carrier—not your usual medical training. But in the field, Army medics have to be able to pick up the wounded, which means knowing how to drive what he describes as a souped-up SUV—only instead of tires, it has tracks.

Justin plans to get enough rank to go from green to gold—enlisted to officer. "I'll have to take additional college courses to get a four-year degree," he says. It'll take him about seven years, including his Army duty. Not bad for someone who once had doubts about joining the military.

Private First Class Justin Platt
Fort Carson, Colorado

correspondence courses, apprenticeship/job training, and flight training. You may be an eligible veteran if you get an Honorable Discharge, you have a High School Diploma or GED, or, in some cases, 12 hours of college credit, AND you meet the necessary requirements related to military service. You MUST have elected to participate in the ADMGIB, which involves giving up $100 of your pay per month for the first twelve months of military service. The monthly benefit paid to you is based on the type of training you take, length of your service, your category, and if the Department of Defense put extra money in your *MGIB* Fund (called "kickers"). You usually have ten years to use your *MGIB* benefits, but the time limit can be less, in some cases, and longer under certain circumstances.

The Selected Reserve Montgomery GI Bill

The Selected Reserve Montgomery GI Bill (SRMGIB) may be available to you if you are a member of the Selected Reserve. The Selected Reserve includes the Army Reserve, Navy Reserve, Air Force Reserve, Marine Corps Reserve and Coast Guard Reserve, and the Army National Guard and the Air National Guard. You may use this education assistance program for degree programs, certificate or correspondence courses, cooperative training, independent study programs, apprenticeship/on-the-job training, and vocational flight training programs. Remedial, refresher, and deficiency training are available under certain circumstances. Eligibility for this program is determined by the Selected Reserve components. VA makes the payments for this program. You may be entitled to receive up to 36 months of education benefits. Your benefit entitlement ends fourteen years from the date of your eligibility for the program, or on the day you leave the Selected Reserve.

Call toll-free 888-GI-BILL-1 for more information, or visit the Web site at www.gibill.va.gov/education/benefits.htm.

The Department of Defense

The U.S. Department of Defense offers a large number of education benefits to those enrolled in the U.S. military or employed by the Department of Defense, including scholarships, grants, tuition assistance, and internships. Visit their Web site at http://web.lmi.org/edugate for complete information.

Tuition Assistance

All branches of the military pay up to 75 percent of tuition for full-time, active-duty enlistees who take courses at community colleges or by correspondence during their tours of duty. Details vary by service.

The Community College of the Air Force

Enlisted Air Force personnel can convert their technical training and military experience into academic credit, earning an associate degree, an occupational instructor's certificate, or a trade school certificate. Participants receive an official transcript from this fully accredited program. You can visit the Community College of the Air Force on line at www.au.af.mil/au/ccaf.

Educational Loan-Repayment Program

The Armed Services can help repay government-insured and other approved loans. Each of the services is free to offer such programs, but individual policies differ.

Other Forms of Tuition Assistance

Each branch of the military offers its own education incentives. To find out more, check with a local recruiting office.

YOU AND THE WORKPLACE

SOME OF YOU WILL GO TO COLLEGE first and then look for jobs. Some of you might work for a few years and then go to college. And many of you will go immediately into the workforce and bypass college altogether. Whenever you become an employee, you'll want to know what you can do to succeed on the job and move to both higher levels of responsibility and more pay.

Chapter 12

JUMP INTO WORK

Almost everyone ends up in the workforce at some point. No matter when you plan to receive that first full-time paycheck, there are some things you'll need to do to prepare yourself for the world of work.

AT EACH GRADE LEVEL, there are specific steps you should take regardless of whether or not you plan to attend college immediately following high school. In fact, college and career timelines should coincide, according to guidance counselors and career specialists, and students should take college-preparatory courses, even if they aren't planning on attending college.

THE COLLEGE/CAREER TIMELINE

The following timeline will help you meet college requirements and prepare you for work. In an effort to make sure that you are adequately preparing for both school and work, incorporate these five steps into your career/college timeline:

1. **Take an aptitude test.** You can do this as early as the sixth grade, but even if you don't do this until high school, it's not too late. By doing so, you will begin to get a feel for what areas you might be good at and enjoy. Your guidance counselor should have a test in his or her office for you to take, or you can try the ASVAB (see page 123). Thousands of high school students take this test every year to discover possible career paths—and taking the ASVAB doesn't require you to join the military!

2. **Beginning in middle school, you should start considering what your options are after high school.** However, if you're only starting to think about this in high school, that's okay, too. Keep a notebook of information gathered from field trips, job-shadowing experiences, mentoring programs, and career fairs to help you make sense of the possibilities open to you. This process should continue through high school. Many schools offer job shadowing and internship programs for students to explore different vocational avenues. Take advantage of these opportunities if you can. Too often, students don't explore the workplace until after they've taken the courses necessary to enter a particular profession, only to discover it wasn't the career they dreamed of after all.

3. **No later than the tenth grade, visit a vocational center to look at the training programs offered.** Some public school systems send students to vocational and career program centers for career exploration.

TAKING A BREAK BETWEEN HIGH SCHOOL AND COLLEGE

Because of the soaring costs of college tuition today, college is no longer a place to "find yourself." It is a costly investment in your future. The career you choose to pursue may or may not require additional education; your research will determine whether or not it's required or preferred. If you decide not to attend college immediately after high school, however, don't consider it to be a closed door. Taking some time off between high school and college is considered perfectly acceptable by employers. Many students simply need a break after thirteen years of schooling. Most experts agree that it's better to be ready and prepared for college; many adults get more out of their classes after they've had a few years to mature.

Source: Street Smart Career Guide: A Step-by-Step Program for Your Career Development.

4. **During your junior and senior years, be sure to create a portfolio of practice resumes, writing samples, and a list of work skills.** This portfolio should also include your high school transcript and letters of recom- mendation. It will serve as a valuable reference tool when it comes time to apply for jobs.

5. **By tenth or eleventh grade, you should begin focusing on a specific career path.** More employers today are looking for employees who have both the education and work experience that relates to the career field for which they're interviewing. If you are looking for part-time employment, you should consider jobs that pertain to your field of study. Until you start interacting with people in the field, you won't have a realistic feel of what's involved in that profession. If you're planning on heading into the workplace right after high school, take a look at the following pages for a list of careers that don't require a four-year degree.

WRITING YOUR RESUME

Resumes are a critical part of getting a job. A resume is an introduction of your skills to a potential employer. For that reason, your resume must stand out in a crowd because some employers receive dozens of resumes each week. A resume that is too long, cluttered, or disorganized may find its way to the "circular file," also known as the trash can. You can avoid this hazard by creating a resume that is short, presentable, and easy to read.

Remember that a resume is a summary of who you are and an outline of your experiences, skills, and goals. While writing it, you may discover some talents that you weren't aware you had and that will help boost your confidence for the job search.

Begin by collecting facts about yourself, including where you went to high school, your past and present jobs, activities, interests, and leadership roles. Next to the individual activities, write down

what responsibilities you had. For example, something as simple as babysitting requires the ability to settle disagreements and supervise others.

Next, decide on how you would like to format your resume. Most hiring managers expect to see one of two types of resumes: chronological or functional. The chronological resume is the most traditional, supplying the reader with a sequential listing (from present to past) of your accomplishments. Because the emphasis here is on past employment experience, high school and college students with little or no employment history might want to avoid this resume type. A functional resume, on the other hand, highlights a person's abilities rather than his or her work history. Entry-level candidates who want to focus on skills rather than credentials should consider using a functional resume.

(Continued on page 135)

CAREERS WITHOUT A FOUR-YEAR DEGREE

Some students spend a few years in the workplace before going to college. Others begin their career with a high school diploma, a vocational certificate, or up to two years of education or training after high school.

With that in mind, sometimes it's easier to know what you don't want rather than what you do want. Take a look at the list below, and check off the careers that interest you. Perhaps you've thought of something you'd like to do that isn't on this list. Well, don't dump your hopes. There are many different levels of training and education that can lead you to the career of your dreams. Since this list is not all-inclusive, you should check with your high school counselor or go on line to research the training you'll need for the job or career you want—without a four-year degree. Then talk to your guidance counselor, teacher, librarian, or career counselor for more information about the careers on the list below or those you've researched on your own.

AGRICULTURE AND NATURAL RESOURCES

High school/vocational diploma
- ❑ Fisher
- ❑ Groundskeeper
- ❑ Logger
- ❑ Pest Controller

Up to two years beyond high school
- ❑ Fish and Game Warden
- ❑ Tree Surgeon

APPLIED ARTS (VISUAL)

High school/vocational diploma
- ❑ Floral Arranger
- ❑ Merchandise Displayer
- ❑ Painter (artist)

Up to two years beyond high school
- ❑ Cartoonist
- ❑ Commercial Artist
- ❑ Fashion Designer
- ❑ Interior Decorator
- ❑ Photographer

APPLIED ARTS (WRITTEN AND SPOKEN)

High school/vocational diploma
- ❑ Proofreader

Up to two years beyond high school
- ❑ Advertising copywriter
- ❑ Legal Assistant

BUSINESS MACHINE/COMPUTER OPERATION

High school/vocational diploma
- ❑ Data Entry
- ❑ Statistical Clerk
- ❑ Telephone Operator
- ❑ Typist

Up to two years beyond high school
- ❑ Computer Operator
- ❑ Motion Picture Projectionist

CONSTRUCTION AND MAINTENANCE

High school/vocational diploma
- ❑ Bricklayer
- ❑ Construction Laborer
- ❑ Elevator Mechanic
- ❑ Floor Covering Installer
- ❑ Heavy Equipment Operator
- ❑ Janitor
- ❑ Maintenance Mechanic

Up to two years beyond high school
- ❑ Building Inspector
- ❑ Carpenter
- ❑ Electrician
- ❑ Insulation Worker

- ❑ Lather
- ❑ Painter (construction)
- ❑ Pipefitter
- ❑ Plumber
- ❑ Roofer
- ❑ Sheet Metal Worker
- ❑ Structural Steel Worker
- ❑ Tile Setter

CRAFTS AND RELATED SERVICES

High school/vocational diploma
- ❑ Baker/Cook/Chef
- ❑ Butcher
- ❑ Furniture Upholsterer
- ❑ Housekeeper (hotel)
- ❑ Tailor/Dressmaker

Up to two years beyond high school
- ❑ Dry Cleaner
- ❑ Jeweler
- ❑ Locksmith
- ❑ Musical Instrument Repairer

CREATIVE/PERFORMING ARTS

High school/vocational diploma
- ❑ Singer
- ❑ Stunt Performer

Up to two years beyond high school
- ❑ Actor/Actress
- ❑ Dancer/Choreographer
- ❑ Musician
- ❑ Writer/Author

EDUCATION AND RELATED SERVICES

High school/vocational diploma
- ❑ Nursery School Attendant
- ❑ Teacher's Aide

ENGINEERING AND RELATED TECHNOLOGIES

High school/vocational diploma
- ❑ Biomedical Equipment Technician
- ❑ Laser Technician

Up to two years beyond high school
- ❑ Aerospace Engineer Technician
- ❑ Broadcast Technician
- ❑ Chemical Laboratory Technician
- ❑ Civil Engineering Technician
- ❑ Computer Programmer
- ❑ Computer Service Technician
- ❑ Electronic Technician
- ❑ Energy Conservation Technician
- ❑ Industrial Engineering Technician
- ❑ Laboratory Tester
- ❑ Mechanical Engineering Technician

- ❑ Metallurgical Technician
- ❑ Pollution Control Technician
- ❑ Quality Control Technician
- ❑ Robot Technician
- ❑ Surveyor (land)
- ❑ Technical Illustrator
- ❑ Tool Designer
- ❑ Weather Observer

FINANCIAL TRANSACTIONS

High school/vocational diploma
- ❑ Accounting Clerk
- ❑ Bank Teller
- ❑ Cashier
- ❑ Payroll Clerk
- ❑ Travel Agent

Up to two years beyond high school
- ❑ Bookkeeper
- ❑ Loan Officer

HEALTH CARE (GENERAL)

High school/vocational diploma
- ❑ Dental Assistant
- ❑ Medical Assistant
- ❑ Nursing/Psychiatric Aide

Up to two years beyond high school
- ❑ Dietetic Technician
- ❑ Nurse (practical)
- ❑ Nurse (registered)
- ❑ Optometric Assistant
- ❑ Physical Therapist's Assistant
- ❑ Physician's Assistant
- ❑ Recreation Therapist

HEALTH-CARE SPECIALTIES AND TECHNOLOGIES

High school/vocational diploma
- ❑ Dialysis Technician

Up to two years beyond high school
- ❑ Dental Hygienist
- ❑ Dental Laboratory Technician
- ❑ EEG Technologist
- ❑ EKG Technician
- ❑ Emergency Medical Technician
- ❑ Medical Laboratory Technician
- ❑ Medical Technologist
- ❑ Nuclear Medicine Technologist
- ❑ Operating Room Technician
- ❑ Optician
- ❑ Radiation Therapy Technologist
- ❑ Radiologic Technologist
- ❑ Respiratory Therapist
- ❑ Sonographer

HOME/BUSINESS EQUIPMENT REPAIR

High school/vocational diploma

- ❑ Air-Conditioning/Refrigeration/Heating Mechanic
- ❑ Appliance Servicer
- ❑ Coin Machine Mechanic

Up to two years beyond high school

- ❑ Communications Equipment Mechanic
- ❑ Line Installer/Splicer
- ❑ Office Machine Servicer
- ❑ Radio/TV Repairer
- ❑ Telephone Installer

INDUSTRIAL EQUIPMENT OPERATIONS AND REPAIR

High school/vocational diploma

- ❑ Assembler
- ❑ Blaster
- ❑ Boilermaker
- ❑ Coal Equipment Operator
- ❑ Compressor House Operator
- ❑ Crater
- ❑ Dock Worker
- ❑ Forging Press Operator
- ❑ Furnace Operator
- ❑ Heat Treater
- ❑ Machine Tool Operator
- ❑ Material Handler
- ❑ Miner
- ❑ Sailor
- ❑ Sewing Machine Operator

Up to two years beyond high school

- ❑ Bookbinder
- ❑ Compositor/Typesetter
- ❑ Electronic Equipment Repairer
- ❑ Electroplater
- ❑ Firefighter
- ❑ Instrument Mechanic
- ❑ Lithographer
- ❑ Machine Repairer
- ❑ Machinist
- ❑ Millwright
- ❑ Molder
- ❑ Nuclear Reactor Operator
- ❑ Patternmaker
- ❑ Photoengraver
- ❑ Power House Mechanic
- ❑ Power Plant Operator
- ❑ Printing Press Operator
- ❑ Stationery Engineer
- ❑ Tool and Die Maker
- ❑ Water Plant Operator
- ❑ Welder
- ❑ Wire Drawer

MANAGEMENT AND PLANNING

High school/vocational diploma

- ❑ Administrative Assistant
- ❑ Food Service Supervisor
- ❑ Postmaster
- ❑ Service Station Manager

Up to two years beyond high school

- ❑ Benefits Manager
- ❑ Building Manager
- ❑ Caterer
- ❑ Contractor
- ❑ Credit Manager
- ❑ Customer Service Coordinator
- ❑ Employment Interviewer
- ❑ Executive Housekeeper
- ❑ Funeral Director
- ❑ Hotel/Motel Manager
- ❑ Importer/Exporter
- ❑ Insurance Manager
- ❑ Manager (small business)
- ❑ Office Manager
- ❑ Personnel Manager
- ❑ Restaurant/Bar Manager
- ❑ Store Manager
- ❑ Supermarket Manager

MARKETING AND SALES

High school/vocational diploma

- ❑ Auctioneer
- ❑ Bill Collector
- ❑ Driver (route)
- ❑ Fashion Model
- ❑ Product Demonstrator
- ❑ Salesperson (general)
- ❑ Sample Distributor

Up to two years beyond high school

- ❑ Claims Adjuster
- ❑ Insurance Worker
- ❑ Manufacturer's Representative
- ❑ Real Estate Agent
- ❑ Sales Manager
- ❑ Travel Agent
- ❑ Travel Guide

PERSONAL AND CUSTOMER SERVICE

High school/vocational diploma

- ❑ Barber
- ❑ Bartender
- ❑ Beautician
- ❑ Child-Care Worker
- ❑ Counter Attendant
- ❑ Dining Room Attendant
- ❑ Electrologist
- ❑ Flight Attendant
- ❑ Host/Hostess
- ❑ Houseparent
- ❑ Manicurist
- ❑ Parking Lot Attendant
- ❑ Porter
- ❑ Private Household Worker
- ❑ Waiter/Waitress

RECORDS AND COMMUNICATIONS

High school/vocational diploma

- ❑ Billing Clerk
- ❑ Clerk (general)
- ❑ File Clerk
- ❑ Foreign Trade Clerk
- ❑ Hotel Clerk
- ❑ Meter Reader
- ❑ Postal Clerk
- ❑ Receptionist
- ❑ Stenographer

Up to two years beyond high school

- ❑ Court Reporter
- ❑ Legal Secretary
- ❑ Library Assistant
- ❑ Library Technician
- ❑ Medical Records Technician
- ❑ Medical Secretary
- ❑ Personnel Assistant
- ❑ Secretary
- ❑ Travel Clerk

SOCIAL AND GOVERNMENT

High school/vocational diploma

- ❑ Corrections Officer
- ❑ Police Officer
- ❑ Security Guard
- ❑ Store Detective

Up to two years beyond high school

- ❑ Detective (police)
- ❑ Hazardous Waste Technician
- ❑ Recreation Leader
- ❑ Personal/Customer Services

STORAGE AND DISPATCHING

High school/vocational diploma

- ❑ Dispatcher
- ❑ Mail Carrier
- ❑ Railroad Conductor
- ❑ Shipping/Receiving Clerk
- ❑ Stock Clerk
- ❑ Tool Crib Attendant
- ❑ Warehouse Worker

Up to two years beyond high school

- ❑ Warehouse Supervisor

VEHICLE OPERATION AND REPAIR

High school/vocational diploma

- ❑ Automotive Painter
- ❑ Bus Driver
- ❑ Chauffeur
- ❑ Diesel Mechanic
- ❑ Farm Equipment Mechanic
- ❑ Forklift Operator
- ❑ Heavy Equipment Mechanic
- ❑ Locomotive Engineer
- ❑ Railroad Braker
- ❑ Refuse Collector
- ❑ Service Station Attendant
- ❑ Taxicab Driver
- ❑ Truck Driver

Up to two years beyond high school

- ❑ Aircraft Mechanic
- ❑ Airplane Pilot
- ❑ Auto Body Repairer
- ❑ Automotive Mechanic
- ❑ Garage Supervisor
- ❑ Motorcycle Mechanic

Parts of a Resume

At the very least, your resume should include the following components:

Heading: Centered at the top of the page should be your name, address, phone number, and e-mail address.

Objective: In one sentence, tell the employer the type of work for which you are looking.

Education: Beginning with your most recent school or program, include the date (or expected date) of completion, the degree or certificate earned, and the address of the institution. Don't overlook any workshops or seminars, self-study, or on-the-job training in which you have been involved. If any courses particularly lend themselves to the type of work for which you are applying, include them. Mention grade point averages and class rank when they are especially impressive.

Skills and abilities: Until you've actually listed these on paper, you can easily overlook many of them. They may be as varied as the ability to work with computers or being captain of the girl's basketball team.

Work experience: If you don't have any, skip this section. If you do, begin with your most recent employer and include the date you left the job, your job title, the company name, and the company address. If you are still employed there, simply enter your start date and "to present" for the date. Include notable accomplishments for each job. High school and college students with little work experience shouldn't be shy about including summer, part-time, and volunteer jobs, such as lifeguarding, babysitting, delivering pizzas, or volunteering at local parks.

Personal: Here's your opportunity to include your special talents and interests as well as notable accomplishments or experiences.

References: Most experts agree that it's best to simply state that references are available upon request. However, if you do decide to list names, addresses, and phone numbers, limit yourself to no more than three. Make sure you inform any people whom you have listed that they may be contacted.

SAMPLE FUNCTIONAL RESUME

Michele A. Thomas
3467 Main Street
Atlanta, Georgia 30308
404-555-3423
E-mail: mthomas_987654321@yahoo.com

OBJECTIVE

Seeking a sales position in the wireless phone industry

EDUCATION

High School Diploma, June 2005

John F. Kennedy High School, Atlanta, Georgia

SKILLS

Computer literate, IBM: MS Works, MS Word, WordPerfect, Netscape; Macintosh: MS Word, Excel

ACTIVITIES/LEADERSHIP

Student Government secretary, 2004–2005

Key Club vice president, 2003–2004

Future Business Leaders of America

AWARDS

Varsity Swim Club (Captain; MVP Junior, Senior; Sportsmanship Award)
Outstanding Community Service Award, 2004

EXPERIENCE

Sales Clerk, The Limited, Atlanta, Georgia; part-time, September 2004 to present

Cashier, Winn-Dixie Supermarkets, Atlanta, Georgia, Summers 2002 and 2003

INTERESTS

Swimming, reading, computers

REFERENCES

Available upon request

SAMPLE COVER LETTER

Take a look at how this student's cover letter applied the facts outlined in her resume to the job to which she's applying. You can use this letter to help you get started on your own cover letters. Text that appears in all caps below indicates the kind of information you need to include in that section. Before you send your letter, proofread it for mistakes and ask a parent or friend you trust to look it over as well.

(DATE)
June 29, 2005

(YOUR ADDRESS)
3467 Main Street
Atlanta, Georgia 30308
Phone: 404-555-3423
E-mail: mthomas_987654321@yahoo.com

(PERSON—BY NAME—TO WHOM YOU'RE SENDING THE LETTER)
Mr. Charles E. Pence
Manager, Human Resources
NexAir Wireless
20201 East Sixth Street
Atlanta, Georgia 30372

Dear Mr. Pence:

(HOW YOU HEARD OF THE POSITION)
Your job announcement in the *Atlanta Gazette* for an entry-level sales position asked for someone who has both computer and sales skills. **(SOMETHING EXTRA THAT WILL INTEREST THE READER)** My training and past job experience fit both of those categories. I also bring an enthusiasm and desire to begin my career in a communications firm such as NexAir.

(WHAT PRACTICAL SKILLS YOU CAN BRING TO THE POSITION)
A few weeks ago, I graduated from John F. Kennedy High School here in Atlanta. While in school, I concentrated on gaining computer skills on both IBM and Macintosh machines and participated in organizations such as the Key Club, in which I was vice president, and the Future Business Leaders of America.

(RELATE PAST EXPERIENCE TO DESIRED JOB)
As you will see from my resume, I worked as a cashier at Winn-Dixie Supermarket for two summers and am currently employed as a sales clerk at The Limited. From these two positions, I have gained valuable customer service skills and an attention to detail, qualities which I am sure are of utmost importance to you as you make your hiring decision.

I would very much like to interview for the position and am available at your convenience. I look forward to hearing from you soon.

Sincerely,

Michele A. Thomas

Resume-Writing Tips

These tips will help as you begin constructing your resume:

- Keep the resume short and simple. Although senior executives may use as many as two or three pages, recent graduates should limit themselves to one page.

- Capitalize headings.

- Keep sentences short; avoid writing in paragraphs.

- Use language that is simple, not flowery or complex.

- Be specific, and offer examples when appropriate.

- Emphasize achievements.

- Be honest.

- Don't include information about salary or wages unless specifically requested.

- Use high-quality, white, beige, or gray, 8 ½" × 11" paper.

- Make good use of white space by leaving adequate side and top margins on the paper.

- Make what you write presentable and use good business style.

- Because your resume should be a reflection of your personality, write it yourself.

- Avoid gimmicks such as colored paper, photos, or clip art.

- Make good use of bullets or asterisks, underlining, and bold print.

- Proofread your work, and have someone you trust proofread it also.

- Be neat and accurate.

- Never send a resume without a cover letter.

The Cover Letter

Every resume should be accompanied by a cover letter. This is often the most crucial part of your job search because the letter will be the first thing that a potential employer reads. When you include a cover letter, you're showing the employer that you care enough to take the time to address him or her personally and that you are genuinely interested in the job.

Always call the company and verify the name and title of the person to whom you are addressing the letter. Although you will want to keep your letter brief, introduce yourself and begin with a statement that will catch the reader's attention. Indicate the position you are applying for and mention if someone referred you or if you are simply responding to a newspaper ad. Draw attention to yourself by including something that will arouse the employer's curiosity about your experience and accomplishments. A cover letter should request something, most commonly an interview. Sign and date your letter. Then follow up with a phone call a few days after you're sure the letter has been received. Persistence pays!

JOB HUNTING 101

High school is a time for taking classes and learning, developing relationships with others, becoming involved in extracurricular activities that teach valuable life skills, and generally preparing for college or a job. Regardless of where you're headed after high school, you need to learn how to create a favorable impression. That can mean setting some clear, attainable goals for yourself, putting them down on paper in the form of a resume and cover letter, and convincing interviewers that you are, indeed, the person for whom they are looking. In short, learn how to sell yourself. A brief course in Job Hunting 101 will help you do just that.

Marketing Yourself

You can use several approaches to market yourself successfully. Networking, the continual process of contacting friends and relatives, is a great way to get information about job openings. Seventy-five percent of the job openings in this country are not advertised but are filled by friends, relatives, and acquaintances of current employees. From the employer's perspective, there is less risk associated with hiring someone recommended by an employee than hiring someone unknown. Networking is powerful. Everyone has a primary network of people they know and talk to frequently. Those acquaintances know and talk to networks of their own, thereby creating a secondary network for you and multiplying the number of individuals who know what you're looking for in a job.

Broadcasting is another marketing method in which you gather a list of companies that interest you and then mail them letters asking for job interviews. Although the rate of return on your mailings is small, two thirds of all job hunters use this approach, and half of those who use it find a job. You will increase your response rate by addressing your letter to a particular person—the one who has the power to hire you—and by following up with a phone call a few days after the letter has been received. To obtain the manager's name, simply call the company and ask the receptionist for the person's name, job title, and correct spelling. Good resources for finding potential employers include referrals, community agencies, job fairs, newspaper ads, trade directories, trade journals, state indexes, the local chamber of commerce, the Yellow Pages, and the Web. The following tips can help as you begin hunting for the perfect job:

- Job-hunting is time-intensive. Do your homework and take it seriously by using every opportunity available to you.

- Prepare yourself for the fact that there will be far more rejections than acceptances.

- Consider taking a temporary job while you continue the job hunt. It will help pay the bills and give you new skills to boost your resume at the same time.

- Research the activities of potential employers and show that you have studied them when you're being interviewed.

- Keep careful records of all contacts and follow-up activities.

- Don't ignore any job leads—act on every tip you get.

- Stay positive.

With all these thoughts in mind, you should be ready to begin the process of making people believe in you, and that's a major part of being successful in your job hunt.

THE JOB INTERVIEW

You can prevent some of the preinterview jitters by adequately preparing. Remember that you have nothing to lose and that you, too, are doing the choosing. Just as you are waiting and hoping to be offered a job, you have the option of choosing whether or not to accept an offer. It's all right to feel somewhat anxious, but keep everything in perspective. This is an adventure, and you are in control. Most important, remember to be yourself. With all of this in mind, consider some of the following points of the interview process:

- Speak up during the interview, and furnish the interviewer with the information he or she needs in order to make an informed decision. It is especially impressive if you can remember the names of people to whom you've been introduced. People like to be called by name, and it shows that you took the initiative to remember them.

- Always arrive a few minutes early for the interview, and look your best. The way you act and dress tells the interviewer plenty about your attitude and personality. Sloppy dress, chewing gum, and cigarettes have no place at an interview and will probably cut your interview short. Instead, dress professionally and appropriately for the job. Avoid heavy makeup, short skirts, jeans, and untidy or flashy clothing of any kind.

The best way to prepare for the interview is to practice. Have a friend or relative play the role of the interviewer, and go over some of the most commonly asked questions. Learn as much as you can about the company you're interviewing with—it pays to do your homework. When you show a potential employer that you've taken the time and initiative to learn about his or her company, you're showing that you will be a motivated and hardworking employee. Employers fear laziness and minimal effort, looking instead for workers who don't always have to be told what to do and when to do it.

Here is a list of interview questions you can expect to have to answer:

- **Tell me a little bit about yourself.** This is your chance to pitch your qualifications for the job in 2 minutes. Provide a few details about your education, previous jobs you've held, and extracurricular activities that relate to the position for which you're interviewing.

- **Are you at your best when working alone or in a group?** The safest answer is "Both." Most companies today cluster their employees into work groups, so you will need strong interpersonal skills. However, on occasion, you may be required to work on projects alone.

- **What did you like the most about your last job? What did you dislike the most about it?** You should always accentuate the positives in an interview, so focus primarily on what you liked. Also be honest about what you disliked, but then explain how facing the negatives helped you grow as an employee.

- **What are your career goals?** Be sure you've done some research on the company and industry before your interview. When this question comes up, talk realistically about how far you believe your skills and talents will take you and what actions you plan to take to ensure this happens, such as pursuing more education.

Take the time to prepare some answers to these commonly asked questions. For instance, if you haven't set at least one career goal for yourself, do it now. Be ready to describe it to the interviewer. Likewise, you should be able to talk about your last job, including what you liked the most and the least. Adapt your answers so they apply to the job for which you are presently interviewing. Other questions that might be asked include:

- What qualifications do you have?

- Why do you want to work for us?

- Do you enjoy school? Why or why not?

- Do you plan to continue your education?

- What do you plan to be doing five years from now?

- What motivates you to do a good job?

If you are seeking a job as a manager, you might respond by saying you liked the varied responsibilities of your past job. Recall that you enjoyed the unexpected challenges and flexible schedule. And when describing what you liked least, make sure you respond with some function or area of responsibility that has nothing to do with the responsibilities of the job you hope to get.

More than likely, you'll be asked to tell the interviewer something about yourself. This is your chance to "toot your horn," but don't ramble. You might ask the interviewer specifically what he or she would like to hear about: your educational background or recent experiences and responsibilities in your present or last job. After he or she chooses, stick to the basics; the next move belongs to the interviewer.

When asked about personal strengths and weaknesses, given that the question is two parts, begin with a weakness so you can end on a strong note with your strengths. Again, try to connect your description of a strength or weakness with the requirements for the job. Naturally, it wouldn't be wise to reveal a serious weakness about yourself, but you can mention how you have changed your shortcomings. You might say, "I like to get my work done fast, but I consciously try to slow down a little to make sure I'm careful and accurate." When it comes to strengths, don't exaggerate, but don't sell yourself short either.

Asking Questions

You can ask questions, too. In fact, the interviewer expects you to ask questions to determine if the job is right for you, just as he or she will be trying to find out if you'll be successful working for his or her company. When you ask questions, it shows that you're interested and want to learn more. When the type of question you ask indicates that you've done your homework regarding the job and the company, your interviewer will be impressed. Avoid asking questions about salary or fringe benefits, anything adversarial, or questions that show you have a negative opinion of the company. It's all right to list your questions on a piece of paper; it's the quality of the question that's important, not whether you can remember it. Here are a few sample questions that you should consider asking if the topics don't come up in your interview:

- What kind of responsibilities come with this job?

- How is the department organized?

- What will be the first project for the new hire to tackle?

- What is a typical career advancement path for a person in this position?

- Who will the supervisor be for this position, and can I meet him or her?

- What is the office environment like? Is it casual or corporate?

- When do you expect to reach a hiring decision?

Following Up

After the interview, follow up with a thank-you note to the interviewer. Not only is it a thoughtful gesture, it triggers the interviewer's memory about you and shows that you have a genuine interest in the job. Your thank-you note should be written in a business letter format and should highlight the key points in your interview.

During the interview process, remember that you will not appeal to everyone who interviews you. If your first experience doesn't work out, don't get discouraged. Keep trying.

SAMPLE THANK-YOU LETTER

After you've interviewed for a job, it's important to reiterate your interest in the position by sending a thank-you letter to those who interviewed you. Take a look at Michele's letter to the manager she interviewed with at NexAir. You can use this letter as a model when the time comes for you to write some thank-you letters.

July 17, 2005

Michele A. Thomas
3467 Main Street
Atlanta, Georgia 30308
Phone: 404-555-3423
E-mail: mthomas_987654321@yahoo.com

Mr. Charles E. Pence
Manager, Human Resources
NexAir Wireless
20201 East Sixth Street
Atlanta, Georgia 30372

Dear Mr. Pence:

It was a pleasure meeting with you Monday to discuss the sales opportunity at NexAir's downtown location. After learning more about the position, it is clear to me that with my background and enthusiasm, I would be an asset to your organization.

As we discussed, my experiences as a cashier at Winn-Dixie Supermarket and as a sales clerk at The Limited have provided me with the basic skills necessary to perform the responsibilities required of a sales representative at NexAir. I believe that with my ability to learn quickly and communicate effectively, I can help NexAir increase sales of its wireless products.

Thank you for the opportunity to interview with your organization. If there is any additional information I can provide about myself, please do not hesitate to call me. I look forward to hearing your decision soon.

Sincerely,

Michele A. Thomas

WHAT EMPLOYERS EXPECT FROM EMPLOYEES

As part of the National City Bank personnel team in Columbus, Ohio, Rose Graham works with Cooperative Business Education (CBE) coordinators in the area who are trying to place high school students in the workplace. When asked what skills she looks for in potential employees, she quickly replies that basic communication skills are at the top of her list. She stresses, "The ability to construct a sentence and put together words cannot be overemphasized." She cites knowledge of the personal computer, with good keyboarding skills, as essential.

In an article published in the *Nashville Business Journal*, Donna Cobble of Staffing Solutions outlined these basic skills for everyday life in the workplace:

Communication. Being a good communicator not only means having the ability to express oneself properly in the English language, but it also means being a good listener. If you feel inferior in any of these areas, it's a good idea to sign up for a public speaking class, read books on the subject, and borrow techniques from professional speakers.

Organization. Organization is the key to success in any occupation or facet of life. The ability to plan, prioritize, and complete a task in a timely fashion is a valuable skill. Check out Chapter 13 for tips on improving your time-management skills.

Problem solving. Companies are looking for creative problem solvers, people who aren't afraid to act on a situation and follow through with their decision. Experience and practice play a major role in your ability to determine the best solution. You can learn these techniques by talking with others about how they solve problems as well as observing others in the problem-solving process.

Sensitivity. In addition to being kind and courteous to their fellow workers, employees need to be sensitive to a coworker's perspective. That might mean putting yourself in the other person's shoes to gain a better understanding of that person's feelings. Employers look for individuals who are able to work on a team instead of those concerned only with their own personal gain.

Judgment. Although closely related to problem solving, good judgment shows up on many different levels in the workplace. It is the ability of a person to assess a situation, weigh the options, consider the risks, and make the necessary decision. Good judgment is built on experience and self-confidence.

Concentration. Concentration is the ability to focus on one thing at a time. Learning to tune out distractions and relate solely to the task at hand is a valuable asset for anyone.

Cooperation. Remember that you're being paid to do a job, so cooperate.

Honesty. Dishonesty shows up in many different ways, ranging from stealing time or property to divulging company secrets. Stay honest.

Initiative. Don't wait to be told exactly what to do. Show some initiative and look around to see what needs to be done next.

Willingness to learn. Be willing to learn how things are done at the company instead of doing things the way you want to do them.

Dependability. Arrive at work on time every day and meet your deadlines.

Enthusiasm. Although not every task you're assigned will be stimulating, show enthusiasm for your work at all times.

Acceptance of criticism. Constructive criticism is necessary for any employee to learn how things should be done. Employees who view criticism as a way to improve themselves will benefit from it.

Loyalty. There is no place for negativity in the workplace. You simply won't be happy working for an employer to whom you're not loyal.

Never fail to show pride in your work, the place where you work, and your appearance. By making these traits a part of your personality and daily performance, you will demonstrate that you are a cut above other employees with equal or better qualifications.

JUMPING ON THE SALARY FAST-TRACK

So the job offer comes, and it's time to talk about money. Unless you are an undiscovered genius, you most likely will start near the bottom of the salary scale if you're heading straight to the workplace after graduating from high school. There's not much room to negotiate a salary since you probably won't be able to say, "Well, I've done this, this, and this. I know what my experience is worth." You will find that most people hiring first-time employees will have a "take-it-or-leave-it" attitude about salary offers. However, according to Amryl Ward, a human resources consultant who has been hiring employees for more than twenty-five years in various human resource positions, there are some things that entry-level employees can do to make themselves more easily hired and, once hired, to get themselves on the fast-track toward more pay:

- **As you interview for the job, be prepared to tell a potential employer why you're worth hiring.** "Bring your skills to the table," says Ward. For instance, you might not think that the job you had during the summer at that big office supply store did anything more than earn you spending money. On the contrary, you learned valuable skills, such as how to be part of a team and how to deal with customers. What about that after-school office job you had? You learned how to answer the phones and how to work with certain software. Think carefully about the jobs you had in high school and what you learned from them. Those are called transferable skills.

- **Once you're hired, be willing to do more than just what the job requires.** Sure, you may be frying fries at the start. But if you come in early and stay late, if you pitch in to help another employee with his or her job, or if you voluntarily clean up the counters and sweep the floor, that says to management, "This employee is a winner. Let's keep him or her in mind the next time a promotion comes up." Soon, you might be managing a crew, then the store.

ON THE JOB

Once you snag that perfect job, there's no time to rest easy. You need to keep your manager happy and instill trust in your coworkers. And at the same time you're doing this, you'll want to watch out for yourself, keep yourself happy, and stay ahead of the learning curve. Here are some ways for you to do just that.

Minding Your Office Etiquette

Okay, so maybe you didn't know which was the salad fork at your cousin Sally's wedding reception. Most likely, though, you can name a few basic rules of etiquette, like not chewing with your mouth open at the dinner table. Now, what about when it comes to the manners you're supposed to have in the workplace? That usually draws a blank if you've never worked in an office setting. How would you know what's the right way to answer the phone or talk to your boss or customers?

Shannon McBride, of the Golden Crescent Tech-Prep Partnership in Victoria, Texas, has seen many students come through his program and land good jobs. He's also seen many of them succeed because they knew how to present themselves in a professional situation. Unfortunately, he can also relate stories of high school graduates who had no clue how to act in the workplace. They didn't realize that when they're working in an office with a group of people, they have to go out of their way to get along and follow the unwritten rules of that workplace. McBride says that means you'll have to size up how others are dressing and match what the office is geared to. For instance, if you work in a business office, most likely you'd wear slacks and a button-down shirt or a nice skirt and top. If you worked in a golf pro shop, you'd wear a golf shirt and shorts. "As much as you want to be an individual," says McBride, "you have to fit in when you're in a business setting. If you want an adult job, you have to act like an adult."

A lot of young people don't grasp how important office etiquette is and blow it off as just some silly rules imposed by adults. But McBride cautions that not following the norms of office etiquette can make or break a job. You can have all the technical talent and know all the latest software applications, but if you're not up on how people dress, talk, and conduct business, your job probably won't last very long. When it comes to getting a job, McBride warns, "First impressions are so important. Bad office etiquette can hurt that first impression." The best advice that we can give is that if you're not sure what the policy is about answering phones, using e-mail or the Internet on the job, or dress codes, ask your boss. He or she won't steer you wrong and will be pleased that you were concerned enough to ask.

Finding a Friendly Face at Work

There you are on the first day of a new job. Everyone looks like they know what they're doing while you stand there feeling really dumb. Even for the most seasoned employee, those first few weeks on the job are tough. Of course, everyone else looks like they know what they're doing because they've been doing it for quite some time. Wouldn't it be nice, though, if you had someone to help you adjust? Someone who would give you those little inside tips everyone else learns with experience. Someone to caution you about things that could go wrong or give you a heads-up when you're doing something that could lead to a reprimand. If you look around the office, you'll find such a person, says Robert Fait, Career Counselor and Instructional Specialist, who is associated with Career and Technology Education in the Katy Independent School district in Katy, Texas.

You might not realize that such a person is a mentor, but in the strict definition of the word, that's what he or she is. Or, as Fait puts it, "Mentors are role models who are willing to assist others with personal education and career goal setting and planning. This caring person shares a listening ear, a comforting shoulder, and an understanding heart." In other words, a mentor is someone who will make you feel comfortable in a new working environment, show you the procedures, and, in the end, help you become more productive.

Unless the company you're working for has a formal mentoring program, mentors don't come with huge signs around their necks that read, "Look here. I'm a mentor. Ask me anything." You have to look for them. Fait advises new employees to look closely at their coworkers and take notice of who demonstrates positive behavior, has strong work habits, and seems trustworthy. Those are the people to approach. "Such workers are usually willing to share their knowledge and insights with others," says Fait.

Who knows? Given some time, you could become a mentor yourself after you've been on the job for a while. Maybe you'll be able to help some new employee who looks kind of bewildered and in need of a friendly hand because you'll remember what it was like to be that new person.

13 chapter

SURVIVAL SKILLS

Whether you're headed to college or work, you're going to come face-to-face with some intimidating stuff after graduation.

Your LEVEL OF STRESS will most likely increase due to the demands of your classes or job and your exposure to alcohol or drugs. Various forms of conflict will arise, and you're going to have to keep up with your own health and nutrition. Seem daunting? It's really not if you keep a level head about you and stick to your core values. This chapter will help you work through the muddier side of life after high school.

SKILLS TO MAKE YOU STRESS-HARDY

Jump out of bed and into the shower. What to wear? Throw that on. Yuck—what's that stain? "Mom, where are my clean socks?" Tick, tock. No time to grab a bite if you want to make the homeroom bell. Skid around the corner and race for the classroom just as the final bell rings. Whoops, forgot your bio book. Sports, clubs, job, homework, friends on the Internet, and finally (sigh) sleep.

Sound like your life? If you're like most high school students, that description probably hits pretty close to home. So now we'll take your already hectic schedule and throw in the fact that you'll soon be graduating and have to figure out what to do with your life. Can you say "stress"?

Some people say that stress actually motivates them to perform better, but we won't talk about those perfect people. For most of you, stress means that you may snap at the dog, slam a few doors, get mad at your dad, and feel down. Maybe you'll even have physical symptoms—upset stomach, rapid heartbeat, sweaty palms, dizziness. The list goes on. Not a good place to be when you're dealing with a huge list of things to do, plus graduation staring you in the face.

How to handle stress has been written about countless times, but out of all the advice that's out there, a few simple pointers can really help you prevent the sweaty palms and nauseated feeling in the pit of your stomach.

- **French fries out, good food in.** Eat at least one hot, balanced meal a day. Healthy, as in veggies, fruits, meats, cheese, grains. Read further along in this chapter for more information about nutrition and health.

- **Sleep.** 7, 8, 10 hours a day. Easier said than done, but well worth it. Sleep will not only get you through high school but also your college and career lives, and it will help you stop feeling like such a frazzled bunch of nerve endings.

- **Hug your dog, cat, rabbit, friend, or mom.** Loneliness breeds stress because then all you've got is yourself and those stressed-out thoughts zooming around in your head.

- **Hang out with friends.** That takes time, but being with people you like and doing fun things eases stress—as long as you don't overdo it.

- **Exercise.** This does not include running down the hall to make the bell. We're talking 20 minutes of heart-pounding perspiration at least three times a week. It's amazing what a little sweat can do to relax you. Believe it or not, good posture helps too.

- **Don't smoke, drink, or use excessive amounts of caffeine.** Whoever told you that partying is the way to relieve stress got it all wrong. Nicotine and alcohol actually take away the things your body needs to fight stress.

- **Simplify your expenses.** Money can be a big stress factor. Think of ways to spend less so that the money you have doesn't have to be stretched so far. Be creative. Share resources. Sell items you no longer use. Maybe put off buying something you've been wanting.

- **Let your feelings out of your head.** It takes time and energy to keep them bottled up inside. Have regular conversations with your parents and siblings so that minor annoyances can be solved when they're still minor.

- **Organize your time.** As in prioritizing and dealing with one small part of your life instead of trying to solve everything in one shot. Read on for more information about time management.

- **Lighten up.** When you've graduated and are into whatever it is you'll end up doing, you'll look back and realize that this was a teensy little part of your life. So look on the bright side. The decisions you'll be making about your future are heavy, but they won't be cut in stone. You can change them if they don't work out.

Stress Busters

Most people get stressed when things are out of control—too many things to do, too many decisions to make, or too much information to digest. If you add not having enough time, enough money, or enough energy to get it all done, you have the perfect recipe for stress.

In the space below, identify what's causing you stress:

_____
_____
_____
_____
_____
_____

Then, choose from these three stress-busting options:

1. **Alter the situation.** Some things you can't control, some things you can. Change the ones you can. If you have too much on your plate and can't possibly do it all, push a few things aside. There's got to be something on the list you can get rid of. (And no, homework is not a choice.) Maybe you need to be able to say no to extra demands. Concentrate on what is important. Make a list of your priorities from the most important to the least, and work your way down.

2. **Avoid the situation—for now.** Step back and ask, "Is this really a problem? Do I really need to solve it now?" This doesn't mean you should procrastinate on things that need to get done. Think of this stress buster as buying some time, taking a break, catching your breath, getting advice, and airing out the situation so that you can deal with it when you're better prepared to handle it.

3. **Accept the situation.** How you perceive your circumstances has a lot to do with how you make decisions about them. Put whatever is stressing you in the perspective of the big picture. How will this really affect me next year or even ten years from now? Look at your circumstances through the lens of your personal values. Think about what feels right to you, not someone else.

Quick Fixes for Stressful Moments

So, you've done all the things we talked about and you're still feeling like you're being pulled in a million directions. If your stressometer has hit the top, use these quick fixes to help you calm down.

- Make the world slow down for a bit. Take a walk. Take a shower. Listen to some soothing music.

- Breathe deeply. Get in tune with the rhythm of your own breathing. Lie or sit down for 15 minutes and just concentrate on relaxing.

- Relax those little knots of tension. Start at your head and work down to your toes.

- Close your eyes and clear your mind. Oops, there comes that nagging thought. Out, out, out! Get rid of the clutter. Imagine yourself in your favorite place: the beach, under a tree, whatever works.

- Close the door to your bedroom, and let out a blood-curdling scream. Walt Whitman knew what he was talking about when he said, "I sound my barbaric yawp over the roofs of the world." Just let your family know what you're doing so they don't come running to your room in fear. You'll be amazed at how much better you feel.

- When all else fails, watch a funny movie. Read the comics. Get in a giggly frame of mind. Those big challenges will quickly be brought down to size.

WINNING THE TIME MANAGEMENT GAME

What is the value of time? Eight dollars an hour? The price of a scholarship because the application is a day late? Time can be a very expensive resource or something you can use to your advantage. Even if you recognize the value of time, managing it is a challenge.

When you live with enough time, life is relaxed and balanced. In order to find that balance, you have to prioritize and plan. Decide what you want and what is important to you. Organize logically and schedule realistically. Overcome obstacles. Change bad habits. Simplify and streamline. Save time when you can.

Sound impossible? It's not easy, but you can do it. The secret is held in a Chinese proverb: The wisdom of life is the elimination of nonessentials.

It's All About Control

The good thing about time is that much of it is yours to do with as you wish. You may feel out of control and as if you must run to keep up with the conflicting demands and expectations of your life. But we all have the same number of hours in each day. The key is in how we spend them. The following tips are designed to help you spend your time wisely and to keep you in control of your life.

Prepare a list of your goals and the tasks necessary to accomplish them. This could be by day, week, month, semester, or even year. You may also want to break the list into sections, such as friends and family, school, work, sports, health and fitness, home, personal development, and college preparation.

Prioritize based on time-sensitive deadlines. Use a grading system to code how important each task is. A is "Do It Now," B is "Do It Soon," C is "Do It Later." Understand the difference between "important" and "urgent."

Be realistic about how much you can really do. Analyze how you spend your time now. What can you cut? How much time do you truly need for each task?

Think ahead. How many times have you underestimated how long it will take to do something? Plan for roadblocks, and give yourself some breathing space.

Accept responsibility. Once you decide to do something, commit yourself to it. That doesn't mean that a task that was on the "A" list can't be moved to the "C" list. But be consistent and specific about what you want to accomplish.

Divide and conquer. You may need to form a committee, delegate tasks to your parents, or ask for help from a friend. That is why it is called time management.

Take advantage of your personal prime time. Don't schedule yourself to get up and do homework at 6 a.m.

if you are a night owl. It won't work. Instead, plan complex tasks when you are most efficient.

Avoid procrastination. There are a million ways to procrastinate. And not one of them is good if you really want to get something done. Have you ever noticed that you always find time to do the things you enjoy?

Do the most unpleasant task first. Get it over with. Then it will be all downhill from there.

Don't over-prepare. That is just another way to procrastinate.

Learn to say no to the demands on your time that you cannot afford.

Be enthusiastic, and share your goals with others.

If you work on too many goals at once, you will overwhelm yourself from the start. Remember, what is important is the quality of the time you spend on a task, not the quantity. It doesn't make any difference if you study for 10 hours if you don't recall a thing you've reviewed. The overall goal is to be productive, efficient, and effective, not just busy. You'll also need to pace yourself. All work and no play makes for an unbalanced person.

Use all the benefits of modern technology to help you manage time. You can save lots of time by using a fax, e-mail, or voice mail. If you don't already use a day planner or calendar, you would be wise to invest in one. Write in all the important deadlines, and refer to it often. Block out commitments you know you have so you won't over-schedule yourself. When you do over-schedule yourself or underestimate the time it takes to accomplish a task, learn from your mistakes. But don't get too down on yourself. Give yourself a pep talk every now and then to keep yourself positive and motivated.

MOVING OUT ON YOUR OWN?

As you consider moving away from home either to a college dorm or your own place, some pretty wonderful expectations of what it no doubt will be like will come floating into your head. No more parental rules. On your own. Making your own decisions. Hamburgers forever. Coming and going when you want to. Wait, what's this? Looks like you're out of clothes to wear. No more cereal bowls—they're all in the sink, and they're dirty. Out of milk and the refrigerator's empty. Yikes! What happened to all those warm, fuzzy thoughts about freedom?

Sure, it's nice to be able to come and go as you please, but before you get too far into that pleasant—and unrealistic—mind mode, here are some thoughts you might want to consider as you make plans to become independent. Ozzie Hashley, a guidance counselor at Clinton Community Schools in Clinton, Michigan, works with juniors and seniors in high school. Here is what he says to inform students about six realities of independent life.

1. **If you rent your own place, have you thought about the extra charges in addition to the rent?** Says Hashley, "Many students think only of paying the rent. They don't realize that they'll be responsible for utilities in many cases. Or the money it will take to wash and dry their clothes."

2. **Subsisting on hamburgers and fries sounds yummy, but as you watch a fast food diet eat its way into your paycheck, you'll most likely think about cooking up something yourself.** What will you cook? Who will buy the food? More importantly, who will do the dishes? Dividing up the responsibilities of preparing food is a big aspect of being on your own, especially when sharing a living space.

3. **Medical insurance may not be on your mind as you prepare to graduate—you're probably on your parents' insurance plans right now.** However, once you are established as independent at age 18 and you're living on your own, insurance becomes a big consideration. If you need health care and don't have medical insurance, the bills will be big. So when you get a job, make sure that you have medical coverage. If you're going off to college after high school, you'll most likely be **covered under your parents' insurance until age 23.**

4. **There's no one to tell you when to come home when you're on your own.** There's also no one to tell you that you're really disorganized when it comes to managing your time. Time management might not sound like a big deal now, but when you have to juggle all the facets of being independent—your job, taking care of your living space and car, your social life—then being able to manage time becomes an important part of life.

5. **Managing your money moves into a whole other realm when you are on your own.** You have to make sure you have enough to pay the rent, your car loan, and insurance, not to mention that movie you wanted to see, the CD you wanted to buy, or those jeans you saw at the mall last week. If you want to eat at the end of the month, budgeting will become an important part of your new independent vocabulary. Ask your parents or an adult you trust to help you set up your budget. Also learn how to balance your checkbook. It's a lot easier to manage your money when you keep track of how much you have in your bank account and how much you spend!

DRUGS AND ALCOHOL: ARE YOU AT RISK?

At risk? Wait a minute. How could you be at risk when the legal drinking age in all fifty states is 21? Chances are, if you're reading this, you're not 21 yet. It's also illegal to smoke or buy any tobacco product before age 18, and possession of any drug for recreational use is illegal, period. So if you drink alcohol before age 21; smoke or buy cigarettes, cigars, or chewing tobacco before age 18; or take any illegal drugs, you could:

- be arrested for driving under the influence (DUI);
- be convicted;
- be required to pay steep fines;
- have your driving privileges suspended;

- get kicked out of school (that's any kind of school, college included);
- get fired;
- go to jail; and/or
- have a criminal record.

A criminal record . . . so what?

Consider this true story. A 29-year-old man who recently received his graduate degree in business was offered a job with a major Fortune-100 corporation. We're talking big bucks, stock options, reserved parking space—the whole nine yards. When the company did a background check and found that he was arrested for a DUI during his freshman year of college, they rescinded their offer. The past can, and will, come back to haunt you. Let's not even think about what would happen down the line if you decide to run for public office.

Think about why you might want to try drinking or doing drugs. For fun? To forget your troubles? To be cool? Are your reasons good enough? Remember the consequences before you make a decision.

How Can I Say No Without Looking Like a Geek?

"It takes a lot more guts to stay sober, awake, and aware than to just get high, get numb, and learn nothing about life," says one former user. "Laugh at people who suggest you drink or take drugs, and then avoid them like the plague."

Friends worth having will respect your decision to say no. And girls—if a guy pressures you to drink or get high, ditch him pronto. You can vice-versa that for guys, too. According to the National Institute on Drug Abuse (NIDA), alcohol and club drugs like GHB or Rohypnol (roofies) make you an easy target for date rape.

The Nitty Gritty

Along with the temporary pleasure they may give you, all drugs (including club drugs, alcohol, and nicotine) have a downside. Alcohol, for example, is a

March 21 & 22, 2007
Counselor Locations

A107	Mrs. Enright
A113	Mr. Mepyans
E167	Ms. Schmeltzer
Library	Mr. Johnson
Library	Ms. Lucente
Library	Mr. Manola
A121	Mrs. Zelisko
A117	Ms. Pembroke

depressant. Even one drink slows down the part of your brain that controls your reasoning. So your judgment gets dull just when you're wondering, "Should I drive my friends home? Should I talk to this guy? Should I have another drink?"

Your body needs about an hour to burn up the alcohol in one drink (one shot of hard liquor, straight or mixed in a cocktail; one glass of wine; or one 12-ounce beer). Nothing, including coffee, will sober you up any faster.

Alcohol helps smart people make bad decisions. In fact, many drugs make you believe that you're thinking even more clearly than usual. Well, guess what? You aren't. Depending on what drug you take, how much, and what you do while you're on it, you're also risking confusion, nausea, headache, sleep problems, depression, paranoia, rape (especially "date rape"), unwanted pregnancy, sexually transmitted diseases (STDs) ranging from herpes to HIV/AIDS, having a baby with a birth defect, memory impairment, persistent psychosis, lung damage, cancer, injuring or killing someone else, and death.

Take a moment now, when your brain is razor sharp, to decide if those consequences are worth the escape you get for 20 minutes one night. You may be saying, "Oh, come on. Only addicts have problems like that." Getting drunk or high doesn't necessarily mean that you're an alcoholic or an addict—but it always means a loss of control.

"So much of addiction is about denial," says one member of Alcoholics Anonymous. "I just didn't think I looked or acted or thought or smelled or lied or cheated or failed like an alcoholic or addict. It was

DID YOU KNOW…

... **that nicotine is as addictive as cocaine and heroin, according to the American Cancer Society?**

... **that drinking a lot of alcohol fast can kill you on the spot, according to Keystone College?**

... **that MDMA (Ecstasy, X, Adam, Clarity, Lover's Speed), according to NIDA, may permanently damage your memory?**

DO I HAVE A PROBLEM?

Take the quiz below to see if you're in real trouble with drugs or alcohol.

1. **Do you look forward to drinking or using drugs?**

2. **Do most of your friends drink or do drugs?**

3. **Do you keep a secret supply of alcohol or drugs?**

4. **Can you drink a lot without appearing drunk?**

5. **Do you "power-hit" to get high faster, by binge-drinking, funneling, or slamming?**

6. **Do you ever drink or do drugs alone, including in a group where no one else is doing so?**

7. **Do you ever drink or use drugs when you hadn't planned to?**

8. **Do you ever have blackouts where you can't remember things that happened when you were drunk or high?**

If you answered yes to any of these questions, you probably need help. If you have a friend who fits the picture, find a respectful way to bring up your concerns. Don't be surprised if he or she tells you to back off—but don't give up, either. If someone in your family has an alcohol or drug problem, be aware that you may be prone to the same tendency.

Source: Keystone College, La Plume, Pennsylvania

when the drugs and alcohol use started to cause problems in multiple areas of my life that I began to think the problem might reside with me. Friends leaving—in disgust—was what opened my eyes."

Where Can I Get Help?

If you think you have a problem, or if you think a friend has a problem, try Alcoholics Anonymous or Narcotics Anonymous. If you're not sure, ask yourself the questions in "Do I Have a Problem?" on the top of this page.

Talk to any adult you trust: maybe your doctor, a clergy member, a counselor, or your parents. Health clinics and hospitals offer information and treatment. The American Cancer Society can help you quit smoking. These are only a few places to turn—check out the Yellow Pages and the Web for more.

Alcoholics Anonymous
212-870-3400
www.aa.org

American Cancer Society
800-ACS-2345
www.cancer.org

Narcotics Anonymous
818-773-9999
www.na.org

So, that's the straight stuff. You're at a tough but wonderful age, when your life is finally your own and your decisions really matter. Think about what you value most—and then make your choices.

CONFLICT: HOW TO AVOID IT OR DEFUSE IT

You're walking along and you see a group of kids up ahead . . . and suddenly you're afraid. Or you're about to talk to someone you have a disagreement with, and already you're tense. Or your boyfriend's jealousy is spooking you. What should you do?

All of these situations involve potential conflicts that could get out of hand. Even if you never get into a violent situation, you'll face conflicts with others, as we all do. Learning to spot the warning signs of violence and how to handle conflicts well will bring you lifelong benefits.

What's Your Style?

What do you do when you're faced with a potential conflict? Do you try to get away, no matter what? Do you find yourself bowing to pressure from others? Do you feel like you have to stand and fight, even if you don't want to? Do you wish you had some new ways to handle conflict?

Different situations call for different strategies. First, let's talk about situations where violence is a real possibility. Most of us get a bad feeling before things get violent, but too often, we ignore the feeling. Trust your gut feeling! And whether you're on the street or in school, Fred Barfoot of the Crime Prevention Association of Philadelphia suggests that you keep in mind these tips for avoiding violence:

- Walk like you're in charge and you know where you're going.

- Stick to lighted areas.

- Travel with a trusted friend when possible. On campus, get an escort from security at night. Loners are targets.

- If a person or group up ahead makes you nervous, cross the street immediately—and calmly—as if you'd intended to anyway.

- Call out to an imaginary friend, "Hey, Joe! Wait up!" and then run toward your "friend," away from whoever is scaring you.

- Go right up to the nearest house and ring the bell. Pretend you're expected: "Hey Joe, it's me!" You can explain later.

- If someone threatens you physically, scream.

- If someone assaults you, scream, kick where it hurts, scratch—anything.

- Don't ever get in a car with someone you don't know well or trust, even if you've seen that person around a lot.

- Strike up a conversation with an innocent bystander if you feel threatened by someone else, just to make yourself less vulnerable for a few minutes.

- Wear a whistle around your neck or carry a personal alarm or pepper spray.

- If someone mugs you, hand over your purse, wallet, jewelry—whatever he or she asks for. None of it is worth your life.

- Don't go along with something your gut says is wrong, no matter who says it's okay.

Remember that it's not a sign of weakness to back down if someone's egging you on to fight. Bill Tomasco, principal of Furness High School in Philadelphia, says that pressure from other kids to fight creates much of the violence in schools. If you're being pushed to fight, show true strength: Know that your opponent has a good side too, speak only to that good side, and don't give in to the pressure of the crowd.

Are You Safe at Home?

Locking doors and windows makes sense—but sometimes the danger lies within. A lot of violence occurs in abusive relationships, says Amy Gottlieb, a marriage family therapist intern at the California Family Counseling Center in Encino. To find out if you're at risk, ask yourself whether your partner, roommate, or family member:

- Uses jealousy to justify controlling you

- Puts you down, humiliates you, or pulls guilt trips on you

- Threatens to reveal your secrets or tells lies about you

- Makes all the decisions

- Frightens you, especially if it's on purpose

- Threatens you in any way

- Makes light of abusive behavior or says you provoked it

If any of these things are going on in your relationship, talk about it to an adult you trust, and ask for help.

Talking It Out

If your instincts tell you to get away from a situation, do it. But you can resolve many actual or potential conflicts face to face and gracefully so that everyone walks away feeling good. Read on for some tips on handling conflict from Kare Anderson, a communications expert in Sausalito, California.

Most of us make the mistake of reacting quickly, thinking only of our own needs, and not listening, says Anderson. Try doing the opposite. First and foremost, think about what you really want from the situation, and keep your goal in mind the whole time. But bring up the other person's concerns first. Then, discuss how the situation affects you both. Offer a solution that will benefit you both—and only then talk about how your solution addresses your own needs.

When the other person is talking, really listen—don't just come up with retorts in your head. Always show that you've heard the person before you give your response, especially if you're talking with someone of a different sex, size, or race. Those differences can distract us so much that we actually hear less. If you're female, you may need to s-l-o-w yourself down. Say less than you think you need to. Guys, don't shut down altogether—keep the communication going.

Even if the other person acts like a jerk, be gracious and respectful. Ask questions instead of criticizing. Let someone save face instead of looking like a fool. If you insult or embarrass someone, you may never have that person's full attention again. In short, treat the other person as you'd like to be treated.

What should you do if you're really angry? One teen said, "Thinking about things calms me down." Another said, "Once in a while, we have to cool off for a day and then come back to the discussion." Anger almost always covers up fear. What are you afraid of? Is the reward you want out of this negotiation bigger than your fear? Focus on that reward. Don't forget to breathe—long, slow breaths.

Think about these strategies often, so you'll be more likely to use them when a situation gets hot, instead of just reacting blindly. Use them to plan for negotiations ahead of time, too. Learning to resolve problems with people takes most of us a lifetime—get a jump on it now!

THE LOWDOWN ON SEXUAL HARASSMENT

Has someone ever looked at you, talked to you, or touched you in a way that gave you the creeps, made you self-conscious about your body, or created a sexual mood when it wasn't appropriate? And did you begin to dread seeing this person because he or she just wouldn't quit?

If so, you've encountered sexual harassment. Sexual harassment is inappropriate behavior that:

- is happening to you because of your sex,

- is unwanted (you don't like it),

- is objectively offensive (to a hypothetical "reasonable" man or woman),

- is either severe, persistent, or pervasive, and

- interferes with your work or school experience.

Paul Edison, a domestic and sexual violence prevention educator in Portland, Oregon, says that mostly—just as with crimes like rape—men harass women. But teenage girls are a bit more likely than older women to sexually harass someone, more girl-on-girl harassment goes on with teens, and guys get harassed, too. In some of the most brutal cases coming to light, gay men (or men perceived to be gay) are the targets.

People who sexually harass others fall into three camps, says Edison. Some just seem to be misguided and insensitive. Others get turned on by harassing someone. And a third group does it to intimidate—for example, to drive someone away from a job or just to make him or her feel bad about himself or herself.

So What Do I Do if Someone's Harassing Me?

Experts in self-defense say the best technique is to name the behavior that's bugging you and request that it stop. You might say, "Your hand is on my knee. Please remove it." If the person doesn't quit, you might try writing a letter spelling out what's bothering you and requesting that the person stop—this way, you've confronted the situation directly and you also have a record of your complaint.

But here's the good news, says Edison: You are not expected to handle harassment on your own, especially if the person harassing you is in a position of authority over you, such as a teacher, sergeant, or boss. The authorities at your school or your job should handle it—but they can't do that unless you tell them what's going on.

If you file a complaint, be prepared to describe what happened, when, and where. And make sure you report your concerns to someone who has clear authority to handle sexual harassment complaints, such as the principal or the personnel director.

Often, the person harassing you will stop as soon as he or she gets the clear message that the behavior isn't okay with you, especially if your complaint goes to someone higher up as well. Edison notes that most harassment cases don't end up involving lawyers and lawsuits. You may choose, in serious cases, to register your complaint with the Office of Civil Rights (if you're being harassed at school) or the Equal Employment Opportunity Commission (if you're being harassed at work). You can also file your complaint on different levels at the same time: for example, with your school and the police.

You have the legal right to a school and workplace free from discrimination based on your race, color, religion, sex, national origin, and—depending on where you live, as state and local laws vary—your sexual orientation. You have the right to protection from retaliation if you file a complaint of harassment. So don't be afraid to report a situation if it truly offends you and interferes with your life.

What if I'm Just Being Hypersensitive?

If someone's words or actions make you uncomfortable, that's all the reason you need to ask that person to stop the behavior, no matter how innocent the behavior may be. Trust your feelings—especially if you find you're trying to convince yourself that nothing is wrong.

What Will Happen to the Person Who Has Been Harassing Me?

If your complaint is successfully handled, says Edison, the main thing that will happen is that the person will stop harassing you. People aren't "charged" with sexual harassment unless their behavior includes criminal conduct. But your harasser may face disciplinary action, loss of privileges, suspension, expulsion, lawsuits, or criminal action, depending on the severity of his or her behavior.

How Can I Avoid Harassing Someone?

Sometimes the line between harmless flirting, joking, or complimenting and harassment is pretty thin. How can you stay on the right side of that line?

First, pay attention to your own motives. Be honest with yourself. Do you enjoy watching someone get uncomfortable when you say or do certain things? Do you feel angry with the person for some reason? Do you enjoy exercising your authority over this person in some way? Do you find yourself obsessing about the person? If any of these are true, whatever you're saying or doing probably isn't harmless.

Even if your motives seem harmless to you, be extraordinarily careful about whom and how you touch. You may be comfortable touching people casually—perhaps you'll touch someone's hand or shoulder in conversation—but remember that other people's boundaries may differ from yours.

Pay attention to the person's reactions to you. Are you getting clear green signals when you do or say things around this person, or does the person seem to shrink away from you? Does the person shut down or seem upset when you do or say certain things? If someone's told you clearly that she or he doesn't like it when you do or say certain things, apologize and stop at once. And remember, no means no.

So, if you're faced with something that feels like sexual harassment, remember to trust your feelings, convey them clearly, and get help promptly if you need it.

STAYING HEALTHY IN SPITE OF YOURSELF

When someone—like your mom—asks if you're eating right, do you ever want to say, "Hey, have you looked at my life lately? Do you see a lot of time there for eating right?" Well, how about exercise—are you getting enough? "Yeah, right. I bench-press my backpack when I'm not doing wind sprints to my next class," may be how you reply.

If you're feeling like you can't escape your stress and fatigue, you might be surprised by how much better you'll feel if you keep active and don't just eat junk. Your workload will seem easier. You'll sleep better. You'll look fantastic. And you can stay healthy—even if time and money are in short supply.

But Really, Who Has Time to Exercise?

As one teen says, "Schoolwork gets in the way, and then I want to relax when I have a moment that isn't filled with schoolwork." You can make time for anything, if you choose to. But if you aren't athletic by nature or school or work keeps you going nonstop, exercise is the first thing to go out the window.

However, you don't have to become a gym rat or run miles to get enough exercise. Longer workouts are great if you do them consistently, but you're better off getting little bits of regular exercise than just doing a huge workout every so often or never doing anything. And by "little bits," we mean 15- to 20-minute chunks. Add that to a fast walk to the bus, a frenzied private dance session in your room, or running up the stairs instead of taking the elevator, and you're exercising!

Regardless of how you choose to pump that muscle in the middle of your chest, the important thing is that you're doing something. You'll not only feel better about yourself, but you'll have increased energy to do other things, like study, go to work, or go out with friends.

What Does "Eating Right" Mean Anyway?

Eating right means eating a balance of good foods in moderate amounts. Your diet needn't be complicated or expensive. Dr. Michele Wilson, a specialist in adolescent medicine at the Children's Hospital of Philadelphia, notes that a teen's diet should be heavy in grains—especially whole grains—and light in sugars and fats. It should include a lot of fruits and vegetables and provide you with plenty of protein, calcium, vitamin A, B vitamins, iron, and zinc. Sound complicated?

Well, what's complicated about a bean burrito with cheese? How about pasta with vegetables, meat, or both in the sauce? A banana or some cantaloupe? Stir-fried vegetables with tofu? Carrot sticks with peanut butter? Yogurt? Cereal with milk and fruit? All of these are cheap, quick to make, and great for you.

One teen swears by microwaveable veggie burgers and adds, "Staying away from deep-fried anything is a good plan." Try to avoid things like chips and sweets, says Dr. Wilson, adding that if you're a vegetarian—and especially if you don't eat dairy products or fish—you should make sure you're getting enough protein and iron. And no matter what your diet, drink water—eight glasses a day.

As Long as I'm in Control of What I Eat, I'm Okay, Right?

That depends. Of course, having no control over what you eat is a problem. But "in control" can be good or bad. How severely do you control what and how you eat? Are you obsessed with getting thinner? Do people who love you tell you that you're too thin, and do you take that as a compliment? Do you ever binge secretly or make yourself throw up after a meal? If any of these are true, you may be suffering from anorexia or bulimia.

According to the National Association of Anorexia Nervosa and Associated Disorders (ANAD), eating disorders affect about 7 million women and 1 million men in this country and can lead to serious health problems—even death. "The thing that convinced me to get help was fear—I had to be hospitalized, as I was literally dying from my anorexia," says one woman. Most Americans who are anorexic or bulimic developed their eating disorders in their teens.

We asked some women being treated for eating disorders what they used to see when they looked in the mirror. "Total ugliness," said one. "The smallest dimple in my flesh looked immense," said another. And a third said, "I got rid of the mirrors because they would set me off to where I wouldn't eat for days." Their advice to teens struggling with an eating disorder? "Treat yourself as you wish your parents had treated you," "Ask people you feel close to not to discuss your weight with you," and "Find ways outside of yourself to feel in control." Above all—get help! That means going to someone you trust, whether it be a parent, relative, sibling, friend, doctor, or teacher. Or call ANAD's national hotline at 847-831-3438 for a listing of support groups and referrals in your area.

So if I Eat Right and Exercise, I'm Healthy?

Well, probably. But Dr. Wilson suggests that you keep a few other things in mind too. If you smoke, drink, or do drugs, you're asking for trouble. Aside from their many scarier side effects, all these habits can steal nutrients that you need. If all this sounds like the recipe for a dull and totally uncool life, remember that feeling and looking great are never boring and that vomiting (or dying) after downing the most tequilas in the fastest time looks really uncool. If you're making short-term decisions that will hurt you in the long run, take some time to figure out why. Good health is priceless—just ask any grandparent.

APPENDICES

NOW THAT YOU HAVE DECIDED what types of opportunities you wish to pursue after graduation, you need a jumping-off point for getting more information. The **Appendices** that follow will provide you with a sampling of additional data to help you with your decision-making process.

NOTE: Because of Thomson Peterson's comprehensive editorial review and because all material comes directly from institution or organization officials, we believe that the information presented in these **Appendices** is accurate. Nonetheless, errors and omissions are possible in a data collection and processing endeavor of this scope. You should check with the specific institution or organization at the time of application to verify pertinent data that may have changed since the publication of this book.

MIDWESTERN STATES

HIGH SCHOOL DIPLOMA TEST REQUIREMENTS

Illinois

Illinois currently does not require high school students to pass a proficiency test in order to receive a high school diploma.

Indiana

Students in grades 3, 6, 8, and 10 are required to take ISTEP+, Indiana's state achievement test. ISTEP+ is a criterion-referenced test, which measures a student's obtained knowledge. These tests are cumulative and are directly linked to the Indiana Academic Standards. For example, the grade 10 test measures what students have learned from kindergarten through the ninth grade.

The grade 10 test is also known as the Graduation Qualifying Examination (GQE). All Indiana students who wish to obtain a state-recognized diploma must take the GQE and receive passing scores in English/language arts and mathematics or meet all waiver requirements. In addition, there is an optional norm-referenced component. School corporations have the option of choosing if they wish to give the norm-referenced portion of the test; however, this decision must be made by the superintendent and be implemented on a corporation-wide basis. This norm-referenced test has no bearing on whether or not a student passes ISTEP+ and subsequently receives a diploma. For more information, call the Indiana Department of Education, Division of Assessment at 317-232-9050 or go to their Web site at www.doe.state.in.us.

Iowa

Iowa currently does not require high school students to pass a proficiency test in order to receive a high school diploma.

Kansas

Kansas currently does not require school students to pass a proficiency test in order to receive a high school diploma.

Michigan

Michigan currently does not require high school students to pass a proficiency test in order to receive a high school diploma.

Minnesota

Minnesota's Graduation Standards have two components: the Basic Standards and the High Standards. The Basic Standards are a "safety net" to make sure that no student graduates without learning the basic skills needed to live and work in today's society. Students must pass tests in reading, mathematics, and writing to show they meet the Basic Standards and in order to be eligible to graduate from a public high school. The reading and mathematics exam is first given in the eighth grade, and the written composition exam is first given in the tenth grade. Students must pass to graduate from a public high school in Minnesota.

The High Standards define what Minnesota students should know, understand, and be able to do to demonstrate an advanced level of learning. The High Standards are organized into ten learning areas: reading, listening, and viewing; writing and speaking; arts and literature; mathematical applications; inquiry (research skills); scientific applications; people and cultures (social studies); decision making; resource management; and world languages. Public high school students from the class of 2002 and beyond must complete 24 of 48 possible standards from the ten learning areas, unless the district's staff and school board agree to reduce the number. Some standards are required for all students, while in some learning areas students may choose the standards they wish to complete. For more information, visit the Web site at www.cfl.state.mn.us.

Missouri

Missouri currently does not require high school students to pass a proficiency test in order to receive a high school diploma. However, individual school districts may or may not require one.

Nebraska

Nebraska currently does not require high school students to pass a proficiency test in order to receive a high school diploma.

North Dakota

North Dakota currently does not require high school students to pass a proficiency test in order to receive a high school diploma. However, all 12th grade students will participate in the North Dakota 12th Grade Assessment as required by state law. This achievement test is designed to access all 12th grade students in their knowledge and skills in reading and mathematics.

Ohio

Any student graduating from a public or chartered nonpublic high school after September 15, 2000, and before September 15, 2006, must pass writing, reading, mathematics, citizenship, and science tests and meet local curriculum requirements in order to receive a diploma. Students graduating after September 15, 2006, will need to pass the new Ohio Graduation Tests (OGT) and meet curriculum requirements in order to receive a diploma. For more information, visit the Ohio Department of Education Web site at www.ode.state. oh.us or call 877-644-6338.

Oklahoma

Oklahoma currently does not require high school students to pass a proficiency test in order to receive a high school diploma.

South Dakota

South Dakota currently does not require high school students to pass a proficiency test in order to receive a high school diploma.

Wisconsin

A state-developed high school graduation test (HSGT) was first administered in 2002. The use of the HSGT as a criterion for graduation applies to the class of 2004. Students who plan to graduate at the end of the 2003–2004 school year are the first class affected. Other criteria will include pupil academic performance and teacher recommendations. The test will cover the four academic content areas of English language arts, mathematics, science, and social studies. For more information, call 608-267-3164 or visit www.dpi.state. wi.us/dpi/oea/hsgtdelay.html.

FOUR-YEAR COLLEGES AND UNIVERSITIES

Illinois

American Academy of Art
332 South Michigan Ave,
Ste. 300
Chicago, IL 60604-4302
312-461-0600
www.aaart.edu/

American InterContinental
University Online
5550 Prairie Stone Pkwy.,
Ste. 400
Hoffman Estates, IL 60192
877-701-3800
www.aiuonline.edu/

Argosy University/Chicago
20 South Clark St., Ste. 300
Chicago, IL 60603
312-201-0200
www.argosyu.edu/

Argosy
University/Schaumburg
1000 North Plaza Dr.,
Ste. 100
Schaumburg, IL 60173
866-290-2777
www.argosyu.edu/

Augustana College
639 38th St.
Rock Island, IL 61201-2296
800-798-8100
www.augustana.edu/

Aurora University
347 South Gladstone Ave.
Aurora, IL 60506-4892
800-742-5281
www.aurora.edu/

Benedictine University
5700 College Rd.
Lisle, IL 60532-0900
888-829-6363
www.ben.edu/

Blackburn College
700 College Ave.
Carlinville, IL 62626-1498
800-233-3550
www.blackburn.edu/

Blessing-Rieman College of
Nursing
Broadway at 11th St.,
POB 7005
Quincy, IL 62305-7005
800-877-9140
www.brcn.edu/

Bradley University
1501 West Bradley Ave.
Peoria, IL 61625-0002
800-447-6460
www.bradley.edu/

Chicago State University
9501 South King Dr.
Chicago, IL 60628
773-995-2000
www.csu.edu/

Christian Life College
400 East Gregory St.
Mount Prospect, IL 60056
847-259-1840
www.christianlifecollege.edu/

Columbia College Chicago
600 South Michigan Ave.
Chicago, IL 60605-1996
312-663-1600
www.colum.edu/

Concordia University
7400 Augusta St.
River Forest, IL 60305-1499
800-285-2668
www.curf.edu/

DePaul University
1 East Jackson Blvd.
Chicago, IL 60604-2287
312-362-8000
www.depaul.edu/

DeVry University
One Tower Ln.
Oakbrook Terrace, IL 60181
630-574-1960
www.devry.edu/

DeVry University
18624 West Creek Dr.
Tinley Park, IL 60477
877-305-8184
www.devry.edu/

DeVry University
1221 North Swift Rd.
Addison, IL 60101-6106
800-346-5420
www.devry.edu/

DeVry University
3300 North Campbell Ave.
Chicago, IL 60618-5994
800-383-3879
www.devry.edu/

DeVry University
2056 Westings Ave., Ste. 40
Naperville, IL 60563-2361
630-428-9086
www.devry.edu/

DeVry University
1075 Tri-State Pkwy., Ste. 800
Gurnee, IL 60031-9126
866-563-3879
www.devry.edu/

DeVry University
385 Airport Rd.
Elgin, IL 60123-9341
847-622-1135
www.devry.edu/

Dominican University
7900 West Division St.
River Forest, IL 60305-1099
800-828-8475
www.dom.edu/

Eastern Illinois University
600 Lincoln Ave.
Charleston, IL 61920-3099
800-252-5711
www.eiu.edu/

East-West University
816 South Michigan Ave.
Chicago, IL 60605-2103
312-939-0111
www.eastwest.edu/

Elmhurst College
190 Prospect Ave.
Elmhurst, IL 60126-3296
800-697-1871
www.elmhurst.edu/

Eureka College
300 East College Ave.
Eureka, IL 61530-1500
888-4-EUREKA
www.eureka.edu/

Governors State University
One University Pkwy.
University Park, IL 60466-
0975
708-534-5000
www.govst.edu/

Greenville College
315 East College, PO Box 159
Greenville, IL 62246-0159
800-345-4440
www.greenville.edu/

Harrington College of Design
200 West Madison St.
Chicago, IL 60606
877-939-4975
www.interiordesign.edu/

Hebrew Theological College
7135 North Carpenter Rd.
Skokie, IL 60077-3263
847-982-2500
www.htcnet.edu/

Illinois College
1101 West College Ave.
Jacksonville, IL 62650-2299
866-464-5265
www.ic.edu/

The Illinois Institute of Art-
Chicago
350 North Orleans
Chicago, IL 60654
800-351-3450
www.ilic.artinstitutes.edu/

The Illinois Institute of Art-
Schaumburg
1000 Plaza Dr.
Schaumburg, IL 60173
800-314-3450
www.ilis.artinstitutes.edu/

Illinois Institute of Technology
3300 South Federal St.
Chicago, IL 60616-3793
800-448-2329
www.iit.edu/

Illinois State University
Normal, IL 61790-2200
309-438-2111
www.ilstu.edu/

Illinois Wesleyan University
PO Box 2900
Bloomington, IL 61702-2900
800-332-2498
www.iwu.edu/

International Academy of
Design & Technology
One North State St., Ste. 400
Chicago, IL 60602-9736
877-ACADEMY
www.iadtchicago.edu/

Judson College
1151 North State St.
Elgin, IL 60123-1498
800-879-5376
www.judsoncollege.edu/

Kendall College
900 North Branch St.
Chicago, IL 60622
877-588-8860
www.kendall.edu/

Knox College
2 East South St.
Galesburg, IL 61401
800-678-KNOX
www.knox.edu/

Lake Forest College
555 North Sheridan Rd.
Lake Forest, IL 60045-2399
800-828-4751
www.lakeforest.edu/

Lakeview College of Nursing
903 North Logan Ave.
Danville, IL 61832
217-443-5238
www.lakeviewcol.edu/

Lewis University
One University Pkwy.
Romeoville, IL 60446
800-897-9000
www.lewisu.edu/

Lexington College
310 South Peoria St., Ste. 512
Chicago, IL 60607-3534
312-226-6294
www.lexingtoncollege.edu/
general-education.htm

Lincoln Christian College
100 Campus View Dr.
Lincoln, IL 62656-2167
888-522-5228
www.lccs.edu/

Loyola University Chicago
820 North Michigan Ave.
Chicago, IL 60611-2196
800-262-2373
www.luc.edu/

MacMurray College
447 East College Ave.
Jacksonville, IL 62650
217-479-7000
www.mac.edu/

McKendree College
701 College Rd.
Lebanon, IL 62254-1299
800-232-7228
www.mckendree.edu/

Midstate College
411 West Northmoor Rd.
Peoria, IL 61614
309-692-4092
www.midstate.edu/

Millikin University
1184 West Main St.
Decatur, IL 62522-2084
800-373-7733
www.millikin.edu/

Monmouth College
700 East Broadway
Monmouth, IL 61462-1998
800-747-2687
www.monm.edu/

Moody Bible Institute
820 North LaSalle Blvd.
Chicago, IL 60610-3284
800-967-4MBI
www.moody.edu/

NAES College
2838 West Peterson Ave.
Chicago, IL 60659-3813
773-761-5000
www.naes.edu/

National-Louis University
122 South Michigan Ave.
Chicago, IL 60603
800-443-5522
www.nl.edu/

North Central College
30 North Brainard St.,
PO Box 3063
Naperville, IL 60566-7063
800-411-1861
www.noctrl.edu/

North Park University
3225 West Foster Ave.
Chicago, IL 60625-4895
800-888-NPC8
www.northpark.edu/

Northeastern Illinois
University
5500 North St Louis Ave.
Chicago, IL 60625-4699
773-583-4050
www.neiu.edu/

Northern Illinois University
De Kalb, IL 60115-2854
815-753-1000
www.niu.edu/

Northwestern University
Evanston, IL 60208
847-491-3741
www.northwestern.edu/

Olivet Nazarene University
One University Ave.
Bourbonnais, IL 60914-2271
800-648-1463
www.olivet.edu/

Principia College
One Maybeck Place
Elsah, IL 62028-9799
800-277-4648 Ext. 2802
www.prin.edu/college/

Quincy University
1800 College Ave.
Quincy, IL 62301-2699
800-688-4295
www.quincy.edu/

Robert Morris College
401 South State St.
Chicago, IL 60605
800-RMC-5960
www.robertmorris.edu/

Rockford College
5050 East State St.
Rockford, IL 61108-2393
800-892-2984
www.rockford.edu/

Roosevelt University
430 South Michigan Ave.
Chicago, IL 60605-1394
877-APPLYRU
www.roosevelt.edu/

Rush University
600 South Paulina
Chicago, IL 60612-3832
312-942-5000
www.rushu.rush.edu/

Saint Anthony College of
Nursing
5658 East State St.
Rockford, IL 61108-2468
815-395-5091
www.sacn.edu/

St. Augustine College
1333-1345 West Argyle
Chicago, IL 60640-3501
773-878-8756
www.staugustinecollege.edu/

Saint Francis Medical Center
College of Nursing
511 NE Greenleaf St.
Peoria, IL 61603-3783
309-655-2596
www.sfmccon.edu/

St. John's College
421 North Ninth St.
Springfield, IL 62702-5317
217-525-5628
www.st-johns.org/education/
schools/nursing/

Saint Xavier University
3700 West 103rd St.
Chicago, IL 60655-3105
800-462-9288
www.sxu.edu/

School of the Art Institute of
Chicago
37 South Wabash
Chicago, IL 60603-3103
800-232-SAIC
www.artic.edu/saic/

Shimer College
PO Box 500
Waukegan, IL 60079-0500
800-215-7173
www.shimer.edu/

Southern Illinois University
Carbondale
Carbondale, IL 62901-4701
618-453-2121
www.siu.edu/siuc/

Southern Illinois University
Edwardsville
Edwardsville, IL 62026-0001
800-447-SIUE
www.siue.edu/

Telshe Yeshiva-Chicago
3535 West Foster Ave.
Chicago, IL 60625-5598
773-463-7738

Trinity Christian College
6601 West College Dr.
Palos Heights, IL 60463-0929
800-748-0085
www.trnty.edu/

Trinity College of Nursing
and Health Sciences
2122-25th Ave.
Rock Island, IL 91201
309-779-7700
www.trinitycollegeqc.edu/

Trinity International
University
2065 Half Day Rd.
Deerfield, IL 60015-1284
800-822-3225
www.tiu.edu/

University of Chicago
5801 Ellis Ave.
Chicago, IL 60637-1513
773-702-1234
www.uchicago.edu/

University of Illinois at Chicago
601 South Morgan St.
Chicago, IL 60607-7128
312-996-7000
www.uic.edu/

University of Illinois at Springfield
One University Plaza
Springfield, IL 62703-5407
888-977-4847
www.uis.edu/

University of Illinois at Urbana-Champaign
601 East John St.
Champaign, IL 61820
217-333-1000
www.uiuc.edu/

University of Phoenix-Chicago Campus
1500 McConner Pkwy.,
Ste. 700
Schaumburg, IL 60173-4399
800-228-7240
www.phoenix.edu/

University of St. Francis
500 Wilcox St.
Joliet, IL 60435-6169
800-735-3500
www.stfrancis.edu/

VanderCook College of Music
3140 South Federal St.
Chicago, IL 60616-3731
800-448-2655
www.vandercook.edu/

West Suburban College of Nursing
3 Erie Ct.
Oak Park, IL 60302
708-763-6530
www.wscn.edu/

Western Illinois University
1 University Cr.
Macomb, IL 61455-1390
877-742-5948
www.wiu.edu/

Wheaton College
501 East College Ave.
Wheaton, IL 60187-5593
800-222-2419
www.wheaton.edu/

Indiana

Anderson University
1100 East Fifth St.
Anderson, IN 46012-3495
800-428-6414
www.anderson.edu/

Ball State University
2000 University Ave.
Muncie, IN 47306-1099
800-482-4BSU
www.bsu.edu/

Bethel College
1001 West McKinley Ave.
Mishawaka, IN 46545-5591
800-422-4101
www.bethelcollege.edu

Butler University
4600 Sunset Ave.
Indianapolis, IN 46208 3485
888-940-8100
www.butler.edu/

Calumet College of Saint Joseph
2400 New York Ave.
Whiting, IN 46394-2195
877-700-9100
www.ccsj.edu/

Crossroads Bible College
601 North Shortridge Rd.
Indianapolis, IN 46219
800-273-2224
www.crossRd.s.edu/

DePauw University
313 South Locust St.
Greencastle, IN 46135-0037
800-447-2495
www.depauw.edu/

DeVry University
Twin Towers,
1000 East 80th Place,
Ste. 222 Mall
Merrillville, IN 46410-5673
219-736-7440
www.devry.edu/

DeVry University
9100 Keystone Crossing,
Ste. 350
Indianapolis, IN 46240-2158
317-581-8854
www.devry.edu/

Earlham College
801 National Rd. West
Richmond, IN 47374-4095
800-327-5426
www.earlham.edu/

Franklin College
101 Branigin Blvd.
Franklin, IN 46131-2623
800-852-0232
www.franklincollege.edu/

Goshen College
1700 South Main St.
Goshen, IN 46526-4794
800-348-7422
www.goshen.edu/

Grace College
200 Seminary Dr.
Winona Lake, IN 46590-1294
800-54 GRACE
www.grace.edu/

Hanover College
PO Box 108
Hanover, IN 47243-0108
800-213-2178
www.hanover.edu/

Huntington University
2303 College Ave.
Huntington, IN 46750-1299
800-642-6493
www.huntington.edu/

Indiana Institute of Technology
1600 East Washington Blvd.
Fort Wayne, IN 46803-1297
888-666-TECH
www.indianatech.edu

Indiana State University
210 North Seventh St.
Terre Haute, IN 47809-1401
800-742-0891
web.indstate.edu/

Indiana University Bloomington
107 S. Indiana Ave.
Bloomington, IN 47405-7000
812-855-4848
www.iub.edu/

Indiana University East
2325 Chester Blvd.
Richmond, IN 47374-1289
800-959-EAST
www.iu.edu/

Indiana University Kokomo
PO Box 9003
Kokomo, IN 46904-9003
888-875-4485
www.iuk.edu/

Indiana University Northwest
3400 Broadway
Gary, IN 46408-1197
800-968-7486
www.iun.edu/

Indiana University South Bend
1700 Mishawaka Ave.,
PO Box 7111
South Bend, IN 46634-7111
877-GO-2-IUSB
www.iusb.edu/

Indiana University Southeast
4201 Grant Line Rd.
New Albany, IN 47150-6405
812-941-2000
www.ius.edu/

Indiana University-Purdue University Fort Wayne
2101 East Coliseum Blvd.
Fort Wayne, IN 46805 1499
260-481-6100
www.ipfw.edu/

Indiana University-Purdue University Indianapolis
355 North Lansing
Indianapolis, IN 46202-2896
317-274-5555
www.Iupul.edu/

Indiana Wesleyan University
4201 South Washington St.
Marion, IN 46953-4974
800-332-6901
www.indwes.edu/

Manchester College
604 East College Ave.
North Manchester, IN 46962-1225
800-852-3648
www.manchester.edu/

Marian College
3200 Cold Spring Rd.
Indianapolis, IN 46222-1997
317-955-6000
www.marian.edu/

Martin University
2171 Avondale Place,
PO Box 18567
Indianapolis, IN 46218-3867
317-543-3235
www.martin.edu/

Oakland City University
138 North Lucretia St.
Oakland City, IN 47660-1099
800-737-5125
www.oak.edu/

Purdue University
West Lafayette, IN 47907
765-494-4600
www.purdue.edu/

Purdue University Calumet
2200 169th St.
Hammond, IN 46323-2094
219-989-2400
www.calumet.purdue.edu/

Purdue University North
Central
1401 South US Hwy. 421
Westville, IN 46391-9542
219-785-5200
www.pnc.edu/

Rose-Hulman Institute of
Technology
5500 Wabash Ave.
Terre Haute, IN 47803-3999
800-248-7448
www.rose-hulman.edu/

Saint Joseph's College
U.S. Hwy. 231, PO Box 890
Rensselaer, IN 47978
800-447-8781
www.saintjoe.edu/

Saint Mary-of-the-Woods
College
Saint Mary-of-the-Woods, IN
47876
800-926-SMWC
www.smwc.edu/

Saint Mary's College
Notre Dame, IN 46556
800-551-7621
www.saintmarys.edu/

Taylor University
236 West Reade Ave.
Upland, IN 46989-1001
800-882-3456
www.taylor.edu/

Taylor University Fort Wayne
1025 West Rudisill Blvd.
Fort Wayne, IN 46807-2197
800-233-3922
www.tayloru.edu/

Tri-State University
1 University Ave.
Angola, IN 46703-1764
800-347-4TSU
www.tristate.edu/

University of Evansville
1800 Lincoln Ave.
Evansville, IN 47722
800-423-8633
www.evansville.edu/

University of Indianapolis
1400 East Hanna Ave.
Indianapolis, IN 46227-3697
800-232-8634
www.uindy.edu/

University of Notre Dame
Notre Dame, IN 46556
574-631-5000
www.nd.edu/

University of Phoenix-
Indianapolis Campus
7999 Knue Rd. Dr., Ste. 150
Indianapolis, IN 46250
800-228-7240
www.phoenix.edu/

University of Saint Francis
2701 Spring St.
Fort Wayne, IN 46808-3994
800-729-4732
www.sf.edu/

University of Southern
Indiana
8600 University Blvd.
Evansville, IN 47712-3590
800-467-1965
www.usi.edu/

Valparaiso University
1700 Chapel Dr.
Valparaiso, IN 46383
888-GO-VALPO
www.valpo.edu/

Wabash College
PO Box 352
Crawfordsville, IN 47933-
0352
800-345-5385
www.wabash.edu/

Iowa

Allen College
1825 Logan Ave.
Waterloo, IA 50703
319-226-2000
www.allencollege.edu/

Briar Cliff University
3303 Rebecca St.
Sioux City, IA 51104-0100
800-662-3303
www.briarcliff.edu/

Buena Vista University
610 West Fourth St.
Storm Lake, IA 50588
800-383-9600
www.bvu.edu/

Central College
812 University St.
Pella, IA 50219-1999
877-462-3689
www.central.edu/

Clarke College
1550 Clarke Dr.
Dubuque, IA 52001-3198
800-383-2345
www.clarke.edu/

Coe College
1220 1st Ave., NE
Cedar Rapids, IA 52402-5092
877-225-5263
www.coe.edu/

Cornell College
600 First St. West
Mount Vernon, IA 52314-1098
800-747-1112
www.cornellcollege.edu/

Divine Word College
102 Jacoby Dr. SW
Epworth, IA 52045-0380
800-553-3321
www.dwci.edu/

Dordt College
498 4th Ave., NE
Sioux Center, IA 51250-1697
800-343-6738
www.dordt.edu/

Drake University
2507 University Ave.
Des Moines, IA 50311-4516
800-44DRAKE
www.drake.edu/

Emmaus Bible College
2570 Asbury Rd.
Dubuque, IA 52001-3097
800-397-2425
www.emmaus.edu/

Faith Baptist Bible College
and Theological Seminary
1900 Northwest 4th St.
Ankeny, IA 50021-2152
888-FAITH 4U
www.faith.edu/

The Franciscan University of
the Prairies
400 North Bluff Blvd.,
PO Box 2967
Clinton, IA 52733-2967
800-242-4153
www.tfu.edu/

Graceland University
1 University Place
Lamoni, IA 50140
866-GRACELAND
www.graceland.edu/

Grand View College
1200 Grandview Ave.
Des Moines, IA 50316-1599
800-444-6083
www.gvc.edu/

Grinnell College
1121 Park St.
Grinnell, IA 50112-1690
800-247-0113
www.grinnell.edu/

Hamilton Technical College
1011 East 53rd St.
Davenport, IA 52807-2653
319-386-3570
www.hamiltontechcollege.com/

Iowa State University of
Science and Technology
Ames, IA 50011
800-262-3810
www.iastate.edu/

Iowa Wesleyan College
601 North Main St.
Mount Pleasant, IA 52641-
1398
800-582-2383
www.iwc.edu/

Loras College
1450 Alta Vista
Dubuque, IA 52004-0178
800-245-6727
www.loras.edu/

Luther College
700 College Dr.
Decorah, IA 52101-1045
800-458-8437
www.luther.edu/

Maharishi University of
Management
1000 North 4th St.
Fairfield, IA 52557
800-369-6480
www.mum.edu/

Mercy College of Health
Sciences
928 Sixth Ave.
Des Moines, IA 50309-1239
800-637-2994
www.mchs.edu/

Morningside College
1501 Morningside Ave.
Sioux City, IA 51106-1751
800-831-0806
www.morningside.edu/

Mount Mercy College
1330 Elmhurst Dr., NE
Cedar Rapids, IA 52402-4797
800-248-4504
www.mtmercy.edu/

Northwestern College
101 Seventh St., SW
Orange City, IA 51041-1996
800-747-4757
www.nwciowa.edu/

Palmer College of
Chiropractic
1000 Brady St.
Davenport, IA 52803-5287
800-722-3648
www.palmer.edu/

Simpson College
701 North C St.
Indianola, IA 50125-1297
800-362-2454
www.simpson.edu/

St. Ambrose University
518 West Locust St.
Davenport, IA 52803-2898
800-383-2627
www.sau.edu/

University of Dubuque
2000 University Ave.
Dubuque, IA 52001-5099
563-589-3000
www.dbq.edu/

The University of Iowa
Iowa City, IA 52242-1316
800-553-4692
www.uiowa.edu/

University of Northern Iowa
1227 West 27th St.
Cedar Falls, IA 50614
800-772-2037
www.uni.edu/

Upper Iowa University
605 Washington St., Box
1857
Fayette, IA 52142-1857
800-553-4150
www.uiu.edu/

Vennard College
PO Box 29
University Park, IA 52595
800-686-8391
www.vennard.edu/

Waldorf College
106 South 6th St.
Forest City, IA 50436-1713
800-292-1903
www.waldorf.edu/

Wartburg College
100 Wartburg Blvd.,
PO Box 1003
Waverly, IA 50677-0903
800-772-2085
www.wartburg.edu/

William Penn University
201 Trueblood Ave.
Oskaloosa, IA 52577-1799
800-779-7366
www.wmpenn.edu/

Kansas

Baker University
Box 65
Baldwin City, KS 66006-0065
800-873-4282
www.bakeru.edu/

Barclay College
607 North Kingman
Haviland, KS 67059-0288
800-862-0226
www.barclaycollege.edu/

Benedictine College
1020 North 2nd St.
Atchison, KS 66002-1499
800-467-5340
www.benedictine.edu/

Bethany College
421 North First St.
Lindsborg, KS 67456-1897
800-826-2281
www.bethanylb.edu/

Bethel College
300 East 27th St.
North Newton, KS 67117
800-522-1887
www.bethelks.edu/

Central Christian College of
Kansas
1200 South Main, PO Box
1403
McPherson, KS 67460-5799
800-835-0078
www.centralchristian.edu/

Emporia State University
1200 Commercial St.
Emporia, KS 66801-5087
877-468-6378
www.emporia.edu/

Fort Hays State University
600 Park St.
Hays, KS 67601-4099
800-628-FHSU
www.fhsu.edu/

Friends University
2100 West University St.
Wichita, KS 67213
800-577-2233
www.friends.edu/

Haskell Indian Nations
University
155 Indian Ave., #5031
Lawrence, KS 66046-4800
785-749-8404
www.haskell.edu/

Kansas State University
Manhattan, KS 66506
785-532-6011
www.ksu.edu/

Kansas Wesleyan University
100 East Claflin Ave.
Salina, KS 67401-6196
800-874-1154
www.kwu.edu/

Manhattan Christian College
1415 Anderson Ave.
Manhattan, KS 66502-4081
877-246-4622
www.mccks.edu/

McPherson College
1600 East Euclid,
PO Box 1402
McPherson, KS 67460-1402
800-365-7402
www.mcpherson.edu/

MidAmerica Nazarene
University
2030 East College Way
Olathe, KS 66062-1899
800-800-8887
www.mnu.edu/

Newman University
3100 McCormick Ave.
Wichita, KS 67213-2097
877-NEWMANU
www.newmanu.edu/

Ottawa University
1001 South Cedar
Ottawa, KS 66067-3399
800-755-5200
www.ottawa.edu/

Pittsburg State University
1701 South Broadway
Pittsburg, KS 66762
800-854-7488
www.pittstate.edu/

Southwestern College
100 College St.
Winfield, KS 67156-2499
800-846-1543
www.sckans.edu/

Sterling College
PO Box 98
Sterling, KS 67579-0098
800-346-1017
www.sterling.edu/

Tabor College
400 South Jefferson
Hillsboro, KS 67063
800-822-6799
www.tabor.edu/

University of Kansas
Lawrence, KS 66045
785-864-2700
www.ku.edu

University of Phoenix-
Wichita Campus
3020 North Cypress Dr.,
Ste. 150
Wichita, KS 67226
800-228-7240
www.phoenix.edu/

University of Saint Mary
4100 South Fourth St.
Leavenworth, KS 66048-5082
800-752-7043
www.stmary.edu/

Washburn University
1700 SW College Ave.
Topeka, KS 66621
785-231-1010
www.washburn.edu/

Wichita State University
1845 North Fairmount
Wichita, KS 67260
800-362-2594
www.wichita.edu/

Michigan

Adrian College
110 South Madison St.
Adrian, MI 49221-2575
800-877-2246
www.adrian.edu/

Albion College
611 East Porter St.
Albion, MI 49224-1831
800-858-6770
www.albion.edu/

Alma College
614 West Superior St.
Alma, MI 48801-1599
800-321-ALMA
www.alma.edu/

Andrews University
Berrien Springs, MI 49104
800-253-2874
www.andrews.edu/

Aquinas College
1607 Robinson Rd., SE
Grand Rapids, MI 49506-1799
800-678-9593
www.aquinas.edu/

Ave Maria College
300 West Forest Ave.
Ypsilanti, MI 48197
866-866-3030
www.avemaria.edu/

Baker College of Allen Park
4500 Enterprise Dr.
Allen Park, MI 48101
313-425-3700
www.baker.edu/

Baker College of Auburn Hills
1500 University Dr.
Auburn Hills, MI 48326-1586
248-340-0600
www.baker.edu/

Baker College of Cadillac
9600 East 13th St.
Cadillac, MI 49601
231-876-3100
www.baker.edu/

Baker College of Clinton
Township
34950 Little Mack Ave.
Clinton Township, MI 48035-
4701
888-272-2842
www.baker.edu/

Baker College of Flint
1050 West Bristol Rd.
Flint, MI 48507-5508
800-964-4299
www.baker.edu/

Baker College of Jackson
2800 Springport Rd.
Jackson, MI 49202
888-343-3683
www.baker.edu/

Baker College of Muskegon
1903 Marquette Ave.
Muskegon, MI 49442-3497
231-777-5200
www.baker.edu/

Baker College of Owosso
1020 South Washington St.
Owosso, MI 48867-4400
800-879-3797
www.baker.edu/

Baker College of Port Huron
3403 Lapeer Rd.
Port Huron, MI 48060-2597
888-262-2442
www.baker.edu/

Calvin College
3201 Burton St., SE
Grand Rapids, MI 49546-4388
800-688-0122
www.calvin.edu/

Central Michigan University
Mount Pleasant, MI 48859
888-292-5366
www.cmich.edu/

Cleary University
3601 Plymouth Rd.
Ann Arbor, MI 48105-2659
888-5-CLEARY
www.cleary.edu/

College for Creative Studies
201 East Kirby
Detroit, MI 48202-4034
800-952-ARTS
www.ccscad.edu/

Concordia University
4090 Geddes Rd.
Ann Arbor, MI 48105-2797
800-253-0680
www.cuaa.edu/

Cornerstone University
1001 East Beltline Ave., NE
Grand Rapids, MI 49525-5897
800-787-9778
www.cornerstone.edu/

Davenport University
550 Lake Dr., Ste. B
Lapeer, MI 48446
800-632-9569
www.davenport.edu/

Davenport University
27650 Dequindre Rd.
Warren, MI 48092-5209
800-632-9569
www.davenport.edu/

Davenport University
643 South Waverly Rd.
Holland, MI 49423
800-632-9569
www.davenport.edu/

Davenport University
415 East Fulton
Grand Rapids, MI 49503
800-632-9569
www.davenport.edu/

Davenport University
220 East Kalamazoo St.
Lansing, MI 48933-2197
800-632-9569
www.davenport.edu/

Davenport University
4123 West Main St.
Kalamazoo, MI 49006-2791
800-632-9569
www.davenport.edu/

Davenport University
2200 Dendrinos Dr., Ste. 110
Traverse City, MI 49684
800-632-9569
www.davenport.edu/

Davenport University
4801 Oakman Blvd.
Dearborn, MI 48126-3799
800-632-9569
www.davenport.edu/

Davenport University
80 Livingston Blvd.
Gaylord, MI 49735
800-632-9569
www.davenport.edu/

Eastern Michigan University
Ypsilanti, MI 48197
800-GO TO EMU
www.emich.edu/

Ferris State University
1201 South State St.
Big Rapids, MI 49307
800-433-7747
www.ferris.edu/

Finlandia University
601 Quincy St.
Hancock, MI 49930-1882
877-202-5491
www.finlandia.edu/

Grace Bible College
1011 Aldon St. SW,
PO Box 910
Grand Rapids, MI 49509-0910
800-968-1887
www.gbcol.edu/

Grand Valley State University
1 Campus Dr.
Allendale, MI 49401-9403
800-748-0246
www.gvsu.edu/

Great Lakes Christian College
6211 West Willow Hwy.
Lansing, MI 48917-1299
800-YES-GLCC
www.glcc.edu/

Hillsdale College
33 East College St.
Hillsdale, MI 49242-1298
517-437-7341
www.hillsdale.edu/

Hope College
141 East 12th St.,
PO Box 9000
Holland, MI 49422-9000
800-968-7850
www.hope.edu/

Kalamazoo College
1200 Academy St.
Kalamazoo, MI 49006-3295
800-253-3602
www.kzoo.edu/

Kettering University
1700 West Third Ave.
Flint, MI 48504-4898
800-955-4464
www.kettering.edu/

Lake Superior State
University
650 W Easterday Ave.
Sault Sainte Marie, MI 49783-
1626
888-800-LSSU
www.lssu.edu/

Lawrence Technological
University
21000 West Ten Mile Rd.
Southfield, MI 48075-1058
800-225-5588
www.ltu.edu/

Madonna University
36600 Schoolcraft Rd.
Livonia, MI 48150-1173
800-852-4951
www.madonna.edu

Marygrove College
8425 West McNichols Rd.
Detroit, MI 48221-2599
866-313-1297
www.marygrove.edu/

Michigan Jewish Institute
25401 Coolidge Hwy.
Oak Park, MI 48237-1304
248-414-6900
www.mji.edu/

Michigan State University
East Lansing, MI 48824
517-355-1855
www.msu.edu/

Michigan Technological
University
1400 Townsend Dr.
Houghton, MI 49931-1295
888-MTU-1885
www.mtu.edu/

Northern Michigan
University
1401 Presque Isle Ave.
Marquette, MI 49855-5301
000-002-9797
www.nmu.edu/

Northwood University
4000 Whiting Dr.
Midland, MI 48640-2398
800-457-7878
www.northwood.edu/

Oakland University
Rochester, MI 48309-4401
800-OAK-UNIV
www.oakland.edu/

Olivet College
320 South Main St.
Olivet, MI 49076-9701
800-456-7189
www.olivetcollege.edu/

Reformed Bible College
3333 East Beltline, NE
Grand Rapids, MI 49525-9749
800-511-3749
www.reformed.edu/

Rochester College
800 West Avon Rd.
Rochester Hills, MI 48307-2764
800-521-6010
www.rc.edu/

Sacred Heart Major Seminary
2701 Chicago Blvd.
Detroit, MI 48206-1799
313-883-8500
www.archdioceseofdetroit.
org/shms/shms.htm

Saginaw Valley State
University
7400 Bay Rd.
University Center, MI 48710
800-968-9500
www.svsu.edu/

Siena Heights University
1247 East Siena Heights Dr.
Adrian, MI 49221-1796
800-521-0009
www.sienahts.edu

Spring Arbor University
106 East Main St.
Spring Arbor, MI 49283-9799
800-968-0011
www.arbor.edu/

University of Detroit Mercy
4001 W McNichols Rd, PO
Box 19900
Detroit, MI 48219-0900
800-635-5020
www.udmercy.edu/

University of Michigan
Ann Arbor, MI 48109
734-764-1817
www.umich.edu/

University of Michigan-
Dearborn
4901 Evergreen Rd.
Dearborn, MI 48128-1491
313-593-5000
www.umd.umich.edu/

University of Michigan-Flint
303 East Kearsley St.
Flint, MI 48502-1950
810-762-3000
www.umflint.edu/

University of Phoenix-Metro
Detroit Campus
5480 Corporate Dr., Ste. 260
Troy, MI 48098-2623
800-228-7240
www.phoenix.edu/

University of Phoenix-West
Michigan Campus
318 River Ridge Dr. NW
Grand Rapids, MI 49544-1683
800-228-7240
www.phoenix.edu/

Walsh College of
Accountancy and Business
Administration
3838 Livernois Rd.,
PO Box 7006
Troy, MI 48007-7006
248-689-8282
www.walshcollege.edu/

Wayne State University
656 West Kirby St.
Detroit, MI 48202
877-978
www.wayne.edu/

Western Michigan University
1903 West Michigan Ave.
Kalamazoo, MI 49008-5202
269-387-1000
www.wmich.edu/

Yeshiva Geddolah of Greater
Detroit Rabbinical College
24600 Greenfield
Oak Park, MI 48237-1544
810-968-3360

Minnesota

Argosy University/Twin Cities
1515 Central Pkwy.
Eagan, MN 55121
888-844-2004
www.argosyu.edu/

The Art Institutes
International Minnesota
15 South 9th St.
Minneapolis, MN 55402-3137
800-777-3643
www.aim.artinstitutes.edu/

Augsburg College
2211 Riverside Ave.
Minneapolis, MN 55454-1351
800-788-5678
www.augsburg.edu/

Bemidji State University
1500 Birchmont Dr., NE
Bemidji, MN 56601-2699
800-652-9747
www.bemidjistate.edu/

Bethany Lutheran College
700 Luther Dr.
Mankato, MN 56001-6163
800-944-3066
www.blc.edu/

Bethel University
3900 Bethel Dr.
St. Paul, MN 55112-6999
800-255-8706
www.bethel.edu/

Capella University
225 South 6th St.
Minneapolis, MN 55402
888-CAPELLA
www.capella.edu/

Carleton College
One North College St.
Northfield, MN 55057-4001
800-995-2275
www.carleton.edu/

College of Saint Benedict
37 South College Ave.
Saint Joseph, MN 56374-2091
800-544-1489
www.csbsju.edu/

College of St. Catherine
2004 Randolph Ave.
St. Paul, MN 55105-1789
651-690-6000
www.stkate.edu/

College of St. Catherine-
Minneapolis
601 25th Ave. South
Minneapolis, MN 55454-1494
800-945-4599
www.stkate.edu/

The College of St.
Scholastica
1200 Kenwood Ave.
Duluth, MN 55811-4199
800-249-6412
www.css.edu/

College of Visual Arts
344 Summit Ave.
St. Paul, MN 55102-2124
800-224-1536
www.cva.edu/

Concordia College
901 South 8th St.
Moorhead, MN 56562
800-699-9897
www.concordiacollege.edu/

Concordia University,
St. Paul
275 Syndicate St. North
St. Paul, MN 55104-5494
800-333-4705
www.csp.edu/

Crossroads College
920 Mayowood Rd., SW
Rochester, MN 55902-2382
800-456-7651
www.crossroadscollege.edu/

Crown College
8700 College View Dr.
St. Bonifacius, MN 55375-9001
800-68-CROWN
www.crown.edu

Gustavus Adolphus College
800 West College Ave.
St. Peter, MN 56082-1498
800-GUSTAVU(S)
www.gustavus.edu/

Hamline University
1536 Hewitt Ave.
St. Paul, MN 55104-1284
800-753-9753
www.hamline.edu/

Macalester College
1600 Grand Ave.
St. Paul, MN 55105-1899
800-231-7974
www.macalester.edu/

Martin Luther College
1995 Luther Ct.
New Ulm, MN 56073
507-354-8221
www.mlc-wels.edu/

Metropolitan State University
700 East 7th St.
St. Paul, MN 55106-5000
651-793-1212
www.metrostate.edu

Minneapolis College of Art
and Design
2501 Stevens Ave. South
Minneapolis, MN 55404-4347
800-874-6223
www.mcad.edu/

Minnesota State University
Mankato
228 Wiecking Center
Mankato, MN 56001
800-722-0544
www.mnsu.edu/

Minnesota State University
Moorhead
1104 7th Ave. South
Moorhead, MN 56563-0002
800-593-7246
www.mnstate.edu/

National American University
1500 West Hwy. 36
Roseville, MN 55113-4035
651-644-1265
www.national.edu/

North Central University
910 Elliot Ave.
Minneapolis, MN 55404-1322
800-289-6222
www.northcentral.edu/

Northwestern College
3003 Snelling Ave. North
St. Paul, MN 55113-1598
800-827-6827
www.nwc.edu/

Oak Hills Christian College
1600 Oak Hills Rd., SW
Bemidji, MN 56601-8832
888-751-8670
www.oakhills.edu/

Pillsbury Baptist Bible
College
315 South Grove Ave.
Owatonna, MN 55060-3097
800-747-4557
www.pillsbury.edu/

St. Cloud State University
720 4th Ave. South
St. Cloud, MN 56301-4498
877-654-7278
www.stcloudstate.edu/

Saint John's University
PO Box 2000
Collegeville, MN 56321
800-544-1489
www.csbsju.edu/

Saint Mary's University of
Minnesota
700 Terrace Heights
Winona, MN 55987-1399
800-635-5987
www.smumn.edu/

St. Olaf College
1520 St. Olaf Ave.
Northfield, MN 55057-1098
800-800-3025
www.stolaf.edu/

Southwest Minnesota State
University
1501 State St.
Marshall, MN 56258-1598
800-642-0684
www.southwest.msus.edu/

University of Minnesota,
Crookston
2900 University Ave.
Crookston, MN 56716-5001
800-862-6466
www.crk.umn.edu/

University of Minnesota,
Duluth
10 University Dr.
Duluth, MN 55812-2496
800-232-1339
www.d.umn.edu/

University of Minnesota,
Morris
600 East 4th St.
Morris, MN 56267-2134
800-992-8863
www.mrs.umn.edu/

University of Minnesota,
Twin Cities Campus
100 Church St., SE
Minneapolis, MN 55455-0213
800-752-1000
www.umn.edu/tc/

University of St. Thomas
2115 Summit Ave.
St. Paul, MN 55105-1096
800-328-6819
www.stthomas.edu/

Walden University
155 Fifth Ave. South
Minneapolis, MN 55401
612-338-7224
www.waldenu.edu/

Winona State University
PO Box 5838
Winona, MN 55987-5838
800-DIAL WSU

Missouri

Avila University
11901 Wornall Rd.
Kansas City, MO 64145-1698
800-GO-AVILA
www.avila.edu/

Baptist Bible College
628 East Kearney
Springfield, MO 65803-3498
417-268-6000
www.baptist.edu/index.htm

Barnes-Jewish College of
Nursing and Allied Health
306 S. Kings Highway Blvd.
St. Louis, MO 63110-1091
314-454-7055
www.barnesjewishcollege.edu

Calvary Bible College and
Theological Seminary
15800 Calvary Rd.
Kansas City, MO 64147-1341
800-326-3960
www.calvary.edu/

Central Bible College
3000 North Grant Ave.
Springfield, MO 65803-1096
800-831-4222
www.cbcag.edu/

Central Christian College of
the Bible
911 Urbandale Dr. East
Moberly, MO 65270-1997
660-263-3900
www.cccb.edu/

Central Methodist University
411 Central Methodist Square
Fayette, MO 65248-1198
660-248-3391
www.centralmethodist.edu/

Central Missouri State
University
PO Box 800
Warrensburg, MO 64093
660-543-4111
www.cmsu.edu/

Cleveland Chiropractic
College-Kansas City Campus
6401 Rockhill Rd.
Kansas City, MO 64131-1181
800-467-2252
www.cleveland.edu/

College of the Ozarks
PO Box 17
Point Lookout, MO 65726
800-222-0525
www.cofo.edu/

Columbia College
1001 Rogers St.
Columbia, MO 65216-0002
800-231-2391
www.ccis.edu/

Conception Seminary
College
PO Box 502
Conception, MO 64433-0502
660-944-3105
www.conceptionabbey.org/

Culver-Stockton College
1 College Hill
Canton, MO 63435-1299
800-537-1883
www.culver.edu/

Deaconess College of
Nursing
6150 Oakland Ave.
St. Louis, MO 63139-3215
800-942-4310
www.deaconess.edu/

DeVry University
1801 Park 270 Dr., Ste. 260
St. Louis, MO 63146-4020
314-542-4222
www.devry.edu/

DeVry University
11224 Holmes Rd.
Kansas City, MO 64131-3698
800-821-3766
www.devry.edu/

DeVry University
City Center Square, 1100
Main St., Ste. 118
Kansas City, MO 64105-2112
816-221-1300
www.devry.edu/

Drury University
900 North Benton Ave.
Springfield, MO 65802-3791
800-922-2274
www.drury.edu/

Evangel University
1111 North Glenstone
Springfield, MO 65802-2191
417-865-2811
www.evangel.edu/

Fontbonne University
6800 Wydown Blvd.
St. Louis, MO 63105-3098
314-862-3456
www.fontbonne.edu/

Global University of the
Assemblies of God
1211 South Glenstone Ave.
Springfield, MO 65804
800-443-1083
www.globaluniversity.edu/

Hannibal-LaGrange College
2800 Palmyra Rd.
Hannibal, MO 63401-1999
800-HLG-1119
www.hlg.edu/

Harris-Stowe State College
3026 Laclede Ave.
St. Louis, MO 63103-2136
314-340-3366
www.hssc.edu/

Kansas City Art Institute
4415 Warwick Blvd.
Kansas City, MO 64111-1874
800-522-5224
www.kcai.edu/

Kansas City College
402 East Bannister Rd., Ste. A
Kansas City, MO 64131
877-582-3963
www.metropolitancollege.edu/

Lester L. Cox College of
Nursing and Health Sciences
1423 North Jefferson
Springfield, MO 65802
417-269-3401
www.coxcollege.edu/

Lincoln University
820 Chestnut
Jefferson City, MO 65102
800-521-5052
www.lincolnu.edu/

Lindenwood University
209 South Kings Highway
St. Charles, MO 63301-1695
636-949-2000
www.lindenwood.edu/

Logan University-College of
Chiropractic
1851 Schoettler Rd., Box 1065
Chesterfield, MO 63006-1065
800-533-9210
www.logan.edu/

Maryville University of Saint
Louis
13550 Conway Rd.
St. Louis, MO 63141-7299
800-627-9855
www.maryville.edu/

Messenger College
PO Box 4050
Joplin, MO 64803
417-624-7070
www.messengercollege.edu/

Missouri Baptist University
One College Park Dr.
St. Louis, MO 63141-8660
877-434-1115
www.mobap.edu/

Missouri Southern State
University
3950 East Newman Rd.
Joplin, MO 64801-1595
866-818-MSSU
www.mssu.edu/

Missouri State University
901 South National
Springfield, MO 65804-0094
800-492-7900
www.smsu.edu/

Missouri Tech
1167 Corporate Lake Dr.
St. Louis, MO 63132-1716
314-569-3600
www.motech.edu/

Missouri Valley College
500 East College
Marshall, MO 65340-3197
660-831-4000
www.moval.edu/

Missouri Western State
University
4525 Downs Dr.
St. Joseph, MO 64507-2294
800-662-7041
www.mwsc.edu/

National American University
4200 Blue Ridge Blvd.
Kansas City, MO 64133-1612
816-353-4554
www.national.edu/

Northwest Missouri State
University
800 University Dr.
Maryville, MO 64468-6001
800-633-1175
www.nwmissouri.edu/

Ozark Christian College
1111 North Main St.
Joplin, MO 64801-4804
800-299-4622
www.occ.edu/

Park University
8700 NW River Park Dr.
Parkville, MO 64152-3795
800-745-7275
www.park.edu/

Research College of Nursing
2300 East Meyer Blvd.
Kansas City, MO 64132
800-842-6776
www.researchcollege.edu/

Rockhurst University
1100 Rockhurst Rd.
Kansas City, MO 64110-2561
800-842-6776
www.rockhurst.edu/

St. Louis Christian College
1360 Grandview Dr.
Florissant, MO 63033-6499
800-887-SLCC
www.slcc4ministry.edu/

St. Louis College of
Pharmacy
4588 Parkview Place
St. Louis, MO 63110-1088
314-367-8700
www.stlcop.edu/

Saint Louis University
221 North Grand Blvd.
St. Louis, MO 63103-2097
800-758-3678
www.slu.edu

Saint Luke's College
4426 Wornall Rd.
Kansas City, MO 64111
816-932-2233
www.saintlukescollege.edu/

Southeast Missouri State
University
One University Plaza
Cape Girardeau, MO 63701-
4799
573-651-2000
www.semo.edu/

Southwest Baptist University
1600 University Ave.
Bolivar, MO 65613-2597
800-526-5859
www.sbuniv.edu/

Stephens College
1200 East Broadway
Columbia, MO 65215-0002
800-876-7207
www.stephens.edu/

Truman State University
100 East Normal St.
Kirksville, MO 63501-4221
660-785-4000
www.truman.edu/

University of Missouri-
Columbia
Columbia, MO 65211
573-882-2121
www.missouri.edu/

University of Missouri-
Kansas City
5100 Rockhill Rd.
Kansas City, MO 64110-2499
800-775-8652
www.umkc.edu/

University of Missouri-Rolla
1870 Miner Cr.
Rolla, MO 65409-0910
800-522-0938
www.umr.edu/

University of Missouri-St.
Louis
One University Blvd.
St. Louis, MO 63121
314-516-5000
www.umsl.edu/

University of Phoenix-Kansas
City Campus
901 East 104th St., Ste. 301
Kansas City, MO 64131-4517
800-228-7240
www.phoenix.edu/

University of Phoenix-
Springfield Campus
1260 E. Kingsley St.
Springfield, MO 65804-7211
800-228-7240
www.phoenix.edu/

University of Phoenix-St.
Louis Campus
Riverport Lakes West, 13801
Riverport Dr., Ste. 102
St. Louis, MO 63043-4828
800-228-7240
www.phoenix.edu/

Washington University in St.
Louis
1 Brookings Dr.
St. Louis, MO 63130-4899
800-638-0700
www.wustl.edu

Webster University
470 East Lockwood Ave.
St. Louis, MO 63119-3194
800-75-ENROL
www.webster.edu/

Westminster College
501 Westminster Ave.
Fulton, MO 65251-1299
800-475-3361
www.westminster-mo.edu/

William Jewell College
500 College Hill
Liberty, MO 64068-1843
888-2JEWELL
www.jewell.edu/

William Woods University
One University Ave.
Fulton, MO 65251-1098
800-995-3159
www.williamwoods.edu/

Nebraska

Bellevue University
1000 Galvin Rd. South
Bellevue, NE 68005-3098
800-756-7920
www.bellevue.edu/

Chadron State College
1000 Main St.
Chadron, NE 69337
308-432-6000
www.csc.edu/

Clarkson College
101 South 42nd St.
Omaha, NE 68131-2739
800-647-5500
www.clarksoncollege.edu/

College of Saint Mary
1901 South 72nd St.
Omaha, NE 68124-2377
800-926-5534
www.csm.edu/

Concordia University
800 North Columbia Ave.
Seward, NE 68434-1599
800-535-5494
www.cune.edu/

Creighton University
2500 California Plaza
Omaha, NE 68178-0001
800-282-5835
www.creighton.edu/

Dana College
2848 College Dr.
Blair, NE 68008-1099
800-444-3262
www.dana.edu/

Doane College
1014 Boswell Ave.
Crete, NE 68333-2430
800-333-6263
www.doane.edu/

Grace University
1311 South Ninth St.
Omaha, NE 68108
800-383-1422
www.graceuniversity.edu/

Hastings College
800 North Turner Ave.
Hastings, NE 68901-7696
800-532-7642
www.hastings.edu/

Midland Lutheran College
900 North Clarkson St.
Fremont, NE 68025-4200
800-642-8382
www.mlc.edu/

Nebraska Christian College
1800 Syracuse Ave.
Norfolk, NE 68701-2458
402-379-5000
www.nechristian.edu/

Nebraska Methodist College
8501 West Dodge Rd.
Omaha, NE 68114-3426
800-335-5510
www.methodistcollege.edu/

Nebraska Wesleyan
University
5000 Saint Paul Ave.
Lincoln, NE 68504-2796
800-541-3818
www.nebrwesleyan.edu/

Peru State College
PO Box 10
Peru, NE 68421
402-872-3815
www.peru.edu/

Union College
3800 South 48th St.
Lincoln, NE 68506-4300
800-228-4600
www.ucollege.edu/

University of Nebraska at
Kearney
905 West 25th St.
Kearney, NE 68849-0001
800-532-7639
www.unk.edu/

University of Nebraska at
Omaha
6001 Dodge St.
Omaha, NE 68182
402-554-2200
www.unomaha.edu/

University of Nebraska
Medical Center
Nebraska Medical Center
Omaha, NE 68198
800-626-8431
www.unmc.edu/

University of Nebraska-
Lincoln
14th and R Streets
Lincoln, NE 68588
800-742-8800
www.unl.edu/

Wayne State College
1111 Main St.
Wayne, NE 68787
402-375-7000
www.wsc.edu/

York College
1125 East 8th St.
York, NE 68467
800-950-9675
www.york.edu/

North Dakota

Dickinson State University
291 Campus Dr.
Dickinson, ND 58601-4896
800-279-4295
www.dsu.nodak.edu/

Jamestown College
6000 College Ln.
Jamestown, ND 58405
800-336-2554
www.jc.edu/

Mayville State University
330 3rd St., NE
Mayville, ND 58257-1299
800-437-4104
www.mayvillestate.edu/

Medcenter One College of
Nursing
512 North 7th St.
Bismarck, ND 58501-4494
701-323-6271
medcenterone.com/college/
nursing.htm

Minot State University
500 University Ave. West
Minot, ND 58707-0002
800-777-0750
www.minotstateu.edu/

North Dakota State
University
1301 North University Ave.
Fargo, ND 58105
800-488-NDSU
www.ndsu.edu/

Trinity Bible College
50 South 6th Ave.
Ellendale, ND 58436-7150
888-TBC-2DAY
www.trinitybiblecollege.edu/

University of Mary
7500 University Dr.
Bismarck, ND 58504-9652
800-288-6279
www.umary.edu/

University of North Dakota
Grand Forks, ND 58202
800-CALL UND
www.und.nodak.edu/

Valley City State University
101 College St., SW
Valley City, ND 58072
800-532-8641
www.vcsu.edu/

Ohio

Allegheny Wesleyan College
2161 Woodsdale Rd.
Salem, OH 44460
800-292-3153
www.awc.edu/

Antioch College
795 Livermore St.
Yellow Springs, OH 45387-1697
800-543-9436
www.antioch-college.edu/

Antioch University McGregor
800 Livermore St.
Yellow Springs, OH 45387-1609
937-769-1818
www.mcgregor.edu/

Art Academy of Cincinnati
1125 Saint Gregory St.
Cincinnati, OH 45202-1799
513-721-5205
www.artacademy.edu/

Ashland University
401 College Ave.
Ashland, OH 44805-3702
800-882-1548
www.exploreashland.com

Baldwin-Wallace College
275 Eastland Rd.
Berea, OH 44017-2088
440-826-2900
www.bw.edu/

Bluffton University
1 University Dr.
Bluffton, OH 45817
800-488-3257
www.bluffton.edu/

Bowling Green State University
Bowling Green, OH 43403
419-372-2531
www.bgsu.edu/

Bryant and Stratton College
1700 East 13th St.
Cleveland, OH 44114-3203
216-771-1700
www.bryantstratton.edu/

Capital University
2199 East Main St.
Columbus, OH 43209-2394
800-289-6289
www.capital.edu/

Case Western Reserve University
10900 Euclid Ave.
Cleveland, OH 44106
216-368-2000
www.case.edu/

Cedarville University
251 North Main St.
Cedarville, OH 45314-0601
800-CEDARVILLE
www.cedarville.edu/

Central State University
1400 Brush Row Rd.,
PO Box 1004
Wilberforce, OH 45384
937-376-6011
www.centralstate.edu/

Cincinnati Christian University
2700 Glenway Ave.,
PO Box 04320
Cincinnati, OH 45204-3200
800-949-4CBC
www.ccuniversity.edu/

Circleville Bible College
1476 Lancaster Pike,
PO Box 458
Circleville, OH 43113-9487
800-701-0222
www.biblecollege.edu/

The Cleveland Institute of Art
11141 East Blvd.
Cleveland, OH 44106-1700
800-223-4700
www.cia.edu/

Cleveland Institute of Music
11021 East Blvd.
Cleveland, OH 44106-1776
216-791-5000
www.cim.edu/

Cleveland State University
2121 Euclid Ave.
Cleveland, OH 44115
888-CSU-OHIO
www.csuohio.edu/

College of Mount St. Joseph
5701 Delhi Rd.
Cincinnati, OH 45233-1670
800-654-9314
www.msj.edu/

The College of Wooster
1189 Beall Ave.
Wooster, OH 44691-2363
800-877-9905
www.wooster.edu/

Columbus College of Art & Design
107 North Ninth St.
Columbus, OH 43215-1758
877-997-2223
www.ccad.edu/

David N. Myers University
112 Prospect Ave.
Cleveland, OH 44115-1096
800-424-3953
www.dnmyers.edu/

Defiance College
701 North Clinton St.
Defiance, OH 43512-1610
800-520-4632
www.defiance.edu/

Denison University
Granville, OH 43023
800-DENISON
www.denison.edu/

DeVry University
1350 Alum Creek Dr.
Columbus, OH 43209-2705
800-426-2206
www.devry.edu/

DeVry University
The Genesis Building, 6000
Lombardo Center
Seven Hills, OH 44131-6907
866-453-3879
www.devry.edu/

DeVry University
200 Public Square, Ste. 150
Cleveland, OH 44114-2301
216-781-8000
www.devry.edu/

Franciscan University of Steubenville
1235 University Blvd.
Steubenville, OH 43952-1763
800-783-6220
www.franciscan.edu/

Franklin University
201 South Grant Ave.
Columbus, OH 43215-5399
877-341-6300
www.franklin.edu/

God's Bible School and College
1810 Young St.
Cincinnati, OH 45202-6838
800-486-4637
www.gbs.edu/

Heidelberg College
310 East Market St.
Tiffin, OH 44883-2462
800-434-3352
www.heidelberg.edu/

Hiram College
Box 67
Hiram, OH 44234-0067
800-362-5280
www.hiram.edu/

John Carroll University
20700 North Park Blvd.
University Heights, OH 44118-4581
216-397-1886
www.jcu.edu/

Kent State University
PO Box 5190
Kent, OH 44242-0001
800-988-KENT
www.kent.edu/

Kenyon College
Gambier, OH 43022-9623
800-848-2468
www.kenyon.edu/

Lake Erie College
391 West Washington St.
Painesville, OH 44077-3389
800-916-0904
www.lec.edu/

Laura and Alvin Siegal College of Judaic Studies
26500 Shaker Blvd.
Beachwood, OH 44122-7116
888-336-2257
www.siegalcollege.edu/

Lourdes College
6832 Convent Blvd.
Sylvania, OH 43560-2898
800-878-3210
www.lourdes.edu/

Malone College
515 25th St., NW
Canton, OH 44709-3897
800-521-1146
www.malone.edu/

Marietta College
215 Fifth St.
Marietta, OH 45750-4000
800-331-7896
www.marietta.edu/

MedCentral College of Nursing
335 Glessner Ave.
Mansfield, OH 44903
877-656-4360
www.medcentral.edu/

Miami University
Oxford, OH 45056
513-529-1809
www.muohio.edu/

Mount Carmel College of
Nursing
127 South Davis Ave.
Columbus, OH 43222
614-234-5800
www.mccn.edu/

Mount Union College
1972 Clark Ave.
Alliance, OH 44601-3993
800-992-6682
www.muc.edu/

Mount Vernon Nazarene
University
800 Martinsburg Rd.
Mount Vernon, OH 43050-9500
866-462-6868
www.mvnu.edu/

Muskingum College
163 Stormont St.
New Concord, OH 43762
800-752-6082
www.muskingum.edu/

Notre Dame College
4545 College Rd.
South Euclid, OH 44121-4293
800-632-1680
www.notredamecollege.edu/

Oberlin College
173 West Lorain St.
Oberlin, OH 44074
800-622-OBIE
www.oberlin.edu/

Ohio Dominican University
1216 Sunbury Rd.
Columbus, OH 43219-2099
800-854-2670
www.ohiodominican.edu/

Ohio Northern University
525 South Main
Ada, OH 45810-1599
888-408-4ONU
www.onu.edu/

The Ohio State University
Enarson Hall,
154 W. 12th Ave.
Columbus, OH 43210
614-292-6446
www.osu.edu/

The Ohio State University at
Lima
4240 Campus Dr.
Lima, OH 45804
419-995-8600
www.lima.osu.edu/

The Ohio State University at
Marion
1465 Mount Vernon Ave.
Marion, OH 43302-5695
740-389-6786
www.marion.ohio-state.edu/

The Ohio State University-
Mansfield Campus
1680 University Dr.
Mansfield, OH 44906-1599
419-755-4011
www.mansfield.osu.edu/

The Ohio State University-
Newark Campus
1179 University Dr.
Newark, OH 43055-1797
740-366-3321
www.newark.osu.edu/

Ohio University
Athens, OH 45701-2979
740-593-1000
www.ohio.edu/

Ohio University-Chillicothe
571 West Fifth St.,
PO Box 629
Chillicothe, OH 45601-0629
740-774-7200
www.ohio.edu/chillicothe/

Ohio University-Eastern
45425 National Rd.
St. Clairsville, OH 43950-9724
740-695-1720
www.eastern.ohiou.edu/

Ohio University-Lancaster
1570 Granville Pike
Lancaster, OH 43130-1097
888-446-4468
www.ohiou.edu/lancaster/

Ohio University-Southern
Campus
1804 Liberty Ave.
Ironton, OH 45638-2214
800-626-0513
www.ohiou.edu/

Ohio University-Zanesville
1425 Newark Rd.
Zanesville, OH 43701-2695
740-453-0762
www.zanesville.ohiou.edu/

Ohio Wesleyan University
61 South Sandusky St.
Delaware, OH 43015
800-922-8953
www.owu.edu/

Otterbein College
1 Otterbein College
Westerville, OH 43081
800-488-8144
www.otterbein.edu/

Pontifical College
Josephinum
7625 North High St.
Columbus, OH 43235-1498
888-252-5812
www.pcj.edu/

Rabbinical College of Telshe
28400 Euclid Ave.
Wickliffe, OH 44092-2523
216-943-5300

Shawnee State University
940 Second St.
Portsmouth, OH 45662-4344
800-959-2SSU
www.shawnee.edu/

Temple Baptist College
11965 Kenn Rd.
Cincinnati, OH 45240
513-851-3800
www.templebaptistcollege.
com/

Tiffin University
155 Miami St.
Tiffin, OH 44883-2161
800-968-6446
www.tiffin.edu/

Tri-State Bible College
506 Margaret St., PO Box 445
South Point, OH 45680-8402
740-377-2520
www.tsbc.edu/

Union Institute & University
440 East McMillan St.
Cincinnati, OH 45206-1925
800-486-3116
www.tui.edu/

The University of Akron
302 Buchtel Common
Akron, OH 44325-0001
800-655-4884
www.uakron.edu/

University of Cincinnati
2624 Clifton Ave.
Cincinnati, OH 45221
513-556-6000
www.uc.edu/

University of Dayton
300 College Park
Dayton, OH 45469-1300
800-837-7433
www.udayton.edu/

The University of Findlay
1000 North Main St.
Findlay, OH 45840-3653
800-548-0932
www.findlay.edu/

University of Phoenix-
Cincinnati Campus
9050 Centre Pointe Dr.
West Chester, OH 45069
800-228-7240
www.phoenix.edu/

University of Phoenix-
Cleveland Campus
5005 Rockside Rd., Ste. 325
Independence, OH 44131-
2194
800-228-7240
www.phoenix.edu/

University of Phoenix-
Columbus Ohio Campus
8425 Pulsar Place
Columbus, OH 43240
800-228-7240
www.phoenix.edu/

University of Rio Grande
218 North College Ave.
Rio Grande, OH 45674
740-245-5353
www.rio.edu/

The University of Toledo
2801 West Bancroft
Toledo, OH 43606-3390
419-530-4636
www.utoledo.edu/

Urbana University
579 College Way
Urbana, OH 43078-2091
800-7-URBANA
www.urbana.edu/

Ursuline College
2550 Lander Rd.
Pepper Pike, OH 44124-4398
888-URSULINE
www.ursuline.edu/

Walsh University
2020 East Maple St., NW
North Canton, OH 44720-
3396
800-362-8846
www.walsh.edu/

Wilberforce University
1055 North Bickett Rd.
Wilberforce, OH 45384
800-367-8568
www.wilberforce.edu/

Wilmington College
Pyle Center Box 1185
Wilmington, OH 45177
800-341-9318
www.wilmington.edu/

Wittenberg University
PO Box 720
Springfield, OH 45501-0720
800-677-7558
www.wittenberg.edu/

Wright State University
3640 Colonel Glenn Hwy.
Dayton, OH 45435
800-247-1770
www.wright.edu/

Xavier University
3800 Victory Pkwy.
Cincinnati, OH 45207
800-344-4698
www.xu.edu/

Youngstown State University
One University Plaza
Youngstown, OH 44555-0001
877-468-6978
www.ysu.edu/

Oklahoma

Bacone College
2299 Old Bacone Rd.
Muskogee, OK 74403-1597
888-682-5514
www.bacone.edu/

Cameron University
2800 West Gore Blvd.
Lawton, OK 73505-6377
888-454-7600
www.cameron.edu/

East Central University
1100 East 14th St.
Ada, OK 74820-6899
580-332-8000
www.ecok.edu/

Hillsdale Free Will Baptist
College
3701 South I-35 Service Rd.,
PO Box 7208
Moore, OK 73160-1208
405-912-9000
www.hc.edu/

Langston University
PO Box 907
Langston, OK 73050-0907
405-466-2231
www.lunet.edu/

Metropolitan College
2901 North Classen Blvd.,
Ste. 200
Oklahoma City, OK 73106
405-528-5000
www.metropolitancollege.edu/

Metropolitan College
4528 South Sheridan Rd.,
Ste. 105
Tulsa, OK 74145-1011
918-627-9300
www.metropolitancollege.edu/

Mid-America Christian
University
3500 Southwest 119th St.
Oklahoma City, OK 73170-4504
405-691-3800
www.macu.edu/

Northeastern State
University
600 North Grand
Tahlequah, OK 74464-2399
918-456-5511
www.nsuok.edu/

Northwestern Oklahoma
State University
709 Oklahoma Blvd.
Alva, OK 73717-2799
580-327-1700
www.nwosu.edu/

Oklahoma Baptist University
500 West University
Shawnee, OK 74804
800-654-3285
www.okbu.edu/

Oklahoma Christian
University
PO Box 11000
Oklahoma City, OK 73136-1100
405-425-5000
www.oc.edu/

Oklahoma City University
2501 North Blackwelder
Oklahoma City, OK 73106-
1402
800-633-7242
www.okcu.edu/

Oklahoma Panhandle State
University
PO Box 430
Goodwell, OK 73939-0430
800-664-6778
www.opsu.edu/

Oklahoma State University
Stillwater, OK 74078
800-852-1255
www.okstate.edu/

Oklahoma Wesleyan
University
2201 Silver Lake Rd.
Bartlesville, OK 74006-6299
918-335-6200
www.okwu.edu/

Oral Roberts University
7777 South Lewis Ave.
Tulsa, OK 74171-0001
800-678-8876
www.oru.edu/

Rogers State University
1701 West Will Rogers Blvd.
Claremore, OK 74017-3252
800-256-7511
www.rsu.edu/

St. Gregory's University
1900 West MacArthur Dr.
Shawnee, OK 74804-2499
888-STGREGS
www.stgregorys.edu/

Southeastern Oklahoma
State University
1405 North 4th Ave.
Durant, OK 74701-0609
800-435-1327
www.sosu.edu/

Southern Nazarene
University
6729 Northwest 39th
Expressway
Bethany, OK 73008
800-648-9899
www.snu.edu/

Southwestern Christian
University
PO Box 340
Bethany, OK 73008-0340
405-789-7661
www.swcu.edu/

Southwestern Oklahoma
State University
100 Campus Dr.
Weatherford, OK 73096-3098
580-772-6611
www.swosu.edu/

University of Central
Oklahoma
100 North University Dr.
Edmond, OK 73034-5209
800-254-4215
www.ucok.edu/

University of Oklahoma
660 Parrington Oval
Norman, OK 73019-0390
800-234-6868
www.ou.edu/

University of Oklahoma
Health Sciences Center
PO Box 26901
Oklahoma City, OK 73190
405-271-4000
www.ouhsc.edu/

University of Phoenix-
Oklahoma City Campus
6501 North Broadway
Extension, Ste. 100
Oklahoma City, OK 73116-
8244
800-228-7240
www.phoenix.edu/

University of Phoenix-Tulsa
Campus
10810 East 45th St., Ste. 103
Tulsa, OK 74146-3801
800-228-7240
www.phoenix.edu/

University of Science and
Arts of Oklahoma
1727 West Alabama
Chickasha, OK 73018
800-933-8726
www.usao.edu/

University of Tulsa
600 South College Ave.
Tulsa, OK 74104-3189
800-331-3050
www.utulsa.edu/

South Dakota

Augustana College
2001 South Summit Ave.
Sioux Falls, SD 57197
800-727-2844
www.augie.edu/

Black Hills State University
1200 University St.
Spearfish, SD 57799
800-255-2478
www.bhsu.edu/

Colorado Technical University
Sioux Falls Campus
3901 West 59th St.
Sioux Falls, SD 57108
605-361-0200
www.ctu-siouxfalls.com/

Dakota State University
820 North Washington
Madison, SD 57042-1799
888-DSU-9988
www.dsu.edu/

Dakota Wesleyan University
1200 West University Ave.
Mitchell, SD 57301-4398
800-333-8506
www.dwu.edu/

Mount Marty College
1105 West 8th St.
Yankton, SD 57078-3724
800-658-4552
www.mtmc.edu/

National American University
321 Kansas City St.
Rapid City, SD 57701
800-843-8892
www.national.edu/

National American
University-Sioux Falls Branch
2801 South Kiwanis Ave.,
Ste. 100
Sioux Falls, SD 57105-4293
800-388-5430
www.national.edu/

Northern State University
1200 South Jay St.
Aberdeen, SD 57401-7198
800-678-5330
www.northern.edu/

Oglala Lakota College
490 Piya Wiconi Rd.
Kyle, SD 57752-0490
605-455-6000
www.olc.edu/

Presentation College
1500 North Main St.
Aberdeen, SD 57401-1299
800-437-6060
www.presentation.edu/

Si Tanka University
333 9th St. SW
Huron, SD 57350-2798
800-710-7159
www.sitanka.edu/

Sinte Gleska University
150 East 2nd St., P.O. Box 105
Rosebud, SD 57555
605-856-8100
www.sinte.edu/

South Dakota School of
Mines and Technology
501 East Saint Joseph
Rapid City, SD 57701-3995
800-544-8162
www.sdsmt.edu/

South Dakota State
University
PO Box 2201
Brookings, SD 57007
800-952-3541
www.sdstate.edu/

The University of South
Dakota
414 East Clark St.
Vermillion, SD 57069-2390
877-269-6837
www.usd.edu/

University of Sioux Falls
1101 West 22nd St.
Sioux Falls, SD 57105-1699
800-888-1047
www.usiouxfalls.edu/

Wisconsin

Alverno College
3400 South 43rd St.,
PO Box 343922
Milwaukee, WI 53234-3922
800-933-3401
www.alverno.edu/

Bellin College of Nursing
725 South Webster Ave.,
PO Box 23400
Green Bay, WI 54305-3400
800-236-8707
www.bcon.edu/

Beloit College
700 College St.
Beloit, WI 53511-5596
800-9-BELOIT
www.beloit.edu/

Cardinal Stritch University
6801 North Yates Rd.
Milwaukee, WI 53217-3985
800-347-8822
www.stritch.edu/

Carroll College
100 North East Ave.
Waukesha, WI 53186-5593
800-CARROLL
www.cc.edu/

Carthage College
2001 Alford Park Dr.
Kenosha, WI 53140-1994
800-351-4058
www.carthage.edu/

Columbia College of Nursing
2121 East Newport Ave.
Milwaukee, WI 53211-2952
800-321-6265
www.ccon.edu/

Concordia University
Wisconsin
12800 North Lake Shore Dr.
Mequon, WI 53097-2402
888-628-9472
www.cuw.edu/

DeVry University
20935 Swenson Dr., Ste. 450
Waukesha, WI 53186-4047
262-798-9889
www.devry.edu/

DeVry University
100 East Wisconsin Ave.,
Ste. 2550
Milwaukee, WI 53202-4107
414-278-7677
www.devry.edu/

Edgewood College
1000 Edgewood College Dr.
Madison, WI 53711-1997
800-444-4861
www.edgewood.edu/

Lakeland College
PO Box 359
Sheboygan, WI 53082-0359
920-565-1000
www.lakeland.edu/

Lawrence University
PO Box 599
Appleton, WI 54912-0599
800-227-0982
www.lawrence.edu/

Maranatha Baptist Bible
College
745 West Main St.
Watertown, WI 53094
800-622-2947
www.mbbc.edu/

Marian College of
Fond du Lac
45 South National Ave.
Fond du Lac, WI 54935-4699
920-923-7600
www.mariancollege.edu/

Marquette University
PO Box 1881
Milwaukee, WI 53201-1881
800-222-6544
www.marquette.edu/

Milwaukee Institute of Art
and Design
273 East Erie St.
Milwaukee, WI 53202-6003
888-749-MIAD
www.miad.edu/

Milwaukee School of
Engineering
1025 North Broadway
Milwaukee, WI 53202-3109
800-332-6763
www.msoe.edu/

Mount Mary College
2900 North Menomonee
River Pkwy.
Milwaukee, WI 53222-4597
414-258-4810
www.mtmary.edu/

Northland College
1411 Ellis Ave.
Ashland, WI 54806-3925
800-753-1040
www.northland.edu/

Ripon College
300 Seward St., PO Box 248
Ripon, WI 54971
800-947-4766
www.ripon.edu/

Silver Lake College
2406 South Alverno Rd.
Manitowoc, WI 54220-9319
920-684-6691
www.sl.edu/

St. Norbert College
100 Grant St.
De Pere, WI 54115-2099
800-236-4878
www.snc.edu/

University of Phoenix-
Wisconsin Campus
20075 Watertower Blvd.
Brookfield, WI 53045-6608
800-228-7240
www.phoenix.edu/

University of Wisconsin-
Eau Claire
PO Box 4004
Eau Claire, WI 54702-4004
715-836-2637
www.uwec.edu/

University of Wisconsin-
Green Bay
2420 Nicolet Dr.
Green Bay, WI 54311-7001
888-367-8942
www.uwgb.edu/

University of Wisconsin-La
Crosse
1725 State St.
La Crosse, WI 54601-3742
608-785-8000
www.uwlax.edu

University of Wisconsin-
Madison
500 Lincoln Dr.
Madison, WI 53706-1380
608-262-1234
www.wisc.edu/

University of Wisconsin-
Milwaukee
PO Box 413
Milwaukee, WI 53201-0413
414-229-1122
www.uwm.edu/

University of Wisconsin-
Oshkosh
800 Algoma Blvd.
Oshkosh, WI 54901
920-424-1234
www.uwosh.edu/

University of Wisconsin-
Parkside
900 Wood Rd., Box 2000
Kenosha, WI 53141-2000
262-595-2345
www.uwp.edu/

University of Wisconsin-
Platteville
1 University Plaza
Platteville, WI 53818-3099
800-362-5515
www.uwplatt.edu/

University of Wisconsin-
River Falls
410 South Third St.
River Falls, WI 54022-5001
715-425-3911
www.uwrf.edu/

University of Wisconsin-
Stevens Point
2100 Main St.
Stevens Point, WI 54481-3897
715-346-0123
www.uwsp.edu/

University of Wisconsin-
Stout
Menomonie, WI 54751
715-232-1122
www.uwstout.edu/

University of Wisconsin-
Superior
Belknap and Catlin,
PO Box 2000
Superior, WI 54880-4500
715-394-8101
www.uwsuper.edu/

University of Wisconsin-
Whitewater
800 West Main St.
Whitewater, WI 53190-1790
262-472-1234
www.uww.edu/

Viterbo University
900 Viterbo Dr.
La Crosse, WI 54601-4797
800-VITERBO
www.viterbo.edu/

Wisconsin Lutheran College
8800 West Bluemound Rd.
Milwaukee, WI 53226-9942
888-WIS LUTH
www.wlc.edu/

TWO-YEAR COLLEGES

Illinois

Black Hawk College
6600 34th Ave.
Moline, IL 61265-5899
309-796-5000
www.bhc.edu/

Career Colleges of Chicago
11 East Adams St., 2nd Fl.
Chicago, IL 60603-6301
312-895-6300
www.careerchi.com/

Carl Sandburg College
2400 Tom L. Wilson Blvd.
Galesburg, IL 61401-9576
309-344-2518
www.sandburg.edu/

City Colleges of Chicago,
Harold Washington College
30 East Lake St.
Chicago, IL 60601-2449
312-553-5600
hwashington.ccc.edu/

City Colleges of Chicago,
Harry S. Truman College
1145 West Wilson Ave.
Chicago, IL 60640-5616
773-907-4000
www.trumancollege.cc/

City Colleges of Chicago,
Kennedy-King College
6800 South Wentworth Ave.
Chicago, IL 60621-3733
773-602-5000
kennedyking.ccc.edu/

City Colleges of Chicago,
Malcolm X College
1900 West Van Buren St.
Chicago, IL 60612-3145
312-850-7000
malcolmx.ccc.edu/

City Colleges of Chicago,
Olive-Harvey College
10001 South Woodlawn Ave.
Chicago, IL 60628-1645
773-291-6100
oliveharvey.ccc.edu/

City Colleges of Chicago,
Richard J. Daley College
7500 South Pulaski Rd.
Chicago, IL 60652-1242
773-838-7500
daley.ccc.edu/

City Colleges of Chicago,
Wilbur Wright College
4300 North Narragansett Ave.
Chicago, IL 60634-1591
773-777-7900
wright.ccc.edu/

College of DuPage
425 Fawell Blvd.
Glen Ellyn, IL 60137-6599
630-942-2800
www.cod.edu/

College of Lake County
19351 West Washington St.
Grayslake, IL 60030-1198
847-543-2000
www.clcillinois.edu/

The College of Office
Technology
1514-20 West Division St.,
Second Fl.
Chicago, IL 60622
773-278-0042
www.cotedu.com/

The Cooking and Hospitality
Institute of Chicago
361 West Chestnut
Chicago, IL 60610-3050
312-944-0882
www.chicnet.org/

Danville Area Community
College
2000 East Main St.
Danville, IL 61832-5199
217-443-3222
www.dacc.cc.il.us/

Elgin Community College
1700 Spartan Dr.
Elgin, IL 60123-7193
847-697-1000
www.elgin.edu/

Fox College
4201 West 93rd St.
Oak Lawn, IL 60453
866-636-7711
www.foxcollege.com/

Gem City College
PO Box 179
Quincy, IL 62301
217-222-0391
www.gemcitycollege.com/

Heartland Community
College
1500 West Raab Rd.
Normal, IL 61761
309-268-8000
www.heartland.edu/

Highland Community College
2998 West Pearl City Rd.
Freeport, IL 61032-9341
815-235-6121
www.highland.edu/

Illinois Central College
One College Dr.
East Peoria, IL 61635-0001
309-694-5011
www.icc.edu/

Illinois Eastern Community
Colleges, Frontier
Community College
Frontier Dr.
Fairfield, IL 62837-2601
618-842-3711
www.iecc.edu/fcc/

Illinois Eastern Community
Colleges, Lincoln Trail
College
11220 State Highway 1
Robinson, IL 62454
618-544-8657
www.iecc.edu/ltc/

Illinois Eastern Community
Colleges, Olney Central
College
305 North West St.
Olney, IL 62450
618-395-7777
www.iecc.edu/occ/

Illinois Eastern Community
Colleges, Wabash Valley
College
2200 College Dr.
Mount Carmel, IL 62863-2657
618-262-8641
www.iecc.edu/wvc/

Illinois Valley Community
College
815 N. Orlando Smith Ave.
Oglesby, IL 61348-9692
815-224-2720
www.ivcc.edu/

ITT Technical Institute
1401 Feehanville Dr.
Mount Prospect, IL 60056
847-375-8800
www.itt-tech.edu/

ITT Technical Institute
7040 High Grove Blvd.
Burr Ridge, IL 60521
630-455-6470
www.itt-tech.edu/

ITT Technical Institute
600 Holiday Plaza Dr.
Matteson, IL 60443
708-747-2571
www.itt-tech.edu/

John A. Logan College
700 Logan College Rd.
Carterville, IL 62918-9900
618-985-3741
www.jalc.edu/

John Wood Community
College
1301 South 48th St.
Quincy, IL 62305-8736
217-224-6500
www.jwcc.edu/

Joliet Junior College
1215 Houbolt Rd.
Joliet, IL 60431-8938
815-729-9020
www.jjc.edu/

Kankakee Community
College
PO Box 888
Kankakee, IL 60901-0888
815-933-0345
www.kcc.cc.il.us/

Kaskaskia College
27210 College Rd.
Centralia, IL 62801-7878
618-545-3000
www.kaskaskia.edu/

Kishwaukee College
21193 Malta Rd.
Malta, IL 60150-9699
815-825-2086
www.kishwaukeecollege.edu/

Lake Land College
5001 Lake Land Blvd.
Mattoon, IL 61938-9366
217-234-5253
www.lakelandcollege.edu/

Lewis and Clark Community
College
5800 Godfrey Rd.
Godfrey, IL 62035-2466
618-466-7000
www.lc.edu/

Lincoln College
715 West Raab Rd.
Normal, IL 61761
800-569-0558
www.lincolncollege.edu/
normal/

Lincoln College
300 Keokuk St.
Lincoln, IL 62656-1699
800-569-0556
www.lincolncollege.edu/

Lincoln Land Community
College
5250 Shepherd Rd.,
PO Box 19256
Springfield, IL 62794-9256
217-786-2200
www.llcc.edu/

MacCormac College
506 South Wabash Ave.
Chicago, IL 60605-1667
312-922-1884
www.maccormac.edu/

McHenry County College
8900 US Highway 14
Crystal Lake, IL 60012-2761
815-455-3700
www.mchenry.edu/

Moraine Valley Community
College
10900 South 88th Ave.
Palos Hills, IL 60465-0937
708-974-4300
www.morainevalley.edu/

Morrison Institute of
Technology
701 Portland Ave.
Morrison, IL 61270-0410
815-772-7218
www.morrison.tec.il.us/

Morton College
3801 South Central Ave.
Cicero, IL 60804-4398
708-656-8000
www.morton.edu/

Northwestern Business
College
4829 North Lipps Ave.
Chicago, IL 60630-2298
800-396-5613
www.northwesternbc.edu/

Oakton Community College
1600 East Golf Rd.
Des Plaines, IL 60016-1268
847-635-1600
www.oakton.edu/

Parkland College
2400 West Bradley Ave.
Champaign, IL 61821-1899
217-351-2200
www.parkland.edu/

Prairie State College
202 South Halsted St.
Chicago Heights, IL 60411-8226
708-709-3516
www.prairiestate.edu/

Rend Lake College
468 North Ken Gray Parkway
Ina, IL 62846-9801
618-437-5321
www.rlc.edu/

Richland Community College
One College Park
Decatur, IL 62521-8513
217-875-7200
www.richland.edu/

Rock Valley College
3301 North Mulford Rd.
Rockford, IL 61114-5699
800-973-7821
www.rockvalleycollege.edu/

Rockford Business College
730 North Church St.
Rockford, IL 61103
815-965-8616
www.rbcsuccess.com/

Sauk Valley Community
College
173 Illinois Route 2
Dixon, IL 61021
815-288-5511
www.svcc.edu/

Shawnee Community
College
8364 Shawnee College Rd.
Ullin, IL 62992-2206
618-634-3200
www.shawneecc.edu/

South Suburban College
15800 South State St.
South Holland, IL 60473-1270
708-596-2000
www.southsuburban
college.edu/

Southeastern Illinois College
3575 College Rd.
Harrisburg, IL 62946-4925
866-338-2742
www.sic.edu/

Southwestern Illinois College
2500 Carlyle Rd.
Belleville, IL 62221-5899
618-235-2700
www.southwestern.cc.il.us/

Spoon River College
23235 North County 22
Canton, IL 61520-9801
309-647-4645
www.spoonrivercollege.net/

Springfield College in Illinois
1500 North Fifth St.
Springfield, IL 62702-2694
800-635-7289
www.sci.edu/

Taylor Business Institute
200 North Michigan Ave.,
Ste. 301
Chicago, IL 60601
312-236-6400

Triton College
2000 5th Ave.
River Grove, IL 60171-1995
800-942-7404
www.triton.cc.il.us/

Waubonsee Community
College
Route 47 at Waubonsee Dr.
Sugar Grove, IL 60554-9799
630-466-7900
www.waubonsee.edu/

Westwood College–Chicago
Du Page
7155 Janes Ave.
Woodridge, IL 60517
630-434-8244
www.westwood.edu/

Westwood College–Chicago
Loop Campus
17 North State St., Ste. 1500
Chicago, IL 60602
312-739-0850
www.westwood.edu/

Westwood College–Chicago
O'Hare Airport
4825 North Scott St., Ste. 100
Schiller Park, IL 60176
847-928-0200
www.westwood.edu/

Westwood College–Chicago
River Oaks
80 River Oaks Dr., Ste. D-49
Calumet City, IL 60409
708-832-1988
www.westwood.edu/

William Rainey Harper
College
1200 West Algonquin Rd.
Palatine, IL 60067-7398
847-925-6000
www.harpercollege.edu/

Worsham College of
Mortuary Science
495 Northgate Parkway
Wheeling, IL 60090-2646
847-808-8444
www.worshamcollege.com/

Indiana

American Trans Air Aviation
Training Academy
7251 West McCarty St.
Indianapolis, IN 46241
800-241-9699
www.aviationtraining.net/

Ancilla College
Union Rd., PO Box 1
Donaldson, IN 46513
574-936-8898
www.ancilla.edu/

Brown Mackie College, Fort
Wayne Campus
4422 East State Blvd.
Fort Wayne, IN 46815
219-484-4400
www.brownmackie.edu/loca-
tions.asp?locid=1

Brown Mackie College,
Merrillville Campus
1000 East 80th Place,
Ste. 101, N
Merrillville, IN 46410
219-769-3321
www.brownmackie.edu/
locations.asp?locid=19

Brown Mackie College,
Michigan City Campus
325 East US Highway 20
Michigan City, IN 46360
800-519-2416
www.brownmackie.edu/
locations.asp?locid=20

Brown Mackie College, South
Bend Campus
1030 East Jefferson Blvd.
South Bend, IN 46617-3123
800-743-2447
www.brownmackie.edu/
locations.asp?locid=2

College of Ct. Reporting
111 West Tenth St., Ste. 111
Hobart, IN 46342
219-942-1459
www.ccredu.com/

Davenport University
8200 Georgia St.
Merrillville, IN 46410
800-632-9569
www.davenport.edu/

Davenport University
7121 Grape Rd.
Granger, IN 46530
800-632-9569
www.davenport.edu/

Davenport University
5727 Solh Ave.
Hammond, IN 46320
800-632-9569
www.davenport.edu/

Holy Cross College
PO Box 308, 54515 State Rd.
033 North
Notre Dame, IN 46556-0308
574-239-8400
www.hcc-nd.edu/

Indiana Business College
550 East Washington St.
Indianapolis, IN 46204
317-264-5656
www.ibcschools.edu/

Indiana Business College
140 East 53rd St.
Anderson, IN 46013
765-644-7514
www.ibcschools.edu/

Indiana Business College
4601 Theatre Dr.
Evansville, IN 47715-4601
812-476-6000
www.ibcschools.edu/

Indiana Business College
830 North Miller Ave.
Marion, IN 46952-2338
765-662-7497
www.ibcschools.edu/

Indiana Business College
6413 North Clinton St.
Fort Wayne, IN 46825
260-471-7667
www.ibcschools.edu/

Indiana Business College
3175 South Third Place
Terre Haute, IN 47802
812-232-4458
www.ibcschools.edu/

Indiana Business College
2 Executive Dr.
Lafayette, IN 47905
765-447-9550
www.ibcschools.edu/

Indiana Business College
2222 Poshard Dr.
Columbus, IN 47203-1843
812-379-9000
www.ibcschools.edu/

Indiana Business College
411 West Riggin Rd.
Muncie, IN 47303
765-288-8681
www.ibcschools.edu/

Indiana Business College
6300 Technology Center Dr.
Indianapolis, IN 46278
317-873-6500
www.ibcschools.edu/
campuses/northwest.asp

Indiana Business College-
Medical
8150 Brookville Rd.
Indianapolis, IN 46239
317-375-8000
www.ibcschools.edu/

International Business
College
7205 Shadeland Station
Indianapolis, IN 46256
317-841-6400
www.intlbusinesscollege.com/

International Business College
5699 Covington Ln.
Fort Wayne, IN 46804
800-589-6363
www.ibcfortwayne.edu/

ITT Technical Institute
9511 Angola Ct.
Indianapolis, IN 46268-1119
800-937-4488
www.itt-tech.edu/

ITT Technical Institute
4919 Coldwater Rd.
Fort Wayne, IN 46825-5532
800-866-4488
www.itt-tech.edu/

ITT Technical Institute
10999 Stahl Rd.
Newburgh, IN 47630-7430
812-858-1600
www.itt-tech.edu/

Ivy Tech State
College–Bloomington
3116 Canterbury Ct.
Bloomington, IN 47404
812-332-1559
www.ivytech.edu/

Ivy Tech State
College–Central Indiana
1 West 26th St., PO Box 1763
Indianapolis, IN 46206-1763
317-921-4800
www.ivytech.edu/

Ivy Tech State
College–Columbus
4475 Central Ave.
Columbus, IN 47203-1868
800-922-4838
www.ivytech.edu/

Ivy Tech State
College–Eastcentral
4301 South Cowan Rd.,
PO Box 3100
Muncie, IN 47302-9448
765-289-2291
www.ivytech.edu/

Ivy Tech State
College–Kokomo
1815 East Morgan St,
PO Box 1373
Kokomo, IN 46903-1373
765-459-0561
www.ivytech.edu/

Ivy Tech State
College–Lafayette
3101 South Creasy Ln.
Lafayette, IN 47905-5266
765-772-9100
www.ivytech.edu/

Ivy Tech State College–North
Central
220 Dean Johnson Blvd.
South Bend, IN 46601
574-289-7001
www.ivytech.edu/

Ivy Tech State
College–Northeast
3800 North Anthony Blvd.
Fort Wayne, IN 46805-1430
800-859-4882
www.ivytech.edu/

Ivy Tech State
College–Northwest
1440 East 35th Ave.
Gary, IN 46409-1499
219-981-1111
www.ivytech.edu/

Ivy Tech State
College–Southcentral
8204 Highway 311
Sellersburg, IN 47172-1829
812-246-3301
www.ivytech.edu/

Ivy Tech State
College–Southeast
590 Ivy Tech Dr., PO Box 209
Madison, IN 47250-1883
812 265 4020
www.ivytech.edu/

Ivy Tech State
College–Southwest
3501 First Ave.
Evansville, IN 47710-3398
812-428-2865
www.ivytech.edu/

Ivy Tech State
College–Wabash Valley
7999 US Highway 41, South
Terre Haute, IN 47802
812-299-1121
www.ivytech.edu/

Ivy Tech State
College–Whitewater
2325 Chester Blvd.
Richmond, IN 47374-1220
765-966-2656
www.ivytech.edu/

Lincoln Technical Institute
1201 Stadium Dr.
Indianapolis, IN 46202-2194
800-554-4465
www.lincolntech.com/

Mid-America College of
Funeral Service
3111 Hamburg Pike
Jeffersonville, IN 47130-9630
800-221-6158
www.mid-america.edu/

Professional Careers Institute
7302 Woodland Dr.
Indianapolis, IN 46278
317-299-6001
www.pcicareers.com/

Sawyer College
3803 East Lincoln Highway
Merrillville, IN 46410
219-736-0436
www.sawyercollege.edu/

Sawyer College
6040 Hohman Ave.
Hammond, IN 46320
219-931-0436
www.sawyercollege.edu/

Vincennes University
1002 North First St.
Vincennes, IN 47591-5202
812-888-8888
www.vinu.edu/

Vincennes University Jasper
Campus
850 College Ave.
Jasper, IN 47546-9393
800-809-VUJC
vujc.vinu.edu/

Iowa

AIB College of Business
2500 Fleur Dr.
Des Moines, IA 50321-1799
800-444-1921
www.aib.edu/

Clinton Community College
1000 Lincoln Blvd.
Clinton, IA 52732-6299
563-244-7001
www.eicc.edu/ccc/

Des Moines Area Community
College
2006 South Ankeny Blvd.
Ankeny, IA 50021-8995
515-964-6200
www.dmacc.edu/

Ellsworth Community
College
1100 College Ave.
Iowa Falls, IA 50126-1199
800-ECC-9235
www.iavalley.cc.ia.us/ecc/

Hamilton College
3165 Edgewood Pkwy, SW
Cedar Rapids, IA 52404
800-728-0481
www.hamiltonia.edu/

Hawkeye Community
College
PO Box 8015
Waterloo, IA 50704-8015
800-670-4769
www.hawkeyecollege.edu/

Indian Hills Community
College
525 Grandview Ave., Bldg #1
Ottumwa, IA 52501-1398
800-726-2585
www.ihcc.cc.ia.us/

Iowa Central Community
College
330 Ave. M
Fort Dodge, IA 50501-5798
515-576-7201
www.iccc.cc.ia.us/

Iowa Lakes Community
College
19 South 7th St.
Estherville, IA 51334-2295
800-521-5054
www.iowalakes.edu/

Iowa Western Community
College
2700 College Rd., Box 4-C
Council Bluffs, IA 51502
800-432-5852
www.iwcc.edu/

Kaplan College
1801 East Kimberly Rd., Ste. 1
Davenport, IA 52807-2095
563-355-3500
www.kaplancollegeia.com/

Kirkwood Community
College
PO Box 2068
Cedar Rapids, IA 52406-2068
800-332-2055
www.kirkwood.cc.ia.us/

Marshalltown Community
College
3700 South Center St.
Marshalltown, IA 50158-4760
866-622-4748
www.marshalltown
communitycollege.com/

Muscatine Community
College
152 Colorado St.
Muscatine, IA 52761-5396
563-288-6001
www.eicc.edu/

North Iowa Area Community
College
500 College Dr.
Mason City, IA 50401-7299
888-GO NIACC
www.niacc.edu/

Northeast Iowa Community
College
Box 400
Calmar, IA 52132-0480
800-728-CALMAR
www.nicc.edu/

Northwest Iowa Community
College
603 West Park St.
Sheldon, IA 51201-1046
800-352-4907
www.nwicc.edu/

Scott Community College
500 Belmont Rd.
Bettendorf, IA 52722-6804
563-441-4001
www.eicc.edu/scc/

Southeastern Community
College, North Campus
1500 West Agency St.,
PO Box 180
West Burlington, IA 52655-
0180
319-752-2731
www.secc.cc.ia.us/

Southeastern Community
College, South Campus
335 Messenger Rd.,
PO Box 6007
Keokuk, IA 52632-6007
319-524-3221
www.secc.cc.ia.us/

Southwestern Community
College
1501 West Townline St.
Creston, IA 50801
800-247-4023
www.swcc.cc.ia.us/

St. Luke's College
2720 Stone Park Blvd.
Sioux City, IA 51104
800-352-4660
stlukescollege.org/

Vatterott College
6100 Thornton Ave., Ste. 290
Des Moines, IA 50321
800-353-7264
www.vatterott-college.edu/

Western Iowa Tech
Community College
4647 Stone Ave.,
PO Box 5199
Sioux City, IA 51102-5199
712-274-6400
www.witcc.edu/

Kansas

Allen County Community
College
1801 North Cottonwood St.
Iola, KS 66749-1607
620-365-5116
www.allencc.net/

Barton County Community
College
245 Northeast 30th Rd.
Great Bend, KS 67530-9283
800-722-6842
www.bartonccc.edu/

Brown Mackie College,
Lenexa Campus
9705 Lenexa Dr.
Lenexa, KS 66215
800-635-9101
www.bmcaec.com/

Brown Mackie College,
Salina Campus
2106 South 9th St.
Salina, KS 67401-2810
800-365-0433
www.brownmackie.edu/
locations.asp?locid=13

Butler County Community
College
901 South Haverhill Rd.
El Dorado, KS 67042-3280
316-321-2222
www.butlercc.edu/

Cloud County Community
College
2221 Campus Dr.,
PO Box 1002
Concordia, KS 66901-1002
800-729-5101
www.cloud.edu/

Coffeyville Community
College
400 West 11th St.
Coffeyville, KS 67337-5063
620-251-7700
www.coffeyville.edu/

Colby Community College
1255 South Range
Colby, KS 67701-4099
785-462-3984
www.colbycc.edu/

Cowley County Community
College and Area
Vocational–Technical School
125 South Second,
PO Box 1147
Arkansas City, KS 67005-1147
800-593-CCCC
www.cowley.cc.ks.us/

Dodge City Community
College
2501 North 14th Ave.
Dodge City, KS 67801-2399
620-225-1321
www.dccc.cc.ks.us/

Donnelly College
608 North 18th St.
Kansas City, KS 66102-4200
913-621-6070
www.donnelly.edu/

Flint Hills Technical College
3301 West 18th Ave.
Emporia, KS 66801
800-711-6947
www.fhtc.kansas.net/

Fort Scott Community
College
2108 South Horton
Fort Scott, KS 66701
800-874-3722
www.fortscott.edu/

Garden City Community
College
801 Campus Dr.
Garden City, KS 67846-6399
316-276-7611
www.gcccks.edu/

Hesston College
Box 3000
Hesston, KS 67062-2093
800-995-2757
www.hesston.edu/

Highland Community College
606 West Main St.
Highland, KS 66035
785-442-6000
www.highlandcc.edu/

Hutchinson Community College
and Area Vocational School
1300 North Plum St.
Hutchinson, KS 67501-5894
800-289-3501
www.hutchcc.edu/

Independence Community
College
Brookside Dr. and College
Ave., PO Box 708
Independence, KS 67301-
0708
800-842-6063
www.indycc.edu/

Johnson County Community
College
12345 College Blvd.
Overland Park, KS 66210-
1299
913-469-8500
www.johnco.cc.ks.us/

Kansas City Kansas
Community College
7250 State Ave.
Kansas City, KS 66112-3003
913-334-1100
www.kckcc.edu/

Labette Community College
200 South 14th St.
Parsons, KS 67357-4299
620-421-6700
www.labette.edu/

Manhattan Area Technical
College
3136 Dickens Ave.
Manhattan, KS 66503-2499
800-352-7575
www.matc.net/

National American University
10310 Mastin
Overland Park, KS 66212
913-217-2900
www.national.edu/

Neosho County Community
College
800 West 14th St.
Chanute, KS 66720-2699
800-729-6222
www.neosho.edu/

North Central Kansas
Technical College
PO Box 507
Beloit, KS 67420
800-658-4655
www.ncktc.tec.ks.us/

Northeast Kansas Technical
College
1501 West Riley St.
Atchison, KS 66002
800-567-4890
www.nektc.net/

Northwest Kansas Technical
College
PO Box 668, 1209 Harrison St.
Goodland, KS 67735
800-316-4127
www.nwktc.org/

Pratt Community College
348 NE State Rd. 61
Pratt, KS 67124-8317
620-672-9800
www.prattcc.edu/

Seward County Community
College
PO Box 1137
Liberal, KS 67905-1137
800-373-9951
www.sccc.edu/

Wichita Area Technical
College
301 South Grove St.
Wichita, KS 67211
316-677-9282
www.wichitatech.com/

Michigan

Alpena Community College
666 Johnson St.
Alpena, MI 49707-1495
989-356-9021
www.alpenacc.edu/

Bay de Noc Community
College
2001 North Lincoln Rd.
Escanaba, MI 49829-2511
800-221-2001
www.baydenoc.cc.mi.us/

Bay Mills Community
College
12214 West Lakeshore Dr.
Brimley, MI 49715
800-844-BMCC
www.bmcc.edu/

Davenport University
1500 North Pine St.
Alma, MI 48801
800-632-9569
www.davenport.edu/

Davenport University
5300 Bay Rd.
Saginaw, MI 48604
800-632-9569
www.davenport.edu/

Davenport University
71180 Van Dyke Rd.
Romeo, MI 48065
800-632-9569
www.davenport.edu/

Davenport University
1231 Cleaver Rd.
Caro, MI 48723
800-632-9569
www.davenport.edu/

Davenport University
3930 Traxler Ct.
Bay City, MI 48706
800-632-9569
www.davenport.edu/

Davenport University
150 Nugent Rd.
Bad Axe, MI 48413
800-632-9569
www.davenport.edu/

Davenport University
3555 East Patrick Rd.
Midland, MI 48642
800-632-9569
www.davenport.edu/

Delta College
1961 Delta Rd.
University Center, MI 48710
800-285-1705
www.delta.edu/

Glen Oaks Community
College
62249 Shimmel Rd.
Centreville, MI 49032-9719
888-994-7818
www.glenoaks.edu/

Gogebic Community College
E-4946 Jackson Rd.
Ironwood, MI 49938
906-932-4231
www.gogebic.edu/

Grand Rapids Community
College
143 Bostwick Ave., NE
Grand Rapids, MI 49503-3201
616-234-4000
www.grcc.edu/

Henry Ford Community
College
5101 Evergreen Rd.
Dearborn, MI 48128-1495
313-845-9615
www.hfcc.edu/

ITT Technical Institute
1905 South Haggerty Rd.
Canton, MI 48188-2025
800-247-4477
www.itt-tech.edu/

ITT Technical Institute
1522 East Big Beaver Rd.
Troy, MI 48083-1905
248-524-1800
www.itt-tech.edu/

ITT Technical Institute
4020 Sparks Dr., SE
Grand Rapids, MI 49546
616-956-1060
www.itt-tech.edu/

Jackson Community College
2111 Emmons Rd.
Jackson, MI 49201-8399
888-522-7344
www.jccmi.edu

Kalamazoo Valley
Community College
PO Box 4070
Kalamazoo, MI 49003-4070
269-488-4400
www.kvcc.edu/

Kellogg Community College
450 North Ave.
Battle Creek, MI 49017-3397
616-965-3931
www.kellogg.edu/

Kirtland Community College
10775 North St Helen Rd.
Roscommon, MI 48653-9699
989-275-5000
www.kirtland.edu/

Lake Michigan College
2755 East Napier
Benton Harbor, MI 49022-1899
616-927-8100
www.lmc.cc.mi.us/

Lansing Community College
PO Box 40010
Lansing, MI 48901-7210
800-644-4LCC
www.lcc.edu/

Lewis College of Business
17370 Meyers Rd.
Detroit, MI 48235-1423
313-862-6300
www.lewiscollege.edu/

Macomb Community College
14500 East Twelve Mile Rd.
Warren, MI 48088-3896
866-622-6624
www.macomb.edu/

Mid Michigan Community
College
1375 South Clare Ave.
Harrison, MI 48625-9447
989-386-6622
www.midmich.cc.mi.us/

Monroe County Community
College
1555 South Raisinville Rd.
Monroe, MI 48161-9047
734-242-7300
www.monroeccc.edu/

Montcalm Community
College
2800 College Dr.
Sidney, MI 48885-9723
989-328-2111
www.montcalm.edu/

Mott Community College
1401 East Court St.
Flint, MI 48503-2089
810-762-0200
www.mcc.edu/

Muskegon Community
College
221 South Quarterline Rd.
Muskegon, MI 49442-1493
231-773-9131
www.muskegon.cc.mi.us/

North Central Michigan
College
1515 Howard St.
Petoskey, MI 49770-8717
888-298-6605
www.ncmc.cc.mi.us/

Northwestern Michigan
College
1701 East Front St.
Traverse City, MI 49686-3061
800-748-0566
www.nmc.edu/

Oakland Community College
2480 Opdyke Rd.
Bloomfield Hills, MI 48304-2266
248-341-2000
www.oaklandcc.edu/

Saginaw Chippewa Tribal
College
2274 Enterprise Dr.
Mount Pleasant, MI 48858
989-775-4123
www.sagchip.org/tribal
college/

Schoolcraft College
18600 Haggerty Rd.
Livonia, MI 48152-2696
734-462-4400
www.schoolcraft.edu/

Southwestern Michigan
College
58900 Cherry Grove Rd.
Dowagiac, MI 49047-9793
800-456-8675
www.swmich.edu/

St. Clair County Community
College
323 Erie St., PO Box 5015
Port Huron, MI 48061-5015
810-984-3881
www.sc4.edu/

Washtenaw Community
College
4800 East Huron River Dr.,
PO Box D-1
Ann Arbor, MI 48106
734-973-3300
www.wccnet.edu/

Wayne County Community
College District
801 West Fort St.
Detroit, MI 48226-3010
313-496-2600
www.wcccd.edu/

West Shore Community
College
PO Box 277, 3000 North
Stiles Rd.
Scottville, MI 49454-0277
231-845-6211
www.westshore.edu/

Minnesota

Academy College
1101 East 78th St., Ste. 100
Minneapolis, MN 55420
800-292-9149
www.academycollege.edu/

Alexandria Technical College
1601 Jefferson St.
Alexandria, MN 56308-3707
888-234-1222
www.alextech.edu/

Anoka Technical College
1355 West Highway 10
Anoka, MN 55303
612-576-4700
www.ank.tec.mn.us/

Anoka-Ramsey Community
College
11200 Mississippi Blvd., NW
Coon Rapids, MN 55433-3470
763-427-2600
www.anokaramsey.edu/

Anoka-Ramsey Community
College, Cambridge Campus
300 Polk St. South
Cambridge, MN 55008-5706
763-689-7000
www.anokaramsey.edu/

Brown College
1440 Northland Dr.
Mendota Heights, MN 55120
800-6BROWN6
www.browncollege.edu/

Central Lakes College
501 West College Dr.
Brainerd, MN 56401-3904
218-855-8000
www.clcmn.edu/

Century College
3300 Century Ave. North
White Bear Lake, MN 55110
800-228-1978
www.century.cc.mn.us/

Dakota County Technical
College
1300 East 145th St.
Rosemount, MN 55068
877-YES-DCTC
www.dctc.edu/

Duluth Business University
4724 Mike Colalillo Dr.
Duluth, MN 55807
800-777-8406
www.dbumn.edu/

Dunwoody College of
Technology
818 Dunwoody Blvd.
Minneapolis, MN 55403
800-292-4625
www.dunwoody.edu/

Fond du Lac Tribal and
Community College
2101 14th St.
Cloquet, MN 55720
800-657-3712
www.fdltcc.edu/

Globe College
7166 North 10th St.
Oakdale, MN 55128
651-730-5100
www.globecollege.com/

Hennepin Technical College
9000 Brooklyn Blvd.
Brooklyn Park, MN 55445
763-425-3800
www.hennepintech.edu/

Herzing College
5700 West Broadway
Minneapolis, MN 55428
800-878-DRAW
www.herzing.edu/

Hibbing Community College
1515 East 25th St.
Hibbing, MN 55746-3300
800-224-4HCC
www.hcc.mnscu.edu/

High-Tech Institute
5100 Gamble Dr.
St. Louis Park, MN 55416
800-987-0110
www.high-techinstitute.com/

Inver Hills Community
College
2500 East 80th St.
Inver Grove Heights, MN
55076-3224
651-450-8500
www.inverhills.edu/

Itasca Community College
1851 Highway 169 East
Grand Rapids, MN 55744
800-996-6422
www.itascacc.edu/

ITT Technical Institute
8911 Columbine Rd.
Eden Prairie, MN 55347
952-914-5300
www.itt-tech.edu/

Lake Superior College
2101 Trinity Rd.
Duluth, MN 55811
800-432-2884
www.lsc.mnscu.edu/

Leech Lake Tribal College
PO Box 180
Cass Lake, MN 56633-0180
888-829-4240
www.lltc.org/

McNally Smith College of
Music
19 Exchange St. East
Saint Paul, MN 55101
800-594-9500
www.mcnallysmith.edu/

Mesabi Range Community
and Technical College
1001 Chestnut St. West
Virginia, MN 55792-3448
218-741-3095
www.mr.mnscu.edu/

Minneapolis Business
College
1711 West County Rd. B
Roseville, MN 55113
800-279-5200
www.mplsbusinesscollege.
com/

Minneapolis Community and
Technical College
1501 Hennepin Ave.
Minneapolis, MN 55403-1779
612-659-6000
www.mcto.mnscu.edu/

Minnesota School of
Business–Brooklyn Center
5910 Shingle Creek Parkway
Brooklyn Center, MN 55430
763-566-7777
www.msbcollege.edu/

Minnesota School of
Business–Plymouth
1455 Country Rd. 101 North
Minneapolis, MN 55447
763-476-2000
www.msbcollege.edu/

Minnesota School of
Business–Richfield
1401 West 76th St.
Richfield, MN 55423
612-861-2000
www.msbcollege.edu/

Minnesota School of
Business–Shakopee
1200 Shakopee Town Square
Shakopee, MN 55379
866-766-1200
www.msbcollege.edu/

Minnesota School of
Business–St. Cloud
1201 2nd St. South
Waite Park, MN 56387
866-403-3333
www.msbcollege.edu/

Minnesota State
College–Southeast Technical
1250 Homer Rd., PO Box 409
Winona, MN 55987
800-372-8164
www.southeastmn.edu/

Minnesota State Community
and Technical College–Detroit
Lakes
900 Highway 34, E
Detroit Lakes, MN 56501
800-492-4836
www.minnesota.edu/

Minnesota State Community
and Technical College–Fergus
Falls
1414 College Way
Fergus Falls, MN 56537-1009
888-MY-MSCTC
www.minnesota.edu/

Minnesota State Community
and Technical
College–Moorhead
1900 28th Ave., South
Moorhead, MN 56560
800-426-5603
www.minnesota.edu/

Minnesota State Community
and Technical
College–Wadena
405 Colfax Ave., SW,
PO Box 566
Wadena, MN 56482
800-247-2007
www.minnesota.edu/

Minnesota West Community
and Technical College
1314 North Hiawatha Ave.
Pipestone, MN 56164
800-658-2330
www.mnwest.mnscu.edu/

National American University
112 West Market
Bloomington, MN 55425
605-394-4800
www.national.edu/

National American University
6120 Earle Brown Dr., Ste. 100
Brooklyn Center, MN 55430
763-560-8377
www.national.edu/

Normandale Community
College
9700 France Ave. South
Bloomington, MN 55431-
4399
866-880-8740
www.normandale.edu/

North Hennepin Community
College
7411 85th Ave. North
Brooklyn Park, MN 55445-
2231
763-424-0702
www.nhcc.edu/

Northland Community and
Technical College–East Grand
Forks
2022 Central Ave., NW
East Grand Forks, MN 56721-
2702
800-451-3441
www.northlandcollege.edu/

Northland Community and
Technical College–Thief River
Falls
1101 Highway One East
Thief River Falls, MN 56701
800-959-6282
www.northlandcollege.edu/

Northwest Technical College
905 Grant Ave., SE
Bemidji, MN 56601-4907
800-942-8324
bemidji.ntcmn.edu/

Northwest Technical Institute
11995 Singletree Ln.
Eden Prairie, MN 55344-5351
800-443-4223
www.nti.edu/

Pine Technical College
900 4th St. SE
Pine City, MN 55063
800-521-7463
www.pinetech.edu/

Rainy River Community
College
1501 Highway 71
International Falls, MN 56649
800-456-3996
www.rrcc.mnscu.edu/

Rasmussen College Eagan
3500 Federal Dr.
Eagan, MN 55122-1346
800-852-6367
www.rasmussen.edu/

Rasmussen College Mankato
501 Holly Ln.
Mankato, MN 56001-6803
507-625-6556
www.rasmussen.edu/

Rasmussen College
Minnetonka
12450 Wayzata Blvd., Ste. 315
Minnetonka, MN 55305-1928
952-545-2000
www.rasmussen.edu/

Rasmussen College St. Cloud
226 Park Ave. South
St. Cloud, MN 56301-3713
320-251-5600
www.rasmussen.edu/

Ridgewater College
PO Box 1097
Willmar, MN 56201-1097
800-722-1151
www.ridgewater.mnscu.edu/

Riverland Community
College
1900 8th Ave., NW
Austin, MN 55912
800-247-5039
www.riverland.cc.mn.us/

Rochester Community and
Technical College
851 30th Ave., SE
Rochester, MN 55904-4999
507-285-7210
www.roch.edu/

Saint Paul College–A
Community & Technical
College
235 Marshall Ave.
St. Paul, MN 55102-1800
800-227-6029
www.saintpaul.edu/

South Central Technical
College
1920 Lee Blvd.
North Mankato, MN 56003
507-389-7200
www.sctc.mnscu.edu/

St. Cloud Technical College
1540 Northway Dr.
St. Cloud, MN 56303-1240
320-654-5000
www.sctc.edu/

Vermilion Community
College
1900 East Camp St.
Ely, MN 55731-1996
800-657-3608
www.vcc.edu/

Missouri

Allied College
500 Northwest Plaza Tower,
Ste. 400
Saint Ann, MO 63074
314-739-4450
www.alliedmedicalcollege.com

Blue River Community
College
20301 East 78 Highway
Independence, MO 64057
816-655-6000
www.kcmetro.edu/

Concorde Career Institute
3239 Broadway
Kansas City, MO 64111-2407
816-531-5223
www.concordecareer
colleges.com/

Cottey College
1000 West Austin
Nevada, MO 64772
888-526-8839
www.cottey.edu/

Crowder College
601 Laclede Ave.
Neosho, MO 64850-9160
866-238-7788
www.crowder.edu/

East Central College
1964 Prairie Dell Rd.
Union, MO 63084
636-583-5193
www.eastcentral.edu/

Heritage College
534 East 99th St.
Kansas City, MO 64131-4203
816-942-5474
www.heritage-education.
com/

Hickey College
940 West Port Plaza, Ste. 101
St. Louis, MO 63146
800-777-1544
www.hickeycollege.com/

High-Tech Institute
9001 State Line Rd.
Kansas City, MO 64114
602-279-9700
www.high-techinstitute.com/

IHM Health Studies Center
2500 Abbott Place
St. Louis, MO 63143-2636
314-768-1234
www.ihmhealthstudies.com/

ITT Technical Institute
1930 Meyer Drury Dr.
Arnold, MO 63010
888-488-1082
www.itt-tech.edu/

ITT Technical Institute
13505 Lakefront Dr.
Earth City, MO 63045-1412
800-235-5488
www.itt-tech.edu/

Jefferson College
1000 Viking Dr.
Hillsboro, MO 63050-2441
636-797-3000
www.jeffco.edu/

Linn State Technical College
One Technology Dr.
Linn, MO 65051-9606
800-743-TECH
www.linnstate.edu/

Longview Community College
500 Southwest Longview Rd.
Lee's Summit, MO 64081-
2105
816-672-2000
www.kcmetro.edu/

Maple Woods Community
College
2601 Northeast Barry Rd.
Kansas City, MO 64156-1299
816-437-3000
www.kcmetro.edu/

Metro Business College
1732 North Kingshighway
Cape Girardeau, MO 63701
573-334-9181
www.metrobusinesscollege.
edu/

Metro Business College
1202 East State Route 72
Rolla, MO 65401
800-467-0785
www.metrobusinesscollege.
edu/

Metro Business College
1407 Southwest Blvd.
Jefferson City, MO 65109
800-467-0786
www.metrobusinesscollege.
edu/

Metropolitan Community
College-Business &
Technology College
1775 Universal Ave.
Kansas City, MO 64120
800-841-7158
www.mccbtc.com/

Midwest Institute
10910 Manchester Rd.
Kirkwood, MO 63122
314-965-8363
www.midwestinstitute.com/

Midwest Institute
4260 Shoreline Dr.
Earth City, MO 63045
314-344-3334
www.midwestinstitute.com/

Mineral Area College
PO Box 1000
Park Hills, MO 63601-1000
573-431-4593
www.mineralarea.edu/

Missouri College
10121 Manchester Rd.
St. Louis, MO 63122-1583
314-821-7700
www.mocollege.com/

Missouri State
University–West Plains
128 Garfield
West Plains, MO 65775
417-255-7255
www.wp.smsu.edu/

Moberly Area Community
College
101 College Ave.
Moberly, MO 65270-1304
800-622-2070
www.macc.edu/

North Central Missouri
College
1301 Main St.
Trenton, MO 64683-1824
800-880-6180
www.ncmissouri.edu/

Ozarks Technical Community
College
PO Box 5958
Springfield, MO 65801
417-895-7000
www.otc.edu/

Patricia Stevens College
330 North Fourth St., Ste. 306
St. Louis, MO 63102
800-871-0949
www.patriciastevenscollege.
edu/

Penn Valley Community
College
3201 Southwest Trafficway
Kansas City, MO 64111
816-759-4000
www.kcmetro.edu/

Pinnacle Career Institute
15329 Kensington Ave.
Kansas City, MO 64147-1212
816-331-5700
www.pcitraining.edu/

Ranken Technical College
4431 Finney Ave.
St. Louis, MO 63113
866-4RANKEN
www.ranken.edu/

Saint Charles Community
College
4601 Mid Rivers Mall Dr.
St. Peters, MO 63376-0975
636-922-8000
www.stchas.edu/

Sanford-Brown College
75 Village Square
Hazelwood, MO 63042
314-731-1101
www.sanford-brown.edu/

Sanford-Brown College
520 East 19th Ave.
North Kansas City, MO 64116
800-456-7222
www.sanford-brown.edu/

Sanford-Brown College
3555 Franks Dr.
St. Charles, MO 63301
314-949-2620
www.sanford-brown.edu/

Sanford-Brown College
1203 Smizer Mill Rd.
Fenton, MO 63026
800-456-7222
www.sanford-brown.edu/

Southeast Missouri Hospital
College of Nursing and
Health Sciences
1819 Broadway
Cape Girardeau, MO 63701
573-334-6825
www.southeastmissouri
hospital.com/college/

Springfield College
1010 West Sunshine
Springfield, MO 65807-2488
800-475-2669
www.Springfield-college.
com/

St. Louis Community College
at Florissant Valley
3400 Pershall Rd.
St. Louis, MO 63135-1499
314-513-4200
www.stlcc.edu/

St. Louis Community College
at Forest Park
5600 Oakland Ave.
St. Louis, MO 63110-1316
314-644-9100
www.stlcc.edu/

St. Louis Community College
at Meramec
11333 Big Bend Blvd.
Kirkwood, MO 63122-5720
314-984-7500
www.stlcc.edu/

State Fair Community
College
3201 West 16th St.
Sedalia, MO 65301-2199
877-311-SFCC
www.sfcc.cc.mo.us/

Three Rivers Community
College
2080 Three Rivers Blvd.
Poplar Bluff, MO 63901-2393
877-TRY-TRCC
www.trcc.edu/

Vatterott College
3925 Industrial Dr.
St. Ann, MO 63074-1807
800-345-6018
www.vatterott-college.edu/

Vatterott College
8955 East 38th Terrace
Kansas City, MO 64129
800-466-3997
www.vatterott-college.com/

Vatterott College
927 East Terra Ln.
O'Fallon, MO 63366
636-978-7488
www.vatterott-college.com/

Vatterott College
12970 Maurer Industrial Dr.
St. Louis, MO 63127
314-843-4200
www.vatterott-college.edu/

Vatterott College
3131 Frederick Ave.
St. Joseph, MO 64506
800-282-5327
www.vatterott-college.com/

Vatterott College
1258 East Trafficway St.
Springfield, MO 65802
800-766-5829
www.vatterott-college.edu/

Wentworth Military Academy
and Junior College
1880 Washington Ave.
Lexington, MO 64067
660-259-2221
www.wma1880.org/

Nebraska

Central Community
College–Columbus Campus
4500 63rd St., PO Box 1027
Columbus, NE 68602-1027
402-564-7132
www.cccneb.edu/

Central Community College–
Grand Island Campus
PO Box 4903
Grand Island, NE 68802-4903
308-398-4222
www.cccneb.edu/

Central Community
College–Hastings Campus
PO Box 1024
Hastings, NE 68902-1024
402-463-9811
www.cccneb.edu/

The Creative Center
10850 Emmet St.
Omaha, NE 68164
888-898-1789
www.thecreativecenter.com/

Hamilton College-Lincoln
1821 K St., PO Box 82826
Lincoln, NE 68501-2826
402-474-5315
www.hamiltonlincoln.com/

Hamilton College-Omaha
3350 North 90th St.
Omaha, NE 68134
800-642-1456
www.hamiltonomaha.edu/

ITT Technical Institute
9814 M St.
Omaha, NE 68127-2056
800-677-9260
www.itt-tech.edu/

Little Priest Tribal College
PO Box 270
Winnebago, NE 68071
402-878-2380
www.lptc.bia.edu/

Metrop...
College...
PO Box 3777...
Omaha, NE 681...
800-228-9553
www.mccneb.edu/

Mid-Plains Community
College
601 West State Farm Rd.
North Platte, NE 69101
800-658-4348
www.mpcca.cc.ne.us/

Myotherapy Institute
6020 South 58th St.
Lincoln, NE 68516
800-896-3363
www.myomassage.net/

Nebraska College of Technical
Agriculture
RR3, Box 23A
Curtis, NE 69025-9205
800-3CURTIS
www.ncta.unl.edu/

Nebraska Indian Community
College
PO Box 428
Macy, NE 68039-0428
888-843-6432
www.thenicc.edu/

Northeast Community
College
801 East Benjamin Ave,
PO Box 469
Norfolk, NE 68702-0469
402-371-2020
www.northeastcollege.com/

Southeast Community
College, Beatrice Campus
4771 W. Scott Rd.
Beatrice, NE 68310-7042
800-233-5027
www.southeast.edu/

Southeast Community
College, Lincoln Campus
8800 O St.
Lincoln, NE 68520-1299
800-642-4075
www.southeast.edu/

Southeast Community
College, Milford Campus
600 State St.
Milford, NE 68405-8498
800-933-7223
www.southeast.edu/

Vatterott College
5318 South 136th St.
Omaha, NE 68137
402-891-9411
www.vatterott-college.edu/

Vatterott College
225 North 80th St.
Omaha, NE 68114
402-392-1300
www.vatterott-college.edu/

Western Nebraska
Community College
371 College Dr.
Sidney, NE 69162
800-348-4435
www.wncc.net/

North Dakota

Aakers Business College
4012 19th Ave., SW
Fargo, ND 58103
800-817-0009
www.aakers-college.com/

Bismarck State College
PO Box 5587
Bismarck, ND 58506-5587
800-445-5073
www.bismarckstate.edu/

Cankdeska Cikana
Community College
PO Box 269
Fort Totten, ND 58335-0269
701-766-4415
www.littlehoop.cc/

Fort Berthold Community
College
PO Box 490
New Town, ND 58763-0490
701-627-4738
www.fbcc.bia.edu/

Lake Region State College
1801 College Dr. North
Devils Lake, ND 58301-1598
800-443-1313
www.lrsc.nodak.edu/

Minot State
University–Bottineau
Campus
105 Simrall Blvd.
Bottineau, ND 58318-1198
800-542-6866
www.misu-b.nodak.edu/

North Dakota State College
of Science
800 North Sixth St.
Wahpeton, ND 58076
800-342-4325
www.ndscs.nodak.edu/

Sitting Bull College
1341 92nd St.
Fort Yates, ND 58538-9701
701-854-3861
www.sittingbull.edu/

Turtle Mountain Community
College
Box 340
Belcourt, ND 58316-0340
701-477-7862
www.turtle-mountain.
cc.nd.us/

United Tribes Technical
College
3315 University Dr.
Bismarck, ND 58504-7596
701-255-3285
www.uttc.edu/

Williston State College
Box 1326
Williston, ND 58802-1326
888-863-9455
www.wsc.nodak.edu/

Ohio

Academy of Court Reporting
2044 Euclid Ave.
Cleveland, OH 44115
216-861-3222
www.acr.edu/

Antonelli College
124 East Seventh St.
Cincinnati, OH 45202-2592
800-505-4338
www.antonellic.com/

The Art Institute of Cincinnati
1171 East Kemper Rd.
Cincinnati, OH 45246
513-751-1206
www.theartinstituteofcincin-
nati.com/

The Art Institute of
Ohio–Cincinnati
1011 Glendale Milford Rd.
Cincinnati, OH 45215
513-771-2821
www.aiohc.aii.edu

ATS Institute of Technology
230 Alpha Park
Highland Heights, OH 44143
440-449-1700
www.atsinstitute.com/

Belmont Technical College
120 Fox Shannon Place
St. Clairsville, OH 43950-9735
740-695-9500
www.btc.edu/

Bohecker's Business College
326 East Main St.
Ravenna, OH 44266
330-297-7319
www.boheckers.com/

Bowling Green State
University–Firelands College
One University Dr.
Huron, OH 44839-9791
419-433-5560
www.firelands.bgsu.edu/

Bradford School
2469 Stelzer Rd.
Columbus, OH 43219
800-678-7981
www.bradfordschool
columbus.edu/

Brown Mackie College, Akron
Campus
2791 Mogadore Rd.
Akron, OH 44312-1596
330-733-8766
www.socaec.com/

Brown Mackie College,
Cincinnati Campus
1011 Glendale-Milford Rd.
Cincinnati, OH 45215
513-771-2424
www.brownmackie.edu/loca-
tions.asp?locid=6

Brown Mackie College,
Findlay Campus
1637 Tiffin Ave.
Findlay, OH 45840
800-842-3687
www.brownmackie.edu

Brown Mackie College, North
Canton Campus
1320 West Maple St., NW
North Canton, OH 44720-
2854
330-494-1214
www.socaec.com/

Bryant and Stratton College
27557 Chardon Rd.
Willoughby Hills, OH 44092
440-944-6800
www.bryantstratton.edu/

Bryant and Stratton College
12955 Snow Rd.
Parma, OH 44130-1013
216-265-3151
www.bryantstratton.edu/

Central Ohio Technical
College
1179 University Dr.
Newark, OH 43055-1767
740-366-1351
www.cotc.edu/

Chatfield College
20918 State Route 251
St. Martin, OH 45118-9705
513-875-3344
www.chatfield.edu/

Cincinnati College of
Mortuary Science
645 West North Bend Rd.
Cincinnati, OH 45224-1462
513-761-2020
www.ccms.edu/

Cincinnati State Technical and
Community College
3520 Central Parkway
Cincinnati, OH 45223-2690
513-569-1500
www.cincinnatistate.edu/

Clark State Community
College
570 East Leffel Ln.,
PO Box 570
Springfield, OH 45501-0570
937-325-0691
www.clarkstate.edu/

Cleveland Institute of
Electronics
1776 East Seventeenth St.
Cleveland, OH 44114-3636
800-243-6446
www.cie-wc.edu/

College of Art Advertising
4343 Bridgetown Rd.
Cincinnati, OH 45211-4427
513-574-1010
www.collegeofart
advertising.com/

Columbus State Community College
Box 1609
Columbus, OH 43216-1609
800-621-6407
www.cscc.edu/

Cuyahoga Community College
700 Carnegie Ave.
Cleveland, OH 44115-2878
800-954-8742
www.tri-c.edu/

Davis College
4747 Monroe St.
Toledo, OH 43623-4307
800-477-7021
daviscollege.edu/

Edison State Community College
1973 Edison Dr.
Piqua, OH 45356-9253
937-778-8600
www.edisonohio.edu/

ETI Technical College of Niles
2076 Youngstown-Warren Rd.
Niles, OH 44446-4398
330-652-9919
www.eti-college.com/

Gallipolis Career College
1176 Jackson Pike, Ste. 312
Gallipolis, OH 45631
800-214-0452
www.gallipoliscareercol-lege.com/

Hocking College
3301 Hocking Parkway
Nelsonville, OH 45764-9588
740-753-3591
www.hocking.edu/

Hondros College
4140 Executive Parkway
Westerville, OH 43081-3855
800-783-0095
www.hondroscollege.com/

International College of Broadcasting
6 South Smithville Rd.
Dayton, OH 45431-1833
937-258-8251
www.icbcollege.com/

ITT Technical Institute
3781 Park Mill Run Dr.
Hilliard, OH 43026
888-483-4888
www.itt-tech.edu/

ITT Technical Institute
14955 Sprague Rd.
Strongsville, OH 44136
800-331-1488
www.itt-tech.edu/

ITT Technical Institute
4750 Wesley Ave.
Norwood, OH 45212
800-314-8324
www.itt-tech.edu/

ITT Technical Institute
1030 North Meridian Rd.
Youngstown, OH 44509-4098
800-832-5001
www.itt-tech.edu/

ITT Technical Institute
3325 Stop 8 Rd.
Dayton, OH 45414-3425
937-454-2267
www.itt-tech.edu/

James A. Rhodes State College
4240 Campus Dr.
Lima, OH 45804-3597
419-995-8000
www.rhodesstate.edu/

Jefferson Community College
4000 Sunset Blvd.
Steubenville, OH 43952-3598
740-264-5591
www.jcc.edu/

Kent State University, Ashtabula Campus
3325 West 13th St.
Ashtabula, OH 44004-2299
440-964-3322
www.ashtabula.kent.edu/

Kent State University, East Liverpool Campus
400 East 4th St.
East Liverpool, OH 43920-3497
330-385-3805
www.kenteliv.kent.edu/

Kent State University, Geauga Campus
14111 Claridon-Troy Rd.
Burton, OH 44021-9500
440-834-4187
www.geauga.kent.edu/

Kent State University, Salem Campus
2491 State Route 45 South
Salem, OH 44460-9412
330-332-0361
www.salem.kent.edu/

Kent State University, Stark Campus
6000 Frank Ave., NW
Canton, OH 44720-7599
330-499-9600
www.stark.kent.edu/

Kent State University, Trumbull Campus
4314 Mahoning Ave., NW
Warren, OH 44483-1998
330-847-0571
www.trumbull.kent.edu/

Kent State University, Tuscarawas Campus
330 University Dr., NE
New Philadelphia, OH 44663-9403
330-339-3391
www.tusc.kent.edu/

Kettering College of Medical Arts
3737 Southern Blvd.
Kettering, OH 45429-1299
800-433-5262
www.kcma.edu/

Lakeland Community College
7700 Clocktower Dr.
Kirtland, OH 44094-5198
440-525-7000
www.lakeland.cc.oh.us/

Lorain County Community College
1005 Abbe Rd., North
Elyria, OH 44035
800-995-5222
www.lorainccc.edu/

Marion Technical College
1467 Mount Vernon Ave.
Marion, OH 43302-5694
740-389-4636
www.mtc.edu/

Mercy College of Northwest Ohio
2221 Madison Ave.
Toledo, OH 43624-1132
888-80-Mercy
www.mercycollege.edu/

Miami University Hamilton
1601 Peck Blvd.
Hamilton, OH 45011-3399
513-785-3000
www.ham.muohio.edu/

Miami University–Middletown Campus
4200 East University Blvd.
Middletown, OH 45042-3497
513-727-3200
www.mid.muohio.edu/

Miami–Jacobs College
PO Box 1433
Dayton, OH 45401-1433
937-461-5174
www.miamijacobs.edu/

National Institute of Technology
2545 Bailey Rd.
Cuyahoga Falls, OH 44221
330-923-9959
www.nationalinstituteof
technology.com/

North Central State College
2441 Kenwood Cr.,
PO Box 698
Mansfield, OH 44901-0698
419-755-4800
www.ncstatecollege.edu/

Northwest State Community College
22-600 State Route 34
Archbold, OH 43502-9542
419-267-5511
www.northweststate.edu

Ohio Business College
1907 North Ridge Rd.
Lorain, OH 44055
888-514-3126
www.ohiobusinesscollege.com

Ohio Business College
4020 Milan Rd.
Sandusky, OH 44870-5894
888-627-8345
www.ohiobusinesscollege.com

Ohio College of Massotherapy
225 Heritage Woods Dr.
Akron, OH 44321
330-665-1084
www.ocm.edu/

Ohio Institute of Photography and Technology
2029 Edgefield Rd.
Dayton, OH 45439-1917
800-932-9698
www.oipt.com/

The Ohio State University
Agricultural Technical
Institute
1328 Dover Rd.
Wooster, OH 44691
330-264-3911
www.ati.ohio-state.edu/

Ohio Technical College
1374 East 51st St.
Cleveland, OH 44103
800-322-7000
www.ohiotechnicalcollege.
com/

Ohio Valley College of
Technology
16808 St. Clair Ave.,
PO Box 7000
East Liverpool, OH 43920
330-385-1070
www.ovct.edu/

Owens Community College
300 Davis St.
Findlay, OH 45840
800-FINDLAY
www.owens.edu/

Owens Community College
PO Box 10000
Toledo, OH 43699-1947
800-GO-OWENS
www.owens.edu/

Professional Skills Institute
20 Arco Dr.
Toledo, OH 43607
419-531-9610
www.proskills.com/

Remington College–
Cleveland Campus
14445 Broadway Ave.
Cleveland, OH 44125
216-475-7520
www.remingtoncollege.edu/

Remington College–
Cleveland West Campus
26350 Brookpark Rd.
North Olmstead, OH 44070
440-777-2560
www.remingtoncollege.edu/

RETS Tech Center
555 East Alex Bell Rd.
Centerville, OH 45459
800-837-7387
www.retstechcenter.com/

Rosedale Bible College
2270 Rosedale Rd.
Irwin, OH 43029-9501
740-857-1311
www.rosedalebible.org/

School of Advertising Art
1725 East David Rd.
Kettering, OH 45440-1612
877-300-9866
www.saacollege.com/

Sinclair Community College
444 West Third St.
Dayton, OH 45402-1460
937-512-2500
www.sinclair.edu/

Southeastern Business
College
504 McCarty Ln.
Jackson, OH 45640
740-286-1554
www.careersohio.com/

Southeastern Business
College
1522 Sheridan Dr.
Lancaster, OH 43130-1303
740-687-6126
www.careersohio.com/

Southeastern Business
College
1855 Western Ave.
Chillicothe, OH 45601-1038
740-774-6300
www.careersohio.com/

Southern State Community
College
100 Hobart Dr.
Hillsboro, OH 45133-9487
937-393-3431
www.sscc.edu/

Southwestern College of
Business
111 West First St.
Dayton, OH 45402-3003
937-224-0061
www.swcollege.net/

Southwestern College of
Business
149 Northland Blvd.
Cincinnati, OH 45246-1122
513-874-0432
www.swcollege.net/

Southwestern College of
Business
632 Vine St., Ste. 200
Cincinnati, OH 45202-4304
513-421-3212
www.swcollege.net/

Southwestern College of
Business
201 East Second St.
Franklin, OH 45005
937-746-6633
www.swcollege.net/

Stark State College of
Technology
6200 Frank Ave., NW
Canton, OH 44720-7299
800-797-8275
www.starkstate.edu/

Stautzenberger College
5355 Southwyck Blvd.
Toledo, OH 43614
800-552-5099
www.sctoday.com/

Technology Education
College
288 South Hamilton Rd.
Columbus, OH 43213-2087
800-838-3233
www.teceducation.com/

Terra State Community
College
2830 Napoleon Rd.
Fremont, OH 43420-9670
419-334-8400
www.terra.edu/

Trumbull Business College
3200 Ridge Rd.
Warren, OH 44484
330-369-3200
www.tbc-trumbullbusiness.
com/

The University of Akron–
Wayne College
1901 Smucker Rd.
Orrville, OH 44667-9192
330-683-2010
www.wayne.uakron.edu/

University of Cincinnati
Clermont College
4200 Clermont College Dr.
Batavia, OH 45103-1785
513-732-5200
www.clc.uc.edu/

University of Cincinnati
Raymond Walters College
9555 Plainfield Rd.
Cincinnati, OH 45236-1007
513-745-5600
www.rwc.uc.edu/

University of Northwestern
Ohio
1441 North Cable Rd.
Lima, OH 45805-1498
419-227-3141
www.unoh.edu/

Vatterott College
5025 East Royalton Rd.
Broadview Heights, OH
44147
800-864-5644
www.vatterott-college.edu/

Virginia Marti College of Art
and Design
11724 Detroit Ave.,
PO Box 580
Lakewood, OH 44107-3002
216-221-8584
www.vmcad.edu/

Washington State
Community College
710 Colegate Dr.
Marietta, OH 45750-9225
740-374-8716
www.wscc.edu/

Wright State University, Lake
Campus
7600 State Route 703
Celina, OH 45822-2921
419-586-0300
www.wright.edu/lake/

Zane State College
1555 Newark Rd.
Zanesville, OH 43701-2626
740-454-2501
www.zanestate.edu/

Oklahoma

Carl Albert State College
1507 South McKenna
Poteau, OK 74953-5208
918-647-1200
www.casc.cc.ok.us/

Community Care College
4242 South Sheridan
Tulsa, OK 74145
918-610-0027
www.communitycare
college.com/

Connors State College
Route 1 Box 1000
Warner, OK 74469-9700
918-463-2931
www.connorsstate.edu/

Eastern Oklahoma State
College
1301 West Main
Wilburton, OK 74578-4999
918-465-2361
www.eosc.edu/

Heritage College of Hair
Design
7100 I-35 Services Rd.,
Ste. 7118
Oklahoma City, OK 73149
405-631-3399

Murray State College
One Murray Campus
Tishomingo, OK 73460-3130
580-371-2371
www.mscok.edu/

Northeastern Oklahoma
Agricultural and Mechanical
College
200 I St., NE
Miami, OK 74354-6434
918-542-8441
www.neoam.cc.ok.us/

Northern Oklahoma College
1220 East Grand Ave.,
PO Box 310
Tonkawa, OK 74653-0310
800-429-5715
www.north-ok.edu/

Oklahoma City Community
College
7777 South May Ave.
Oklahoma City, OK 73159-
4419
405-682-1611
www.okccc.edu/

Oklahoma State University,
Oklahoma City
900 North Portland
Oklahoma City, OK 73107-
6120
405-947-4421
www.osuokc.edu/

Oklahoma State University,
Okmulgee
1801 East Fourth St.
Okmulgee, OK 74447-3901
800-722-4471
www.osu-okmulgee.edu/

Platt College
3801 South Sheridan Rd.
Tulsa, OK 74145-111
918-663-9000
www.plattcollege.org/

Platt College
309 South Ann Arbor Ave.
Oklahoma City, OK 73128
405-946-7799
www.plattcollege.org/

Redlands Community
College
1300 South Country Club Rd.
El Reno, OK 73036-5304
405-262-2552
www.redlandscc.edu/

Rose State College
6420 Southeast 15th St.
Midwest City, OK 73110-2799
405-733-7673
www.rose.edu/

Seminole State College
PO Box 351
Seminole, OK 74818-0351
405-382-9950
www.ssc.cc.ok.us/

Southwestern Oklahoma
State University at Sayre
409 East Mississippi St.
Sayre, OK 73662-1236
580-928-5533
www.swosu.edu/sayre/

Spartan College of
Aeronautics and Technology
8820 East Pine St., PO Box
582833
Tulsa, OK 74158-2833
918-836-6886
www.spartan.edu/

Tulsa Community College
6111 East Skelly Dr.
Tulsa, OK 74135-6198
918-595-7000
www.tulsacc.edu/

Tulsa Welding School
2545 East 11th St.
Tulsa, OK 74104-3909
800-WELD-PRO
www.weldingschool.com/

Vatterott College
555 South Memorial Dr.
Tulsa, OK 74112
888-857-4016
www.vatterott-college.edu/

Vatterott College
4629 Northwest 23rd St.
Oklahoma City, OK 73127
888-948-0088
www.vatterott-college.edu/

Western Oklahoma State
College
2801 North Main St.
Altus, OK 73521-1397
580-477-2000
www.wosc.edu/

South Dakota

Kilian Community College
300 East 6th St.
Sioux Falls, SD 57103
800-888-1147
www.kilian.edu/

Lake Area Technical Institute
230 11th St. Northeast
Watertown, SD 57201
800-657-4344
www.lati.tec.sd.us/

Mitchell Technical Institute
821 North Capital
Mitchell, SD 57301
800-952-0042
mti.tec.sd.us/

National American University
2700 Doolittle Dr.
Ellsworth AFB, SD 57706
605-923-5856
www.national.edu/

Sisseton-Wahpeton
Community College
Old Agency Box 689
Sisseton, SD 57262
605-698-3966
www.swc.tc/

Southeast Technical Institute
2320 N. Career Ave.
Sioux Falls, SD 57107-1301
605-367-7624
www.southeasttech.com/

Western Dakota Technical
Institute
800 Mickelson Dr.
Rapid City, SD 57703
800-544-8765
www.westerndakotatech.org/

Wisconsin

Blackhawk Technical College
PO Box 5009
Janesville, WI 53547-5009
800-472-0024
www.blackhawk.edu/

Bryant and Stratton College
1300 North Jackson St.
Milwaukee, WI 53202-2608
414-276-5200
www.bryantstratton.edu/

Chippewa Valley Technical
College
620 West Clairemont Ave.
Eau Claire, WI 54701-6162
800-547-2882
www.cvtc.edu/

College of Menominee
Nation
PO Box 1179
Keshena, WI 54135
715-799-5600
www.menominee.edu/

Fox Valley Technical College
1825 North Bluemound,
PO Box 2277
Appleton, WI 54912-2277
920-735-5600
www.fvtc.edu/

Gateway Technical College
3520 30th Ave.
Kenosha, WI 53144-1690
262-564-2200
www.gtc.edu/

Herzing College
5218 East Terrace Dr.
Madison, WI 53718
800-582-1227
www.herzing.edu/Madison

ITT Technical Institute
470 Security Blvd.
Green Bay, WI 54313
888-884-3626
www.itt-tech.edu/

ITT Technical Institute
6300 West Layton Ave.
Greenfield, WI 53220-4612
414-282-9494
www.itt-tech.edu/

Lac Coute Oreilles Ojibwa
Community College
13466 West Trepania Rd.
Hayward, WI 54843-2181
888-526-6221
www.lco.edu/

Lakeshore Technical College
1290 North Ave.
Cleveland, WI 53015-1414
888-GO TO LTC
www.gotoltc.com/

Madison Area Technical College
3550 Anderson St.
Madison, WI 53704-2599
608-246-6100
www.matcmadison.edu/matc

Madison Media Institute
2702 Agriculture Dr., Ste. 1
Madison, WI 53718
800-236-4997
www.madisonmedia.com/

Mid-State Technical College
500 32nd St. North
Wisconsin Rapids, WI 54494-5599
888-575-6782
www.mstc.edu/

Milwaukee Area Technical College
700 West State St.
Milwaukee, WI 53233-1443
414-297-6600
matc.edu

Moraine Park Technical College
235 North National Ave,
PO Box 1940
Fond du Lac, WI 54936-1940
920-922-8611
www.morainepark.edu/

Nicolet Area Technical College
Box 518
Rhinelander, WI 54501-0518
715-365-4410
www.nicoletcollege.edu/

Northcentral Technical College
1000 West Campus Dr.
Wausau, WI 54401-1899
715-675-3331
www.ntc.edu/

Northeast Wisconsin Technical College
2740 W Mason St.,
PO Box 19042
Green Bay, WI 54307-9042
800-422-6982
www.nwtc.edu/

Southwest Wisconsin Technical College
1800 Bronson Blvd.
Fennimore, WI 53809-9778
608-822-3262
www.swtc.edu/

University of Wisconsin–Baraboo/Sauk County
1006 Connie Rd.
Baraboo, WI 53913-1015
608-356-8351
www.baraboo.uwc.edu/

University of Wisconsin–Barron County
1800 College Dr.
Rice Lake, WI 54868-2497
715-234-8176
www.barron.uwc.edu/

University of Wisconsin–Fond du Lac
400 University Dr.
Fond du Lac, WI 54935
920-929-3600
www.fdl.uwc.edu/

University of Wisconsin–Fox Valley
1478 Midway Rd.
Menasha, WI 54952
888-INFOUWC
www.uwfoxvalley.uwc.edu/

University of Wisconsin–Manitowoc
705 Viebahn St.
Manitowoc, WI 54220-6699
920-683-4700
www.manitowoc.uwc.edu/

University of Wisconsin–Marathon County
518 South Seventh Ave.
Wausau, WI 54401-5396
888-367-8962
www.uwmc.uwc.edu/

University of Wisconsin–Marinette
750 West Bay Shore
Marinette, WI 54143-4299
715-735-4300
www.uwc.edu/

University of Wisconsin–Marshfield/Wood County
2000 West 5th St.
Marshfield, WI 54449
715-389-6500
marshfield.uwc.edu/

University of Wisconsin–Richland
1200 Highway 14 West
Richland Center, WI 53581
608-647-6186
richland.uwc.edu/

University of Wisconsin–Rock County
2909 Kellogg Ave.
Janesville, WI 53546-5699
888-INFO-UWC
rock.uwc.edu/

University of Wisconsin–Sheboygan
One University Dr.
Sheboygan, WI 53081-4789
920-459-6600
www.sheboygan.uwc.edu/

University of Wisconsin–Washington County
400 University Dr.
West Bend, WI 53095-3699
262-335-5200
www.washington.uwc.edu/

University of Wisconsin–Waukesha
1500 University Dr.
Waukesha, WI 53188-2799
414-521-5200
www.waukesha.uwc.edu/

Waukesha County Technical College
800 Main St.
Pewaukee, WI 53072-4601
888-892-WCTC
www.wctc.edu/

Western Wisconsin Technical College
304 6th St. North,
PO Box C-908
La Crosse, WI 54602-0908
800-248-9982
www.wwtc.edu/

Wisconsin Indianhead Technical College
505 Pine Ridge Dr.
Shell Lake, WI 54871
800-243-9482
www.witc.edu/

VOCATIONAL/CAREER COLLEGES

Illinois

Black Hawk College
6600 34th Ave.
Moline, IL 61265-5899
309-796-5000
www.bhc.edu/

Capital Area School of Practical Nursing
2201 Toronto Rd.
Springfield, IL 62707
217-585-2160

Capri Oak Forest School of Beauty Culture
15815 South Robroy Dr.
Oak Forest, IL 60452
708-687-3020
www.capribeautyschool.com

Career Colleges of Chicago
11 East Adams St., 2nd Fl.
Chicago, IL 60603-6301
312-895-6300
www.careerchi.com/

Carl Sandburg College
2400 Tom L. Wilson Blvd.
Galesburg, IL 61401-9576
309-344-2518
www.sandburg.edu/

Center For Employment Training–Chicago
3301 West Arthington, Ste. 101
Chicago, IL 60624
408-287-7924

City Colleges of Chicago, Harold Washington College
30 East Lake St.
Chicago, IL 60601-2449
312-553-5600
hwashington.ccc.edu/

City Colleges of Chicago, Harry S. Truman College
1145 West Wilson Ave.
Chicago, IL 60640-5616
773-907-4000
www.trumancollege.cc/

City Colleges of Chicago, Kennedy-King College
6800 South Wentworth Ave.
Chicago, IL 60621-3733
773-602-5000
kennedyking.ccc.edu/

City Colleges of Chicago, Malcolm X College
1900 West Van Buren St.
Chicago, IL 60612-3145
312-850-7000
malcolmx.ccc.edu/

City Colleges of Chicago, Olive-Harvey College
10001 South Woodlawn Ave.
Chicago, IL 60628-1645
773-291-6100
oliveharvey.ccc.edu/

City Colleges of Chicago, Richard J. Daley College
7500 South Pulaski Rd.
Chicago, IL 60652-1242
773-838-7500
daley.ccc.edu/

City Colleges of Chicago, Wilbur Wright College
4300 North Narragansett Ave.
Chicago, IL 60634-1591
773-777-7900
wright.ccc.edu/

College of DuPage
425 Fawell Blvd.
Glen Ellyn, IL 60137-6599
630-942-2800
www.cod.edu/

College of Lake County
19351 West Washington St.
Grayslake, IL 60030-1198
847-543-2000
www.clcillinois.edu/

The College of Office Technology
1514-20 West Division St., Second Fl.
Chicago, IL 60622
773-278-0042
www.cotedu.com/

The Cooking and Hospitality Institute of Chicago
361 West Chestnut
Chicago, IL 60610-3050
312-944-0882
www.chicnet.org/

Danville Area Community College
2000 East Main St.
Danville, IL 61832-5199
217-443-3222
www.dacc.cc.il.us/

Educators of Beauty
128 South Fifth St.
Rockford, IL 61104
800-424-7678

Elgin Community College
1700 Spartan Dr.
Elgin, IL 60123-7193
847-697-1000
www.elgin.edu/

Environmental Technical Institute
1101 West Thorndale Ave.
Itasca, IL 60143-1334
630-285-9100
www.eticampus.com

Environmental Technical Institute–Blue Island Campus
13010 South Division St.
Blue Island, IL 60406-2606
708-285-0707
www.eticampus.com

Fox College
4201 West 93rd St.
Oak Lawn, IL 60453
708-636-7700
www.foxcollege.com/

Gem City College
PO Box 179
Quincy, IL 62301
217-222-0391
www.gemcitycollege.com/

Heartland Community College
1500 West Raab Rd.
Normal, IL 61761
309-268-8000
www.heartland.edu/

Highland Community College
2998 West Pearl City Rd.
Freeport, IL 61032-9341
815-235-6121
www.highland.edu/

Illinois Central College
One College Dr.
East Peoria, IL 61635-0001
309-694-5011
www.icc.edu/

Illinois Eastern Community Colleges, Frontier Community College
Frontier Dr.
Fairfield, IL 62837-2601
618-842-3711
www.iecc.edu/fcc/

Illinois Eastern Community Colleges, Lincoln Trail College
11220 State Hwy. 1
Robinson, IL 62454
618-544-8657
www.iecc.edu/ ltc/

Illinois Eastern Community Colleges, Olney Central College
305 North West St.
Olney, IL 62450
618-395-7777
www.iecc.edu/occ/

Illinois Eastern Community Colleges, Wabash Valley College
2200 College Dr.
Mount Carmel, IL 62863-2657
618-262-8641
www.iecc.edu/wvc/

Illinois School of Health Careers
220 South State St., #600
Chicago, IL 60004
312-913-1230
www.SchoolofHealthCareers.com

Illinois Valley Community College
815 N. Orlando Smith Ave.
Oglesby, IL 61348-9692
815-224-2720
www.ivcc.edu/

Illinois Welding School
5901 Washington St.
Bartonville, IL 61607
309-633-0379
www.illinoisweldingschool.com

John A. Logan College
700 Logan College Rd.
Carterville, IL 62918-9900
618-985-3741
www.jalc.edu/

John Wood Community College
1301 South 48th St.
Quincy, IL 62305-8736
217-224-6500
www.jwcc.edu/

Joliet Junior College
1215 Houbolt Rd.
Joliet, IL 60431-8938
815-729-9020
www.jjc.edu/

Kankakee Community
College
PO Box 888
Kankakee, IL 60901-0888
815-933-0345
www.kcc.cc.il.us/

Kaskaskia College
27210 College Rd.
Centralia, IL 62801-7878
618-545-3000
www.kaskaskia.edu/

Kishwaukee College
21193 Malta Rd.
Malta, IL 60150-9699
815-825-2086
www.kishwaukeecollege.edu/

Lake Land College
5001 Lake Land Blvd.
Mattoon, IL 61938-9366
217-234-5253
www.lakelandcollege.edu/

Lewis and Clark Community
College
5800 Godfrey Rd.
Godfrey, IL 62035-2466
618-466-7000
www.lc.edu/

Lincoln College
300 Keokuk St.
Lincoln, IL 62656-1699
217-732-3155
www.lincolncollege.edu/

Lincoln Land Community
College
5250 Shepherd Rd.,
PO Box 19256
Springfield, IL 62794-9256
217-786-2200
www.llcc.edu/

Lincoln Technical Institute
7320 West Agatite Ave.
Norridge, IL 60656-9975
312-625-1535

MacCormac College
506 South Wabash Ave.
Chicago, IL 60605-1667
312-922-1884
www.maccormac.edu/

McHenry County College
8900 US Hwy. 14
Crystal Lake, IL 60012-2761
815-455-3700
www.mchenry.edu/

Midwest Technical Institute
405 N. Limit St.
Lincoln, IL 62656-0506
800-504-8882
www.midwest-school.com

Moraine Valley Community
College
10900 South 88th Ave.
Palos Hills, IL 60465-0937
708-974-4300
www.morainevalley.edu/

Morton College
3801 South Central Ave.
Cicero, IL 60804-4398
708-656-8000
www.morton.edu/

Northwestern Business
College
4829 North Lipps Ave.
Chicago, IL 60630-2298
773-777-4220
www.northwesternbc.edu/

Oakton Community College
1600 East Golf Rd.
Des Plaines, IL 60016-1268
847-635-1600
www.oakton.edu/

Olympia College
6880 Frontgate Rd., Ste. 400
Burr Ridge, IL 60527
630-920-1102

Olympia College
247 South State St., Ste. 400
Chicago, IL 60604

Parkland College
2400 West Bradley Ave.
Champaign, IL 61821-1899
217-351-2200
www.parkland.edu/

Pivot Point Beauty School
1791 West Howard St.
Chicago, IL 60626
773-465-0170

Pivot Point International
Cosmetology Research
Center
525 Busse Rd.
Elk Grove Villiage, IL 60007-
2116
708-490-5900

Prairie State College
202 South Halsted St.
Chicago Heights, IL 60411-
8226
708-709-3500
www.prairiestate.edu/

Rend Lake College
468 North Ken Gray Pkwy.
Ina, IL 62846-9801
618-437-5321
www.rlc.edu/

Richland Community College
One College Park
Decatur, IL 62521-8513
217-875-7200
www.richland.edu/

Rock Valley College
3301 North Mulford Rd.
Rockford, IL 61114-5699
815-921-7821
www.rockvalleycollege.edu/

Rockford Business College
730 North Church St.
Rockford, IL 61103
815-965-8616
www.rbcsuccess.com/

Rosel School of Cosmetology
2444 West Devon Ave.
Chicago, IL 60659
773-508-5600

Sanford-Brown College
1101 Eastport Plaza Dr.
Collinsville, IL 62234
618-931-0300
www.sanford-brown.edu/

Sauk Valley Community
College
173 Illinois Route 2
Dixon, IL 61021
815-288-5511
www.svcc.edu/

Shawnee Community
College
8364 Shawnee College Rd.
Ullin, IL 62992-2206
618-634-3200
www.shawneecc.edu/

South Suburban College
15800 South State St.
South Holland, IL 60473-
1270
708-596-2000
www.southsuburban
college.edu/

Southeastern Illinois College
3575 College Rd.
Harrisburg, IL 62946-4925
618-252-5400
www.sic.edu/

Southwestern Illinois College
2500 Carlyle Rd.
Belleville, IL 62221-5899
618-235-2700
www.southwestern.cc.il.us/

Spoon River College
23235 North County 22
Canton, IL 61520-9801
309-647-4645
www.spoonrivercollege.net/

Triton College
2000 5th Ave.
River Grove, IL 60171-1995
708-456-0300
www.triton.cc.il.us/

Undergraduate School of
Cosmetology
300 West Carpenter St.
Springfield, IL 62702
217-753-8552
www.uscart.com

Universal Technical Institute
601 Regency Dr.
Glendale Heights, IL 60139-
2208
630-529-2662
www.uticorp.com

Waubonsee Community
College
Route 47 at Waubonsee Dr.
Sugar Grove, IL 60554-9799
630-466-7900
www.waubonsee.edu/

William Rainey Harper
College
1200 West Algonquin Rd.
Palatine, IL 60067-7398
847-925-6000
www.harpercollege.edu/

Zarem/Golde ORT Technical
Institute
3050 West Touhy Ave.
Chicago, IL 60645
773-761-5900

Indiana

Ancilla College
Union Rd., PO Box 1
Donaldson, IN 46513
574-936-8898
www.ancilla.edu/

Brown Mackie College, Fort
Wayne Campus
4422 East State Blvd.
Fort Wayne, IN 46815
219-484-4400
www.brownmackie.edu/

Brown Mackie College,
Merrillville Campus
1000 East 80th Place,
Ste. 101, N
Merrillville, IN 46410
219-769-3321
www.brownmackie.edu/

Brown Mackie College,
Michigan City Campus
325 East US Hwy. 20
Michigan City, IN 46360
219-877-3100
www.brownmackie.edu/
locations.asp?locid=20

Brown Mackie College, South
Bend Campus
1030 East Jefferson Blvd.
South Bend, IN 46617-3123
574-237-0774
www.brownmackie.edu/

Decker College
6825 Hillsdale Ct.
Indianapolis, IN 46250
www.deckercollege.edu

Hair Fashions by Kaye
Beauty College
6316 East 82nd St.
Indianapolis, IN 46250
317-576-8000

Horizon Career College
8315 Virginia St., Ste. A
Merrillville, IN 46410
219-756-6811

Indiana Business College
140 East 53rd St.
Anderson, IN 46013
765-644-7514
www.ibcschools.edu/

Indiana Business College
2222 Poshard Dr.
Columbus, IN 47203-1843
812-379-9000
www.ibcschools.edu/

Indiana Business College
4601 Theatre Dr.
Evansville, IN 47715-4601
812-476-6000
www.ibcschools.edu/

Indiana Business College
6413 North Clinton St.
Fort Wayne, IN 46825
260-471-7667
www.ibcschools.edu/

Indiana Business College
550 East Washington St.
Indianapolis, IN 46204
317-264-5656
www.ibcschools.edu/

Indiana Business College
2 Executive Dr.
Lafayette, IN 47905
765-447-9550
www.ibcschools.edu/

Indiana Business College
830 North Miller Ave.
Marion, IN 46952-2338
765-662-7497
www.ibcschools.edu/

Indiana Business College
411 West Riggin Rd.
Muncie, IN 47303
765-288-8681
www.ibcschools.edu/

Indiana Business College
3175 South Third Place
Terre Haute, IN 47802
812-232-4458
www.ibcschools.edu/

Indiana Business College-
Medical
8150 Brookville Rd.
Indianapolis, IN 46239
317-375-8000
www.ibcschools.edu/

International Business
College
5699 Covington Lane
Fort Wayne, IN 46804
219-459-4500
www.ibcfortwayne.edu/

International Business
College
7205 Shadeland Station
Indianapolis, IN 46256
317-841-6400
www.intlbusinesscollege.com

Ivy Tech State College–
Bloomington
3116 Canterbury Ct.
Bloomington, IN 47404
812-332-1559
www.ivytech.edu/

Ivy Tech State College–
Central Indiana
1 West 26th St., PO Box 1763
Indianapolis, IN 46206-1763
317-921-4800
www.ivytech.edu/

Ivy Tech State College–
Columbus
4475 Central Ave.
Columbus, IN 47203-1868
812-372-9925
www.ivytech.edu/

Ivy Tech State College–
Eastcentral
4301 South Cowan Rd.,
PO Box 3100
Muncie, IN 47302-9448
765-289-2291
www.ivytech.edu/

Ivy Tech State College–
Kokomo
1815 East Morgan St.,
PO Box 1373
Kokomo, IN 46903-1373
765-459-0561
www.ivytech.edu/

Ivy Tech State College–
Lafayette
3101 South Creasy Lane
Lafayette, IN 47905-5266
765-772-9100
www.ivytech.edu/

Ivy Tech State College–North
Central
220 Dean Johnson Blvd.
South Bend, IN 46601
574-289-7001
www.ivytech.edu/

Ivy Tech State College–
Northeast
3800 North Anthony Blvd.
Fort Wayne, IN 46805-1430
260-482-9171
www.ivytech.edu/

Ivy Tech State College–
Northwest
1440 East 35th Ave.
Gary, IN 46409-1499
219-981-1111
www.ivytech.edu/

Ivy Tech State College–
Southcentral
8204 Hwy. 311
Sellersburg, IN 47172-1829
812-246-3301
www.ivytech.edu/

Ivy Tech State College–
Southeast
590 Ivy Tech Dr., PO Box 209
Madison, IN 47250-1883
812-265-4028
www.ivytech.edu/

Ivy Tech State College–
Southwest
3501 First Ave.
Evansville, IN 47710-3398
812-426-2865
www.ivytech.edu/

Ivy Tech State College–
Wabash Valley
7999 US Hwy. 41, South
Terre Haute, IN 47802
812-299-1121
www.ivytech.edu/

Ivy Tech State College–
Whitewater
2325 Chester Blvd.
Richmond, IN 47374-1220
765-966-2656
www.ivytech.edu/

Lincoln Technical Institute
1201 Stadium Dr.
Indianapolis, IN 46202-2194
317-632-5553
www.lincolntech.com/

Merrillville Beauty College
48 West 67th Place
Merrillville, IN 46410
219-769-2232

Professional Careers Institute
7302 Woodland Dr.
Indianapolis, IN 46278
317-299-6001
www.pcicareers.com/

Sawyer College
6040 Hohman Ave.
Hammond, IN 46320
219-931-0436
www.sawyercollege.edu/

Sawyer College
3803 East Lincoln Hwy.
Merrillville, IN 46410
219-736-0436
www.sawyercollege.edu/

Vincennes University
1002 North First St.
Vincennes, IN 47591-5202
812-888-8888
www.vinu.edu/

Iowa

AIB College of Business
2500 Fleur Dr.
Des Moines, IA 50321-1799
515-244-4221
www.aib.edu/

Des Moines Area Community
College
2006 South Ankeny Blvd.
Ankeny, IA 50021-8995
515-964-6200
www.dmacc.edu/

Ellsworth Community
College
1100 College Ave.
Iowa Falls, IA 50126-1199
641-648-4611
www.iavalley.cc.ia.us/ecc/

Hamilton College
3165 Edgewood Pkwy, SW
Cedar Rapids, IA 52404
319-363-0481
www.hamiltonia.edu/

Hawkeye Community
College
PO Box 8015
Waterloo, IA 50704-8015
319-296-2320
www.hawkeyecollege.edu/

Indian Hills Community
College
525 Grandview Ave., Bldg #1
Ottumwa, IA 52501-1398
641-683-5111
www.ihcc.cc.ia.us/

Iowa Central Community
College
330 Ave. M
Fort Dodge, IA 50501-5798
515-576-7201
www.iccc.cc.ia.us/

Iowa Lakes Community
College
19 South 7th St.
Estherville, IA 51334-2295
712-362-2604
www.iowalakes.edu/

Iowa School of Beauty
3305 70th St.
Des Moines, IA 50322
515-278-9939

Iowa Western Community
College
2700 College Rd., Box 4-C
Council Bluffs, IA 51502
712-325-3200
www.iwcc.edu/

Kaplan College
1801 East Kimberly Rd., Ste. 1
Davenport, IA 52807-2095
563-355-3500
www.kaplancollegeia.com/

Kirkwood Community
College
PO Box 2068
Cedar Rapids, IA 52406-2068
319-398-5411
www.kirkwood.cc.ia.us/

La' James College of
Hairstyling
6322 University Ave.
Cedar Falls, IA 50613
319-277-2150
www.lajames.net

La' James College of
Hairstyling
6336 Hickman Rd.
Des Moines, IA 50322
515-278-2208
www.lajames.net

La' James College of
Hairstyling
227 East Market St.
Iowa City, IA 52240
319-337-7109
www.lajames.net

Marshalltown Community
College
3700 South Center St.
Marshalltown, IA 50158-4760
641-752-7106
www.marshalltown
communitycollege.com/

Muscatine Community
College
152 Colorado St.
Muscatine, IA 52761-5396
563-288-6001
www.eicc.edu/

North Iowa Area Community
College
500 College Dr.
Mason City, IA 50401-7299
641-423-1264
www.niacc.edu/

Northeast Iowa Community
College
Box 400
Calmar, IA 52132-0480
563-562-3263
www.nicc.edu/

Northwest Iowa Community
College
603 West Park St.
Sheldon, IA 51201-1046
712-324-5061
www.nwicc.edu/

Professional Cosmetology
Institute
627 Main St.
Ames, IA 50010
515-232-7250

Southeastern Community
College, North Campus
1500 West Agency St.,
PO Box 180
West Burlington, IA 52655-
0180
319-752-2731
www.secc.cc.ia.us/

Southwestern Community
College
1501 West Townline St.
Creston, IA 50801
641-782-7081
www.swcc.cc.ia.us/

Vatterott College
6100 Thornton Ave., Ste. 290
Des Moines, IA 50321
515-309-9000
www.vatterott-college.edu/

Western Iowa Tech
Community College
4647 Stone Ave.,
PO Box 5199
Sioux City, IA 51102-5199
712-274-6400
www.witcc.edu/

Kansas

Allen County Community
College
1801 North Cottonwood St.
Iola, KS 66749-1607
620-365-5116
www.allencc.net/

American Academy of Hair
Design
901 SW 37th St.
Topeka, KS 66611
913-267-5800

Barton County Community
College
245 Northeast 30th Rd.
Great Bend, KS 67530-9283
620-792-2701
www.bartonccc.edu/

Brown Mackie College,
Lenexa Campus
9705 Lenexa Dr.
Lenexa, KS 66215
913-768-1900
www.bmcaec.com/

Brown Mackie College,
Salina Campus
2106 South 9th St.
Salina, KS 67401-2810
785-825-5422
www.brownmackie.edu/loca-
tions.asp?locid=13

Butler County Community
College
901 South Haverhill Rd.
El Dorado, KS 67042-3280
316-321-2222
www.butlercc.edu/

Cloud County Community
College
2221 Campus Dr.,
PO Box 1002
Concordia, KS 66901-1002
785-243-1435
www.cloud.edu/

Coffeyville Community
College
400 West 11th St.
Coffeyville, KS 67337-5063
620-251-7700
www.coffeyville.edu/

Colby Community College
1255 South Range
Colby, KS 67701-4099
785-462-3984
www.colbycc.edu/

Cowley County Community
College and Area
Vocational–Technical School
125 South Second,
PO Box 1147
Arkansas City, KS 67005-
1147
620-442-0430
www.cowley.cc.ks.us/

Dodge City Community
College
2501 North 14th Ave.
Dodge City, KS 67801-2399
620-225-1321
www.dccc.cc.ks.us/

Donnelly College
608 North 18th St.
Kansas City, KS 66102-4298
913-621-6070
www.donnelly.edu/

Fort Scott Community
College
2108 South Horton
Fort Scott, KS 66701
316-223-2700
www.fortscott.edu/

Garden City Community
College
801 Campus Dr.
Garden City, KS 67846-6399
910-276-7611
www.gcccks.edu/

Highland Community College
606 West Main St.
Highland, KS 66035
785-442-6000
www.highlandcc.edu/

Hutchinson Community
College and Area Vocational
School
1300 North Plum St.
Hutchinson, KS 67501-5894
620-665-3500
www.hutchcc.edu/

Independence Community
College
Brookside Dr. and College Ave.,
PO Box 708
Independence, KS 67301-
0708
620-331-4100
www.indycc.edu/

Johnson County Community
College
12345 College Blvd.
Overland Park, KS 66210-
1299
913-469-8500
www.johnco.cc.ks.us/

Kansas City Area Technical
School
2220 North 59th St.
Kansas City, KS 66104
913-596-5500

Kansas City Kansas
Community College
7250 State Ave.
Kansas City, KS 66112-3003
913-334-1100
www.kckcc.edu/

Labette Community College
200 South 14th St.
Parsons, KS 67357-4299
620-421-6700
www.labette.edu/

Manhattan Area Technical
College
3136 Dickens Ave.
Manhattan, KS 66503-2499
913-587-2800
www.matc.net/

Neosho County Community
College
800 West 14th St.
Chanute, KS 66720-2699
620-431-2820
www.neosho.edu/

North Central Kansas
Technical College
PO Box 507
Beloit, KS 67420
913-738-2276
www.ncktc.tec.ks.us/

Northwest Kansas Technical
College
PO Box 668, 1209 Harrison St.
Goodland, KS 67735
785-899-3641
www.nwktc.org/

Pratt Community College
348 NE State Rd. 61
Pratt, KS 67124-8317
620-672-9800
www.prattcc.edu/

Salina Area Technical School
2562 Scanlan Ave.
Salina, KS 67401
785-825-2261

Seward County Community
College
PO Box 1137
Liberal, KS 67905-1137
620-624-1951
www.sccc.edu/

Southwest Kansas Technical
School
2215 North Kansas
Liberal, KS 67905-1599
316-626-3819
www.usd480.net/swkts/

Wichita Area Technical
College
301 South Grove St.
Wichita, KS 67211
316-677-9282
www.wichitatech.com/

Xenon International School
of Hair Design
3804 West Douglas
Wichita, KS 67203
316-943-5516

Michigan

Alpena Community College
666 Johnson St.
Alpena, MI 49707-1495
989-356-9021
www.alpenacc.edu/

Bay de Noc Community
College
2001 North Lincoln Rd.
Escanaba, MI 49829-2511
906-786-5802
www.baydenoc.cc.mi.us/

Bay Mills Community
College
12214 West Lakeshore Dr.
Brimley, MI 49715
906-248-3354
www.bmcc.edu/

Chic University of
Cosmetology
1735 Four Mile, NE
Grand Rapids, MI 49525
616-363-9853

David Pressley Professional
School of Cosmetology
1127 South Washington St.
Royal Oak, MI 48067
248-548-5090

Delta College
1961 Delta Rd.
University Center, MI 48710
989-686-9000
www.delta.edu/

Detroit Business
Institute–Southfield
23077 Greenfield Rd.,
Ste. LL28
Southfield, MI 48075
248-552-6300

Douglas J. Educational Center
333 Albert St., Ste. 110
East Lansing, MI 48823
517-333-9656
www.douglasj.com

Glen Oaks Community
College
62249 Shimmel Rd.
Centreville, MI 49032-9719
616-467-9945
www.glenoaks.edu/

Gogebic Community College
E-4946 Jackson Rd.
Ironwood, MI 49938
906-932-4231
www.gogebic.edu/

Grand Rapids Community
College
143 Bostwick Ave., NE
Grand Rapids, MI 49503-
3201
616-234-4000
www.grcc.edu/

Henry Ford Community
College
5101 Evergreen Rd.
Dearborn, MI 48128-1495
313-845-9615
www.hfcc.edu/

Irene's Myomassology
Institute
26061 Franklin Rd.
Southfield, MI 48034
248-350-1400
www.myomassology.com

Jackson Community College
2111 Emmons Rd.
Jackson, MI 49201-8399
517-787-0800
www.jccmi.edu

Kalamazoo Valley
Community College
PO Box 4070
Kalamazoo, MI 49003-4070
269-488-4400
www.kvcc.edu/

Kellogg Community College
450 North Ave.
Battle Creek, MI 49017-3397
616-965-3931
www.kellogg.edu/

Kirtland Community College
10775 North St Helen Rd.
Roscommon, MI 48653-9699
989-275-5000
www.kirtland.edu/

Lake Michigan College
2755 East Napier
Benton Harbor, MI 49022-1899
616-927-8100
www.lmc.cc.mi.us/

Lansing Community College
PO Box 40010
Lansing, MI 48901-7210
517-483-1957
www.lcc.edu/

Lawton School
20755 Greenfield Rd., #300
Southfield, MI 48075
248-569-7787

Lewis College of Business
17370 Meyers Rd.
Detroit, MI 48235-1423
313-862-6300
www.lewiscollege.edu/

Macomb Community College
14500 East Twelve Mile Rd.
Warren, MI 48088-3896
586-445-7000
www.macomb.edu/

Michigan College of Beauty
3498 Rochester Rd.
Troy, MI 48083
313-528-0303

Michigan Institute of
Aeronautics
Willow Run Airport East Side,
47884 D St.
Belleville, MI 48111
734-483-3758

Mid Michigan Community
College
1375 South Clare Ave.
Harrison, MI 48625-9447
989-386-6622
www.midmich.cc.mi.us/

Monroe County Community
College
1555 South Raisinville Rd.
Monroe, MI 48161-9047
734-242-7300
www.monroeccc.edu/

Montcalm Community
College
2800 College Dr.
Sidney, MI 48885-9723
989-328-2111
www.montcalm.edu/

Mott Community College
1401 East Court St.
Flint, MI 48503-2089
810-762-0200
www.mcc.edu/

Muskegon Community
College
221 South Quarterline Rd.
Muskegon, MI 49442-1493
231-773-9131
www.muskegon.cc.mi.us/

National Institute of
Technology
23400 Michigan Ave.,
Ste. 200
Dearborn, MI 48124
313-562-4228
www.nitschools.com

National Institute of
Technology
26555 Evergreen Rd., #500
Southfield, MI 48076
248-799-9933
www.nitschools.com

North Central Michigan
College
1515 Howard St.
Petoskey, MI 49770-8717
231-348-6600
www.ncmc.cc.mi.us/

Northwestern Michigan
College
1701 East Front St.
Traverse City, MI 49686-3061
231-995-1000
www.nmc.edu/

Northwestern Technological
Institute
24567 Northwestern Hwy.,
Ste. 200
Southfield, MI 48075
248-358-4006

Oakland Community College
2480 Opdyke Rd.
Bloomfield Hills, MI 48304-2266
248-341-2000
www.oaklandcc.edu/

Olympia Career Training
Institute
1750 Woodworth St., NE
Grand Rapids, MI 49505
616-364-8464
www.cci.edu

Olympia Career Training
Institute
5349 West Main
Kalamazoo, MI 49009
616-681-9616
www.olympia-institute.com

Olympia Career Training
Institute
2620-2630 Remico St., SW
Wyoming, MI 49509-9990
616-538-3170
www.olympia-institute.com

St. Clair County Community
College
323 Erie St., PO Box 5015
Port Huron, MI 48061-5015
810-984-3881
www.sc4.edu/

Schoolcraft College
18600 Haggerty Rd.
Livonia, MI 48152-2696
734-462-4400
www.schoolcraft.edu/

Southwestern Michigan
College
58900 Cherry Grove Rd.
Dowagiac, MI 49047-9793
269-782-1000
www.swmich.edu/

Specs Howard School of
Broadcast Arts
19900 West Nine Mile Rd.,
Ste. 115
Southfield, MI 48075-5273
248-358-9000
www.specshoward.edu

Virginia Farrell Beauty School
22925 Woodward Ave.
Ferndale, MI 48220
313-424-9123

Washtenaw Community
College
4800 East Huron River Dr.,
PO Box D-1
Ann Arbor, MI 48106
734-973-3300
www.wccnet.edu/

Wayne County Community
College District
801 West Fort St.
Detroit, MI 48226-3010
313-496-2600
www.wcccd.edu/

West Shore Community
College
PO Box 277, 3000 North
Stiles Rd.
Scottville, MI 49454-0277
231-845-6211
www.westshore.edu/

Minnesota

Alexandria Technical College
1601 Jefferson St.
Alexandria, MN 56308-3707
320-762-0221
www.alextech.edu/

Anoka Technical College
1355 West Hwy. 10
Anoka, MN 55303
612-576-4700
www.ank.tec.mn.us/

Anoka-Ramsey Community
College
11200 Mississippi Blvd., NW
Coon Rapids, MN 55433-3470
763-427-2600
www.anokaramsey.edu/

Anoka-Ramsey Community
College, Cambridge Campus
300 Polk St. South
Cambridge, MN 55008-5706
763-689-7000
www.anokaramsey.edu/

Aveda Institute–Minneapolis
400 Central Ave.
Minneapolis, MN 55414
612-378-7404
www.aveda.com

Brown College
1440 Northland Dr.
Mendota Heights, MN 55120
651-905-3400
www.browncollege.edu/

Central Lakes College
501 West College Dr.
Brainerd, MN 56401-3904
218-855-8000
www.clcmn.edu/

Century College
3300 Century Ave. North
White Bear Lake, MN 55110
651-779-3200
www.century.cc.mn.us/

Dakota County Technical
College
1300 East 145th St.
Rosemount, MN 55068
651-423-8000
www.dctc.edu/

Duluth Business University
4724 Mike Colalillo Dr.
Duluth, MN 55807
218-722-4000
www.dbumn.edu/

Dunwoody College of
Technology
818 Dunwoody Blvd.
Minneapolis, MN 55403
612-374-5800
www.dunwoody.edu/

Fond du Lac Tribal and
Community College
2101 14th St.
Cloquet, MN 55720
218-879-0800
www.fdltcc.edu/

Globe College
7166 North 10th St.
Oakdale, MN 55128
651-730-5100
www.globecollege.com/

Hennepin Technical College
9000 Brooklyn Blvd.
Brooklyn Park, MN 55445
763-425-3800
www.hennepintech.edu/

Hibbing Community College
1515 East 25th St.
Hibbing, MN 55746-3300
218-262-7200
www.hcc.mnscu.edu/

High-Tech Institute
5100 Gamble Dr.
St. Louis Park, MN 55416
763-560-9700
www.high-techinstitute.com/

Inver Hills Community
College
2500 East 80th St.
Inver Grove Heights, MN
55076-3224
651-450-8500
www.inverhills.edu/

Itasca Community College
1851 Hwy. 169 East
Grand Rapids, MN 55744
218-327-4460
www.itascacc.edu/

Lake Superior College
2101 Trinity Rd.
Duluth, MN 55811
218-733-7600
www.lsc.mnscu.edu/

McNally Smith College of
Music
19 Exchange St. East
Saint Paul, MN 55101
651-291-0177
www.mcnallysmith.edu/

Mesabi Range Community
and Technical College
1001 Chestnut St. West
Virginia, MN 55792-3448
218-741-3095
www.mr.mnscu.edu/

Minneapolis Business
College
1711 West County Rd. B
Roseville, MN 55113
612-636-7406
www.mplsbusinesscollege.com

Minneapolis Community and
Technical College
1501 Hennepin Ave.
Minneapolis, MN 55403-
1779
612-659-6000
www.mctc.mnscu.edu/

Minneapolis School of
Massage and Bodywork
81 Lowry Ave. NE
Minneapolis, MN 55418
612-788-8907
www.mplsschoolof
massage.org

Minnesota School of
Business–Brooklyn Center
5910 Shingle Creek Pkwy
Brooklyn Center, MN 55430
763-566-7777
www.msbcollege.edu/

Minnesota School of
Business–Plymouth
1455 Country Rd. 101 North
Minneapolis, MN 55447
763-476-2000
www.msbcollege.edu/

Minnesota School of
Business–Richfield
1401 West 76th St.
Richfield, MN 55423
612-861-2000
www.msbcollege.edu/

Minnesota State
College–Southeast Technical
1250 Homer Rd., PO Box 409
Winona, MN 55987
507-453-2700
www.southeastmn.edu/

Minnesota State Community
and Technical College–Detroit
Lakes
900 Hwy. 34, E
Detroit Lakes, MN 56501
218-846-7444
www.minnesota.edu/

Minnesota State Community
and Technical College–Fergus
Falls
1414 College Way
Fergus Falls, MN 56537-1009
218-739-7500
www.minnesota.edu/

Minnesota State Community
and Technical
College–Moorhead
1900 28th Ave., South
Moorhead, MN 56560
218-236-6277
www.minnesota.edu/

Minnesota State Community
and Technical
College–Wadena
405 Colfax Ave., SW,
PO Box 566
Wadena, MN 56482
218-631-7800
www.minnesota.edu/

Normandale Community
College
9700 France Ave. South
Bloomington, MN 55431-
4399
952-487-8200
www.normandale.edu/

North Hennepin Community
College
7411 85th Ave. North
Brooklyn Park, MN 55445-
2231
763-424-0702
www.nhcc.edu/

Northland Community and
Technical College–East Grand
Forks
2022 Central Ave., NW
East Grand Forks, MN
56721-2702
218-773-3441
www.northlandcollege.edu/

Northland Community and
Technical College–Thief River
Falls
1101 Hwy. One East
Thief River Falls, MN 56701
218-681-0701
www.northlandcollege.edu/

Northwest Technical College
905 Grant Ave., SE
Bemidji, MN 56601-4907
218-755-4270
bemidji.ntcmn.edu/

Pine Technical College
900 4th St. SE
Pine City, MN 55063
320-629-5100
www.pinetech.edu/

Rainy River Community
College
1501 Hwy. 71
International Falls, MN
56649
218-285-7722
www.rrcc.mnscu.edu/

Rasmussen College St. Cloud
226 Park Ave. South
St. Cloud, MN 56301-3713
320-251-5600
www.rasmussen.edu/

Regency Beauty Academy
40 Hwy. 10
Blaine, MN 55434
612-784-9102

Ridgewater College
PO Box 1097
Willmar, MN 56201-1097
320-235-5114
www.ridgewater.mnscu.edu/

Riverland Community
College
1900 8th Ave., NW
Austin, MN 55912
507-433-0600
www.riverland.cc.mn.us/

Rochester Community and
Technical College
851 30th Ave., SE
Rochester, MN 55904-4999
507-285-7210
www.roch.edu/

St. Cloud Regency Beauty
Academy
912 West Saint Germain St.
St. Cloud, MN 56301
320-251-0500

St. Cloud Technical College
1540 Northway Dr.
St. Cloud, MN 56303-1240
320-654-5000
www.sctc.edu/

Saint Paul College–A
Community & Technical
College
235 Marshall Ave.
St. Paul, MN 55102-1800
651-846-1600
www.saintpaul.edu/

Scot-Lewis School of
Cosmetology
9801 James Cr.
Bloomington, MN 55431
612-881-8662

Summit Academy
Opportunities
Industrialization Center
935 Olson Memorial Hwy.
Minneapolis, MN 55405
612-377-0150
www.saoic.com

Vermilion Community
College
1900 East Camp St.
Ely, MN 55731-1996
218-365-7200
www.vcc.edu/

Missouri

Al-Med Academy
10963 St. Charles Rock Rd.
St. Louis, MO 63074
314-739-4450

Allied College South
645 Gravois Bluffs Blvd.
Fenton, MO 63026
636-296-8787
www.hightechschools.edu

Concorde Career Institute
3239 Broadway
Kansas City, MO 64111-2407
816-531-5223
www.concordecareer
colleges.com/

Crowder College
601 Laclede Ave.
Neosho, MO 64850-9160
417-451-3223
www.crowder.edu/

East Central College
1964 Prairie Dell Rd.
Union, MO 63084
636-583-5193
www.eastcentral.edu/

Franklin Technology Center
2020 Iowa St.
Joplin, MO 64804
417-625-5260

IHM Health Studies Center
2500 Abbott Place
St. Louis, MO 63143-2636
314-768-1234
www.ihmhealthstudies.com/

Jefferson College
1000 Viking Dr.
Hillsboro, MO 63050-2441
636-797-3000
www.jeffco.edu/

Linn State Technical College
One Technology Dr.
Linn, MO 65051-9606
573-897-5000
www.linnstate.edu/

Longview Community
College
500 Southwest Longview Rd.
Lee's Summit, MO 64081-
2105
816-672-2000
www.kcmetro.edu/

Maple Woods Community
College
2601 Northeast Barry Rd.
Kansas City, MO 64156-1299
816-437-3000
www.kcmetro.edu/

Metropolitan Community
College-Business &
Technology College
1775 Universal Ave.
Kansas City, MO 64120
816-482-5210
www.mccbtc.com/

Mineral Area College
PO Box 1000
Park Hills, MO 63601-1000
573-431-4593
www.mineralarea.edu/

Missouri College
10121 Manchester Rd.
St. Louis, MO 63122-1583
314-821-7700
www.mocollege.com/

Missouri College of
Cosmetology North
1035 W. Kearney
Springfield, MO 65803
417-887-6511

Missouri State
University–West Plains
128 Garfield
West Plains, MO 65775
417-255-7255
www.wp.smsu.edu/

Moberly Area Community
College
101 College Ave.
Moberly, MO 65270-1304
660-263-4110
www.macc.edu/

National Academy of Beauty
Arts
157 Concord Plaza
St. Louis, MO 63128
314-842-3616

North Central Missouri
College
1301 Main St.
Trenton, MO 64683-1824
660-359-3948
www.ncmissouri.edu/

Ozarks Technical Community
College
PO Box 5958
Springfield, MO 65801
417-895-7000
www.otc.edu/

Patricia Stevens College
330 North Fourth St., Ste. 306
St. Louis, MO 63102
314-421-0949
www.patriciastevenscollege.
edu/

Patsy and Rob's Academy of
Beauty
18 NW Plaza
St. Ann, MO 63074
314-298-8808

Penn Valley Community
College
3201 Southwest Trafficway
Kansas City, MO 64111
816-759-4000
www.kcmetro.edu/

Pinnacle Career Institute
15329 Kensington Ave.
Kansas City, MO 64147-1212
816-331-5700
www.pcitraining.edu/

Ranken Technical College
4431 Finney Ave.
St. Louis, MO 63113
314-371-0233
www.ranken.edu/

Saint Charles Community
College
4601 Mid Rivers Mall Dr.
St. Peters, MO 63376-0975
636-922-8000
www.stchas.edu/

St. Louis College of Health
Careers
4484 West Pine Blvd.
St. Louis, MO 63108
314-652-0300

St. Louis Community College
at Forest Park
5600 Oakland Ave.
St. Louis, MO 63110-1316
314-644-9100
www.stlcc.edu/

St. Louis Community College
at Meramec
11333 Big Bend Blvd.
Kirkwood, MO 63122-5720
314-984-7500
www.stlcc.edu/

Sanford-Brown College
1203 Smizer Mill Rd.
Fenton, MO 63026
636-349-4900
www.sanford-brown.edu/

Sanford-Brown College
75 Village Square
Hazelwood, MO 63042
314-731-1101
www.sanford-brown.edu/

Sanford-Brown College
520 East 19th Ave.
North Kansas City, MO 64116
816-472-7400
www.sanford-brown.edu/

Sanford-Brown College
3555 Franks Dr.
St. Charles, MO 63301
314-949-2620
www.sanford-brown.edu/

Springfield College
1010 West Sunshine
Springfield, MO 65807-2488
417-864-7220
www.Springfield-college.
com/

State Fair Community
College
3201 West 16th St.
Sedalia, MO 65301-2199
660-530-5800
www.sfcc.cc.mo.us/

Three Rivers Community
College
2080 Three Rivers Blvd.
Poplar Bluff, MO 63901-2393
573-840-9600
www.trcc.edu/

Vatterott College
12970 Maurer Industrial Dr.
St. Louis, MO 63127
314-843-4200
www.vatterott-college.edu/

Nebraska

Central Community College–
Grand Island Campus
PO Box 4903
Grand Island, NE 68802-4903
308-398-4222
www.cccneb.edu/

Hamilton College-Lincoln
1821 K St., PO Box 82826
Lincoln, NE 68501-2826
402-474-5315
www.hamiltonlincoln.com/

Hamilton College-Omaha
3350 North 90th St.
Omaha, NE 68134
402-572-8500
www.hamiltonomaha.edu/

Little Priest Tribal College
PO Box 270
Winnebago, NE 68071
402-878-2380
www.lptc.bia.edu/

Metropolitan Community
College
PO Box 3777
Omaha, NE 68103-0777
402-457-2400
www.mccneb.edu/

Mid-Plains Community
College
601 West State Farm Rd.
North Platte, NE 69101
308-535-3600
www.mpcca.cc.ne.us/

Nebraska College of Technical
Agriculture
RR3, Box 23A
Curtis, NE 69025-9205
308-367-4124
www.ncta.unl.edu/

Nebraska Indian Community
College
PO Box 428
Macy, NE 68039-0428
402-837-5078
www.thenicc.edu/

Northeast Community
College
801 East Benjamin Ave.,
PO Box 469
Norfolk, NE 68702-0469
402-371-2020
www.northeastcollege.com/

Western Nebraska
Community College
371 College Dr.
Sidney, NE 69162
308-254-5450
www.wncc.net/

North Dakota

Bismarck State College
PO Box 5587
Bismarck, ND 58506-5587
701-224-5400
www.bismarckstate.edu/

Cankdeska Cikana
Community College
PO Box 269
Fort Totten, ND 58335-0269
701-766-4415
www.littlehoop.cc/

Fort Berthold Community
College
PO Box 490
New Town, ND 58763-0490
701-627-4738
www.fbcc.bia.edu/

Lake Region State College
1801 College Dr. North
Devils Lake, ND 58301-1598
701-662-1600
www.lrsc.nodak.edu/

Minot State University–
Bottineau Campus
105 Simrall Blvd.
Bottineau, ND 58318-1198
701-228-2277
www.misu-b.nodak.edu/

North Dakota State College
of Science
800 North Sixth St.
Wahpeton, ND 58076
701-671-2401
www.ndscs.nodak.edu/

Sitting Bull College
1341 92nd St.
Fort Yates, ND 58538-9701
701-854-3861
www.sittingbull.edu/

Turtle Mountain Community
College
Box 340
Belcourt, ND 58316-0340
701-477-7862
www.turtle-mountain.cc.nd.us/

United Tribes Technical
College
3315 University Dr.
Bismarck, ND 58504-7596
701-255-3285
www.uttc.edu/

Williston State College
Box 1326
Williston, ND 58802-1326
701-774-4200
www.wsc.nodak.edu/

Ohio

Akron Adult Vocational
Services
147 Park St.
Akron, OH 44308
330-761-1385

American School of
Technology
2100 Morse Rd.
Columbus, OH 43229-6665

Antonelli College
124 East Seventh St.
Cincinnati, OH 45202-2592
513-241-4338
www.antonellic.com/

Belmont Technical College
120 Fox Shannon Place
St. Clairsville, OH 43950-
9735
740-695-9500
www.btc.edu/

Bowling Green State
University–Firelands College
One University Dr.
Huron, OH 44839-9791
419-433-5560
www.firelands.bgsu.edu/

Bradford School
2469 Stelzer Rd.
Columbus, OH 43219
614-416-6200
www.bradfordschool
columbus.edu/

Brown Aveda Institute
8816 Mentor Ave.
Mentor, OH 44060
440-255-9494, ext. 212
www.brownaveda.com

Brown Mackie College, Akron
Campus
2791 Mogadore Rd.
Akron, OH 44312-1596
330-733-8766
www.socaec.com/

Brown Mackie College,
Cincinnati Campus
1011 Glendale-Milford Rd.
Cincinnati, OH 45215
513-771-2424
www.brownmackie.edu/

Brown Mackie College, North
Canton Campus
1320 West Maple St., NW
North Canton, OH 44720-
2854
330-494-1214
www.socaec.com/

Bryant and Stratton College
12955 Snow Rd.
Parma, OH 44130-1013
216-265-3151
www.bryantstratton.edu/

Butler County JVS District–D.
Russel Lee Career Center and
Manchester Technical Center
3603 Hamilton-Middletown Rd.
Hamilton, OH 45011
513-868-6300
www.butlercountyjvs.com

Central Ohio Technical
College
1179 University Dr.
Newark, OH 43055-1767
740-366-1351
www.cotc.edu/

Cincinnati State Technical and Community College
3520 Central Pkwy
Cincinnati, OH 45223-2690
513-569-1500
www.cincinnatistate.edu/

Clark State Community College
570 East Leffel Lane,
PO Box 570
Springfield, OH 45501-0570
937-325-0691
www.clarkstate.edu/

Cleveland Institute of Dental-Medical Assistants
1836 Euclid Ave., Room 401
Cleveland, OH 44115-2285
216-241-2930

Cleveland Institute of Dental-Medical Assistants
5733 Hopkins Rd.
Mentor, OH 44060
440-946-9530

Cleveland Municipal School District Adult and Continuing Education
4600 Detroit Ave.
Cleveland, OH 44102
216-634-2157
www.cmsdnet.net

Columbus Paraprofessional Institute
1900 East Grandville Rd.,
Building A, Ste. 210
Columbus, OH 43229
614-891-5030

Columbus State Community College
Box 1609
Columbus, OH 43216-1609
614-287-2400
www.cscc.edu/

Cuyahoga Community College
700 Carnegie Ave.
Cleveland, OH 44115-2878
216-987-6000
www.tri-c.edu/

Davis College
4747 Monroe St.
Toledo, OH 43623-4307
419-473-2700
daviscollege.edu/

Delaware JVS District
4565 Columbus Pike
Delaware, OH 43015
614-548-0708

Eastland Career Center
4300 Amalgamated Place
Groveport, OH 43112
614-836-4541

Edison State Community College
1973 Edison Dr.
Piqua, OH 45356-9253
937-778-8600
www.edisonohio.edu/

Ehove Career Center
316 West Mason Rd.
Milan, OH 44846
419-499-4663

ETI Technical College of Niles
2076 Youngstown-Warren Rd.
Niles, OH 44446-4398
330-652-9919
www.eti-college.com/

Gallia-Jackson-Vinton JVS District
PO Box 157
Rio Grande, OH 45674
740-245-5334

Gallipolis Career College
1176 Jackson Pike, Ste. 312
Gallipolis, OH 45631
740-446-4367
www.gallipoliscareer
college.com/

Great Oaks Institute of Technology and Career Development
3254 E. Kemper Rd.
Cincinnati, OH 45246
513-771-8925, ext. 5799
www.greatoaks.com

Health Occupations Program–Columbus Public School
100 Arcadia Ave.
Columbus, OH 43202
614-365-6000
www.columbus.k12.oh.us/
north_ed/index

Hocking College
3301 Hocking Pkwy
Nelsonville, OH 45764-9588
740-753-3591
www.hocking.edu/

Inner State Beauty School
5150 Mayfield Rd.
Lyndhurst, OH 44124
216-442-4500

Institute of Medical and Dental Technology
375 Glensprings Dr., Ste. 201
Cincinnati, OH 45246
513-851-8500

James A. Rhodes State College
4240 Campus Dr.
Lima, OH 45804-3597
419-995-8000
www.rhodesstate.edu/

Jefferson Community College
4000 Sunset Blvd.
Steubenville, OH 43952-3598
740-264-5591
www.jcc.edu/

Kent State University, Ashtabula Campus
3325 West 13th St.
Ashtabula, OH 44004-2299
440-964-3322
www.ashtabula.kent.edu/

Kent State University, East Liverpool Campus
400 East 4th St.
East Liverpool, OH 43920-3497
330-385-3805
www.kenteliv.kent.edu/

Kent State University, Geauga Campus
14111 Claridon-Troy Rd.
Burton, OH 44021-9500
440-834-4187
www.geauga.kent.edu/

Kent State University, Salem Campus
2491 State Route 45 South
Salem, OH 44460-9412
330-332-0361
www.salem.kent.edu/

Kent State University, Stark Campus
6000 Frank Ave., NW
Canton, OH 44720-7599
330-499-9600
www.stark.kent.edu/

Kent State University, Trumbull Campus
4314 Mahoning Ave., NW
Warren, OH 44483-1998
330-847-0571
www.trumbull.kent.edu/

Kent State University, Tuscarawas Campus
330 University Dr., NE
New Philadelphia, OH 44663-9403
330-339-3391
www.tusc.kent.edu/

Kettering College of Medical Arts
3737 Southern Blvd.
Kettering, OH 45429-1299
937-395-8601
www.kcma.edu/

Lakeland Community College
7700 Clocktower Dr.
Kirtland, OH 44094-5198
440-525-7000
www.lakeland.cc.oh.us/

Lorain County Community College
1005 Abbe Rd., North
Elyria, OH 44035
440-365-5222
www.lorainccc.edu/

Marion Technical College
1467 Mount Vernon Ave.
Marion, OH 43302-5694
740-389-4636
www.mtc.edu/

Mercy College of Northwest Ohio
2221 Madison Ave.
Toledo, OH 43624-1132
419-251-1313
www.mercycollege.edu/

Miami University Hamilton
1601 Peck Blvd.
Hamilton, OH 45011-3399
513-785-3000
www.ham.muohio.edu/

Miami University–Middletown Campus
4200 East University Blvd.
Middletown, OH 45042-3497
513-727-3200
www.mid.muohio.edu/

Miami–Jacobs College
PO Box 1433
Dayton, OH 45401-1433
937-461-5174
www.miamijacobs.edu/

Mid-East Ohio Vocational School District Adult Ed
400 Richards Rd.
Zanesville, OH 43701
740-455-3111

North Central State College
2441 Kenwood Cr.,
PO Box 698
Mansfield, OH 44901-0698
419-755-4800
www.ncstatecollege.edu/

Northwest State Community
College
22-600 State Route 34
Archbold, OH 43502-9542
419-267-5511
www.northweststate.edu

O. C. Collins Career Center
11627 State Route 243
Chesapeake, OH 45619

Ohio Business College
4020 Milan Rd.
Sandusky, OH 44870-5894
419-627-8345
www.ohiobusinesscollege.com

Ohio Institute of
Photography and Technology
2029 Edgefield Rd.
Dayton, OH 45439-1917
937-294-6155
www.oipt.com/

Ohio State Beauty Academy
57 Town Square
Lima, OH 45801
419-229-7896

Ohio State School of
Cosmetology
5970 Westerville Rd.
Westerville, OH 43081
614-890-3535

Ohio Technical College
1374 East 51st St.
Cleveland, OH 44103
216-881-1700
www.ohiotechnicalcollege.com

Ohio Valley College of
Technology
16808 St. Clair Ave.,
PO Box 7000
East Liverpool, OH 43920
330-385-1070
www.ovct.edu/

Owens Community College
PO Box 10000
Toledo, OH 43699-1947
419-661-7000
www.owens.edu/

Portage Lakes Career Center
4401 Shriver Rd.
Green, OH 44232-0248
330-896-8200
www.plcc.K12.oh.us

Professional Skills Institute
20 Arco Dr.
Toledo, OH 43607
419-531-9610
www.proskills.com/

Remington College–
Cleveland Campus
14801 Broadway Ave.
Cleveland, OH 44137
216-475-7520

RETS Tech Center
555 East Alex Bell Rd.
Centerville, OH 45459
937-433-3410
www.retstechcenter.com/

Riggs LeMar Beauty College
3464 Hudson Dr.
Cuyahoga Falls, OH 44221
330-945-4045

Sanford-Brown Institute
17535 Rosbough Dr., Ste. 100
Middleburg Heights, OH
44130
440-239-9640

Scioto County Joint
Vocational School District
PO Box 766
Lucasville, OH 45648
740-259-5522

Sinclair Community College
444 West Third St.
Dayton, OH 45402-1460
937-512-2500
www.sinclair.edu/

Southern State Community
College
100 Hobart Dr.
Hillsboro, OH 45133-9487
937-393-3431
www.sscc.edu/

Southwestern College of
Business
149 Northland Blvd.
Cincinnati, OH 45246-1122
513-874-0432
www.swcollege.net/

Southwestern College of
Business
201 East Second St.
Franklin, OH 45005
937-746-6633
www.swcollege.net/

Stark State College of
Technology
6200 Frank Ave., NW
Canton, OH 44720-7299
330-494-6170
www.starkstate.edu/

TDDS
1688 North Pricetown Rd.
Diamond, OH 44412-9608
330-538-2216
www.tdds.com

Technology Education
College
288 South Hamilton Rd.
Columbus, OH 43213-2087
614-759-7700
www.teceducation.com/

Terra State Community
College
2830 Napoleon Rd.
Fremont, OH 43420-9670
419-334-8400
www.terra.edu/

Trumbull Business College
3200 Ridge Rd.
Warren, OH 44484
330-369-3200
www.tbc-trumbullbusiness.
com/

Trumbull County JVS District
528 Educational Hwy.
Warren, OH 44483
330-847-0503

The University of Akron–
Wayne College
1901 Smucker Rd.
Orrville, OH 44667-9192
330-683-2010
www.wayne.uakron.edu/

University of Cincinnati
Clermont College
4200 Clermont College Dr.
Batavia, OH 45103-1785
513-732-5200
www.clc.uc.edu/

University of Cincinnati
Raymond Walters College
9555 Plainfield Rd.
Cincinnati, OH 45236-1007
513-745-5600
www.rwc.uc.edu/

University of Northwestern
Ohio
1441 North Cable Rd.
Lima, OH 45805-1498
419-227-3141
www.unoh.edu/

Vatterott College
5025 East Royalton Rd.
Broadview Heights, OH
44147
440-526-1660
www.vatterott-college.edu/

Virginia Marti College of Art
and Design
11724 Detroit Ave.,
PO Box 580
Lakewood, OH 44107-3002
216-221-8584
www.vmcad.edu/

Washington State
Community College
710 Colegate Dr.
Marietta, OH 45750-9225
740-374-8716
www.wscc.edu/

Zane State College
1555 Newark Rd.
Zanesville, OH 43701-2626
740-454-2501
www.zanestate.edu/

Oklahoma

Advance Barber College
5301 S. Pennsylvania Ave.
Oklahoma City, OK 73119
405-685-0172

Autry Technology Center
1201 West Willow St.
Enid, OK 73703
405-242-2750

Canadian Valley Technology
Center
6505 E. Hwy. 66
El Reno, OK 73036
405-262-2629
www.cvvt.org

Career Point Business School
3138 South Garnett
Tulsa, OK 74146
918-622-4100

Carl Albert State College
1507 South McKenna
Poteau, OK 74953-5208
918-647-1200
www.casc.cc.ok.us/

Central Oklahoma Area
Vocational Technical School
3 Court Cr.
Drumright, OK 74030
918-352-2551

City College, Inc.
1370 North Interstate Dr.
Norman, OK 73072
405-329-5627

Community Care College
4242 South Sheridan
Tulsa, OK 74145
918-610-0027
www.communitycare
college.com/

Connors State College
Route 1, Box 1000
Warner, OK 74469-9700
918-463-2931
www.connorsstate.edu/

Demarge College South
9301 S. Western
Oklahoma City, OK 73139
405-692-2900
www.demarge.edu

Eastern Oklahoma State
College
1301 West Main
Wilburton, OK 74578-4999
918-465-2361
www.eosc.edu/

Francis Tuttle Area Vocational
Technical Center
12777 North Rockwell Ave.
Oklahoma City, OK 73142-
2789
405-717-7799
www.francistuttle.com

Gordon Cooper Area
Vocational Technical School
1. John C. Bruton Blvd.
Shawnee, OK 74801
405-273-7493

Great Plains Area Vocational-
Technical School
4500 West Lee Blvd.
Lawton, OK 73505
405-355-6371
www.gpv.org

Green Country Technology
Center
PO Box 1217
Okmulgee, OK 74447
918-758-0840 Ext. 221

Indian Capital Area
Vocational-Technical
School–Bill Willis Campus
1400 South Hensley Dr.
Tahlequah, OK 74464
918-456-2594

Indian Capital Technology
Center–Muskogee
2403 N. 41st St. E
Muskogee, OK 74403
918-687-6383 Ext. 212
www.icavts.tec.ok.us

Kiamichi Area Vocational Tech
School School District 7–
McAlester
301 Kiamichi Dr.
McAlester, OK 74501
918-426-0940

Kiamichi Area Vocational Tech
School–Durant
810 Waldron Rd.
Durant, OK 74701
405-924-7081

Meridian Technology Center
1312 South Sangre Rd.
Stillwater, OK 74074
405-377-3333
www.meridian-technology.
com

Metro Area Vocational
Technical School District 22
1900 Springlake Dr.
Oklahoma City, OK 73111
405-424-8324
www.metrotech.org

Metro Technology Centers–
South Bryant Campus
4901 S. Bryant
Oklahoma City, OK 73129
405-424-8324
www.metrotech.org

Metropolitan College of
Legal Studies
4528 South Sheridan Rd.,
Ste. 105
Tulsa, OK 74145
918-627-9300

Murray State College
One Murray Campus
Tishomingo, OK 73460-3130
580-371-2371
www.mscok.edu/

Northeastern Oklahoma
Agricultural and Mechanical
College
200 I St., NE
Miami, OK 74354-6434
918-542-8441
www.neoam.cc.ok.us/

Northern Oklahoma College
1220 East Grand Ave.,
PO Box 310
Tonkawa, OK 74653-0310
580-628-6200
www.north-ok.edu/

Oklahoma City Community
College
7777 South May Ave.
Oklahoma City, OK 73159-
4419
405-682-1611
www.okccc.edu/

Oklahoma Health Academy
1939 N. Moore Ave.
Moore, OK 73160
405-912-2777

Oklahoma State University,
Oklahoma City
900 North Portland
Oklahoma City, OK 73107-
6120
405-947-4421
www.osuokc.edu/

Pioneer Area Vocational
Technical School
2101 North Ash
Ponca City, OK 74601
405-762-8336

Platt College
309 South Ann Arbor Ave.
Oklahoma City, OK 73128
405-946-7799
www.plattcollege.org/

Platt College
3801 South Sheridan
Tulsa, OK 74145
918-663-9000

Pontotoc Technology Center
601 West 33rd
Ada, OK 74820
580-310-2200
www.pontotoc.com

Redlands Community College
1300 South Country Club Rd.
El Reno, OK 73036-5304
405-262-2552
www.redlandscc.edu/

Rose State College
6420 Southeast 15th St.
Midwest City, OK 73110-2799
405-733-7673
www.rose.edu/

Sand Springs Beauty College
28 East Second St.
Sand Springs, OK 74063
918-245-6627

Seminole State College
PO Box 351
Seminole, OK 74818-0351
405-382-9950
www.ssc.cc.ok.us/

Spartan College of
Aeronautics and Technology
8820 East Pine St.,
PO Box 582833
Tulsa, OK 74158-2833
918-836-6886
www.spartan.edu/

Tulsa Community College
6111 East Skelly Dr.
Tulsa, OK 74135-6198
918-595-7000
www.tulsacc.edu/

Tulsa County Area Vocational
Technical School District 18
Memorial
3420 South Memorial Dr.
Tulsa, OK 74145
918-828-5200

Tulsa Welding School
2545 East 11th St.
Tulsa, OK 74104-3909
918-587-6789
www.weldingschool.com/

Vatterott College
4629 Northwest 23rd St.
Oklahoma City, OK 73127
405-945-0088
www.vatterott-college.edu/

Vatterott College
555 South Memorial Dr.
Tulsa, OK 74112
918-835-8288
www.vatterott-college.edu/

Wes Watkins Area Vocational-
Technical Center
Route 2, Box 159-1
Wetumka, OK 74883
405-452-5500

Western Oklahoma State
College
2801 North Main St.
Altus, OK 73521-1397
580-477-2000
www.wosc.edu/

South Dakota

Kilian Community College
300 East 6th St.
Sioux Falls, SD 57103
605-221-3100
www.kilian.edu/

Lake Area Technical Institute
230 11th St. Northeast
Watertown, SD 57201
605-882-5284
www.lati.tec.sd.us/

Mitchell Technical Institute
821 North Capital
Mitchell, SD 57301
605-995-3024
mti.tec.sd.us/

Sisseton-Wahpeton
Community College
Old Agency Box 689
Sisseton, SD 57262
605-698-3966
www.swc.tc/

Southeast Technical Institute
2320 N. Career Ave.
Sioux Falls, SD 57107-1301
605-367-7624
www.southeasttech.com/

Western Dakota Technical
Institute
800 Mickelson Dr.
Rapid City, SD 57703
605-394-4034
www.westerndakotatech.org/

Wisconsin

Blackhawk Technical College
PO Box 5009
Janesville, WI 53547-5009
608-758-6900
www.blackhawk.edu/

Chippewa Valley Technical
College
620 West Clairemont Ave.
Eau Claire, WI 54701-6162
715-833-6200
www.cvtc.edu/

College of Menominee
Nation
PO Box 1179
Keshena, WI 54135
715-799-5600
www.menominee.edu/

Fox Valley Technical College
1825 North Bluemound, PO
Box 2277
Appleton, WI 54912-2277
920-735-5600
www.fvtc.edu/

Gateway Technical College
3520 30th Ave.
Kenosha, WI 53144-1090
262-564-2200
www.gtc.edu/

Herzing College
5218 East Terrace Dr.
Madison, WI 53718
608-249-6611
www.herzing.edu/madison

Lakeshore Technical College
1290 North Ave.
Cleveland, WI 53015-1414
920-693-1000
www.gotoltc.com/

Madison Area Technical
College
3550 Anderson St.
Madison, WI 53704-2599
608-246-6100
www.matcmadison.edu/
matc/

Martin's School of Hair
Design
2575 West Mason St.
Green Bay, WI 54304
920-494-1430

Martin's School of Hair
Design
1034 South 18th St.
Manitowoc, WI 54220
920-684-0177

Mid-State Technical College
500 32nd St. North
Wisconsin Rapids, WI 54494-
5599
715-422-5300
www.mstc.edu/

Milwaukee Area Technical
College
700 West State St.
Milwaukee, WI 53233-1443
414-297-6600
matc.edu

Moraine Park Technical
College
235 North National Ave,
PO Box 1940
Fond du Lac, WI 54936-1940
920-922-8611
www.morainepark.edu/

Nicolet Area Technical
College
Box 518
Rhinelander, WI 54501-0518
715-365-4410
www.nicoletcollege.edu/

Northcentral Technical
College
1000 West Campus Dr.
Wausau, WI 54401-1899
715-675-3331
www.ntc.edu/

Northeast Wisconsin
Technical College
2740 W Mason St.,
PO Box 19042
Green Bay, WI 54307-9042
920-498-5400
www.nwtc.edu/

Scientific College of Beauty
and Barbering
310 Westgate Mall
Madison, WI 53711
608-271-4204

Southwest Wisconsin
Technical College
1800 Bronson Blvd.
Fennimore, WI 53809-9778
608-822-3262
www.swtc.edu/

Waukesha County Technical
College
800 Main St.
Pewaukee, WI 53072-4601
262-691-5566
www.wctc.edu/

Western Wisconsin Technical
College
304 6th St. North,
PO Box C-908
La Crosse, WI 54602-0908
608-785-9200
www.wwtc.edu/

Wisconsin Indianhead
Technical College
505 Pine Ridge Dr.
Shell Lake, WI 54871
715-468-2815
www.witc.edu/

SCHOLARSHIPS AND FINANCIAL AID

Illinois

Golden Apple Foundation

100 scholars are selected annually. Scholars receive $7,000 a year for 4 years. Applicants must be between 17 and 21 and maintain a GPA of 2.5. Eligible applicants must be residents of Illinois studying in Illinois. The deadline is December 1. Recipients must agree to teach in high-need Illinois schools. **Award:** Forgivable loan for use in freshman, sophomore, junior, or senior years; renewable. **Number:** up to 100. **Amount:** $7000. **Eligibility Requirements:** Applicant must be age 17-21; enrolled or expecting to enroll full-time at a four-year institution or university; resident of Illinois and studying in Illinois. Applicant must have 2.5 GPA or higher. Available to U.S. and non-U.S. citizens. **Application Requirements:** Application, autobiography, essay, interview, photo, references, test scores, transcript. **Application Deadline:** December 1. **Contact:** Pat Kilduff, Director of Recruitment and Placement, Golden Apple Foundation, 8 South Michigan Ave., Ste. 700, Chicago, IL 60603-3318. **Phone:** 312-407-0006 Ext. 105. **E-mail:** kilduff@goldenapple.org

Higher Education License Plate Program–HELP

Need-based grants for students at Illinois institutions participating in program whose funds are raised by sale of special license plates commemorating the institutions. Deadline: June 30. Must be Illinois resident. May be eligible to receive the grant for the equivalent of 10 semesters of full-time enrollment. **Award:** Grant for use in freshman, sophomore, junior, or senior years; not renewable. **Number:** 175–200. **Amount:** up to $2000. **Eligibility Requirements:** Applicant must be enrolled or expecting to enroll full or part-time at a two-year or four-year institution or university; resident of Illinois and studying in Illinois. Available to U.S. citizens. **Application Requirements:** Financial need analysis, FAFSA. **Application Deadline:** June 30. **Contact:** College Zone Counselor, Illinois Student Assistance Commission (ISAC), 1755 Lake Cook Rd., Deerfield, IL 60015-5209. **Phone:** 800-899-4722. **E-mail:** collegezone@isac.org

Illinois College Savings Bond Bonus Incentive Grant Program

Program offers holders of Illinois College Savings Bonds a $20 grant for each year of bond maturity payable upon bond redemption if at least 70% of proceeds are used to attend college in Illinois. May not be used by students attending religious or divinity schools. **Award:** Grant for use in freshman, sophomore, junior, senior, graduate, or postgraduate years; not renewable. **Number:** 1200–1400. **Amount:** $40–$440. **Eligibility Requirements:** Applicant must be enrolled or expecting to enroll full or part-time at a two-year, four-year, or technical institution or university and studying in Illinois. Available to U.S. citizens. **Application Requirements:** Application. **Application Deadline:** Continuous. **Contact:** College Zone Counselor, Illinois Student Assistance Commission (ISAC), 1755 Lake Cook Rd., Deerfield, IL 60015-5209. **Phone:** 800-899-4722. **E-mail:** collegezone@isac.org

Illinois Department of Public Health Center for Rural Health

Scholarship for Illinois students studying to be a nurse practitioner, physician assistant, or certified nurse midwife. Funding available for up to two years. Must fulfill an obligation to practice full-time in a designated shortage area as an allied healthcare professional in Illinois for one year for each year of scholarship funding. Failure to fulfill the obligation will require repayment to the state three times the amount of the scholarship received for each unfulfilled year of obligation plus 7% interest per year. **Award:** Scholarship for use in freshman, sophomore, junior, or senior years; renewable. **Number:** 20. **Amount:** $7500–$15,000. **Eligibility Requirements:** Applicant must be enrolled or expecting to enroll at a two-year or four-year institution or university and resident of Illinois. Available to U.S. citizens. **Application Requirements:** Application. **Contact:** Marcia Franklin, Department of Public Health. **Phone:** 217-782-1624

Illinois Department of Public Health Center for Rural Health

Scholarship for Illinois students pursuing a certificate, diploma, or degree in nursing and demonstrating financial need. Scholarship provides up to four years of financial aid in return for full-or part-time employment as a licensed practical or registered nurse in Illinois upon graduation. Must remain employed in Illinois for a period equivalent to the educational time that was supported by the scholarship. Application deadline is May 31. **Award:** Scholarship for use in freshman, sophomore, junior, or senior years; renewable. **Number:** varies. **Amount:** varies. **Eligibility Requirements:** Applicant must be enrolled or expecting to enroll at a two-year or four-year institution or university and resident of Illinois. Available to U.S. citizens. **Application Requirements:** Application, financial need analysis. **Application Deadline:** May 31. **Contact:** College Zone Counselor, Illinois Student Assistance Commission (ISAC), 1755 Lake Cook Rd., Deerfield, IL 60015-5209. **Phone:** 800-899-4722. **E-mail:** collegezone@isac.org

Illinois Department of Rehabilitation Services Education Benefits

If you have a physical or mental disability, and have been approved for vocational training by the Office of Rehabilitation you may be eligible to receive financial assistance to be used at any accredited Illinois college or technical school. Must be Illinois resident and demonstrate financial need. See Web site: http://www.dhs.state.il.us. **Award:** Scholarship for use in freshman, sophomore, junior, or senior years; renewable. **Number:** varies. **Amount:** varies. **Eligibility Requirements:** Applicant must be enrolled or expecting to enroll at a two-year, four-year, or technical institution or university; resident of Illinois and studying in Illinois. Applicant must be hearing impaired, learning disabled, physically disabled, or visually impaired. Available to U.S. citizens. **Application Requirements:** Application, financial need analysis. **Application Deadline:** Continuous. **Contact:** Paul Worrall, Counselor, Illinois Student Assistance Commission (ISAC), 1755 Lake Cook Rd., Deerfield, IL 60015-5209. **Phone:** 800-843-6154

Illinois Department of Veterans' Affairs

One-time award for spouse, child, or step-child of veterans who are missing in action or were a prisoner of war. Must be enrolled at a state-supported school in Illinois. Candidate must be U.S. citizen. Must apply and be accepted before beginning of school. Also for children and spouses of veterans who are determined to be 100% disabled as established by the Veterans Administration. **Award:** Scholarship for use in freshman, sophomore, junior, senior, or graduate years; renewable. **Number:** varies. **Amount:** varies. **Eligibility Requirements:** Applicant must be enrolled or expecting to enroll full or part-time at a two-year or four-year institution or university; resident of Illinois and studying in Illinois. Available to U.S. citizens. Applicant or parent must meet one or more of the following requirements: general military experience; retired from active duty; disabled or killed as a result of military service; prisoner of war; or missing in action. **Application Requirements:** Application. **Application Deadline:** Continuous. **Contact:** Ms. Tracy Mahan, Grants Section, Illinois Department of Veterans' Affairs, 833 South Spring St., Springfield, IL 62794-9432. **Phone:** 217-782-3564

Illinois Future Teachers Corps Program

Scholarships available for students planning to become teachers in Illinois. Students must be Illinois residents enrolled or accepted as a junior or above in a Teacher Education Program at an Illinois college or university. By receiving award, students agree to teach for 5 years at either a public, private, or parochial Illinois preschool, or at a public elementary or secondary school. For an application and further information, visit http://www.collegezone.com. **Award:** Forgivable loan for use in junior, senior, or graduate years; renewable. **Number:** 1150. **Amount:** $5000–$15,000. **Eligibility Requirements:** Applicant must be enrolled or expecting to enroll full or part-time at a four-year institution or university; resident of Illinois and studying in Illinois. Available to U.S. citizens. **Application Requirements:** Application, financial need analysis, FAFSA. **Application Deadline:** March 1. **Contact:** College Zone Counselor, Illinois Student Assistance Commission (ISAC), 1755 Lake Cook Rd., Deerfield, IL 60015-5209. **Phone:** 800-899-4722. **E-mail:** collegezone@isac.org

Illinois General Assembly Scholarship

Scholarships available for Illinois students enrolled at an Illinois four-year state-supported college. Must contact the General Assembly member from your district for eligibility criteria. **Award:** Scholarship for use in freshman, sophomore, junior, or senior years. **Number:** varies. **Amount:** varies. **Eligibility**

Requirements: Applicant must be enrolled or expecting to enroll at a four-year institution or university; resident of Illinois and studying in Illinois. Available to U.S. citizens. **Application Requirements:** Application. **Contact:** College Zone Counselor, Illinois Student Assistance Commission (ISAC), 1755 Lake Cook Rd., Deerfield, IL 60015-5209. **Phone:** 800-899-4722. **E-mail:** collegezone@isac.org

Illinois Monetary Award Program

Award for eligible students attending Illinois public universities, private colleges and universities, community colleges, and some proprietary institutions. Applicable only to tuition and fees. Based on financial need. Applicants are encouraged to apply as soon after January 1st as possible. **Award:** Grant for use in freshman, sophomore, junior, or senior years; not renewable. **Number:** 135,000–145,000. **Amount:** up to $4968. **Eligibility Requirements:** Applicant must be enrolled or expecting to enroll full or part-time at a two-year, four-year, or technical institution or university; resident of Illinois and studying in Illinois. Available to U.S. citizens. **Application Requirements:** Financial need analysis, FAFSA online. **Application Deadline:** Continuous. **Contact:** College Zone Counselor, Illinois Student Assistance Commission (ISAC), 1755 Lake Cook Rd., Deerfield, IL 60015-5209. **Phone:** 800-899-4722. **E-mail:** collegezone@isac.org

Illinois National Guard Grant Program

Award for qualified National Guard personnel, which pays tuition and fees at Illinois public universities and community colleges. Must provide documentation of service. Applications are due October 1 of the academic year for full year, March 1 for second/third term, or June 15 for the summer term. **Award:** Grant for use in freshman, sophomore, junior, senior, graduate, or postgraduate years; renewable. **Number:** 2000–3000. **Amount:** $1300–$1700.

Eligibility Requirements: Applicant must be enrolled or expecting to enroll full or part-time at a two-year or four-year institution or university; resident of Illinois and studying in Illinois. Available to U.S. citizens. Applicant must have served in the Air Force National Guard or Army National Guard. **Application Requirements:** Application, documentation of service. **Application Deadline:** varies. **Contact:** College Zone Counselor, Illinois Student Assistance Commission (ISAC), 1755 Lake Cook Rd.
Deerfield, IL 60015-5209.
Phone: 800-899-4722.
E-mail: collegezone@isac.org

Illinois Special Education Teacher Tuition Waiver

Tuition waiver for up to four years for Illinois teacher or student pursuing a career in special education. Must be enrolled in an eligible Illinois institution and seeking certification in any area of special education. Must teach in Illinois for two years upon gaining certification.
Award: Forgivable loan for use in freshman, sophomore, junior, senior, or graduate years; renewable.
Number: 250. **Eligibility Requirements:** Applicant must be enrolled or expecting to enroll at a four-year institution or university; resident of Illinois and studying in Illinois. Available to U.S. citizens.
Application Requirements: Application. **Application Deadline:** March 1. **Contact:** College Zone Counselor, Illinois Student Assistance Commission (ISAC), 1755 Lake Cook Rd., Deerfield, IL 60015-5209. **Phone:** 800-899-4722.
E-mail: collegezone@isac.org

Illinois State Treasurer's Office

Scholarships awarded annually to Illinois high school seniors who plan to enroll as full-time students in agriculture or agriculture-related studies in an Illinois institution and be committed to pursuing a career in agriculture or an agriculture-related field. **Award:** Scholarship for use in freshman year; not renewable.
Number: 5. **Amount:** $2500.
Eligibility Requirements: Applicant must be high school student; planning to enroll or expecting to enroll full-time at a two-year, four-year, or technical institution or university; resident of Illinois and studying in Illinois. Applicant must have 2.5 GPA or higher. Available to U.S. citizens. **Application Requirements:** Application, essay, references, test scores, transcript, goal statement, list of activities. **Application Deadline:** April 15. **Contact:** Mindy Varley, Scholarships, Illinois State Treasurer's Office, One West Old State Capitol Plaza, Ste. 814, Springfield, IL 62701.
Phone: 217-558-6215.
E-mail: mvarley@treasurer.state.il.us

Illinois Student Assistance Commission (ISAC)

Award for dependents of police, fire, and corrections officers killed or disabled in line of duty. Provides for tuition and fees at approved Illinois institutions. Must be resident of Illinois. Continuous deadline. Provide proof of status. For information and application, go to Web site: http://www.collegezone. **Award:** Grant for use in freshman, sophomore, junior, senior, graduate, or postgraduate years; renewable.
Number: 50–55. **Amount:** $3000–$4000. **Eligibility Requirements:** Applicant must be enrolled or expecting to enroll at a two-year, four-year, or technical institution or university; resident of Illinois and studying in Illinois. Applicant or parent of applicant must have employment or volunteer experience in police/firefighting. Available to U.S. citizens.
Application Requirements: Application, proof of status.
Application Deadline: Continuous.
Contact: College Zone Counselor, Illinois Student Assistance Commission (ISAC), 1755 Lake Cook Rd., Deerfield, IL 60015-5209.
Phone: 800-899-4722.
E-mail: collegezone@isac.org

Illinois Student-to-Student Program of Matching Grants

Award provides matching funds for need-based grants at participating Illinois public universities and community colleges. Deadlines are set by each institution. Contact financial aid office at the institution in which you are enrolled for eligibility. **Award:** Grant for use in freshman, sophomore, junior, or senior years; not renewable. **Number:** 2000–4000. **Amount:** $300–$500. **Eligibility Requirements:** Applicant must be enrolled or expecting to enroll full or part-time at a two-year or four-year institution or university; resident of Illinois and studying in Illinois. Available to U.S. citizens. **Application Requirements:** Application, financial need analysis. **Application Deadline:** varies. **Contact:** College Zone Counselor, Illinois Student Assistance Commission (ISAC), 1755 Lake Cook Rd., Deerfield, IL 60015-5209, **Phone:** 800-899-4722.
E-mail: collegezone@isac.org

Illinois Veteran Grant Program–IVG

Award for qualified veterans for tuition and fees at Illinois public universities and community colleges. Must provide documentation of service (DD214). Deadline is continuous. **Award:** Grant for use in freshman, sophomore, junior, senior, or graduate years; renewable. **Number:** 11,000–13,000. **Amount:** $1400–$1600. **Eligibility Requirements:** Applicant must be enrolled or expecting to enroll full or part-time at a two-year or four-year institution or university; resident of Illinois and studying in Illinois. Available to U.S. citizens. Applicant must have general military experience. **Application Requirements:** Application, documentation of service. **Application Deadline:** Continuous. **Contact:** College Zone Counselor, Illinois Student Assistance Commission (ISAC), 1755 Lake Cook Rd., Deerfield, IL 60015-5209.
Phone: 800-899-4722.
E-mail: collegezone@isac.org

Merit Recognition Scholarship (MRS) Program

Award for Illinois high school seniors graduating in the top 4% of their class and attending Illinois postsecondary institution or one of the nation's four approved Military Service Academies. Students scoring in the top 4% in one of the college entrance tests among Illinois residents are also eligible. Contact for application procedures. **Award:** Scholarship for use in freshman year; not renewable. **Number:** 5000–6000. **Amount:** up to $1000. **Eligibility Requirements:** Applicant must be high school student; planning to enroll or expecting to enroll full or part-time at a two-year or four-year institution or university; resident of Illinois and studying in Illinois. Applicant must have 3.5 GPA or higher. Available to U.S. citizens. **Application Requirements:** Application. **Application Deadline:** Continuous. **Contact:** College Zone Counselor, Illinois Student Assistance Commission (ISAC), 1755 Lake Cook Rd., Deerfield, IL 60015-5209. **Phone:** 800-899-4722. **E-mail:** collegezone@isac.org

Minority Teachers of Illinois Scholarship Program

Award for minority students planning to teach at an approved Illinois preschool, elementary, or secondary school. Deadline: March 1. Must be Illinois resident. **Award:** Forgivable loan for use in freshman, sophomore, junior, senior, graduate, or postgraduate years; renewable. **Number:** 450–550. **Amount:** up to $5000. **Eligibility Requirements:** Applicant must be American Indian/Alaska Native, Asian/Pacific Islander, Black (non-Hispanic), or Hispanic; enrolled or expecting to enroll full or part-time at a two-year or four-year institution or university; resident of Illinois and studying in Illinois. Applicant must have 2.5 GPA or higher. Available to U.S. citizens. **Application Requirements:** Application. **Application Deadline:** March 1. **Contact:** College Zone Counselor Illinois Student Assistance Commission (ISAC), 1755 Lake Cook Rd., Deerfield, IL 60015-5209. **Phone:** 800-899-4722. **E-mail:** collegezone@isac.org

Silas Purnell Illinois Incentive for Access Program

Award for eligible first-time freshmen enrolling in approved Illinois institutions. One-time grant of up to $500 may be used for any educational expense. Using the FAFSA, applicants are encouraged to apply as quickly as possible after January 1st preceding the academic year. **Award:** Grant for use in freshman year; not renewable. **Number:** 19,000–22,000. **Amount:** $300–$500. **Eligibility Requirements:** Applicant must be enrolled or expecting to enroll full or part-time at a two-year, four-year, or technical institution or university; resident of Illinois and studying in Illinois. Available to U.S. citizens. **Application Requirements:** Financial need analysis, FAFSA online. **Application Deadline:** Continuous. **Contact:** College Zone Counselor, Illinois Student Assistance Commission (ISAC), 1755 Lake Cook Rd., Deerfield, IL 60015-5209. **Phone:** 800-899-4722. **E-mail:** collegezone@isac.org

Veterans' Children Educational Opportunities

Award is provided to each child age 18 or younger of a veteran who died or became totally disabled as a result of service during World War I, World War II, Korean, or Vietnam War. Must be an Illinois resident and studying in Illinois. Death must be service-connected. Disability must be rated 100% for two or more years. **Award:** Grant for use in freshman year; not renewable. **Number:** varies. **Amount:** up to $250. **Eligibility Requirements:** Applicant must be age 10-18; enrolled or expecting to enroll at an institution or university; resident of Illinois and studying in Illinois. Available to U.S. citizens. Applicant or parent must meet one or more of the following requirements: general military experience; retired from active duty; disabled or killed as a result of military service; prisoner of war; or missing in action. **Application Requirements:** Application. **Application Deadline:** June 30. **Contact:** Ms. Tracy Mahan, Grants Section, Illinois Department of Veterans' Affairs, 833 South Spring St., Springfield, IL 62794-9432. **Phone:** 217-782-3564

Indiana

Culture Connection

Culture Connection Foundation Scholarship
Scholarships available for students in single parent families. May be used for undergraduate or graduate study. Those interested in foreign languages, culture, and ethnic studies are encouraged to apply. Application deadline is August 1. **Award:** Scholarship for use in freshman, sophomore, junior, senior, or graduate years; renewable. **Number:** 1000. **Amount:** $4700. **Eligibility Requirements:** Applicant must be enrolled or expecting to enroll full or part-time at a two-year, four-year, or technical institution or university and single. Applicant must have 2.5 GPA or higher. Available to U.S. and non-U.S. citizens. **Application Requirements:** Application, essay, financial need analysis, interview, references, self-addressed stamped envelope, test scores, transcript, birth certificate, divorce decree. **Application Deadline:** August 1. **Contact:** Anna Leis, National Program Director, Culture Connection, 8888 Keystone Crossing, Ste. 1300, Indianapolis, IN 46240. **Phone:** 317-547-7055. **E-mail:** annaleis@thecultureconnection.com

Department of Veterans Affairs Free Tuition for Children of POW/MIA's in Vietnam

Renewable award for residents of Indiana who are the children of veterans declared missing in action or prisoner-of-war after January 1, 1960. Provides tuition at Indiana state-supported institutions for undergraduate study. **Award:** Grant for use in freshman, sophomore, junior, senior, graduate, or postgraduate years; renewable. **Number:** varies. **Amount:** varies. **Eligibility Requirements:** Applicant must be enrolled or expecting to enroll at a two-year or four-year institution or university; resident of Indiana and studying in Indiana. Available to U.S. citizens. Applicant or parent must meet one or more of the following requirements: general military experience; retired from active duty; disabled or killed as a result of military service; prisoner of war; or missing in action. **Application Requirements:** Application. **Application Deadline:** Continuous. **Contact:** Jon Brinkley, State Service Officer, Indiana Department of Veterans' Affairs, 302 West Washington St., Room E-120, Indianapolis, IN 46204-2738. **Phone:** 317-232-3910. **E-mail:** jbrinkley@dva.state.in.us

Indiana Department of Veterans' Affairs

Child of Disabled Veteran Grant or Purple Heart Recipient Grant is a free tuition at Indiana state-supported colleges or universities for children of disabled veterans or Purple Heart recipients. Must submit Form DD214 or service record. **Award:** Grant for use in freshman, sophomore, junior, senior, graduate, or postgraduate years; renewable. **Number:** varies. **Amount:** varies. **Eligibility Requirements:** Applicant must be enrolled or expecting to enroll full or part-time at a two-year or four-year institution or university; resident of Indiana and studying in Indiana. Available to U.S. citizens. Applicant or parent must meet one or more of the following requirements: general military experience; retired from active duty; disabled or killed as a result of military service; prisoner of war; or missing in action. **Application Requirements:** Application. **Application Deadline:** Continuous. **Contact:** Jon Brinkley, State Service Officer, Indiana Department of Veterans' Affairs, 302 West Washington St., Room E-120, Indianapolis, IN 46204-2738. **Phone:** 317-232-3910. **E-mail:** jbrinkley@dva.state.in.us

Indiana Freedom of Choice Grant

The Freedom of Choice Grant is a need-based, tuition-restricted program for students attending Indiana private institutions seeking a first undergraduate degree. It is awarded in addition to the Higher Education Award. Students (and parents of dependent students) who are U.S.

citizens and Indiana residents must file the FAFSA yearly by the March 10 deadline. **Award:** Grant for use in freshman, sophomore, junior, or senior years; not renewable. **Number:** 10,000–11,830. **Amount:** $200–$5915. **Eligibility Requirements:** Applicant must be enrolled or expecting to enroll full-time at a four-year institution or university; resident of Indiana and studying in Indiana. Available to U.S. citizens. **Application Requirements:** Application, financial need analysis, FAFSA. **Application Deadline:** March 10. **Contact:** Grants Counselor, State Student Assistance Commission of Indiana (SSACI), 150 West Market St., Ste. 500, Indianapolis, IN 46204-2805. **Phone:** 317-232-2350. **E-mail:** grants@ssaci.state.in.us

Indiana Higher Education Award

The Higher Education Award is a need-based, tuition-restricted program for students attending Indiana public, private, or proprietary institutions seeking a first undergraduate degree. Students (and parents of dependent students) who are U.S. citizens and Indiana residents must file the FAFSA yearly by the March 10 deadline. **Award:** Grant for use in freshman, sophomore, junior, or senior years; not renewable. **Number:** 38,000–43,660. **Amount:** $200–$4700. **Eligibility Requirements:** Applicant must be enrolled or expecting to enroll full-time at a two-year, four-year, or technical institution or university; resident of Indiana and studying in Indiana. Available to U.S. citizens. **Application Requirements:** Application, financial need analysis, FAFSA. **Application Deadline:** March 10. **Contact:** Grants Counselor, State Student Assistance Commission of Indiana (SSACI), 150 West Market St., Ste. 500, Indianapolis, IN 46204-2805. **Phone:** 317-232-2350. **E-mail:** grants@ssaci.state.in.us

Indiana Minority Teacher and Special Education Services Scholarship Program

For Black or Hispanic students seeking teaching certification or for

students seeking special education teaching certification or occupational or physical therapy certification. Must be a U.S. citizen and Indiana resident enrolled full-time in an eligible Indiana institution. Must teach in an Indiana-accredited elementary or secondary school after graduation. Contact institution for application and deadline. Minimum 2.0 GPA required. **Award:** Scholarship for use in freshman, sophomore, junior, or senior years; not renewable. **Number:** 280–370. **Amount:** $1000–$4000. **Eligibility Requirements:** Applicant must be Black (non-Hispanic) or Hispanic; enrolled or expecting to enroll full-time at a four-year institution or university; resident of Indiana and studying in Indiana. Available to U.S. citizens. **Application Requirements:** Application, financial need analysis. **Application Deadline:** Continuous. **Contact:** Ms. Yvonne Heflin, Director, Special Programs, State Student Assistance Commission of Indiana (SSACI), 150 West Market St., Ste. 500, Indianapolis, IN 46204-2805. **Phone:** 317-232-2350. **E-mail:** grants@ssaci.state.in.us

Indiana National Guard Supplemental Grant

The award is a supplement to the Indiana Higher Education Grant program. Applicants must be members of the Indiana National Guard. All Guard paperwork must be completed prior to the start of each semester. The FAFSA must be received by March 10. Award covers certain tuition and fees at select public colleges. **Award:** Grant for use in freshman, sophomore, junior, or senior years; not renewable. **Number:** 503–925. **Amount:** $200–$6516. **Eligibility Requirements:** Applicant must be enrolled or expecting to enroll full or part-time at a two-year or four-year institution or university; resident of Indiana and studying in Indiana. Available to U.S. citizens. Applicant must have served in the Air Force National Guard or Army National Guard. **Application Requirements:** Application. **Application Deadline:** March 10.

Contact: Grants Counselor, State Student Assistance Commission of Indiana (SSACI), 150 West Market St., Ste. 500, Indianapolis, IN 46204-2805. **Phone:** 317-232-2350. **E-mail:** grants@ssaci.state.in.us

Indiana Nursing Scholarship Fund

Need-based tuition funding for nursing students enrolled full- or part-time at an eligible Indiana institution. Must be a U.S. citizen and an Indiana resident and have a minimum 2.0 GPA or meet the minimum requirements for the nursing program. Upon graduation, recipients must practice as a nurse in an Indiana health care setting for two years. **Award:** Scholarship for use in freshman, sophomore, junior, or senior years; not renewable. **Number:** 490–690. **Amount:** $200–$5000. **Eligibility Requirements:** Applicant must be enrolled or expecting to enroll full or part-time at a two-year or four-year institution or university; resident of Indiana and studying in Indiana. Available to U.S. citizens. **Application Requirements:** Application, financial need analysis. **Application Deadline:** Continuous. **Contact:** Ms. Yvonne Heflin, Director, Special Programs, State Student Assistance Commission of Indiana (SSACI), 150 West Market St., Ste. 500, Indianapolis, IN 46204-2805. **Phone:** 317-232-2350

Indiana Wildlife Federation Endowment

A $1000 scholarship will be awarded to an Indiana resident accepted for the study or already enrolled for the study of resource conservation or environmental education at the undergraduate level. For more details see Web site: http://www.indianawildlife.org. **Award:** Scholarship for use in sophomore, junior, or senior years; not renewable. **Number:** 1. **Amount:** $1000. **Eligibility Requirements:** Applicant must be enrolled or expecting to enroll full-time at a four-year institution or university; resident of Indiana and studying in Indiana. Available to U.S. citizens.

Application Requirements: Application. **Application Deadline:** April 30. Application available at Web site.

Part-time Grant Program

Program is designed to encourage part-time undergraduates to start and complete their associate or baccalaureate degrees or certificates by subsidizing part-time tuition costs. It is a term-based award that is based on need. State residency requirements must be met and a FAFSA must be filed. Eligibility is determined at the institutional level subject to approval by SSACI. **Award:** Grant for use in freshman, sophomore, junior, or senior years; not renewable. **Number:** 4680–6700. **Amount:** $50–$4000. **Eligibility Requirements:** Applicant must be enrolled or expecting to enroll part-time at a two-year, four-year, or technical institution or university; resident of Indiana and studying in Indiana. Available to U.S. citizens. **Application Requirements:** Application, financial need analysis. **Application Deadline:** Continuous. **Contact:** Grants Counselor, State Student Assistance Commission of Indiana (SSACI), 150 West Market St., Ste. 500, Indianapolis, IN 46204-2805. **Phone:** 317-232-2350. **E-mail:** grants@ssaci.state.in.us

State Student Assistance Commission of Indiana (SSACI)

The Hoosier Scholar Award is a $500 nonrenewable award. Based on the size of the senior class, one to three scholars are selected by the guidance counselor(s) of each accredited high school in Indiana. The award is based on academic merit and may be used for any educational expense at an eligible Indiana institution of higher education. **Award:** Scholarship for use in freshman year; not renewable. **Number:** 790–840. **Amount:** $500. **Eligibility Requirements:** Applicant must be high school student; planning to enroll or expecting to enroll full-time at a two-year or four-year institution or university; resident of Indiana and studying in Indiana. Applicant must have 3.5 GPA or

higher. Available to U.S. citizens. **Application Requirements:** References. **Application Deadline:** March 10. **Contact:** Ms. Ada Sparkman, Program Coordinator, State Student Assistance Commission of Indiana (SSACI), 150 West Market St., Ste. 500, Indianapolis, IN 46204-2805. **Phone:** 317-232-2350

Twenty-first Century Scholars Award

Income-eligible 7th graders who enroll in the program, fulfill a pledge of good citizenship, and complete the Affirmation Form are guaranteed tuition for four years at any participating public institution. If the student attends a private institution, the state will award an amount comparable to that of a public institution. If the student attends a participating proprietary school, the state will award a tuition scholarship equal to that of Ivy Tech State College. FAFSA and affirmation form must be filed yearly by March 10. Applicant must be resident of Indiana. **Award:** Scholarship for use in freshman, sophomore, junior, or senior years; not renewable. **Number:** 2800–8100. **Amount:** $1000–$6516. **Eligibility Requirements:** Applicant must be enrolled or expecting to enroll full-time at a two-year, four-year, or technical institution or university; resident of Indiana and studying in Indiana. Applicant must have 2.5 GPA or higher. Available to U.S. citizens. **Application Requirements:** Application, financial need analysis, affirmation form. **Application Deadline:** March 10. **Contact:** Twenty-first Century Scholars Program Counselors, State Student Assistance Commission of Indiana (SSACI), 150 West Market St., Ste. 500, Indianapolis, IN 46204-2805. **Phone:** 317-233-2100

Iowa

Iowa College Student Aid Commission

Up to four scholarships ranging from $500 to $1000 will be awarded to students graduating from an Iowa high school. Must actively participate at the Iowa State Fair. For more details see Web site: http://www.iowacollegeaid.org. **Award:** Scholarship for use in freshman year; not renewable. **Number:** up to 4. **Amount:** $500–$1000. **Eligibility Requirements:** Applicant must be high school student; planning to enroll or expecting to enroll at an institution or university; resident of Iowa and studying in Iowa. Available to U.S. citizens. **Application Requirements:** Application, essay, financial need analysis, references, transcript. **Application Deadline:** May 1. **Contact:** Brenda Easter, Director, Special Programs, Iowa College Student Aid Commission, 200 10th St., 4th Fl., Des Moines, IA 50309-3609. **Phone:** 515-242-3380

Iowa Division of Vocational Rehabilitation Services

Provides vocational rehabilitation services to individuals with disabilities who need these services in order to maintain, retain, or obtain employment compatible with their disabilities. Must be Iowa resident. **Award:** Grant for use in freshman, sophomore, junior, senior, graduate, or postgraduate years; renewable. **Number:** up to 5000. **Amount:** $500–$4000. **Eligibility Requirements:** Applicant must be enrolled or expecting to enroll full or part-time at a two-year, four-year, or technical institution or university and resident of Iowa. Applicant must be hearing impaired, learning disabled, physically disabled, or visually impaired. Available to U.S. and non-U.S. citizens. **Application Requirements:** Application, interview. **Application Deadline:** Continuous. **Contact:** Ralph Childers, Policy and Workforce Initiatives Coordinator, Iowa Division of Vocational Rehabilitation Services, Division of Vocational Rehabilitation Services, 510 East 12th St., Des Moines, IA 50319. **Phone:** 515-281-4151. **E-mail:** rchilders@dvrs.state.ia.us

Iowa Foster Child Grants

Grants renewable up to four years will be awarded to students graduating from an Iowa high school who are in Iowa foster care under the care and custody of the Iowa Department of Human Service. Must have a minimum GPA of 2.25 and have applied to an accredited Iowa college or university. For more details see Web site: http://www.iowacollegeaid.org. **Award:** Grant for use in freshman year; renewable. **Number:** varies. **Amount:** $2000–$4200. **Eligibility Requirements:** Applicant must be high school student; planning to enroll or expecting to enroll at a two-year or four-year institution or university; resident of Iowa and studying in Iowa. Available to U.S. citizens. **Application Requirements:** Application. **Application Deadline:** April 15. **Contact:** Brenda Easter, Director, Special Programs, Iowa College Student Aid Commission, 200 10th St., 4th Fl., Des Moines, IA 50309-3609. **Phone:** 515-242-3380

Iowa Grants

Statewide need-based program to assist high-need Iowa residents. Recipients must demonstrate a high level of financial need to receive awards ranging from $100 to $1,000. Awards are prorated for students enrolled for less than full-time. Awards must be used at Iowa postsecondary institutions. **Award:** Grant for use in freshman, sophomore, junior, or senior years; not renewable. **Number:** varies. **Amount:** $100–$1000. **Eligibility Requirements:** Applicant must be enrolled or expecting to enroll full or part-time at a two-year, four-year, or technical institution or university; resident of Iowa and studying in Iowa. Available to U.S. citizens. **Application Requirements:** Application, financial need analysis. **Application Deadline:** Continuous.

Contact: Julie Leeper, Director, State Student Aid Programs, Iowa College Student Aid Commission, 200 10th St., 4th Fl., Des Moines, IA 50309-3609. **Phone:** 515-242-3370. **E-mail:** icsac@max.state.ia.us

Iowa National Guard Education Assistance Program

Program provides postsecondary tuition assistance to members of Iowa National Guard Units. Must study at a postsecondary institution in Iowa. Contact for additional information. **Award:** Grant for use in freshman, sophomore, junior, or senior years; not renewable. **Number:** varies. **Amount:** up to $1200. **Eligibility Requirements:** Applicant must be enrolled or expecting to enroll full or part-time at a two-year, four-year, or technical institution or university; resident of Iowa and studying in Iowa. Available to U.S. citizens. Applicant must have served in the Air Force National Guard or Army National Guard. **Application Requirements:** Application. **Application Deadline:** Continuous. **Contact:** Julie Leeper, Director, State Student Aid Programs, Iowa College Student Aid Commission, 200 10th St., 4th Fl., Des Moines, IA 50309-3609. **Phone:** 515-242-3370. **E-mail:** icsac@max.state.ia.us

Iowa Teacher Forgivable Loan Program

Forgivable loan assists students who will teach in Iowa secondary schools. Must be an Iowa resident attending an Iowa postsecondary institution. Contact for additional information. **Award:** Forgivable loan for use in freshman, sophomore, junior, or senior years; not renewable. **Number:** varies. **Amount:** $2686. **Eligibility Requirements:** Applicant must be enrolled or expecting to enroll full or part-time at a four-year institution or university; resident of Iowa and studying in Iowa. Applicant or parent of applicant must have employment or volunteer experience in teaching. Available to U.S. citizens. **Application Requirements:** Application, financial need analysis.

Application Deadline: Continuous. **Contact:** Brenda Easter, Special Programs Administrator, Iowa College Student Aid Commission, 200 10th St., 4th Fl., Des Moines, IA 50309-3609. **Phone:** 515-242-3380. **E-mail:** icsac@max.state.ia.us

Iowa Tuition Grant Program

Program assists students who attend independent postsecondary institutions in Iowa. Iowa residents currently enrolled, or planning to enroll, for at least three semester hours at one of the eligible Iowa postsecondary institutions may apply. Awards currently range from $100 to $4000. Grants may not exceed the difference between independent college and university tuition and fees and the average tuition and fees at the three public Regent universities. **Award:** Grant for use in freshman, sophomore, junior, or senior years; not renewable. **Number:** varies. **Amount:** $100–$4000. **Eligibility Requirements:** Applicant must be enrolled or expecting to enroll full or part-time at a two-year or four-year institution; resident of Iowa and studying in Iowa. Available to U.S. citizens. **Application Requirements:** Application, financial need analysis. **Application Deadline:** July 1. **Contact:** Julie Leeper, Director, State Student Aid Programs, Iowa College Student Aid Commission, 200 10th St., 4th Fl., Des Moines, IA 50309-3609. **Phone:** 515-242-3370. **E-mail:** icsac@max.state.ia.us

Iowa Vocational/Technical Tuition Grant Program

Program provides need-based financial assistance to Iowa residents enrolled in career education (vocational-technical), and career option programs at Iowa area community colleges. Grants range from $150 to $650, depending on the length of program, financial need, and available funds. **Award:** Grant for use in freshman or sophomore years; not renewable. **Number:** varies. **Amount:** $150–$650. **Eligibility Requirements:** Applicant must be enrolled or expecting to enroll full or part-time at a technical institution; resident of

Iowa and studying in Iowa. Available to U.S. citizens. **Application Requirements:** Application, financial need analysis. **Application Deadline:** July 1. **Contact:** Julie Leeper, Director, State Student Aid Programs, Iowa College Student Aid Commission, 200 10th St., 4th Fl., Des Moines, IA 50309-3609. **Phone:** 515-242-3370. **E-mail:** icsac@max.state.ia.us

State of Iowa Scholarship Program

Program provides recognition and financial honorarium to Iowa's academically talented high school seniors. Honorary scholarships are presented to all qualified candidates. Approximately 1700 top-ranking candidates are designated State of Iowa Scholars every March, from an applicant pool of nearly 5000 high school seniors. Must be used at an Iowa postsecondary institution. Minimum 3.5 GPA required. **Award:** Scholarship for use in freshman year; not renewable. **Number:** up to 1700. **Amount:** up to $400. **Eligibility Requirements:** Applicant must be high school student; planning to enroll or expecting to enroll full-time at a two-year, four-year, or technical institution or university; resident of Iowa and studying in Iowa. Applicant must have 3.5 GPA or higher. Available to U.S. citizens. **Application Requirements:** Application, test scores. **Application Deadline:** November 1. **Contact:** Julie Leeper, Director, State Student Aid Programs, Iowa College Student Aid Commission, 200 10th St., 4th Fl., Des Moines, IA 50309-3609. **Phone:** 515-242-3370. **E-mail:** icsac@max.state.ia.us

Kansas

Kansas Commission on Veterans Affairs

The Kansas Educational Benefits for Children of MIA, POW, and Deceased Veterans of the Vietnam War is a full-tuition scholarship awarded to students who are children of veterans. Must show proof

of parent's status as missing in action, prisoner-of-war, or killed in action in the Vietnam War. Kansas residence required of veteran at time of entry to service. Must attend a state-supported postsecondary school. **Award:** Scholarship for use in freshman, sophomore, junior, or senior years; not renewable. **Eligibility Requirements:** Applicant must be enrolled or expecting to enroll at a two-year, four-year, or technical institution or university and studying in Kansas. Available to U.S. citizens. Applicant or parent must meet one or more of the following requirements: general military experience; retired from active duty; disabled or killed as a result of military service; prisoner of war; or missing in action. **Application Requirements:** Application, report of casualty, birth certificate, school acceptance letter. **Application Deadline:** Continuous. **Contact:** Tony Floyd, Program Director, Kansas Commission on Veterans Affairs, 700 Southwest Jackson, Jayhawk Tower, #701, Topeka, KS 66603. **Phone:** 785-291-3422. **E-mail:** kcva004@ink.org

Kansas National Guard Educational Assistance Program

Service scholarship for enlisted soldiers in the Kansas National Guard. Pays up to 100% of tuition and fees based on funding. Must attend a state-supported institution. Recipients will be required to serve in the KNG for three months for every semester of benefits after the last payment of state tuition assistance. Must not have over 15 years of service at time of application. Deadlines are January 15 and August 20. Contact KNG Education Services Specialist for further information. Must be Kansas resident. **Award:** Scholarship for use in freshman, sophomore, junior, or senior years; not renewable. **Number:** up to 400. **Amount:** $250–$3500. **Eligibility Requirements:** Applicant must be enrolled or expecting to enroll full or part-time at a two-year, four-year, or technical institution or university; resident of Kansas and studying in Kansas. Available to U.S.

citizens. Applicant must have served in the Air Force National Guard or Army National Guard. **Application Requirements:** Application. **Application Deadline:** varies. **Contact:** Steve Finch, Education Services Specialist, Kansas National Guard Educational Assistance Program, Attn: AGKS-DOP-ESO, The Adjutant General of Kansas, 2800 South West Topeka Blvd., Topeka, KS 66611-1287. **Phone:** 785-274-1060. **E-mail:** steve.finch@ks.ngb.army.mil

Michigan

Inter-Tribal Council of Michigan, Inc.
Renewable award provides free tuition for Native-American of one-quarter or more blood degree who attend a Michigan public college or university. Must be a Michigan resident for at least one year. For more details and deadlines contact college financial aid office. **Award:** Scholarship for use in freshman, sophomore, junior, senior, graduate, or postgraduate years; renewable. **Number:** varies. **Amount:** varies. **Eligibility Requirements:** Applicant must be American Indian/Alaska Native; enrolled or expecting to enroll full or part-time at a two-year or four-year institution or university; resident of Michigan and studying in Michigan. Available to U.S. and Canadian citizens. **Application Requirements:** Application, Dr.r's license. **Application Deadline:** Continuous. **Contact:** Christin McKerchie, Executive Assistant to Programs, Inter-Tribal Council of Michigan, Inc., 405 East Easterday Ave., Sault Ste. Marie, MI 49783. **Phone:** 906-632-6896. **E-mail:** christin@itcmi.org

Michigan Bureau of Student Financial Assistance
Grant for part-time, needy, independent undergraduates at an approved, degree-granting Michigan college or university. Eligibility is limited to two years. Must be Michigan resident. Deadlines determined by college. **Award:** Grant for use in freshman, sophomore, junior, or senior years; not renewable. **Number:** varies. **Amount:** up to $600. **Eligibility Requirements:** Applicant must be enrolled or expecting to enroll part-time at a two-year or four-year institution or university; resident of Michigan and studying in Michigan. Available to U.S. citizens. **Application Requirements:** Application, financial need analysis. **Contact:** Program Director, Michigan Bureau of Student Financial Assistance, PO Box 30466, Lansing, MI 48909-7966

Michigan Competitive Scholarship
Awards limited to tuition. Must maintain a C average and meet the college's academic progress requirements. Must file Free Application for Federal Student Aid. Deadline: March 1. Must be Michigan resident. Renewable award of $1300 for undergraduate study at a Michigan institution. **Award:** Scholarship for use in freshman, sophomore, junior, or senior years; renewable. **Number:** varies. **Amount:** $100–$1300. **Eligibility Requirements:** Applicant must be enrolled or expecting to enroll at a two-year or four-year institution or university; resident of Michigan and studying in Michigan. Available to U.S. citizens. **Application Requirements:** Application, financial need analysis, test scores, FAFSA. **Application Deadline:** March 1. **Contact:** Scholarship and Grant Director, Michigan Bureau of Student Financial Assistance, PO Box 30466, Lansing, MI 48909

Michigan Educational Opportunity Grant
Need-based program for Michigan residents who are at least half-time undergraduates attending public Michigan colleges. Must maintain good academic standing. Deadline determined by college. Award of up to $1000. **Award:** Grant for use in freshman, sophomore, junior, or senior years; not renewable. **Number:** varies. **Amount:** up to $1000.

Eligibility Requirements: Applicant must be enrolled or expecting to enroll full or part-time at a two-year or four-year institution or university; resident of Michigan and studying in Michigan. Available to U.S. citizens. **Application Requirements:** Application, financial need analysis. **Application Deadline:** varies. **Contact:** Program Director, Michigan Bureau of Student Financial Assistance, PO Box 30466, Lansing, MI 48909-7966

Michigan Merit Award
Scholarship for students scoring well on state's standardized assessment tests. Students will have four years from high school graduation to use the award. **Award:** Scholarship for use in freshman year; not renewable. **Number:** varies. **Amount:** $1000–$2500. **Eligibility Requirements:** Applicant must be high school student; planning to enroll or expecting to enroll full or part-time at a two-year, four-year, or technical institution or university and resident of Michigan. Available to U.S. citizens. **Application Requirements:** Test scores. **Contact:** Program Director, Michigan Bureau of Student Financial Assistance, PO Box 30466, Lansing, MI 48909-7966

Michigan Nursing Scholarship
For students enrolled in an LPN, associate degree in nursing, or bachelor of science in nursing programs. Colleges determine application procedure and select recipients. Recipients must fulfill in-state work commitment or repay scholarship. **Award:** Scholarship for use in freshman, sophomore, junior, or senior years; renewable. **Number:** varies. **Amount:** up to $4000. **Eligibility Requirements:** Applicant must be enrolled or expecting to enroll full or part-time at a two-year or four-year institution or university; resident of Michigan and studying in Michigan. Available to U.S. citizens. **Contact:** Program Director, Michigan Bureau of Student Financial Assistance, PO Box 30466, Lansing, MI 48909-7966

Michigan Tuition Grants

Need-based program. Students must attend a Michigan private, nonprofit, degree-granting college. Must file the Free Application for Federal Student Aid and meet the college's academic progress requirements. Deadline: March 1. Must be Michigan resident. Renewable award of $2000. **Award:** Grant for use in freshman, sophomore, junior, or senior years; renewable. **Number:** varies. **Amount:** $100–$2750. **Eligibility Requirements:** Applicant must be enrolled or expecting to enroll at a two-year or four-year institution or university; resident of Michigan and studying in Michigan. Available to U.S. citizens. **Application Requirements:** Application, financial need analysis, FAFSA. **Application Deadline:** March 1. **Contact:** Scholarship and Grant Director, Michigan Bureau of Student Financial Assistance, PO Box 30466, Lansing, MI 48909-7966

Michigan Veterans Trust Fund

Tuition grant of $2,800 for children of Michigan veterans who died on active duty or subsequently declared 100% disabled as the result of service-connected illness or injury. Must be 17 to 25 years old, be a Michigan resident, and attend a private or public institution in Michigan. **Award:** Grant for use in freshman, sophomore, junior, or senior years; renewable. **Number:** varies. **Amount:** up to $2800. **Eligibility Requirements:** Applicant must be age 17-25; enrolled or expecting to enroll full-time at a two-year, four-year, or technical institution or university; resident of Michigan and studying in Michigan. Applicant or parent must meet one or more of the following requirements: general military experience; retired from active duty; disabled or killed as a result of military service; prisoner of war; or missing in action. **Application Requirements:** Application. **Application Deadline:** Continuous. **Contact:** Phyllis Ochis, Department of Military and Veterans Affairs, Michigan Veterans Trust Fund, 2500 South Washington Ave., Lansing, MI 48913. **Phone:** 517-483-5469

Tuition Incentive Program (TIP)

Award for Michigan residents who receive or have received Medicaid for required period of time through the Family Independence Agency. Scholarship provides two years tuition towards an associate's degree at a Michigan college or university. Apply before graduating from high school or earning General Education Development diploma. **Award:** Scholarship for use in freshman or sophomore years; renewable. **Number:** varies. **Eligibility Requirements:** Applicant must be high school student; planning to enroll or expecting to enroll full or part-time at a two-year or four-year institution or university; resident of Michigan and studying in Michigan. Available to U.S. citizens. **Application Requirements:** Application, financial need analysis. **Application Deadline:** Continuous. **Contact:** Program Director, Michigan Bureau of Student Financial Assistance, PO Box 30466, Lansing, MI 48909

Minnesota

Donaldson Company

Scholarships for children of U.S. employees of Donaldson Company, Inc. Any form of accredited postsecondary education is eligible. Application deadline is March 12. **Award:** Scholarship for use in freshman, sophomore, junior, or senior years; renewable. **Amount:** $1000–$3000. **Eligibility Requirements:** Applicant must be enrolled or expecting to enroll full-time at a two-year, four-year, or technical institution or university. Applicant or parent of applicant must be affiliated with Donaldson Company. Available to U.S. citizens. **Application Requirements:** Application, essay, financial need analysis, references, transcript. **Application Deadline:** March 12. **Contact:** Norm Linnell, Vice President, General Counsel, and Secretary, Donaldson Company, PO Box 1299, Minneapolis, MN 55440. **Phone:** 952-887-3631. **E-mail:** nlinnell@mail.donaldson.com

Minnesota Department of Health

This program offers loan repayment to registered nurse and licensed practical nurse students who agree to practice in a Minnesota nursing home or an Intermediate Care Facility for persons with mental retardation for a minimum 3-year service obligation after completion of training. Candidates must apply while still in school. **Award:** Grant for use in freshman, sophomore, junior, or senior years; not renewable. **Number:** 25–35. **Amount:** $3000–$4000. **Eligibility Requirements:** Applicant must be enrolled or expecting to enroll full or part-time at a two-year, four-year, or technical institution or university. Available to U.S. citizens. **Application Requirements:** Application, essay. **Application Deadline:** Continuous. **Contact:** Karen Welter, Minnesota Department of Health, 121 East Seventh Place, Ste. 460, PO Box 64975, St. Paul, MN 55164-0975. **Phone:** 651-282-6302. **E-mail:** karen.welter@health.state.mn.us

Minnesota Department of Military Affairs

Awarded to high school seniors who enlist in the Minnesota National Guard. The award recognizes demonstrated leadership, community services and potential for success in the Minnesota National Guard. For more information, applicant may contact any Minnesota army national guard recruiter at 1-800-go-guard or visit the Web site http://www.dma.state.mn.us. **Award:** Scholarship for use in freshman year; not renewable. **Number:** 30. **Amount:** $1000. **Eligibility Requirements:** Applicant must be high school student and planning to enroll or expecting to enroll full or part-time at a two-year, four-year, or technical institution or university. Available to U.S. and non-U.S. citizens. Applicant must have served in the Air Force National Guard or Army National Guard. **Application Requirements:** Essay, references, transcript. **Application Deadline:** March 15. **Contact:** Barbara O'Reilly,

Education Services Officer, Minnesota Department of Military Affairs, Veterans Services Building, 20 West 12th St., St. Paul, MN 55155-2098. **Phone:** 651-282-4508. **E-mail:** barbara.oreilly@mn.ngb.army.mil

Minnesota Department of Veterans' Affairs

War orphans may qualify for $750 per year. Must have lost parent through service-related death. Children of deceased veterans may qualify for free tuition at State university, college, or vocational or technical schools, but not at University of Minnesota. Must have been resident of Minnesota for at least two years. **Award:** Grant for use in freshman, sophomore, junior, or senior years; renewable. **Number:** varies. **Amount:** $750. **Eligibility Requirements:** Applicant must be enrolled or expecting to enroll full or part-time at a two-year, four-year, or technical institution or university; resident of Minnesota and studying in Minnesota. Available to U.S. citizens. Applicant or parent must meet one or more of the following requirements: general military experience; retired from active duty; disabled or killed as a result of military service; prisoner of war; or missing in action. **Application Requirements:** Application, financial need analysis. **Application Deadline:** Continuous. **Contact:** Terrence Logan, Management Analyst IV, Minnesota Department of Veterans' Affairs, 20 West 12th St., Second Fl., St. Paul, MN 55155-2079. **Phone:** 651-296-2562

Minnesota Higher Education Services Office

Renewable tuition waiver for Minnesota residents. Waives all or part of non-resident tuition surcharge at public institutions in Iowa, Kansas, Michigan, Missouri, Nebraska, North Dakota, South Dakota, and Wisconsin. Deadline is last day of academic term. **Award:** Scholarship for use in freshman, sophomore, junior, senior, graduate, or postgraduate years; renewable.

Number: varies. **Amount:** varies. **Eligibility Requirements:** Applicant must be enrolled or expecting to enroll full or part-time at a two-year, four-year, or technical institution or university; resident of Minnesota and studying in Iowa, Kansas, Michigan, Missouri, Nebraska, North Dakota, South Dakota, or Wisconsin. Available to U.S. citizens. **Application Requirements:** Application. **Application Deadline:** varies. **Contact:** Minnesota Higher Education Services Office, 1450 Energy Park Dr., Ste. 350, St. Paul, MN 55108-5227, **Phone:** 651-642-0567 Ext. 1

Minnesota Indian Scholarship Office

One time award for Minnesota Native-American. Applicant must be one quarter Native-American and a resident of Minnesota. Must re-apply for scholarship annually. **Award:** Scholarship for use in freshman, sophomore, junior, or senior years; not renewable. **Number:** varies. **Amount:** up to $3300. **Eligibility Requirements:** Applicant must be American Indian/Alaska Native; enrolled or expecting to enroll full or part-time at a two-year, four-year, or technical institution or university; resident of Minnesota and studying in Minnesota. Available to U.S. citizens. **Application Requirements:** Application, financial need analysis. **Application Deadline:** July 1. **Contact:** Lea Perkins, Director, Minnesota Indian Scholarship Office, Minnesota Department of Education, 1500 Hwy. 36W, Roseville, MN 55113-4266. **Phone:** 800-657-3927. **E-mail:** cfl.indianeducation@state.mn.us

Minnesota Safety Officers' Survivor Program

Grant for eligible survivors of Minnesota public safety officer killed in the line of duty. Safety officers who have been permanently or totally disabled in the line of duty are also eligible. Must be used at a Minnesota institution participating in State Grant Program. Write for

details. Must submit proof of death or disability and Public Safety Officers Benefit Fund Certificate. Must apply each year. Can be renewed for four years. **Award:** Grant for use in freshman, sophomore, junior, or senior years; not renewable. **Amount:** up to $8096. **Eligibility Requirements:** Applicant must be enrolled or expecting to enroll full or part-time at a two-year, four-year, or technical institution or university and studying in Minnesota. Applicant or parent of applicant must have employment or volunteer experience in police/fire-fighting. Available to U.S. citizens. **Application Requirements:** Application, proof of death/disability. **Application Deadline:** Continuous. **Contact:** Minnesota Higher Education Services Office, 1450 Energy Park Dr., Ste. 350, St. Paul, MN 55108-5227. **Phone:** 651-642-0567 Ext. 1

Minnesota State Grant Program

Need-based grant program available for Minnesota residents attending Minnesota colleges. Student covers 46% of cost with remainder covered by Pell Grant, parent contribution and state grant. Students apply with FAFSA and college administers the program on campus. **Award:** Grant for use in freshman, sophomore, junior, or senior years; not renewable. **Number:** 71,000–75,000. **Amount:** $100–$7662. **Eligibility Requirements:** Applicant must be age 17; enrolled or expecting to enroll full or part-time at a two-year, four-year, or technical institution or university; resident of Minnesota and studying in Minnesota. Available to U.S. citizens. **Application Requirements:** Application, financial need analysis. **Application Deadline:** varies. **Contact:** Minnesota Higher Education Services Office, 1450 Energy Park Dr., Ste. 350, St. Paul, MN 55108. **Phone:** 651-642-0567 Ext. 1

Minnesota State Veterans' Dependents Assistance Program

Tuition assistance to dependents of persons considered to be prisoner-of-war or missing in action after August 1, 1958. Must be Minnesota resident attending Minnesota two- or four-year school. **Award:** Scholarship for use in freshman, sophomore, junior, or senior years; renewable. **Number:** varies. **Amount:** varies. **Eligibility Requirements:** Applicant must be enrolled or expecting to enroll at a two-year or four-year institution; resident of Minnesota and studying in Minnesota. Available to U.S. citizens. Applicant or parent must meet one or more of the following requirements: general military experience; retired from active duty; disabled or killed as a result of military service; prisoner of war; or missing in action. **Application Requirements:** Application. **Application Deadline:** Continuous. **Contact:** Minnesota Higher Education Services Office, 1450 Energy Park Dr., Ste. 350, St. Paul, MN 55108-5227

Minnesota VA Educational Assistance for Veterans

One-time $750 stipend given to veterans who have used up all other federal funds, yet have time remaining on their delimiting period. Applicant must be a Minnesota resident and must be attending a Minnesota college or university, but not the University of Minnesota. **Award:** Grant for use in freshman, sophomore, junior, or senior years; not renewable. **Number:** varies. **Amount:** $750. **Eligibility Requirements:** Applicant must be enrolled or expecting to enroll full or part-time at a two-year, four-year, or technical institution or university; resident of Minnesota and studying in Minnesota. Available to U.S. citizens. Applicant must have general military experience. **Application Requirements:** Application, financial need analysis. **Application Deadline:** Continuous. **Contact:** Terrence Logan, Management Analyst IV, Minnesota Department of Veterans' Affairs, 20 West 12th St., Second Fl., St. Paul, MN 55155-2079. **Phone:** 651-296-2562

Postsecondary Child Care Grant Program

One-time grant available for students not receiving MFIP. Based on financial need. Cannot exceed actual child care costs or maximum award chart (based on income). Must be Minnesota resident. For use at Minnesota two- or four-year school, including public technical colleges. **Award:** Grant for use in freshman, sophomore, junior, or senior years; not renewable. **Number:** varies. **Amount:** $100–$2200. **Eligibility Requirements:** Applicant must be enrolled or expecting to enroll full or part-time at a two-year, four-year, or technical institution or university; resident of Minnesota and studying in Minnesota. Available to U.S. citizens. **Application Requirements:** Application, financial need analysis. **Application Deadline:** Continuous. **Contact:** Minnesota Higher Education Services Office, 1450 Energy Park Dr., Ste. 350, St. Paul, MN 55108-5227 **Phone:** 651-642-0567 Ext. 1

Missouri

Marguerite Ross Barnett Memorial Scholarship

Applicant must be employed (at least 20 hours per week) and attending school part-time. Must be Missouri resident and enrolled at a participating Missouri postsecondary school. Awards not available during summer term. Minimum age is 18. **Award:** Scholarship for use in freshman, sophomore, junior, or senior years; not renewable. **Number:** varies. **Amount:** $900–$1700. **Eligibility Requirements:** Applicant must be age 18; enrolled or expecting to enroll part-time at a two-year or four-year institution or university; resident of Missouri and studying in Missouri. Available to U.S. citizens. **Application Requirements:** Application, financial need analysis. **Application Deadline:** April 1. **Contact:** MDHE Information Center, Missouri Department of Higher

Education, 3515 Amazonas Dr., Jefferson City, MO 65109. **Phone:** 800-473-6757 Ext. 1. **E-mail:** icweb@dhe.mo.gov

Missouri College Guarantee Program

Available to Missouri residents attending Missouri colleges full-time. Minimum 2.5 GPA required. Must have participated in high school extracurricular activities. **Award:** Scholarship for use in freshman, sophomore, junior, or senior years; not renewable. **Number:** varies. **Amount:** $100–$4900. **Eligibility Requirements:** Applicant must be enrolled or expecting to enroll full-time at a two-year or four-year institution or university; resident of Missouri and studying in Missouri. Applicant must have 2.5 GPA or higher. Available to U.S. citizens. **Application Requirements:** Financial need analysis, test scores. **Application Deadline:** April 1. **Contact:** MDHE Information Center, Missouri Department of Higher Education, 3515 Amazonas Dr., Jefferson City, MO 65109. **Phone:** 800-473-6757 Ext. 1. **E-mail:** icweb@dhe.mo.gov

Missouri Department of Elementary and Secondary Education

Award may be used any year up to four years at an approved, participating Missouri institution. Scholarship is for minority Missouri residents in teaching programs. Recipients must commit to teach for five years in a Missouri public elementary or secondary school. Graduate students must teach math or science. Otherwise, award must be repaid. **Award:** Scholarship for use in freshman, sophomore, junior, senior, or graduate years; renewable. **Number:** 100. **Amount:** $3000. **Eligibility Requirements:** Applicant must be American Indian/Alaska Native, Asian/Pacific Islander, Black (non-Hispanic), or Hispanic; enrolled or expecting to enroll full-time at a two-year or four-year institution or university; resident of Missouri and studying in Missouri. Applicant must have 3.0 GPA or higher. Available to U.S. citizens. **Application Requirements:** Application, essay, financial need analysis, references, test scores, transcript. **Application Deadline:** February 15. **Contact:** Laura Harrison, Administrative Assistant II, Missouri Department of Elementary and Secondary Education, PO Box 480, Jefferson City, MO 65102-0480. **Phone:** 573-751-1668. **E-mail:** laura.harrison@dese.mo.gov

Missouri Department of Health and Senior Services

Forgivable loans for Missouri residents attending Missouri institutions pursuing a degree as a primary care physician or dentist, studying for a bachelors degree as a dental hygienist, or a master of science degree in nursing leading to certification as an Advanced Practice Nurse. To be forgiven participant must work in a Missouri health professional shortage area. **Award:** Forgivable loan for use in freshman, sophomore, junior, senior, graduate, or postgraduate years; not renewable. **Number:** varies. **Amount:** $3000–$25,000. **Eligibility Requirements:** Applicant must be enrolled or expecting to enroll full or part-time at a four-year institution or university; resident of Missouri and studying in Missouri. Available to U.S. citizens. **Application Requirements:** Application, Dr.r's license. **Application Deadline:** July 1. **Contact:** Kristie Frank, Health Program Representative, Missouri Department of Health and Senior Services, PO Box 570, Jefferson City, MO 65102-0570, **Phone:** 800-891-7415. **E-mail:** frank@dhss.mo.gov

Missouri Department of Higher Education

Available to Missouri residents attending Missouri colleges or universities full-time. Must be undergraduates with financial need. May reapply for up to a maximum of ten semesters. Free Application for Federal Student Aid (FAFSA) or a renewal must be received by the federal processor by April 1 to be considered. **Award:** Grant for use in freshman, sophomore, junior, or senior years; not renewable. **Number:** varies. **Amount:** $100–$1500. **Eligibility Requirements:** Applicant must be enrolled or expecting to enroll full-time at a two-year, four-year, or technical institution or university; resident of Missouri and studying in Missouri. Available to U.S. citizens. **Application Requirements:** Financial need analysis. **Application Deadline:** April 1. **Contact:** MDHE Information Center, Missouri Department of Higher Education, 3515 Amazonas Dr., Jefferson City, MO 65109. **Phone:** 800-473-6757 Ext. 1. **E-mail:** icweb@dhe.mo.gov

Missouri Higher Education Academic Scholarship (Bright Flight)

Awards of $2000 for Missouri high school seniors. Must be in top 3% of Missouri SAT or ACT scorers. Must attend Missouri institution as full-time undergraduate. May reapply for up to ten semesters. Must be Missouri resident and U.S. citizen. **Award:** Scholarship for use in freshman, sophomore, junior, or senior years; not renewable. **Number:** varies. **Amount:** $2000. **Eligibility Requirements:** Applicant must be high school student; planning to enroll or expecting to enroll full-time at a two-year, four-year, or technical institution or university; resident of Missouri and studying in Missouri. Available to U.S. citizens. **Application Requirements:** Test scores. **Application Deadline:** July 31. **Contact:** MDHE Information Center, Missouri Department of Higher Education, 3515 Amazonas Dr., Jefferson City, MO 65109. **Phone:** 800-473-6757 Ext. 1 **E-mail:** icweb@dhe.mo.gov

Missouri Teacher Education Scholarship (General)

Nonrenewable award for Missouri high school seniors or Missouri resident college students. Must attend approved teacher training program at a participating Missouri institution. Must rank in top 15 % of high school class on ACT/SAT. Merit-based award. Recipients must commit to teach in Missouri for five years at a public elementary or secondary school or award must be repaid. **Award:** Scholarship for use in freshman, sophomore, junior, or senior years; not renewable. **Number:** 200–240. **Amount:** $2000. **Eligibility Requirements:** Applicant must be enrolled or expecting to enroll full-time at a two-year or four-year institution or university; resident of Missouri and studying in Missouri. Applicant must have 3.5 GPA or higher. Available to U.S. citizens. **Application Requirements:** Application, essay, references, test scores, transcript. **Application Deadline:** February 15. **Contact:** Laura Harrison, Administrative Assistant II, Missouri Department of Elementary and Secondary Education, PO Box 480, Jefferson City, MO 65102-0480, **Phone:** 573-751-1668. **E-mail:** laura.harrison@dese.mo.gov

Rural Missouri, Inc.

The grant is from the Department of Labor. Renewable grant to low income seasonal farm workers and their dependents for tuition assistance. Must be a resident of Missouri. Must be paid wages for doing farm work. High school seniors may apply. Must attend a Missouri school. Minimum 2.5 GPA required. **Award:** Grant for use in freshman, sophomore, junior, or senior years; renewable. **Number:** varies. **Amount:** up to $3000. **Eligibility Requirements:** Applicant must be age 16; enrolled or expecting to enroll at a two-year, four-year, or technical institution or university; resident of Missouri and studying in Missouri. Applicant or parent of applicant must have employment or volunteer experience in agriculture, farming, or migrant worker. Applicant must have 2.5 GPA or higher. **Application Requirements:** Application. **Application Deadline:** Continuous. **Contact:** Lynn Hatfield, Program Director, Rural Missouri, Inc., 1014 Northeast Dr., Jefferson City, MO 65109. **Phone:** 800-234-4971. **E-mail:** lynn@rmiinc.org

Nebraska

Nebraska National Guard

Renewable award for members of the Nebraska National Guard. Pays 75% of enlisted soldier's tuition until he or she has received a baccalaureate degree. **Award:** Scholarship for use in freshman, sophomore, junior, or senior years; renewable. **Number:** up to 1200. **Eligibility Requirements:** Applicant must be enrolled or expecting to enroll full or part-time at a two-year, four-year, or technical institution or university; resident of Nebraska and studying in Nebraska. Applicant must have served in the Air Force National Guard or Army National Guard. **Application Requirements:** Application. **Application Deadline:** Continuous. **Contact:** Cindy York, Administrative Assistant, Nebraska National Guard, 1300 Military Rd., Lincoln, NE 68508-1090. **Phone:** 402-309-7143

State of Nebraska Coordinating Commission for Postsecondary Education

Available to undergraduates attending a participating postsecondary institution in Nebraska. Available to Pell Grant recipients only. Nebraska residency required. Awards determined by each participating institution. Contact financial aid office at institution for application and additional information. **Award:** Grant for use in freshman, sophomore, junior, or senior years; not renewable. **Number:** varies. **Amount:** $100–$1032. **Eligibility Requirements:** Applicant must be enrolled or expecting to enroll full or part-time at a two-year, four-year, or technical institution or university; resident of Nebraska and studying in Nebraska. Available to U.S. citizens. **Application Requirements:** Application, financial need analysis. **Application Deadline:** Continuous. **Contact:** Financial Aid Office at college or university

North Dakota

North Dakota Department of Transportation

Educational grants for civil or construction engineering, or civil engineering technology, are awarded to students who have completed one year of course study at an institution of higher learning in North Dakota. Recipients must agree to work for the Department for a period of time at least equal to the grant period or repay the grant at 6% interest. Minimum 2.0 GPA required. **Award:** Grant for use in sophomore, junior, or senior years; renewable. **Number:** varies. **Amount:** $1000–$6000. **Eligibility Requirements:** Applicant must be enrolled or expecting to enroll full-time at a four-year, or technical institution and studying in North Dakota. Available to U.S. citizens. **Application Requirements:** Application, financial need analysis, interview, transcript. **Application Deadline:** Continuous. **Contact:** Lorrie Pavlicek, Human Resources Manager, North Dakota Department of Transportation, 503 38th St. South, Fargo, ND 58103. **Phone:** 701-239-8934. **E-mail:** lpavlice@state.nd.us

North Dakota Scholars Program

Provides scholarships equal to cost of tuition at the public colleges in North Dakota for North Dakota residents. Must score at or above the 95th percentile on ACT and rank in top twenty percent of high school graduation class. Must take ACT in fall. For high school seniors with a minimum 3.5 GPA. Application deadline is the October or June ACT test date. **Award:** Scholarship for use in freshman, sophomore, junior, or senior years; renewable. **Number:** 20. **Amount:** varies. **Eligibility Requirements:** Applicant must be high school student; planning to enroll or expecting to enroll full-time at a two-year or four-year institution or university; resident of North Dakota and studying in North Dakota. Applicant must have 3.5

GPA or higher. Available to U.S. citizens. **Application Requirements:** Test scores. **Application Deadline:** varies. **Contact:** Peggy Wipf, Director of Financial Aid, State of North Dakota, Bismarck, ND 58505-0230 **Phone:** 701-328-4114
North Dakota State Student Incentive Grant Program
Aids North Dakota residents attending an approved college or university in North Dakota. Must be enrolled in a program of at least nine months in length. **Award:** Grant for use in freshman, sophomore, junior, or senior years; not renewable. **Number:** 2500–2600. **Amount:** up to $600. **Eligibility Requirements:** Applicant must be enrolled or expecting to enroll full-time at a two-year or four-year institution or university; resident of North Dakota and studying in North Dakota. Available to U.S. citizens. **Application Requirements:** Financial need analysis, FAFSA. **Application Deadline:** March 15. **Contact:** Peggy Wipf, Director of Financial Aid, State of North Dakota, 600 East Blvd., Department 215, Bismarck, ND 58505-0230. **Phone:** 701-328-4114

North Dakota University System

Forgivable loan for individuals who received their education degree from a North Dakota public institution and teach in North Dakota at grade levels and/or content areas identified by the Department of Public Instruction as having a teacher shortage. Funding recipients are eligible to have indebtedness reduced for up to $1000 per year for every consecutive year they teach in a teacher shortage area for up to three years. Applications are available on Web site: http://www.ndus.nodak.edu/students/financial-aid. **Award:** Forgivable loan for use in freshman, sophomore, junior, or senior years; renewable. **Number:** 100–175. **Amount:** up to $1000. **Eligibility Requirements:** Applicant must be enrolled or expecting to enroll at a four-year institution or university; resident of North Dakota and studying in North Dakota. Applicant or parent of applicant must have employment or volunteer experience in teaching. Available to U.S. citizens. **Application Requirements:** Application, financial need analysis. **Contact:** Peggy Wipf, Director of Financial Aid, North Dakota University System, 600 East Blvd., Department 215, Bismarck, ND 58505-0230. **Phone:** 701-328-4114. **E-mail:** peggy.wipf@ndus.nodak.edu

State of North Dakota

Assists Native-American North Dakota residents in obtaining a college education. Priority given to full-time undergraduate students and those having a 3.5 GPA or higher. Certification of tribal enrollment required. For use at North Dakota institution. **Award:** Scholarship for use in freshman, sophomore, junior, senior, or graduate years; renewable. **Number:** up to 150. **Amount:** $600–$900. **Eligibility Requirements:** Applicant must be American Indian/Alaska Native; enrolled or expecting to enroll at a two-year or four-year institution or university; resident of North Dakota and studying in North Dakota. Applicant must have 3.5 GPA or higher. **Application Requirements:** Application, financial need analysis, transcript, proof of tribal enrollment. **Application Deadline:** July 15. **Contact:** Rhonda Schauer, Coordinator of American Indian Higher Education, State of North Dakota, 600 East Blvd., Department 215, Bismarck, ND 58505-0230. **Phone:** 701-328-9661

Ohio

Accountancy Board of Ohio

Program intended for minority students or students with financial need. Applicant must be enrolled as accounting major at an accredited Ohio college or university in a five-year degree program. Applicant must be an Ohio resident. Please refer to Web site for further details: http://acc.ohio.gov/educasst.html. **Award:** Scholarship for use in sophomore, junior, or senior years; not renewable. **Number:** varies.

Amount: $7700. **Eligibility Requirements:** Applicant must be enrolled or expecting to enroll at a four-year institution or university; resident of Ohio and studying in Ohio. Available to U.S. citizens. **Application Requirements:** Application, financial need analysis, transcript, FAFSA. **Application Deadline:** varies. **Contact:** Kay Sedgmer, Scholarship Secretary, Accountancy Board of Ohio, Accountancy Board of Ohio, 77 South High St., 18th Fl., Columbus, OH 43266-0301. **Phone:** 614-466-4135. **E-mail:** kay.sedgmer@acc.state.oh.us

Ohio Academy of Science/Ohio Environmental Education Fund

Merit-based, non-renewable, tuition-only scholarships given to undergraduate students admitted to Ohio state or private colleges and universities who can demonstrate their knowledge and commitment to careers in environmental sciences or environmental engineering. Must be in their final year of a program in a two-year or four-year institution. Sophomores in a four-year institution are not eligible. **Award:** Scholarship for use in sophomore or senior years; not renewable. **Number:** 18. **Amount:** $1250–$2500. **Eligibility Requirements:** Applicant must be enrolled or expecting to enroll full or part-time at a two-year or four-year institution or university; resident of Ohio and studying in Ohio. Applicant must have 3.0 GPA or higher. Available to U.S. citizens. **Application Requirements:** Application, essay, references, self-addressed stamped envelope, transcript. **Application Deadline:** July 1. **Contact:** Mr. Lynn E. Elfner, CEO, Ohio Academy of Science/Ohio Environmental Education Fund, 1500 West Third Ave., Ste. 228, Columbus, OH 43212-2817. **Phone:** 614-488-2228. **E-mail:** oas@iwaynet.net

Ohio Board of Regents

Award for academically outstanding Ohio residents planning to attend an

approved Ohio college. Must be a high school senior intending to enroll full-time. Award is renewable for up to four years. Must rank in upper quarter of class or have a minimum GPA of 3.5. **Award:** Scholarship for use in freshman, sophomore, junior, or senior years; renewable. **Number:** 1000. **Amount:** $2205. **Eligibility Requirements:** Applicant must be high school student; planning to enroll or expecting to enroll full-time at a two-year or four-year institution; resident of Ohio and studying in Ohio. Applicant must have 3.5 GPA or higher. Available to U.S. citizens. **Application Requirements:** Application, test scores, transcript. **Application Deadline:** February 23. **Contact:** Sarina Wilks, Program Administrator, Ohio Board of Regents, PO Box 182452, Columbus, OH 43218-2452. **Phone:** 614-752-9528. **E-mail:** swilks@regents.state.oh.us

Ohio Department of Education

Renewable award for graduating high school seniors who demonstrate outstanding academic achievement. Each Ohio high school receives applications by January of each year. School can submit one application for every 200 students in the senior class. Application deadline is the second Friday in March. **Award:** Scholarship for use in freshman, sophomore, junior, or senior years; renewable. **Number:** varies. **Amount:** up to $1500. **Eligibility Requirements:** Applicant must be high school student; planning to enroll or expecting to enroll at a two-year or four-year institution or university and resident of Ohio. Applicant must have 3.5 GPA or higher. Available to U.S. citizens. **Application Requirements:** Application, test scores. **Application Deadline:** varies. **Contact:** Byrd Program Office, Ohio Department of Education, 25 South Front St., Second Fl., Columbus, OH 43215. **Phone:** 614-466-4590

Ohio Instructional Grant

Award for low- and middle-income Ohio residents attending an approved college or school in Ohio or Pennsylvania. Must be enrolled full-time and have financial need. Average award is $630. May be used for any course of study except theology. **Award:** Grant for use in freshman, sophomore, junior, or senior years; renewable. **Number:** varies. **Amount:** $78–$5466. **Eligibility Requirements:** Applicant must be enrolled or expecting to enroll full-time at a two-year or four-year institution or university; resident of Ohio and studying in Ohio or Pennsylvania. Available to U.S. citizens. **Application Requirements:** Application, financial need analysis. **Application Deadline:** October 1. **Contact:** Charles Shahid, Assistant Director, Ohio Board of Regents, PO Box 182452, Columbus, OH 43218-2452. **Phone:** 614-644-5959. **E-mail:** cshahid@regents.state.oh.us

Ohio Missing in Action and Prisoners of War Orphans Scholarship

Renewable award aids children of Vietnam conflict servicemen who have been classified as missing in action or prisoner of war. Must be an Ohio resident, be 16-21, and be enrolled full-time at an Ohio college. Full tuition awards. **Award:** Scholarship for use in freshman, sophomore, junior, or senior years; renewable. **Number:** 1–5. **Amount:** varies. **Eligibility Requirements:** Applicant must be age 16-21; enrolled or expecting to enroll full-time at a two-year or four-year institution; resident of Ohio and studying in Ohio. Available to U.S. citizens. Applicant or parent must meet one or more of the following requirements: general military experience; retired from active duty; disabled or killed as a result of military service; prisoner of war; or missing in action. **Application Requirements:** Application. **Application Deadline:** July 1. **Contact:** Sarina Wilks, Program Administrator, Ohio Board of Regents, PO Box 182452, Columbus, OH 43218-2452. **Phone:** 614-752-9528. **E-mail:** swilks@regents.state.oh.us

Ohio National Guard

Scholarships are for undergraduate studies at an approved Ohio post-secondary institution. Applicants must enlist for six years of Selective Service Reserve Duty in the Ohio National Guard. Scholarship pays 100% instructional and general fees for public institutions and an average of cost of public schools is available for private schools. Must be 18 years of age or older. Award is renewable. Deadlines: July 1, November 1, February 1, April 1. **Award:** Scholarship for use in freshman, sophomore, junior, or senior years; renewable. **Number:** 3500–8000. **Amount:** up to $3000. **Eligibility Requirements:** Applicant must be age 18; enrolled or expecting to enroll full or part-time at a two-year, four-year, or technical institution or university and studying in Ohio. Available to U.S. citizens. Applicant must have served in the Air Force National Guard or Army National Guard. **Application Requirements:** Application. **Application Deadline:** varies. **Contact:** Mrs. Toni Davis, Grants Administrator, Ohio National Guard, 2825 West Dublin Granville Rd., Columbus, OH 43235-2789. **Phone:** 614-336-7032. **E-mail:** toni.davis@tagoh.org

Ohio Safety Officers College Memorial Fund

Renewable award covering up to full tuition is available to children and surviving spouses of peace officers and fire fighters killed in the line of duty in any state. Children must be under 26 years of age. Must be an Ohio resident and enroll full-time or part-time at an Ohio college or university. **Award:** Scholarship for use in freshman, sophomore, junior, or senior years; renewable. **Number:** 50–65. **Amount:** varies. **Eligibility Requirements:** Applicant must be age 25 or under; enrolled or expecting to enroll full or part-time at a two-year or four-year institution or university; resident of Ohio and studying in Ohio. Applicant or parent of applicant must have employment or volunteer experience in police/firefighting. Available to

U.S. citizens. **Application Requirements: Application Deadline:** Continuous. **Contact:** Barbara Metheney, Program Administrator, Ohio Board of Regents, PO Box 182452, Columbus, OH 43218-2452. **Phone:** 614-752-9535. **E-mail:** bmethene@regents.state.oh.us

Ohio Student Choice Grant Program

Renewable award available to Ohio residents attending private colleges within the state. Must be enrolled full-time in a bachelor's degree program. Do not apply to state. Check with financial aid office of college. **Award:** Grant for use in freshman, sophomore, junior, or senior years; renewable. **Number:** varies. **Amount:** up to $1002. **Eligibility Requirements:** Applicant must be enrolled or expecting to enroll full-time at a four-year institution; resident of Ohio and studying in Ohio. Available to U.S. citizens. **Application Requirements: Application Deadline:** Continuous. **Contact:** Barbara Metheney, Program Administrator, Ohio Board of Regents, PO Box 182452, Columbus, OH 43218-2452, **Phone:** 614-752-9535. **E-mail:** bmethene@regents.state.oh.us

Ohio War Orphans Scholarship

Aids Ohio residents attending an eligible college in Ohio. Must be between the ages of 16-21, the child of a disabled or deceased veteran, and enrolled full-time. Renewable up to five years. Amount of award varies. Must include Form DD214. **Award:** Scholarship for use in freshman, sophomore, junior, or senior years; renewable. **Number:** 300–450. **Amount:** varies. **Eligibility Requirements:** Applicant must be age 16-21; enrolled or expecting to enroll full-time at a two-year or four-year institution; resident of Ohio and studying in Ohio. Available to U.S. citizens. Applicant or parent must meet one or more of the following requirements: general military experience; retired from active duty; disabled or killed as a result of

military service; prisoner of war; or missing in action. **Application Requirements:** Application. **Application Deadline:** July 1. **Contact:** Sarina Wilks, Program Administrator, Ohio Board of Regents, PO Box 182452, Columbus, OH 43218-2452.
Phone: 614-752-9528. **E-mail:** swilks@regents.state.oh.us

Part-time Student Instructional Grant

Renewable grants for part-time undergraduates who are Ohio residents. Award amounts vary. Must attend an Ohio institution. **Award:** Grant for use in freshman, sophomore, or junior years; renewable. **Number:** varies. **Amount:** varies. **Eligibility Requirements:** Applicant must be enrolled or expecting to enroll part-time at a two-year or four-year institution or university; resident of Ohio and studying in Ohio. Available to U.S. citizens. **Application Requirements:** Application, financial need analysis. **Application Deadline:** Continuous. **Contact:** Barbara Metheney, Program Administrator, Ohio Board of Regents, PO Box 182462, Columbus, OH 43218-2452.
Phone: 614-752-9535. **E-mail:** bmethene@regents.state.oh.us

Oklahoma

Future Teacher Scholarship-Oklahoma

Open to outstanding Oklahoma high school graduates who agree to teach in shortage areas. Must rank in top 15% of graduating class or score above 85th percentile on ACT or similar test, or be accepted in an educational program. Students nominated by institution. Reapply to renew. Must attend college/university in Oklahoma. Contact institution's financial aid office for application deadline. **Award:** Scholarship for use in freshman, sophomore, junior, senior, or graduate years; not renewable. **Number:** varies. **Amount:** up to $1500. **Eligibility**

Requirements: Applicant must be enrolled or expecting to enroll full or part-time at a two-year or four-year institution or university; resident of Oklahoma and studying in Oklahoma. Available to U.S. and non-U.S. citizens. **Application Requirements:** Application, essay, test scores, transcript. **Application Deadline:** Continuous. **Contact:** Oklahoma State Regents for Higher Education, PO Box 108850, Oklahoma City, OK 73101-8850.
Phone: 800-858-1840

Oklahoma State Regents for Higher Education

Encourages students of high academic ability to attend institutions in Oklahoma. Renewable up to four years. ACT or SAT scores must fall between 99.5 and 100th percentiles, or applicant must be designated as a National Merit scholar or finalist. **Award:** Scholarship for use in freshman, sophomore, junior, or senior years; renewable. **Number:** varies. **Amount:** $3500–$5500. **Eligibility Requirements:** Applicant must be high school student; planning to enroll or expecting to enroll full time at a two-year or four-year institution or university and studying in Oklahoma. Available to U.S. and non-U.S. citizens. **Application Requirements:** Application, test scores, transcript. **Application Deadline:** Continuous. **Contact:** Oklahoma State Regents for Higher Education, PO Box 108850, Oklahoma City, OK 73101-8850.
Phone: 800-858-1840.
E-mail: studentinfo@osrhe.edu

Oklahoma Tuition Aid Grant

Award for Oklahoma residents enrolled at an Oklahoma institution at least part time each semester in a degree program. May be enrolled in two- or four-year or approved vocational-technical institution. Award of up to $1000 per year. Application is made through FAFSA. **Award:** Grant for use in freshman, sophomore, junior, senior, or graduate years; renewable. **Number:** 23,000. **Amount:** $200–$1000. **Eligibility Requirements:** Applicant must be enrolled or expecting to enroll full

or part-time at a two-year, four-year, or technical institution or university; resident of Oklahoma and studying in Oklahoma. Available to U.S. citizens. **Application Requirements:** Application, financial need analysis, FAFSA. **Application Deadline:** April 30. **Contact:** Oklahoma State Regents for Higher Education, PO Box 3020, Oklahoma City, OK 73101-3020. **Phone:** 405-225-9456.
E-mail: otaginfo@otag.org

Regional University Baccalaureate Scholarship

Renewable award for Oklahoma residents attending one of 11 participating Oklahoma public universities. Must have an ACT composite score of at least 30 or be a National Merit semifinalist or commended student. In addition to the award amount, each recipient will receive a resident tuition waiver from the institution. Must maintain a 3.25 GPA. Deadlines vary depending upon the institution attended. **Award:** Scholarship for use in freshman, sophomore, junior, or senior years; renewable. **Number:** varies. **Amount:** $3000. **Eligibility Requirements:** Applicant must be enrolled or expecting to enroll full-time at an institution or university; resident of Oklahoma and studying in Oklahoma. Available to U.S. and non-U.S. citizens. **Application Requirements:** Application. **Application Deadline:** varies. **Contact:** Oklahoma State Regents for Higher Education, PO Box 108850, Oklahoma City, OK 73101-8850. **Phone:** 800-858-1840.
E-mail: studentinfo@osrhe.edu

South Dakota

Haines Memorial Scholarship

One-time scholarship for South Dakota public university students who are sophomores, juniors, or seniors having at least a 2.5 GPA and majoring in a teacher education program. Include resume with application. Must be South Dakota resident. **Award:** Scholarship for use in sophomore, junior, or senior years; not renewable. **Number:** 1. **Amount:** $2150. **Eligibility Requirements:** Applicant must be enrolled or expecting to enroll at an institution or university; resident of South Dakota and studying in South Dakota. Applicant must have 2.5 GPA or higher. **Application Requirements:** Application, autobiography, essay. **Application Deadline:** February 25. **Contact:** South Dakota Board of Regents, 306 East Capitol Ave., Ste. 200, Pierre, SD 57501-3159

South Dakota Aid to Dependents of Deceased Veterans

Program provides free tuition for children of deceased veterans who are under the age of 25, are residents of South Dakota, and whose mother or father was killed in action or died of other causes while on active duty. ("Veteran" for this purpose is as defined by South Dakota Codified Laws.) Parent must have been a bona fide resident of SD for at least six months immediately preceding entry into active service. Eligibility is for state-supported schools only. Must use SDDVA form E-12 available at financial aid offices. **Award:** Scholarship for use in freshman, sophomore, junior, or senior years; not renewable. **Number:** varies. **Amount:** varies. **Eligibility Requirements:** Applicant must be age 24 or under; enrolled or expecting to enroll at a two-year or four-year institution; resident of South Dakota and studying in South Dakota. Available to U.S. citizens. Applicant or parent must meet one or more of the following requirements: general military experience; retired from active duty; disabled or killed as a result of military service; prisoner of war; or missing in action. **Application Requirements:** Application. **Application Deadline:** varies. **Contact:** Dr. Lesta Turchen, Senior Administrator, South Dakota Board of Regents, 306 East Capitol Ave., Ste. 200, Pierre, SD 57501-3159. **Phone:** 605-773-3455. **E-mail:** info@sdbor.edu

South Dakota Board of Regents

Children and spouses of prisoners of war, or of persons listed as missing in action, are entitled to attend a state-supported school without the payment of tuition or mandatory fees provided they are not eligible for equal or greater federal benefits. Must use SDDVA form E-12 available at financial aid offices. Must be a South Dakota resident intending to study in South Dakota. **Award:** Scholarship for use in freshman, sophomore, junior, or senior years; not renewable. **Number:** varies. **Amount:** varies. **Eligibility Requirements:** Applicant must be enrolled or expecting to enroll at an institution or university; resident of South Dakota and studying in South Dakota. Available to U.S. citizens. Applicant or parent must meet one or more of the following requirements: general military experience; retired from active duty; disabled or killed as a result of military service; prisoner of war; or missing in action. **Application Requirements:** Application. **Application Deadline:** varies. **Contact:** Dr. Lesta Turchen, Senior Administrator, South Dakota Board of Regents, 306 East Capitol Ave., Ste. 200, Pierre, SD 57501-3159. **Phone:** 605-773-3455. **E-mail:** info@sdbor.edu

South Dakota Board of Regents Senior Citizens Tuition Assistance

Award for tuition assistance for any postsecondary academic year of study to senior citizens age 65 and older. Write for further details. Must be a South Dakota resident and attend a school in South Dakota. **Award:** Scholarship for use in freshman, sophomore, junior, or senior years; not renewable. **Number:** varies. **Amount:** varies. **Eligibility Requirements:** Applicant must be age 65; enrolled or expecting to enroll at an institution or university; resident of South Dakota and studying in South Dakota. **Application Requirements:** Application. **Application Deadline:** Continuous. **Contact:** South Dakota Board of Regents, 306 East Capitol Ave., Ste. 200, Pierre, SD 57501-3159

South Dakota Board of Regents State Employee Tuition Assistance

Award for South Dakota state employees for any postsecondary academic year of study in South Dakota institution. Must be U.S. citizen. Write for requirements and other details. **Award:** Scholarship for use in freshman, sophomore, junior, or senior years; not renewable. **Number:** varies. **Amount:** varies. **Eligibility Requirements:** Applicant must be enrolled or expecting to enroll at an institution or university; resident of South Dakota and studying in South Dakota. Applicant or parent of applicant must have employment or volunteer experience in designated career field. Available to U.S. citizens. **Application Deadline:** Continuous. **Contact:** South Dakota Board of Regents, 306 East Capitol Ave., Ste. 200, Pierre, SD 57501-3159

South Dakota Education Benefits for National Guard Members

Guard members who meet the requirements for admission are eligible for a 50% reduction in undergraduate tuition charges at any state-supported school for up to a maximum of four academic years. Provision also covers one program of study, approved by the State Board of Education, at any state vocational school. Must be state resident and member of the SD Army or Air Guard throughout period for which benefits are sought. Must contact financial aid office for full details and forms at time of registration. **Award:** Scholarship for use in freshman, sophomore, junior, or senior years; not renewable. **Number:** varies. **Amount:** varies. **Eligibility Requirements:** Applicant must be enrolled or expecting to enroll at a two-year, four-year, or technical institution or university; resident of South Dakota and studying in South Dakota. Available to U.S. citizens. Applicant must have served in the Air Force National Guard or Army National Guard. **Application Requirements:** Application. **Application Deadline:** varies. **Contact:** Dr. Lesta Turchen, Senior Administrator, South Dakota

Board of Regents, 306 East Capitol Ave., Ste. 200, Pierre, SD 57501-3159. **Phone:** 605-773-3455. **E-mail:** info@sdbor.edu

South Dakota Education Benefits for Veterans

Certain veterans are eligible for free undergraduate tuition assistance at state-supported schools provided they are not eligible for educational payments under the GI Bill or any other federal educational program. Contact financial aid office for full details and forms. May receive one month of free tuition for each month of qualifying service (minimum one year, maximum four years). Must be resident of South Dakota. **Award:** Scholarship for use in freshman, sophomore, junior, or senior years; not renewable. **Number:** varies. **Amount:** varies. **Eligibility Requirements:** Applicant must be enrolled or expecting to enroll at an institution or university; resident of South Dakota and studying in South Dakota. Available to U.S. citizens. Applicant must have general military experience. **Application Requirements:** Application, DD Form 214. **Application Deadline:** varies. **Contact:** Dr. Lesta Turchen, Senior Administrator, South Dakota Board of Regents, 306 East Capitol Ave., Ste. 200, Pierre, SD 57501-3159. **Phone:** 605-773-3455. **E-mail:** info@sdbor.edu

South Dakota Opportunity Scholarship

Provides $5000 over 4 years to a qualifying South Dakota student who completes the high school course known as the Regents Scholar curriculum with no final grade below a C and high school cumulative GPA of 3.0. Must attend a NCA-accredited institution in South Dakota. Must have ACT composite score of 24 or higher, or a combined SAT score of 1110. Initial submission of application and transcript should be by June 1. See Web site for application and information: http://www.sdbor.edu. **Award:** Scholarship for use in freshman, sophomore, junior, or senior years; renewable. **Number:** 1000.

Amount: up to $1000. **Eligibility Requirements:** Applicant must be enrolled or expecting to enroll full-time at a four-year institution or university; resident of South Dakota and studying in South Dakota. Applicant must have 3.0 GPA or higher. Available to U.S. citizens. **Application Requirements:** Application, test scores, transcript. **Application Deadline:** September 1. **Contact:** Dr. Lesta Turchen, Senior Administrator, South Dakota Board of Regents, 306 East Capitol Ave., Ste. 200, Pierre, SD 57501-3159. **Phone:** 605-773-3455. **E-mail:** info@sdbor.edu

Wisconsin

Department of Military Affairs

Renewable award for active members of the Wisconsin National Guard in good standing, who successfully complete a course of study at a qualifying school. Award covers full tuition, excluding fees, not to exceed undergraduate tuition charged by University of Wisconsin-Madison. Must have a minimum 2.0 GPA. **Award:** Grant for use in freshman, sophomore, junior, or senior years; renewable. **Number:** up to 4000. **Amount:** up to $1927. **Eligibility Requirements:** Applicant must be enrolled or expecting to enroll full or part-time at a two-year, four-year, or technical institution or university and resident of Wisconsin. Available to U.S. citizens. Applicant must have served in the Air Force National Guard or Army National Guard. **Application Requirements:** Application. **Application Deadline:** Continuous. **Contact:** Karen Behling, Tuition Grant Administrator, Department of Military Affairs, PO Box 14587, Madison, WI 53708-0587. **Phone:** 608-242-3159. **E-mail:** karen.behling@dma.state.wi.us

Minnesota-Wisconsin Reciprocity Program

Wisconsin residents may attend a Minnesota public institution and pay the reciprocity tuition charged by Minnesota institution. All programs are eligible except doctoral programs in medicine, dentistry, and veterinary medicine. Please refer to Web site for further details: http://www.heab.state.wi.us **Award:** Scholarship for use in freshman, sophomore, junior, or senior years; renewable. **Number:** varies. **Amount:** varies. **Eligibility Requirements:** Applicant must be enrolled or expecting to enroll full or part-time at a two-year, four-year, or technical institution or university; resident of Wisconsin and studying in Minnesota. Available to U.S. citizens. **Application Requirements:** Application. **Application Deadline:** Continuous. **Contact:** Cindy Lehrman, Wisconsin Higher Educational Aids Board, PO Box 7885, Madison, WI 53707-7885. **Phone:** 608-267-2209. **E-mail:** cindy.lehrman@heab.state.wi.us

Minority Retention Grant

Provides financial assistance to African-American, Native-American, Hispanic, and former citizens of Laos, Vietnam, and Cambodia, for study in Wisconsin. Must be Wisconsin resident, enrolled at least half-time in a two-year or four-year nonprofit college, and must show financial need. Please refer to Web site for further details: http://www.heab.state.wi.us **Award:** Grant for use in sophomore, junior, senior, or graduate years; not renewable. **Number:** varies. **Amount:** $250–$2500. **Eligibility Requirements:** Applicant must be American Indian/Alaska Native, Asian/Pacific Islander, Black (non-Hispanic), or Hispanic; enrolled or expecting to enroll full or part-time at a two-year, four-year, or technical institution; resident of Wisconsin and studying in Wisconsin. Available to U.S. and non-U.S. citizens. **Application Requirements:** Application, financial need analysis. **Application Deadline:** Continuous.

Contact: Mary Lou Kuzdas, Program Coordinator, Wisconsin Higher Educational Aids Board, PO Box 7885, Madison, WI 53707-7885. **Phone:** 608-267-2212. **E-mail:** mary.kuzdas@heab.state.wi.us

Nursing Student Loan Program

Provides forgivable loans to students enrolled in a nursing program. Must be a Wisconsin resident studying in Wisconsin. Application deadline is last day on which student is enrolled. Please refer to Web site for further details: http://www.heab.state.wi.us **Award:** Forgivable loan for use in freshman, sophomore, junior, or senior years; renewable. **Number:** 150–1800. **Amount:** $250–$3000. **Eligibility Requirements:** Applicant must be enrolled or expecting to enroll full or part-time at a two-year, four-year, or technical institution or university; resident of Wisconsin and studying in Wisconsin. Available to U.S. citizens. **Application Requirements:** Application, financial need analysis. **Contact:** Cindy Lehrman, Program Coordinator, Wisconsin Higher Educational Aids Board, PO Box 7885 Madison, WI 53707-7885. **Phone:** 608-267-2209. **E-mail:** cindy.lehrman@heab.state.wi.us

Talent Incentive Program Grant

Assists residents of Wisconsin who are attending a nonprofit institution in Wisconsin and have substantial financial need. Must meet income criteria, be considered economically and educationally disadvantaged and be enrolled at least half-time. Please refer to Web site for further details: http://www.heab.state.wi.us **Award:** Grant for use in freshman, sophomore, junior, or senior years; renewable. **Number:** varies. **Amount:** $250–$1800. **Eligibility Requirements:** Applicant must be enrolled or expecting to enroll full or part-time at a two-year, four-year, or technical institution or university; resident of Wisconsin and studying in Wisconsin. Available to U.S. citizens. **Application Requirements:** Financial need analysis, nomination.

Application Deadline: Continuous. **Contact:** John Whitt, Program Coordinator, Wisconsin Higher Educational Aids Board, PO Box 7885 Madison, WI 53707-7885. **Phone:** 608-266-1665. **E-mail:** john.whitt@heab.state.wi.us

Teacher of the Visually Impaired Loan Program

Provides forgivable loans to students who enroll in programs that lead to be certified as a teacher of the visually impaired or an orientation and mobility instructor. Must be a Wisconsin resident. For study in Wisconsin, Illinois, Iowa, Michigan, and Minnesota. Please refer to Web site for further details: http://www.heab.state.wi.us **Award:** Forgivable loan for use in freshman, sophomore, junior, senior, graduate, or postgraduate years; not renewable. **Number:** varies. **Amount:** $250–$10,000. **Eligibility Requirements:** Applicant must be enrolled or expecting to enroll full or part-time at a two-year, four-year, or technical institution or university; resident of Wisconsin and studying in Illinois, Iowa, Michigan, Minnesota, or Wisconsin. Available to U.S. citizens. **Application Requirements:** Application, financial need analysis. **Application Deadline:** Continuous. **Contact:** John Whitt, Program Coordinator, Wisconsin Higher Educational Aids Board, PO Box 7885, Madison, WI 53707-7885. **Phone:** 608-266-0888. **E-mail:** john.whitt@heab.state.wi.us

Wisconsin Academic Excellence Scholarship

Renewable award for high school seniors with the highest GPA in graduating class. Must be a Wisconsin resident. Award covers tuition for up to four years. Must maintain 3.0 GPA for renewal. Scholarships of up to $2250 each. Must attend a nonprofit Wisconsin institution full-time. Please refer to Web site for further details: http://www.heab.state.wi.us **Award:** Scholarship for use in freshman, sophomore, junior, or senior years; renewable. **Number:** 3445.

Amount: up to $2250. **Eligibility Requirements:** Applicant must be enrolled or expecting to enroll full-time at a two-year, four-year, or technical institution or university; resident of Wisconsin and studying in Wisconsin. Applicant must have 3.5 GPA or higher. Available to U.S. citizens. **Application Requirements:** Transcript. **Application Deadline:** Continuous. **Contact:** Alice Winters, Program Coordinator, Wisconsin Higher Educational Aids Board, PO Box 7885, Madison, WI 53707-7885. **Phone:** 608-267-2213. **E-mail:** alice.winters@heab.state.wi.us

Wisconsin Department of Veterans Affairs

Up to 100% tuition and fee reimbursement for Wisconsin veterans who were discharged from active duty within the last 10 years. Undergraduate courses must be completed at accredited Wisconsin schools. Those attending Minnesota public colleges, universities, and technical schools that have a tuition reciprocity agreement with Wisconsin also may qualify. Must meet military service requirements. Application must be received no later than 60 days after the completion of the course. **Award:** Grant for use in freshman, sophomore, junior, or senior years; renewable. **Number:** varies. **Amount:** varies. **Eligibility Requirements:** Applicant must be enrolled or expecting to enroll full-time at a two-year, four-year, or technical institution or university; resident of Wisconsin and studying in Minnesota or Wisconsin. Available to U.S. citizens. Applicant must have general military experience. **Application Requirements:** Application. **Application Deadline:** varies. **Contact:** Mike Keatley, Grants Coordinator, Wisconsin Department of Veterans Affairs, PO Box 7843, Madison, WI 53707-7843. **Phone:** 608-266-1311

Wisconsin Department of Veterans Affairs Retraining Grants

Renewable award for veterans, unmarried spouses of deceased veterans, or dependents of deceased veterans. Must be resident of Wisconsin and attend an institution in Wisconsin. Veteran must be recently unemployed and show financial need. Must enroll in a vocational or technical program that can reasonably be expected to lead to employment. Course work at four-year colleges or universities does not qualify as retraining. **Award:** Grant for use in freshman or sophomore years; renewable. **Number:** varies. **Amount:** up to $3000. **Eligibility Requirements:** Applicant must be enrolled or expecting to enroll full or part-time at a technical institution; resident of Wisconsin and studying in Wisconsin. Applicant or parent must meet one or more of the following requirements: general military experience; retired from active duty; disabled or killed as a result of military service; prisoner of war; or missing in action. **Application Requirements:** Application, financial need analysis. **Application Deadline:** varies. **Contact:** Mike Keatley, Grants Coordinator, Wisconsin Department of Veterans Affairs, PO Box 7843, Madison, WI 53707-7843. **Phone:** 608-266-1311

Wisconsin Higher Educational Aids Board

One-time award available to residents of Wisconsin who have severe or profound hearing or visual impairment. Must be enrolled at least half-time at a nonprofit institution. If the handicap prevents the student from attending a Wisconsin school, the award may be used out-of-state in a specialized college. Please refer to Web site for further details: http://www.heab.state.wi.us **Award:** Grant for use in freshman, sophomore, junior, or senior years; not renewable. **Number:** varies. **Amount:** $250–$1800. **Eligibility Requirements:** Applicant must be enrolled or expecting to enroll full or part-time at a two-year, four-year, or technical institution or university and resident of Wisconsin. Applicant must be hearing impaired or visually impaired. Available to U.S. citizens. **Application Requirements:** Application, financial need analysis. **Application Deadline:** Continuous. **Contact:** Sandra Thomas, Program Coordinator, Wisconsin Higher Educational Aids Board, PO Box 7885, Madison, WI 53707-7885.

Phone: 608-266-0888. **E-mail:** sandy.thomas@heab.state.wi.us

Wisconsin Higher Education Grants (WHEG)

Grants for residents of Wisconsin attending a campus of the University of Wisconsin or Wisconsin Technical College. Must be enrolled at least half-time and show financial need. Please refer to Web site for further details: http://www.heab.state.wi.us **Award:** Grant for use in freshman, sophomore, junior, or senior years; not renewable. **Number:** varies. **Amount:** $250–$2500. **Eligibility Requirements:** Applicant must be enrolled or expecting to enroll full or part-time at a two-year, four-year, or technical institution or university; resident of Wisconsin and studying in Wisconsin. Available to U.S. citizens. **Application Requirements:** Application, financial need analysis. **Application Deadline:** Continuous. **Contact:** Sandra Thomas, Program Coordinator, Wisconsin Higher Educational Aids Board, PO Box 7885, Madison, WI 53707-7885. **Phone:** 608-266-0888. **E-mail:** sandy.thomas@heab.state.wi.us

Wisconsin Native American Student Grant

Grants for Wisconsin residents who are at least one-quarter American-Indian. Must be attending a college or university within the state. Please refer to Web site for further details: http://www.heab.state.wi.us **Award:** Grant for use in freshman, sophomore, junior, senior, graduate, or postgraduate years; not renewable. **Number:** varies. **Amount:** $250–$1100. **Eligibility Requirements:** Applicant must be American Indian/Alaska Native; enrolled or expecting to enroll full or part-time at a two-year, four-year, or technical institution or university; resident of Wisconsin and studying in Wisconsin. Available to U.S. citizens. **Application Requirements:** Application, financial need analysis. **Application Deadline:** Continuous. **Contact:** Sandra Thomas, Program Coordinator, Wisconsin Higher Educational Aids Board, PO Box 7885, Madison, WI 53707-7885. **Phone:** 608-266-0888. **E-mail:** sandy.thomas@heab.state.wi.us

Wisconsin Tuition Grant Program

Available to Wisconsin residents who are enrolled at least half-time in degree or certificate programs at independent, nonprofit colleges or universities in Wisconsin. Must show financial need. Please refer to Web site for further details: http://www.heab.state.wi.us **Award:** Grant for use in freshman, sophomore, junior, or senior years; not renewable. **Number:** varies. **Amount:** varies. **Eligibility Requirements:** Applicant must be enrolled or expecting to enroll full or part-time at a four-year institution or university; resident of Wisconsin and studying in Wisconsin. Available to U.S. and non-U.S. citizens. **Application Requirements:** Application, financial need analysis. **Application Deadline:** Continuous. **Contact:** Mary Lou Kuzdas, Program Coordinator, Wisconsin Higher Educational Aids Board, PO Box 7885, Madison, WI 53707-7005. **Phone:** 608-267-2212. **E-mail:** mary.kuzdas@heab.state.wi.us

Wisconsin Veterans Part-time Study Reimbursement Grant

Open only to Wisconsin veterans. Renewable for continuing study. Contact office for more details. Application deadline is no later than sixty days after the course completion. Veterans may be reimbursed up to 100% of tuition and fees. **Award:** Grant for use in freshman, sophomore, junior, or senior years; renewable. **Number:** varies. **Amount:** $300–$2000. **Eligibility Requirements:** Applicant must be enrolled or expecting to enroll part-time at an institution or university; resident of Wisconsin and studying in Wisconsin. Available to U.S. citizens. Applicant or parent must meet one or more of the following requirements: general military experience; retired from active duty; disabled or killed as a result of military service; prisoner of war; or missing in action. **Application Requirements:** Application. **Application Deadline:** varies. **Contact:** Mike Keatley, Grants Coordinator, Wisconsin Department of Veterans Affairs, PO Box 7843, Madison, WI 53707-7843. **Phone:** 608-266-1311

SUMMER OPPORTUNITIES

Illinois

Center for American Archeology/Archeology Field School
Kampsville, IL
General Information: Coed residential academic program established in 1968.
Contact: Mary Pirkl, Director of Education, PO Box 366, Kampsville, IL 62053
Phone: 618-653-4316
Fax: 618-653-4232
E-mail: caa@caa-archeology.org
Web site: www.caa-archeology.org

Center for Talent Development Summer Academic Program
Evanston, IL
General Information: Coed residential and day academic program established in 1983.
Contact: Susie Hoffmann, Summer Program Coordinator, 617 Dartmouth Place, Evanston, IL 60208
Phone: 847-491-3782
Fax: 847-467-4283
E-mail: ctd@northwestern.edu
Web site: www.ctd.northwestern.edu

Emagination Computer Camps
Lake Forest, IL
General Information: Coed residential and day academic program established in 1982.
Contact: Ms. Kathi Rigg, Director, 110 Winn St., Ste. 207, Woburn, MA 01801
Phone: 888-226-6733
Fax: 781-933-0749
E-mail: camp@computercamps.com
Web site: www.computercamps.com

iD Tech Camps–Lake Forest College
Evanston, IL
General Information: Coed residential and day academic program established in 1999.
Contact: Client Service Representatives, 1885 Winchester Blvd., Ste. 201, Campbell, CA 95008
Phone: 888-709-TECH

Fax: 408-871-2228
E-mail: requests@internaldrive.com
Web site: www.internaldrive.com

iD Tech Camps–Northwestern University
Chicago, IL
General Information: Coed residential and day academic program established in 1999.
Contact: Client Service Representatives, 1885 Winchester Blvd., Ste. 201, Campbell, CA 95008
Phone: 888-709-TECH
Fax: 408-871-2228
E-mail: requests@internaldrive.com
Web site: www.internaldrive.com

Junior Statesmen Summer School–Northwestern University
Evanston, IL
General Information: Coed residential academic program established in 1995.
Contact: Matt Randazzo, National Summer School Director, 400 South El Camino Real, Ste. 300, San Mateo, CA 94402
Phone: 650-347-1600
Fax: 650-347-7200
E-mail: jsa@jsa.org
Web site: www.jsa.org/summer

Northwestern University's College Preparation Program
Evanston, IL
General Information: Coed residential and day academic program established in 1987.
Contact: Stephanie Teterycz, Director of Summer Sessions, 405 Church St., Evanston, IL 60208
Phone: 847-467-6703
Fax: 847-491-3660
E-mail: cpp@northwestern.edu
Web site: www.northwestern.edu/collegeprep

Northwestern University's National High School Institute
Evanston, IL
General Information: Coed residential academic and arts program established in 1931.
Contact: Nick Kanel, Department Assistant, 617 Noyes St., Evanston, IL 60208
Phone: 800-662-NHSI

Fax: 847-467-1057
E-mail: nhsi@northwestern.edu
Web site: www.northwestern.edu/nhsi

Power Chord Academy
Chicago, IL
General Information: Coed residential academic and arts program.
Contact: Mr. Bryan J. Wrzesinski, 7336 Santa Monica Blvd., #107, Los Angeles, CA 90046
Phone: 800-897-6677
Fax: 775-306-7923
E-mail: bryan@powerchordacademy.com
Web site: www.powerchordacademy.com

University of Chicago–Insight
Chicago, IL
General Information: Coed residential and day academic program established in 1998.
Contact: Ms. Sarah López, Summer Session Office Administrative Assistant, The Graham School of General Studies, Summer Sessions Office, 1427 East 60th St., Chicago, IL 60637
Phone: 773-834-3792
Fax: 773-702-6814
E-mail: slopez@uchicago.edu
Web site: summer.uchicago.edu/

University of Chicago–Research in the Biological Sciences
Chicago, IL
General Information: Coed residential academic program established in 1999.
Contact: Ms. Sarah López, Summer Session Office, Graham School of General Studies, Summer Sessions Office, 1427 East 60th St., Chicago, IL 60637
Phone: 773-834-3792
Fax: 773-702-6814
E-mail: slopez@uchicago.edu
Web site: summer.uchicago.edu/

University of Chicago–Summer Quarter for High School Students
Chicago, IL
General Information: Coed residential and day academic program established in 1999.
Contact: Ms. Sarah López, Summer

Session Office Administrative Assistant, Graham School of General Studies, Summer Sessions Office, 1427 East 60th St., Chicago, IL 60637
Phone: 773-834-3792
Fax: 773-702-6814
E-mail: slopez@uchicago.edu
Web site: summer.uchicago.edu/

Indiana

Seminar for Top Engineering Prospects (STEP)
West Lafayette, IN
General Information: Coed residential academic program.
Contact: Dr. P. K. Imbrie, Honors Program Director, 1286 Engineering Administration, West Lafayette, IN 47907
Phone: 765-494-3976
Fax: 765-494-5819
E-mail: frehonor@ecn.purdue.edu
Web site: https://engineering.purdue.edu/ENE/SpecialPrograms/ProspectiveStudents/step

Iowa

Grinnell Summer Institute
Grinnell, IA
General Information: Coed residential academic program established in 1983.
Contact: Jim Sumner, Dean of Admissions/Financial Aid, Office of Admissions, 1103 Park St., Grinnell, IA 50112-0810
Phone: 800-247-0113
Fax: 641-269-4800
E-mail: sumnerj@grinnell.edu
Web site: www.grinnell.edu/

Iowa Young Writers' Studio
Iowa City, IA
General Information: Coed residential academic and arts program established in 1999.
Contact: Ms. Trish Walsh, Director, C215 Seashore Hall, Iowa City, IA 52242-1402
Phone: 319-335-4209
Fax: 319-335-4743
E-mail: iyws@uiowa.edu
Web site: www.uiowa.edu/~iyws

Kansas

Future Astronaut Training Program
Hutchinson, KS
General Information: Coed residential academic program established in 1985.
Contact: Mrs. Laurie Givan, Camp Registrar, 1100 North Plum, Hutchinson, KS 67501
Phone: 800-397-0330 ext. 323
Fax: 620-662-3693
E-mail: laurieg@cosmo.org
Web site: www.cosmo.org

Mars Academy
Hutchinson, KS
General Information: Coed residential academic program established in 2003.
Contact: Mrs. Laurie Givan, Education Registrar, 1100 North Plum, Hutchinson, KS 67501
Phone: 800-397-0330 ext. 323
Fax: 620-662-3693
E-mail: laurieg@cosmo.org
Web site: www.cosmo.org

Michigan

iD Tech Camps–University of Michigan
Ann Arbor, MI
General Information: Coed residential and day academic program established in 1999.
Contact: Client Service Representatives, 1885 Winchester Blvd., Ste. 201, Campbell, CA 95008
Phone: 888-709-TECH
Fax: 408-871-2228
E-mail: requests@internaldrive.com
Web site: www.internaldrive.com

Interlochen Arts Camp
Interlochen, MI
General Information: Coed residential arts program established in 1928.
Contact: Ms. Amy Packard, Director of Admissions, PO Box 199, Interlochen, MI 49643
Phone: 231-276-7472
Fax: 231-276-7464
E-mail: admissions@interlochen.org
Web site: www.interlochen.org/

Michigan Technological University American Indian Workshop
Houghton, MI
General Information: Coed residential academic program established in 1988.
Contact: Ms. Karla Korpela, Youth Programs Associate Coordinator, 1400 Townsend Dr., Houghton, MI 49931-1295
Phone: 906-487-2219
Fax: 906-487-3101
E-mail: yp@mtu.edu
Web site: www.mtu.edu/

Michigan Technological University Explorations in Engineering Workshop
Houghton, MI
General Information: Coed residential academic program established in 1988.
Contact: Karla Korpela, Youth Programs Associate Coordinator, 1400 Townsend Dr., Houghton, MI 49931-1295
Phone: 906-487-2219
Fax: 906-487-3101
E-mail: yp@mtu.edu
Web site: www.mtu.edu/

Michigan Technological University Orchestra Fellowship Program
Houghton, MI
General Information: Coed residential arts program established in 1994.
Contact: Peter Larsen, Youth Programs Coordinator, 1400 Townsend Dr., Houghton, MI 49931-1295
Phone: 906-487-2219
Fax: 906-487-3101
E-mail: yp@mtu.edu
Web site: www.mtu.edu/

Michigan Technological University Summer Youth Program
Houghton, MI
General Information: Coed residential and day academic and arts program established in 1973.
Contact: Karla Korpela, Youth Programs Associate Coordinator, 1400 Townsend Dr., Houghton, MI 49931
Phone: 906-487-2219
Fax: 906-487-3101
E-mail: yp@mtu.edu
Web site: www.mtu.edu/

Summer Discovery at Michigan

Ann Arbor, MI

General Information: Coed residential academic program established in 1991.

Contact: The Musiker Family, Director, 1326 Old Northern Blvd., Roslyn Village, NY 11576

Phone: 888-878-6637

Fax: 516-625-3438

E-mail: discovery@summerfun.com

Web site: www.summerfun.com

Minnesota

Carleton College Summer Writing Program

Northfield, MN

General Information: Coed residential academic program established in 1976.

Contact: Becky Fineran-Gardner, Director of Summer Academic Programs, 1 North College St., Northfield, MN 55057-4016

Phone: 507-646-4038

Fax: 507-646-4540

E-mail: swp@carleton.edu

Web site: www.carleton.edu/summer

iD Tech Camps–University of Minnesota

Minneapolis, MN

General Information: Coed residential and day academic program established in 1999.

Contact: Client Service Representatives, 1885 Winchester Blvd., Ste. 201, Campbell, CA 95008

Phone: 888-709-TECH

Fax: 408-871-2228

E-mail: requests@internaldrive.com

Web site: www.internaldrive.com

Wilderness Dance Camp

Bloomington, MN

General Information: Coed residential arts program established in 1997.

Contact: Ms. Chandra Saign, Director, 10251 Lyndale Ave. South, Bloomington, MN 55420

Phone: 952-884-6009

E-mail: info@dancecamp.org

Web site: www.dancecamp.org/

Missouri

Washington University High School Summer Scholars Program

St. Louis, MO

General Information: Coed residential academic program established in 1988.

Contact: Ms. Marsha Hussung, Director, High School Summer Scholars Program, Campus Box 1145, 1 Brookings Dr., St. Louis, MO 63130

Phone: 314-935-6834

Fax: 314-935-4847

E-mail: mhussung@wustl.edu

Web site: ucollege.wustl.edu/hssp

Washington University in St. Louis, School of Art–Portfolio Plus

St. Louis, MO

General Information: Coed residential and day arts program established in 2004.

Contact: Katerina Papageorgio, Assistant Dean of Undergraduate Programs, Washington University in St. Louis, School of Art, Box 1031, One Brookings Dr., St. Louis, MO 63130

Phone: 314-935-6500

Fax: 314-935-6500

E-mail: sumart@art.wustl.edu

Web site: www.artsci.wustl.edu/~artweb/washUSoa/

Ohio

The Grand River Summer Academy

Austinburg, OH

General Information: Coed residential and day academic program established in 1990.

Contact: Sam Corabi, Director of Admission, 3042 College St., Austinburg, OH 44010

Phone: 440-275-2811 ext. 25

Fax: 440-275-1825

E-mail: academy@grandriver.org

Web site: www.grandriver.org

Junior Statesmen Symposium on Ohio State Politics and Government

Columbus, OH

General Information: Coed residential academic program established in 1998.

Contact: Matt Randazzo, National

Summer School Director, 400 South El Camino Real, Ste. 300, San Mateo, CA 94402

Phone: 650-347-1600

Fax: 650-347-7200

E-mail: jsa@jsa.org

Web site: www.jsa.org/summer

Miami University Junior Scholars Program

Oxford, OH

General Information: Coed residential academic program established in 1982.

Contact: Dr. Robert S. Smith, Director, 301 South Patterson Ave., Room 202, Oxford, OH 45056-3414

Phone: 513-529-5825

Fax: 513-529-1498

E-mail: juniorscholars@muohio.edu

Web site: www.muohio.edu/JuniorScholars/

The Summer Institute for the Gifted at Oberlin College

Oberlin, OH

General Information: Coed residential academic program.

Contact: Dr. Stephen Gessner, Director, River Plaza, 9 West Broad St., Stamford, CT 06902-3788

Phone: 866-303-4744

Fax: 203-399-5598

E-mail: sig.info@aifs.com

Web site: www.giftedstudy.com

Wisconsin

Milwaukee School of Engineering (MSOE)–Discover the Possibilities

Milwaukee, WI

General Information: Coed residential academic program established in 1999.

Contact: Ms. Linda Levandowski, Special Events Coordinator MSOE, 1025 North Broadway, Milwaukee, WI 53202

Phone: 800-332-6763

Fax: 414-277-7475

E-mail: levandow@msoe.edu

Web site: www.msoe.edu/admiss/summer

Milwaukee School of Engineering (MSOE)–Focus on Nursing

Milwaukee, WI

General Information: Coed residential academic program established in 2004.

Contact: Ms. Linda Levandowski, Special Events Coordinator, MSOE, 1025 North Broadway, Milwaukee, WI 53202
Phone: 800-332-6763
Fax: 414-277-7475
E-mail: levandow@msoe.edu
Web site: www.msoe.edu/admiss/summer

Milwaukee School of Engineering (MSOE)–Focus on the Possibilities
Milwaukee, WI
General Information: Coed residential academic program established in 1999.
Contact: Ms. Linda Levandowski, Special Events Coordinator, MSOE, 1025 North Broadway, Milwaukee, WI 53202
Phone: 800-332-6763
Fax: 414-277-7475
E-mail: levandow@msoe.edu
Web site: www.msoe.edu/admiss/summer

SuperCamp–University of Wisconsin at Parkside
Kenosha, WI
General Information: Coed residential academic program established in 1981.
Contact: Enrollments Department, 1725 South Coast Hwy., Oceanside, CA 92054
Phone: 800-285-3276
Fax: 760-722-3507
E-mail: info@supercamp.com
Web site: www.supercamp.com

University of Wisconsin–Green Bay Youth Opportunities
Green Bay, WI
General Information: Coed residential and day academic and arts program established in 1965.
Contact: Mona Christensen, Director of Youth Opportunities, 2420 Nicolet Dr., Green Bay, WI 54311-7001
Phone: 920-465-CAMP (2267)
Fax: 920-465-2552

E-mail: summercamps@uwgb.edu
Web site: www.uwgbsummercamps.com

World Affairs Seminar
Whitewater, WI
General Information: Coed residential academic program established in 1977.
Contact: Mr. Frederick R. Luedke, General Manager, 800 West Main St., University of Wisconsin-Whitewater, Whitewater, WI 53190
Phone: 888-404-4049
Fax: 262-472-5210
E-mail: was@uww.edu
Web site: www.worldaffairsseminar.org

NOTES

NOTES

NOTES